The Collected Poems
of
THOMAS MERTON

The
Collected
Poems
of
THOMAS
MERTON

A NEW DIRECTIONS BOOK

Grateful acknowledgment is made to the editors and publishers of books in which some of the material in this volume first appeared or from whom permission to reprint has been obtained. *Columbia Poetry: An Anthology of Students' Verse* (Copyright 1939 by The Trustees of the Merton Legacy Trust), Columbia University Press; *Open Poetry* (Copyright © 1973 by The Trustees of the Merton Legacy Trust), Simon & Schuster. By Thomas Merton, *The Asian Journal of Thomas Merton* (Copyright © 1968, 1970, 1973 by The Trustees of the Merton Legacy Trust; Copyright © 1973, 1975 by New Directions Publishing Corporation), New Directions; *The Behavior of Titans* (Copyright © 1961 by The Abbey of Gethsemani, Inc.), New Directions; *Clement of Alexandria* (All rights reserved), New Directions; *Conjectures of a Guilty Bystander* (Copyright © 1965, 1966 by The Abbey of Gethsemani), Doubleday & Company; *My Argument with the Gestapo* (Copyright © 1968 by Thomas Merton; Copyright © 1969 by The Abbey of Gethsemani, Inc.), Doubleday & Company and New Directions; *Mystics and Zen Masters* (Copyright © 1961, 1962, 1964, 1965, 1966, 1967 by The Abbey of Gethsemani), Farrar, Straus & Giroux; *Reflections on Love: Eight Sacred Poems* (Copyright © 1966 by Robert Williams); *The Sign of Jonas* (Copyright 1953 by The Abbey of Our Lady of Gethsemani), Doubleday & Company and Harcourt Brace Jovanovich; *The Way of Chuang Tzu* (Copyright © 1965 by The Abbey of Gethsemani), New Directions. By Nicanor Parra, *Poems & Antipoems* (Copyright © 1959, 1961, 1962, 1965, 1966, 1967 by Nicanor Parra), New Direc-

First published clothbound by New Directions in 1977
and as NDP504 in 1980.
Published simultaneously in Canada by
George J. McLeod, Ltd, Toronto
Manufactured in the United States of America

New Directions Books are published for James Laughlin
by New Directions Publishing Corporation,
80 Eighth Avenue, New York 10011

ISBN 0–8112–0769–2 pbk.

CONTENTS

EARLY POEMS
(1940–42)

Geography comes to an end,
Compass has lost all earthly north,
Horizons have no meaning
Nor roads an explanation:

THE PHILOSOPHERS

As I lay sleeping in the park,
Buried in the earth,
Waiting for the Easter rains
To drench me in their mirth
And crown my seedtime with some sap and growth,

Into the tunnels of my ears
Two anaesthetic voices came.
Two mandrakes were discussing life
And Truth and Beauty in the other room.

"Body is truth, truth body. Fat is all
We grow on earth, or all we breed to grow."
Said one mandrake to the other.
Then I heard his brother:
"Beauty is troops, troops beauty. Dead is all
We grow on earth, or all we breed to grow."

As I lay dreaming in the earth,
Enfolded in my future leaves,
My rest was broken by these mandrakes
Bitterly arguing in their frozen graves.

DIRGE FOR THE WORLD JOYCE DIED IN

Now ravel up the roots of workman oak trees
And rack apart the knotted limbs of earth:

Ravish the kingdoms of the breeding sun
And scan their ruins for a devil's birth.

Rescue the usurers from the living sea:
Their dead love runs like life, in copper wire.
Their nervousness draws polar fire of metal
To blast the harvest of our prettiest year.

The doctors in their disinfected city
Count the course their shining zodiacs go,
Nor listen to the worms red work devour them
Curled where some tooth is planted in the jaw.

Suffer no drug to slack his idiot eyestring
Receiving, dumb to prayer, the ascetic blade
Sent to stab out and blind that volunteer:
Proud spy in the cursing kingdom of the dead!

TWO BRITISH AIRMEN

(Buried with ceremony in the Teutoburg Forest)

Long buried, ancient men-at-arms
Beneath the beechtrees and the farms
Sleep, and syntax locks their glory
In the old pages of a story.

"We knew that battle when it was
A curious clause in Tacitus,
But were not able to construe
Our graves were in this forest too;
And, buried, never thought to have found
Such strange companions, underground."

"—Bring his flag, and wrap, and lay him
Under a cross that shows no name,
And, in the same ground make his grave
As those long-lost Romans have.
Let him a speechless exile be
From England and his century,
Nor question these old strangers, here,
Inquisitive, around his bier."

Lower, and let the bugle's noise
Supersede the Parson's voice
Who values at too cheap a rate
These men as "servants of their state."
Lower, and let the bombers' noise
Supersede the deacon's voice:
None but perfunctory prayers were said
For the unquiet spirits of these dead.

POEM

Here is the man of the islands,
Proud as a king of congas,
Sharp as fightingcocks' swords
And bitter as their blood.

Shaking his coat, of feathers black as rum,
He comes to the edge of the sea,
And challenges the crested sun.

And studies, with his eyes of grains of corn,
The jealous strut
Of Sunjazz on the burning Caribbean.

The swordplay of his walking shadow
Wars with the meat-eating birds,
Who leave him, in their unprophetic flight,
King of the cliff.

And there he stands,
With his back to where the tropics drum the country,
And threatens, face to face, his oracle
The nameless mask of noon.

POEM

Light plays like a radio in the iron tree;
Green farms fear the night behind me
Where lightnings race across the western world.

Life, like a woman in the moving wheat,
Runs from the staring sky
That bends upon the earth like a reflector.

The last column of sun
Is enfiladed in the battle-colored woods.
Rain fills the valley with a noise of tractors,
(For the tanks are come),

Until the land lies murdered in my naked windows
And the whole horizon's compass
Thrashes with the winds, like harvesters
Pulling down my million acre prairie.

At last, when restless doors fall still,
And let me out to trample the wet light,

I breathe in anguish
Cold and hunger on the watersmelling sky.

Earth turns up with a dark flash, where my spade
Digs the lovely stranger's grave;
And poppies show like blood.

The woman I saw fleeing through the bended wheat:
I know I'll find her dead.

THE CITY'S SPRING

Though jealous March, in marble skies
Prisoned our April Saturdays,
This air is full of courtesies.

The walls, that wept with arrowy rain,
Turn a new presence to the sun.
Flowers and friendly days are in.

The bended lanes are loud with cries,
And are become our Italies,
And bring sweet songs and strawberries.

DIRGE FOR THE CITY OF MIAMI

Oh what wealth of stucco flowers
Will save your memory for two hours
When those dishonest faces fade

That bloom until the gangster's dead?
Where will you find an iron wreath
Appropriate to such a death?

The simple grapefruit in the grove
Shine like the face of childish love
And sunflowers lean toward the south
With the confidence of early youth.
But oh, the red hibiscus paints
This garden with the blood of saints,
And a copper apple in the foliage
Is the fine fruit of the tree of knowledge.

Never did the drunkard think
To taste such bitterness in his drink
And there the gentle murderer stands,
And sadly, sadly wipes his hands:
There the forger and the thief
And the bank robber bow in grief
While up and down the perjurer goes,
Picking his nose, picking his nose.

The weary thief, the limping whore
Lie down upon the windy shore:
They'll find no place to rest their heads
Until they're dead, until they're dead.
Yet jungles full of golden bells,
(The lemon groves) will ring their knells
While all the downcast palms recall
The tears that Magdalen let fall.

So from these nameless mounds infer
Some derelict, some passenger,
Some gentle creature buried there,
For all the downcast palms recall
The tears that Magdalen let fall.

LA COMPARSA EN ORIENTE

(A Conga)

Drums of the early evening wake
The mountain full of ore, and the canebrake.
Up at Cobre tall tambores call
One who rings gangarias with a nail,
One with feathers for sleeves,
One whose arms are birds,
One with a mouth full of great fires
And lights instead of words.

One with a tobaccoleaf hat
Rings his drum like a bell,
And brings the saints of heaven, with claves,
Down from the starlit hill;
A black angel beats an asses jaw
And (tick tick) a white the claves
While the sodality of the blessed virgin
Follow after, carrying flowers.

Five angels beating bongos,
Seven saints ringing their bells,
Wear coats made out of paper money
And shoes made out of shells.
They clatter like a box of nickles,
Holding candletowers, on fire:
They whirl these as solemn as wise men,
Paper temples in the air.

Lights fly like birds behind the cane
And shot flies after, but in gourds,
When the comparsa goes off to the plains
With fires in her mouth, but no words:
For ten angels ring gangarias

When the comparsa goes away,
With all the mountain people and pilgrims
Dancing down to Camaguey.

Then pray for us, Mother of Jesus,
Caridad, Merced,
Queen of Cobre and of the three towers
That watch over Camaguey:
The ten angels are playing gangarias
And the comparsa goes away.

THE STRIFE BETWEEN THE POET AND AMBITION

Money and fame break in the room
And find the poet all alone.
They lock the door, so he won't run,
And turn the radio full-on
And beat the poor dope like a drum.

"Better sing your snatch of song
Before that ostrich voice is dumb,
Better hit your share of gong
Before the sounding brass is mum:
Tomorrow, tomorrow Death will come
And find you sitting dumb and senseless
With your epics unbegun,
And take away your pens and pencils—

There'll be no sculptures on your tomb
And other bards will occupy
Your seven-fifty sitting room."

"Pardon, sirs, my penny face
Bowed to your dollar presences,
Curtsying to Famous Verse,
Flattering wealth with smiles and smirks,
Choking down my hopeless tears!
For someone stole my crate of birds,
And busted up the music box
In which I kept my market flocks
Of bull-ideas and mental bears
And my poetic pocketfox,
My case of literary deers,
My eagle-vans to bat the airs!
They broke the cages and let go
My aviary of metric birds,
And all the diction in my zoo
Was let out by the amateurs!
The fishpond of my Friday words
Is fished out by the days and years.
My whole menagerie of verse
Is ruined by these sly monsieurs!"

The days and years run down the beach
And throw his ideas in the air
And wind his similes up to pitch
And bat his verses out of reach.
He mopes along the empty shore
With gullcries in his windfilled ear.
The hours and minutes, playing catch
With every image they can snatch,
Bat his metaphors to the birds
And cheer him with these bullying words:
"Better sing your snatch of song
Before that ostrich voice is dumb:
Better whack your share of gong
Before the sounding brass is mum:

Tomorrow, tomorrow Death will come
And find your epics unbegun:
There'll be no statues on your tomb,
And other bards will occupy
Your seven-fifty sitting room!"

HYMN TO COMMERCE

Blacker and whiter than the pages of his ledger
The dreaming trader turns to stone,
Because he hears the wind's voice sing this song:
"You shall set sail from the steps of the Exchange
And word will return, 'Lost with all hands.'
You shall set sail from the steps of the Sub-Treasury
And pass grand central at the fall of night
And never be heard of again."

The banker and the shipwright and the craven trader
Can spread their plans, and talk their mathematics
Among the ladders and the stanchions of the skinny ships,
The cargoliners like a leafless forest, on the ways.
But when the steel trees sing like harpstrings in the
        windstorm
Their minds roll up like blueprints,
And they blow away.

Blacker and whiter than the pages of his ledger
The dreaming trader turns to stone:
"You shall set sail from the steps of the Exchange:
Word will return, 'Lost with all hands.'
You shall set sail from the steps of the Sub-Treasury
And pass grand central at the fall of night

And founder in the dark sargassos of your own intolerable
     mind
And never be heard of again."

FROM THE SECOND CHAPTER OF A VERSE HISTORY OF THE WORLD

Minotaur

There was a time when the young girls
of this city
had to put on their pink dresses and
take arms full of
flowers and go up the gangplank
on to a ship, and that
ship carried them away to an island
from which they never
returned. For at that time we were
ruled from the
throne where Aegean Minos sat in-
extricate in the midst of
his house. He was the king of
the monsters.

Your shoes untie, your mantle you untwitch
Your stocking is all runs, you gaudy bitch
Sang to his muse some poet, but I don't know which.
And thus begin upon the precious page
To spread the holiday feast of grief once more,
To shed the policy vest of life, and wear,
Unweft, unbuckled and unstrung,
Starspeckled sweaters in the sun so brave

Their flap flap pleasure on the air to wave
And take their jolly sport upon the hero's grave.

Last Monday the Colonial boss proclaim
The little dames is shot to kingdom come:
Missee no likee, but lobbylinth allee same
Is waiting in the Isle of Crete where Byron was a bum.
Then fires went out, on each Athenian hearth
And patriotism swept the strings of mostly Spartan harps.

Thus grief constricted many a Greekish tongue
And wits that day were lean as starving cats
Which found no words at all to fit the most unhappy facts.

The official poems read over
the loudspeakers
were particularly mediocre. Art
was confounded no end;
verse, for the moment, was hushed.
Rhetoric had gone dead.
Logic had failed.
Music was without speech.
Painting stood inarticulate,
history amazed,
tragedy taken aback,
mimes all tied up,
comedy mum.
Politics struck a couple of
hasty attitudes,
science wore itself to
a shadow
explaining to
boyscouts
no new mistakes
in burying

of the dead,
first aid to old antiques,
and to new bones
immediate assistance,
and here and there
a marble tomb.

Then up went the ropes, down came the planks:
The custom officers sent in their reports,
The dock officials swept the air with speeches,
At which the national guard would often fire
A feu de joie upon their modern guns.
A band of raw recruits from nearby barracks
Sounded the notes of no civilian march
With too many bugles, too few harps and lyres,
Too few flutes, but oh, what a wealth of the worst
Drums, and drums, and (some of them broken) drums.
There was a farewell host of diplomats,
Of presidents, past presidents, vice gerents,
Pro consuls, delegates and governors,
Few simple legates, many classy mayors.
Right at the edge of the fancy crowd I saw
The blind Homer discuss with little truth
The target on the black-as-monday gunwales
Of this expensive ship: Explosive shape
Which even now would bear our daisy daughters
To the cow-president in his Cretan cage!

See how they chop the vessel from the wharf!
She lurches through the tugs into the harbor,
Lists above the launches draped in black
So full of official grief.
She heels and jibes among the motor boats
Upon the winey harbor of Piraeus,

And heads into the cruel, dazzling south
Bearing the pride of all our private schools.

Arms full of cornflowers, grouped in their sororities,
With honor students slightly to one side
The fairest wights of all our wienie roasts
Are off to picnic with the Cretan brute.
So screech of whistles crowns the city's gates,
Combining with the sorry shriek of fifes,
And the great row of a kitchen of kettledrums.
Bugles, immune from preciosity,
Protest against the sad trombone's lament,
Commend the shrill and bullying cornet,
For at this moment orchestras assume
The air and swagger of some drunk police.
See, see our sisters' overloaded boat.
O see the little jailbait dames are carried off to Crete!

The jaunty ship shall hop to Crete where all the monsters are.
The roaring poet sun shall play the hot sea like a lyre,
And twang the copper coastal ridge like any vocal wire:
And then our exile daughters lift their voices in
        a choir: (song)

Those were the days when the little dames
Of our city went up into the ships with a pile of
Flowers, to take away to Crete:
For from the center of Crete we were ruled, from the
Center of Minos' impenetrable house.

Whose teeth shearing away with a sidewise
Motion devoured the white bread of our land.
Unto these last upon the precious pane
Unwarp the scarf of holiday love once more
Unweave the garb of polity judge unswear

Unweft unbothered and unswung
Starspeckled bonnet in the sun to have
Her flap flap sport upon the soldiers' grave.
The shoestring bust, the mantle is untwitch
Your stocking is unlace, you gaudy bitch,
Yell to muse your writer, but I scarce remember which.

Last Monday when the curious boss proclaim
Them bonny girls was shot to kingdom come
(Missee no likee lobbylinth allee same)
The isles of Crete, the isles of Crete where Byron was a bum.
The fires went out on the Athenian hearth
And patriotism swept the string on mostly Spartan harps.

Up went the ropes, down went the planks
The custom officers sent in their reports.

The dock officials swept the air with speeches of farewell
At which the military police would fire
A feu de joie upon their ultramodern rifles.
A band of raw recruits from some marine barracks
Sounded the notes of no civilian march
With too few bugles, too few trumps and timbals
Too few lyres but a wealth of the worst
Drum playing since the defeat of the Marne.
There was a farewell host of diplomats
Of residents, vice regents, post gerents
Proper-bailiffs, Paene-manciples,
Almost presidents, and many classy mayors.

Standing at the edge of the crowd I saw a subaltern
Discuss with little acumen a target
Painted upon the red-as-welcome gunwales
Of this expensive vessel, (or, explosive shape),
Which soon should take our daisy daughters to their
      Cretan fate.

Bend, bend my pretty boughs
And throw my sighs away like leaves.
Scatter upon the land my tears like rain,
Soften the hard earth where no pity lives.
Bend, bend my pretty boughs,
And throw away my sighs like leaves.

When summer with a herd of heifer clouds
Did rain gold rain of blossoms on our woods,
And stocked the wheatfields with young ears, and green
    ungarnered goods,
Then was prepared no bridal veil,
Was taught no epithalamium.
Spring had been kind to no avail,
Our winter was already come.
Bend, bend, my pretty boughs,
And throw away my sighs like leaves;
Scatter upon the land my tears like rain,
And soften the hard earth where no pity lives.
Bend, bend, my pretty boughs,
And throw away my sighs like leaves.

Once there was laughter in the house at Athens
And songs at evening on Hymettus hill,
The roll of childish skate upon the concrete
And clatter of childish hoop upon the earth,
Or gentler cadences where some played house upon the hearth.
Once there was laughter in the house at Athens
And songs at evening on Hymettus hill,
While soon shot up this brave and innocent childhood
Into longlegged, gentle gangling girl.
She combed and combed her cornsilk hair
And stared into her glass.

With blue shoebutton eyes
And ran less awkward to the Hi-Y dance.

But all the while at home mama made good
Fatal and most political intentions,
The sergeant's Cretan plan: so cruel a term
To all the hopes of Athens olive-crowned,
To all the speechless loves of kids
So desperate and kind.
For while to one another younglings laughed
Nodded and pointed like flowers in a field in a wind
Across the floor of the disinfected Gym,
And danced an untaught dance to the tune
Of an untaught violin,
In the separate homes of each particular girl
Mothers wrapped up and put in trunks some smocks.

Junipers and simple linens, camping clothes
All coarse and proper for the labyrinth,
All grey and pleasing to the minotaur,
All colorless to show the tones of grief!

HYMN OF NOT MUCH PRAISE
FOR NEW YORK CITY

When the windows of the West Side clash like cymbals in the
    setting sunlight,
And when wind wails amid the East Side's aerials,
And when, both north and south of thirty-fourth street,
In all the dizzy buildings,
The elevators clack their teeth and rattle the bars of their cages,
Then the children of the city,
Leaving the monkey-houses
    of their office-buildings and apartments,
With the greatest difficulty open their mouths, and sing:

"Queen among the cities of the Earth: New York!
Rich as a cake, common as a doughnut,
Expensive as a fur and crazy as cocaine,
We love to hear you shake
Your big face like a shining bank
Letting the mad world know you're full of dimes!

"This is your night to make maraccas out of all that metal
money
Paris is in the prison-house, and London dies of cancer.
This is the time for you to whirl,
Queen of our hopped-up peace,
And let the excitement of your somewhat crippled congas
Supersede the waltzes of more shining
Capitals that have been bombed.

"Meanwhile we, your children,
Weeping in our seasick zoo of windows while you dance,
Will gobble aspirins,
And try to keep our cage from caving in.
All the while our minds will fill with these petitions,
Flowering quietly in between our gongs of pulse.
These will have to serve as prayers:

" 'O lock us in the safe jails of thy movies!
Confine us to the semiprivate wards and white asylums
Of the unbearable cocktail parties, O New York!
Sentence us for life to the penitentiaries of thy bars and
nightclubs,
And leave us stupefied forever by the blue, objective lights
That fill the pale infirmaries of thy restaurants,
And the clinics of thy schools and offices,
And the operating-rooms of thy dance-halls.

" 'But never give us any explanations, even when we ask,
Why all our food tastes of iodoform,

And even the freshest flowers smell of funerals.
No, never let us look about us long enough to wonder
Which of the rich men, shivering in the overheated office,
And which of the poor men, sleeping face-down on the
    Daily Mirror,
Are still alive, and which are dead.' "

TOWER OF BABEL

The Political Speech

    History is a dialogue between
    forward and backward
    going inevitably forward
    by the misuse of words.

Now the function of the word is:
To designate first the machine,
Then what the machine produces
Then what the machine destroys.
Words show us these things not only in order to mean them
But in order to provoke them
And to incorporate us in their forward movement:
Doing, making, destroy or rather
Being done, being made, being destroyed.
Such is history.

The forgotten principle is that the machine
Should always destroy the maker of the machine
Being more important than the maker
Insofar as man is more important than God.
Words also reflect this principle

Though they are meant to conceal it
From the ones who are too young to know.

Thus words have no essential meaning.
They are means of locomotion
From backward to forward
Along an infinite horizontal plane,
Created by the history which they themselves destroy.
They are the makers of our only reality
The backward-forward working of the web
The movement into the web.

NOMBRIL WALKETH ON THE LOAM

Nombril walketh on the loam
Feeling pretty nasty
Saturday he come upon
Mister Periphrastic:
"Mister, scrap your Theodore,
Dumb today, tomorrow senseless,
Can you write no better verse
They'll take away your pencils.

Pardon me my farthing face,
Pardon you your poundish presence
They took away my birdish box
I use for keeping flocks of pheasants
Robbed me of my case of bears,
Stole away my pocketfox
Indeed the sly unknown monsieurs
Have treat me mighty shabby
Stolen from me rather badly
Treated me like dogs."

Nombril walketh on the sand
Flying mean and close,
Scuds around to pester mister
Smacks him in the nose:
"Mister clap your theaters
Alms today, tomorrow boons,
Meanwhile I snatch your writing pen
Like I warned you once.

Pardon me my penny presence,
Pardon you your Dieu me sauve
I picked up a dirty word that
Fits you like a glove,.
They took away my crate of geese
They all unwound my mouses pen
They foxed my box of antelopes."

LENT

(A Fragment)

Close, eyes, and soul, come home!
Senses will seem to perish, in the desert:
Thought will pretend to live on punishment, among the empty
    tombs.

'Til pride, amid the rocks and sepulchers of Thebes, lies quiet.
The thoughts that foraged for him, kept him fed,
Find in the stones no sustenance,
And scatter to another country, and a milder weather.

Sight will, it seems, dwell idle in her gates:
Not watch the shafts of the sharp sun

Nor feel the little thorn-light of the moon.
Sound will sit lifeless in our ears' small shell,
(Once crowded, and amazed with din of vendors,
The clamors in the stricken galleries,
The clangor of the dead man's funeral bell.)
And skill, forsake these fingers if you will.

SACRED HEART 2

(A Fragment–)

Geography comes to an end,
Compass has lost all earthly north,
Horizons have no meaning
Nor roads an explanation:
I cannot even hope for any special borealis
To rouse my darkness with a brief "Hurray"!

O flaming Heart,
Unseen and unimagined in this wilderness,
You, You alone are real, and here I've found You.
Here will I love and praise You in a tongueless death,
Until my white devoted bones,
Long bleached and polished by the winds of this Sahara,
Relive at Your command,
Rise and unfold the flowers of their everlasting spring.

THIRTY POEMS
(1944)

Virgini Mariae, Reginae Poetarum
Sanctissimae Dei Genitrici Ac Semper

LENT IN A YEAR OF WAR

One of you is a major, made of cord and catskin,

But never dreams his eyes may come to life and thread
The needle-light of famine in a waterglass.

One of you is the paper Jack of Sprites
And will not cast his sentinel voice
Spiraling up the dark ears of the wind
Where the prisoner's yell is lost.

"What if it was our thumbs put out the sun
When the Lance and Cross made their mistake?
You'll never rob us our Eden of drumskin shelters,
You, with the bite of John the Baptist's halter,
Getting away in the basket of Paul,
Loving the answer of death, the mother of Lent!"

Thus, in the evening of their sinless murders,
Jack and the Major, sifting the stars for a sign
See the north-south horizon parting like a string!

THE FLIGHT INTO EGYPT

Through every precinct of the wintry city
Squadroned iron resounds upon the streets;
Herod's police

Make shudder the dark steps of the tenements
At the business about to be done.

Neither look back upon Thy starry country,
Nor hear what rumors crowd across the dark
Where blood runs down those holy walls,
Nor frame a childish blessing with Thy hand
Towards that fiery spiral of exulting souls!

Go, Child of God, upon the singing desert,
Where, with eyes of flame,
The roaming lion keeps thy road from harm.

PROPHET

I met a traveller from the holy desert,
Honeycomb, beggarbread eater,
Lean from drinking rain
That lies in the windprints of rocks.

He had been where
The winds of spring were cats
Running in the rigging of our trees.

He had already seen our new year's storms
Crowding the woods like wrestlers,
Fencing where the morning turns to water
On all our flashing pastures.

And he had also seen the rays of our sun,
Taken in a branchy cage,
Move and sing; those rays in shining choirs,

Telling the time when our woods' Saint Savior's promise,
Flashing like a crossflag in the sky,
Would come disarm our Lent.

I met a traveller from the holy desert.

THE DARK MORNING

This is the black day when
Fog rides the ugly air:
Water wades among the buildings
To the prisoner's curled ear.

Then rain, in thin sentences,
Slakes him like danger,
Whose heart is his Germany
Fevered with anger.

This is the dark day when
Locks let the enemy in
Through all the coiling passages of
(Curled ear) my prison!

SONG FOR OUR LADY OF COBRE

The white girls lift their heads like trees,
The black girls go
Reflected like flamingoes in the street.

The white girls sing as shrill as water,
The black girls talk as quiet as clay.

The white girls open their arms like clouds,
The black girls close their eyes like wings:
Angels bow down like bells,
Angels look up like toys,

Because the heavenly stars
Stand in a ring:
And all the pieces of the mosaic, earth,
Get up and fly away like birds.

THE NIGHT TRAIN

In the unreason of a rainy midnight
France blooms along the windows
Of my sleepy bathysphere,
And runs to seed in a luxuriance of curious lights.

Escape is drawn straight through my dream
And shines to Paris, clean as a violin string,
While spring tides of commotion,
(The third-class pianos of the Orient Express)
Fill up the hollow barrels of my ears.

Cities that stood, by day, as gay as lancers
Are lost, in the night, like old men dying.
At a point where polished rails branch off forever
The steels lament, like crazy ladies.
We wake, and weep the deaths of the cathedrals
That we have never seen,

Because we hear the jugulars of the country
Fly in the wind, and vanish with a cry.

At once the diplomats start up, as white as bread,
Buckle the careless cases of their minds
That just fell open in the sleeper:

For, by the rockets of imaginary sieges
They see to read big, terrible print,
Each in the other's face,

That spells the undecoded names
Of the assassins they will recognise too late:
The ones that seem to be secret police,
Now all in place, all armed, in the obvious ambush.

SAINT JASON

This is the night the false Saint Jason
Wakes in fear from his cannibal sleep,
And drenches the edges of his eyes
With his tears' iron overflow;

For the flying scream of his dead woman
Opened the stitches of his skin,
And Jason bounced in the burly wind
Like a man of sack and string.

"What do you want, in the windows of your wound
Where Judas' money shines
By daggers' waterlight?"

"—I want the martyrs' eyes, as tight as shells,
In death's pretended sleep."

"What does it mean sunlight weeps in your door
Like an abandoned child?"

"—It means the heavyhanded storm,
Whirling and ploughing the wet woods,
Has filled with terrible speech
The stone doors of my feast:

The feast of the false Saint Jason's first communion."

THE MESSENGER

There is some sentry at the rim of winter
Fed with the speech the wind makes
In the grand belfries of the sleepless timber.

He understands the lasting strife of tears,
And the way the world is strung;
He waits to warn all life with the tongue of March's bugle,
Of the coming of the warrior sun.

When spring has garrisonned up her army of water,
A million grasses leave their tents, and stand in rows
To see their invincible brother.
Mending the winter's ruins with their laughter,
The flowers go out to their undestructive wars.

Walk in the woods and be witnesses,
You, the best of these poor children.

When Gabriel hit the bright shore of the world,
Yours were the eyes saw some
Star-sandalled stranger walk like lightning down the air,
The morning the Mother of God
Loved and dreaded the message of an angel.

THE REGRET

When cold November sits among the reeds like an unlucky
    fisher

And ducks drum up as sudden as the wind
Out of the rushy river,
We slowly come, robbed of our rod and gun,
Walking amid the stricken cages of the trees.

The stormy weeks have all gone home like drunken hunters,
Leaving the gates of the grey world wide open to December.
But now there is no speech of branches in these broken jails.
Acorns lie over the earth, no less neglected
Than our unrecognizable regret:
And here we stand as senseless as the oaks,
As dumb as elms.

And though we seem as grave as jailers, yet we did not come
    to wonder
Who picked the locks of the past days, and stole our summer.
(We are no longer listeners for curious saws, and secret keys!)

We are indifferent to seasons,
And stand like hills, deaf.
And never hear the last of the escaping year
Go ducking through the bended branches like a leaf.

POEM

Watching, among the rifled branches, for the sun, our hero,
(Sing, wind, too tuneless in the slender trees)

We think about a whiter day, the marble temples
And the hills, our girls,
The even lovelier skies,
The horses of Poseidon, the lifting seas,
All grave, and clean, and wiser than the glassy mornings.

Watching, among the colored rocks, the sea, our happy
    swimmer,
(Sing, winds, more clearly on the Greek acropoli)

We think about the cries of drowners and the shine of armor,
While the hills, our citadels,
The strict, immovable trees,
    (More marble than the marching winner
    Who winters in our corridors of discontent)
Grow cloudy, in the teeth of the command.

Waiting, among the rifled temples for the light, our savior,
(Play, winds, in this too voiceless choir of columns)

We think about the whiter colonnades, the wiser city,
While the green hills, our shambles,
The burning olive gardens,
Have made the country blinder than the smoky temples,
Louder and harsher than the foamy sea.

Waiting among the rifled branches for the sun, our hero,
Sing, wind, too tuneless in the slender trees!

34

AUBADE: LAKE ERIE

When sun, light handed, sows this Indian water
With a crop of cockles,
The vines arrange their tender shadows
In the sweet leafage of an artificial France.

Awake, in the frames of windows, innocent children,
Loving the blue, sprayed leaves of childish life,
Applaud the bearded corn, the bleeding grape,
And cry:
"Here is the hay-colored sun, our marvelous cousin,
Walking in the barley,
Turning the harrowed earth to growing bread,
And splicing the sweet, wounded vine.
Lift up your hitch-hiking heads
And no more fear the fever,
You fugitives, and sleepers in the fields,
Here is the hay-colored sun!"

And when their shining voices, clean as summer,
Play, like churchbells over the field,
A hundred dusty Luthers rise from the dead, unheeding,
Search the horizon for the gap-toothed grin of factories,
And grope, in the green wheat,
Toward the wood winds of the western freight.

FOR MY BROTHER:
REPORTED MISSING IN ACTION, 1943

Sweet brother, if I do not sleep
My eyes are flowers for your tomb;
And if I cannot eat my bread,

My fasts shall live like willows where you died.
If in the heat I find no water for my thirst,
My thirst shall turn to springs for you, poor traveller.

Where, in what desolate and smokey country,
Lies your poor body, lost and dead?
And in what landscape of disaster
Has your unhappy spirit lost its road?

Come, in my labor find a resting place
And in my sorrows lay your head,
Or rather take my life and blood
And buy yourself a better bed—
Or take my breath and take my death
And buy yourself a better rest.

When all the men of war are shot
And flags have fallen into dust,
Your cross and mine shall tell men still
Christ died on each, for both of us.

For in the wreckage of your April Christ lies slain,
And Christ weeps in the ruins of my spring:
The money of Whose tears shall fall
Into your weak and friendless hand,
And buy you back to your own land:
The silence of Whose tears shall fall
Like bells upon your alien tomb.
Hear them and come: they call you home.

IPHIGENIA: POLITICS

The stairs lead to the room as bleak as glass
Where fancy turns the statues.

The empty chairs are dreaming of a protocol,
The tables, of a treaty;
And the world has become a museum.

(The girl is gone,
Fled from the broken altar by the beach,
From the unholy sacrifice when calms became a trade-wind.)

The palaces stare out from their uncurtained trouble,
And windows weep in the weak sun.
The women fear the empty upper rooms
More than the streets as grey as guns
Or the swordlight of the wide unfriendly esplanade.

Thoughts turn to salt among those shrouded chairs
Where, with knives no crueller than pens, or promises,
Took place the painless slaying of the leader's daughter.

O, humbler than the truth she bowed her head,
And scarcely seemed, to us, to die.
But after she was killed she fled, alive, like a surprise,
Out of the glass world, to Diana's Tauris.

Then wind cheered like a hero in the tackle of the standing
    ships
And hurled them bravely on the swords and lances of the
    wintry sea—
While wisdom turned to salt upon the broken piers.

This is the way the ministers have killed the truth,
    our daughter,
Steps lead back into the rooms we fear to enter;
Our minds are bleaker than the hall of mirrors:

And the world has become a museum.

THE WINTER'S NIGHT

When, in the dark, the frost cracks on the window
The children awaken, and whisper.
One says the moonlight grated like a skate
Across the freezing river.
Another hears the starlight breaking like a knifeblade
Upon the silent, steelbright pond.
They say the trees are stiller than the frozen water
From waiting for a shouting light, a heavenly message.

Yet it is far from Christmas, when a star
Sang in the pane, as brittle as their innocence!
For now the light of early Lent
Glitters upon the icy step—
"We have wept letters to our patron saints,
(The children say) yet slept before they ended."

Oh, is there in this night no sound of strings, of singers?
None coming from the wedding, no, nor Bridegroom's
      messenger?
(The sleepy virgins stir, and trim their lamps.)

The moonlight rings upon the ice as sudden as a footstep;
Starlight clinks upon the dooryard stone, too like a latch,
And the children are, again, awake,
And all call out in whispers to their guardian angels.

DEATH

Where are the merchants and the money-lenders
Whose love sang in the wires between the seaports and the
      inland granaries?

Is the old trader any safer than the sailor sent to drown
Crossing the world's end in a wooden schooner?

Where are the generals who sacked the sunny cities
And burned the cattle and the grain?
Or is the politician any safer in his offices
Than a soldier shot in the eye?

Take time to tremble lest you come without reflection
To feel the furious mercies of my friendship,
(Says death) because I come as quick as intuition.

Cliffs of your hangovers were never half so dizzy as my
       infinite abyss:
Flesh cannot wrestle with the waters that are in the earth,
Nor spirit rest in icy clay!

More than the momentary night of faith, to the lost dead,
Shall be their never-ending midnight:

Yet all my power is conquered by a child's "Hail Mary"
And all my night forever lightened by one waxen candle!

HOLY COMMUNION: THE CITY

"What light will, in your eyes, like an archangel,
Soon stand armed,
O you who come with looks more lowly than the dewy valleys,
And kneel like lepers on the step of Bethlehem?

    "Although we know no hills, no country rivers,
    Here in the jungles of our waterpipes and iron ladders,

Our thoughts are quieter than rivers,
Our loves are simpler than the trees,
Our prayers deeper than the sea.

"What wounds had furrowed up our dry and fearful spirit
Until the massbells came like rain to make them vineyards?

"Now, brighter on our minds' bright mountains
Than the towns of Israel,
Shall shine desire!

"O Glory, be not swift to vanish like the wine's slight savor,
And still lie lightly, Truth, upon our tongues,
For Grace moves, like the wind,
The armies of the wheat our secret hero!
And Faith sits in our hearts like fire,
And makes them smile like suns,

"While we come back from lovely Bethlehem
To burn down Harlem with the glad Word of Our Savior."

THE COMMUNION

O sweet escape! O smiling flight!
O what bright secret breaks our jails of flesh?
For we are fled, among the shining vineyards,
And ride in praises in the hills of wheat,
To find our hero, in His tents of light!
O sweet escape! O smiling flight!

O sweet escape! O smiling flight!
The vineyards break our fetters with their laughter!

40

Our souls walk home as quiet as skies.
The snares that death, our subtle hunter, set,
Are all undone by beams of light!
O sweet escape! O smiling flight!

O sweet escape! O smiling flight!
Unlock our dark! And let us out of night!
And set us free to go to prison in this vineyard,
(Where, in the vines, the sweet and secret sun
Works our eternal rescue into wine)
O sweet escape! O smiling flight!

We'll rob Your vines, and raid Your hills of wheat,
Until you lock us, Jesus in Your jails of light!
O sweet escape! O smiling flight!

EVENING

Now, in the middle of the limpid evening,
The moon speaks clearly to the hill.
The wheatfields make their simple music,
Praise the quiet sky.

And down the road, the way the stars come home,
The cries of children
Play on the empty air, a mile or more,
And fall on our deserted hearing,
Clear as water.

They say the sky is made of glass,
They say the smiling moon's a bride.
They say they love the orchards and apple trees,

The trees, their innocent sisters, dressed in blossoms,
Still wearing, in the blurring dusk,
White dresses from that morning's first communion.

And, where blue heaven's fading fire last shines
They name the new come planets
With words that flower
On little voices, light as stems of lilies.

And where blue heaven's fading fire last shines,
Reflected in the poplar's ripple,
One little, wakeful bird
Sings like a shower.

THE VINE

When wind and winter turn our vineyard
To a bitter Calvary,
What hands come out and crucify us
Like the innocent vine?

How long will starlight weep as sharp as thorns
In the night of our desolate life?
How long will moonlight fear to free the naked prisoner?
Or is there no deliverer?

A mob of winds, on Holy Thursday, come like murderers
And batter the walls of our locked and terrified souls.
Our doors are down, and our defense is done.
Good Friday's rains, in Roman order,
March, with sharpest lances, up our vineyard hill.

More dreadful than St. Peter's cry
When he was being swallowed in the sea,
Cries out our anguish: "O! We are abandoned!"
When in our life we see the ruined vine
Cut open by the cruel spring,
Ploughed by the furious season!

As if we had forgotten how the whips of winter
And the cross of April
Would all be lost in one bright miracle.
For look! The vine on Calvary is bright with branches!
See how the leaves laugh in the light,
And how the whole hill smiles with flowers:
And know how all our numbered veins must run
With life, like the sweet vine, when it is full of sun.

THE EVENING OF THE VISITATION

Go, roads, to the four quarters of our quiet distance,
While you, full moon, wise queen,
Begin your evening journey to the hills of heaven,
And travel no less stately in the summer sky
Than Mary, going to the house of Zachary.

The woods are silent with the sleep of doves,
The valleys with the sleep of streams,
And all our barns are happy with peace of cattle gone to rest.
Still wakeful, in the fields, the shocks of wheat
Preach and say prayers:
You sheaves, make all your evensongs as sweet as ours,
Whose summer world, all ready for the granary and barn,
Seems to have seen, this day,
Into the secret of the Lord's Nativity.

Now at the fall of night, you shocks
Still bend your heads like kind and humble kings
The way you did this golden morning when you saw God's
    Mother passing,
While all our windows fill and sweeten
With the mild vespers of the hay and barley.

You moon and rising stars, pour on our barns and houses
Your gentle benedictions.
Remind us how our Mother, with far subtler and more holy
    influence,
Blesses our rooves and eaves,
Our shutters, lattices and sills,
Our doors, and floors, and stairs, and rooms, and bedrooms,
Smiling by night upon her sleeping children:
O gentle Mary! Our lovely Mother in heaven!

IN MEMORY OF THE SPANISH
POET FEDERICO GARCIA LORCA

Where the white bridge rears up its stamping arches
Proud as a colt across the clatter of the shallow river,
The sharp guitars
Have never forgotten your name.

Only the swordspeech of the cruel strings
Can pierce the minds of those who remain,
Sitting in the eyeless ruins of the houses,
The shelter of the broken wall.

A woman has begun to sing:
O music the color of olives!

Her eyes are darker than the deep cathedrals;
Her words come dressed as mourners,
In the gate of her shadowy voice,
Each with a meaning like a sheaf of seven blades!

The spires and high Giraldas, still as nails
Nailed in the four cross roads,
Watch where the song becomes the color of carnations,
And flowers like wounds in the white dust of Spain.

(Under what crossless Calvary lie your lost bones,
    Garcia Lorca?
What white Sierra hid your murder in a rocky valley?)

In the four quarters of the world, the wind is still,
And wonders at the swordplay of the fierce guitar:
The voice has turned to iron in the naked air,
More loud and more despairing than a ruined tower.

(Under what crossless Calvary lie your lost bones,
    Garcia Lorca?
What white Sierra hid your murder in a rocky valley?)

THE TRAPPIST ABBEY: MATINS

(Our Lady of Gethsemani, Kentucky)

When the full fields begin to smell of sunrise
And the valleys sing in their sleep,
The pilgrim moon pours over the solemn darkness
Her waterfalls of silence,
And then departs, up the long avenue of trees.

The stars hide, in the glade, their light, like tears,
And tremble where some train runs, lost,
Baying in eastward mysteries of distance,
Where fire flares, somewhere, over a sink of cities.

Now kindle in the windows of this ladyhouse, my soul,
Your childish, clear awakeness:
Burn in the country night
Your wise and sleepless lamp.
For, from the frowning tower, the windy belfry,
Sudden the bells come, bridegrooms,
And fill the echoing dark with love and fear.

Wake in the windows of Gethsemani, my soul, my sister,
For the past years, with smokey torches, come,
Bringing betrayal from the burning world
And bloodying the glade with pitch flame.

Wake in the cloisters of the lonely night, my soul, my sister,
Where the apostles gather, who were, one time, scattered,
And mourn God's blood in the place of His betrayal,
And weep with Peter at the triple cock-crow.

THE BLESSED VIRGIN MARY
COMPARED TO A WINDOW

Because my will is simple as a window
And knows no pride of original earth,
It is my life to die, like glass, by light:
Slain in the strong rays of the bridegroom sun.

Because my love is simple as a window
And knows no shame of original dust,

I longed all night, (when I was visible) for dawn my death:
When I would marry day, my Holy Spirit:
And die by transsubstantiation into light.

For light, my lover, steals my life in secret.
I vanish into day, and leave no shadow
But the geometry of my cross,
Whose frame and structure are the strength
By which I die, but only to the earth,
And am uplifted to the sky my life.

When I become the substance of my lover,
(Being obedient, sinless glass)
I love all things that need my lover's life,
And live to give my newborn Morning to your quiet rooms,

—Your rooms, that would be tombs,
Or vaults of night, and death, and terror,
Fill with the clarity of living Heaven,
Shine with the rays of God's Jerusalem:
O shine, bright Sions!

Because I die by brightness and the Holy Spirit,
The sun rejoices in your jail, my kneeling Christian,
(Where even now you weep and grin
To learn, from my simplicity, the strength of faith.)

Therefore do not be troubled at the judgments of the thunder.
Stay still and pray, still stay, my other son,
And do not fear the armies and black ramparts
Of the advancing and retreating rains:
I'll let no lightning kill your room's white order.

Although it is the day's last hour,
Look with no fear:

For the torn storm lets in, at the world's rim,
Three streaming rays as straight as Jacob's ladder:

And you shall see the sun, my Son, my Substance,
Come to convince the world of the day's end, and of the night,
Smile to the lovers of the day in smiles of blood:
For through my love, He'll be their Brother,
My light—the Lamb of their Apocalypse.

ARIADNE AT THE LABYRINTH

Patient, in the fire of noon,
Hands, that hold the thread, crossed,
Ariadne's a Barbadian flower,
And grows by the Labyrinth door.

Under the blue, airy-waters of evening,
Hands folded like white petals,
Watching for the bold adventurer,
Ariadne waits as calm as coral,
Silent as some plant of undersea.

Drums ring at the city's edge:
The speechless hills put on crowns of dark flame;
Dancing citizens fly like little flags
Amid the glad volcano of their congas.
But Ariadne's eyes are lakes
Beside the maze's starwhite wall:

For in the Caribbean midnight
Of her wild and gentle wisdom, she foreknows
And solves the maze's cruel algebra.

But when white morning
Runs with a shout along the jagged mountains
Strength of a cotton thread draws out to Ariadne
The Bravest Soldier, the Wisest Judge,
The Mightiest King!

DIRGE FOR THE PROUD WORLD

Where is the marvelous thief
Who stole harvests from the angry sun
And sacked, with his bright sight, the land?

Where he lies dead, the quiet earth unpacks him
And wind is waving in the earth's revenge:
Fields of barley, oats and rye.

Where is the millionaire
Who squandered the bright spring?
Whose lies played in the summer evening sky
Like cheap guitars?
Who spent the golden fortunes of the fall
And died as bare as a tree?

His heart lies open like a treasury,
Filled up with grass, and generous flowers.

Where is the crazy gambler
Amid the nickels of whose blood have fallen
Heavy half-dollars of his last of life?
Where is he gone?

The burning bees come walk, as bright as jewels
Upon that flowering, dark sun:
The bullet wound in his unmoving lung.

Oh you who hate the gambler or his enemy,
Remember how the bees
Pay visits to the patient dead
And borrow honey from their charitable blood.

You who have judged the gambler or his enemy
Remember this, before the proud world's funeral.

THE HOLY SACRAMENT OF THE ALTAR

You senses, never still, but shrill as children,
Become more humble and more low:
Learn adoration, where our sceret life,
Our Corpus Christi,
Here lives uplifted in His golden window.

Eyes, in your murky night, know new simplicity.
Your ears and iron voices, leave your wars.
Hands, have one action more: wash yourselves clean, and then
    be still.

And all you senses, waiting here, reborn by water,
Stay wakeful in these joyful attitudes,
Attentive to the wheat our holy Stranger:
He is bright heaven's open door.

Look where the Lamb bends all His brightness
Low as our dim and puny lights
Although His fleece is full of sun.
Not all the universe can comprehend
His glory's equal, nor His light's,
Who loves us so, He won't outshine our winking candles!

Be kindled, intellect, although your strongest lamps are
    night-lights
By the beams of this wonderful Sun!
Created wisdom makes at best a metal monstrance, for
    His crown,
And those stiff rays look like no living light:
They are no more than golden spikes, and golden thorns!

But where is reason at the Lamb's bright feast?
Reason and knowledge have bought oxen and they cannot
    come.
Thrift and prudence give their own excuses,
And justice has a wife, and must stay home.

To the cold corners of the earth rise up and go:
Find beggar Faith, and bring him to the holy table.
He shall sit down among the good apostles,
And weep with Peter at the washing of the feet.

His bread shall be the smiles of Pity's human face:
He'll eat, and live with God, at least in longing, ever after:
His wine shall be the mortal blood of Mercy, Love and Peace:
And, having drunk, he'll hear the martyr's joyful laughter.

AN ARGUMENT: OF THE PASSION OF CHRIST

*"And what one of you, by taking thought, can add to his stature one
cubit?"* St. Matthew, vi. 27.

i

The furious prisoner of the womb,
Rebellious, in the jaws of life,

Learns, from the mother's conscious flesh,
The secret laws of blood and strife.

The demon raging at the breast,
Arrayed in cries, and crowned with tears,
Has sucked the magics of the east,
The doubts of the philosophers.

In the red straits of his arteries,
Love runs, lost and ravening;
Nothingness feeds upon itself
And swells up to a mighty king!

Wit walks out, in envy's mask;
Love will hide, and be a lecher.
Adultery, by taking thought,
Adds a cubit to his stature,

Until we scan the wastes of death,
And wind blows through our cage of bones;
Sight leaves the sockets of the skull,
And love runs mad among the stones!

ii

The worm that watched within the womb
Was standing guard at Jesus' tomb,
And my first angry, infant breath
Stood wakeful, lest He rise from death.
My adolescence, like the wolf,
Fled to the edges of the gulf
And searched the ruins of the night
To hide from Calvary's iron light:
But in the burning jaws of day

I saw the barren Judas Tree;
For, to the caverns of my pride
Judas had come, and there was paid!

iii

Seeds of the three hours' agony
Fell on good earth, and grew from me,
And, cherished by my sleepless cares
Flowered with God's blood, and Mary's tears.
My curious love found its reward
When Love was scourged in Pilate's yard:
Here was the work my hands had made:
A thorny crown, to cut His head.
The growth of thoughts that made me great
Lay on His cross, and were its weight;
And my desires lay, turned to stones,
And where He fell, cut to the bone.
The sharpnesses of my delight
Were spikes run through His hands and feet,
And from the sweetness of my will
Their sponge drew vinegar and gall.

iv

The cry that rent the temple veil
And split the earth as deep as hell
And echoed through the universe,
Sounds, in bombardments, down to us.
There is no ear that has not heard
The deathless cry of murdered God:
No eye that has not looked upon
The lance of the crucifixion:

And yet that cry beats at the ears
Of old, deaf-mute interpreters,
Whose querulous and feeble cries
Drown stronger voices, and whose eyes
Will let no light of lances in:
They still will clamor for a sign!

ST. AGNES: A RESPONSORY

Cujus pulchritudinem
Sol et luna mirantur . . .
    Hear with what joy this child of God
    Plays in the perfect garden of her martyrdom,
Ipsi soli servo fidem.

    Spending the silver of her little life
    To bring her Bridegroom these bright flowers
    Of which her arms are full.

Cujus pulchritudinem . . .
    With what white smiles
    She buys the Popes their palliums,
    And lavishes upon our souls the lambs of her confession!
Sol et luna mirantur,
Ipsi soli servo fidem.

    Her virtues, with their simple strings,
    Play to the Lover hidden in the universe,
Cujus pulchritudinem . . .
    Who smiles into the sun His looking-glass,
    And fills it with his glorious face:

Who utters the round moon's recurring O
And drowns our dusks in peace.
Ipsi soli servo fidem!

The Roman captain's work is done:
Now he may tear his temples down—
Her charity has flown to four horizons, like the swiftest
    doves,

Where all towns sing like springtime, with their newborn bells
Pouring her golden name out of their crucibles.

THE HOLY CHILD'S SONG

When midnight occupied the porches of the Poet's reason
Sweeter than any bird
He heard the Holy Child.

SONG

"When My kind Father, kinder than the sun,
With looks and smiles bends down
And utters My bodily life,
My flesh, obeying, praises Heaven like a smiling cloud.
Then I become the laughter of the watercourses.
I am the gay wheatfields, the serious hills:
I fill the sky with words of light, and My incarnate songs
Fly in and out the branches of My childish voice
Like thrushes in a tree.

"And when My Mother, pretty as a church,
Takes Me upon her lap, I laugh with love,

Loving to live in her flesh, which is My house—and full of
    light!
(Because the sky My Spirit enters in at all the windows)
O, then what songs and what incarnate joys
Dance in the bright rays of My childish voice!

> "In winter when the birds put down their flutes
> And wind plays sharper than a fife upon the icy rain,
> I sit in this crib,
> And laugh like fire, and clap My golden hands:
> To view my friends the timid beasts—
> Their great brown flanks, muzzles and milky breath!

"Therefore come, shepherds, from your rocky hill,
And bend about My crib in wonder and adore My joy.
My glances are as good as wine.
The little rivers of My smile
Will wash away all ruins from your eyes,
As I lift up My hands,
As white as blackthorn blossoms,
And charm and kiss you with My seven sacraments.

"This seeming winter is your spring
When skies put off their armor:
Because My Heart already holds
The secret mortal wound,
By which I shall transform all deserts into garden-ground:
And there the peaceful trees,
All day say credos, being full of leaves—
And I will come and be your noon-day sun,
And make your shadows palaces of moving light:
And you will show Me your flowers."

When midnight occupied the porches of the Poet's reason
Sweeter than any bird
He heard the Holy Child.

THE SPONGE FULL OF VINEGAR

When Romans gambled in the clash of lancelight,
Dicing amid the lightnings for the unsewn mantle,
Thirst burned crimson, like a crosswise firebird
Even in the eyes of dying Christ.
But the world's gall, and all its rotten vinegar
Reeked in the sponge, flamed on His swollen mouth,
And all was paid in poison, in the taste of our feasts!

O Lord! When I lie breathless in Thy churches
Knowing it is Thy glory goes again
Torn from the wise world in the daily thundercracks of
        massbells,
I drink new fear from the four clean prayers I ever gave Thee!
For even the Word of Thy Name, caught from Thy grace,
And offered up out of my deepest terror,
Goes back gallsavored of flesh.
Even the one good sacrifice,
The thirst of heaven, comes to Thee: vinegar!
Reeks of the death-thirst manlife found in the forbidden apple.

A MAN IN THE DIVIDED SEA
(1946)

Virgini Mariae Immaculatae
Poetarum Reginae
Dominae Monachorum Beatissimae
Salvatoris Matri

SONG

(From Crossportion's Pastoral)

The bottom of the sea has come
And builded in my noiseless room
The fishes' and the mermaids' home,

Whose it is most, most hell to be
Out of the heavy-hanging sea
And in the thin, thin changeable air

Or unroom sleep some other where;
But play their coral violins
Where waters most lock music in:

The bottom of my room, the sea.
Full of voiceless curtaindeep
There mermaid somnambules come sleep
Where fluted half-lights show the way,

And there, there lost orchestras play
And down the many quarterlights come
To the dim mirth of my aquadrome:
The bottom of my sea, the room.

POEM: 1939

The white, the silent stars
Drive their wheeling ring,

Crane down out of the tall black air
To hear the swanworld sing.

But the long, deep knife is in,
(O bitter, speechless earth)
Throat grows tight, voice thin,
Blood gets no regrowth,

As night devours our days,
Death puts out our eyes,
Towns dry up and flare like tongues
But no voice prophesies.

THE MAN IN THE WIND

Here is the man who fancies Arab ponies,
Captain April, walking like the wind,
Breeding the happy swordlight of the sun.

Secret, in his looks and manner,
He's not as inattentive to the music as he seems,
That jangles in the empty doorways.

But his well-tempered spirit,
Rapt in the middle of a harmony,
Flies to a breathless wedding with the Palisades.

Then his five senses, separate as their numbers,
Scatter, like birds, from in front of his steps,
And instantly return, like water,
To the common Bermuda of the flashing river.

The mathematics of the air describes a perfect silence,
And Captain April's mind, leaning out of its own
    amazing windows,
Dies in a swirl of doves.

ARIADNE

All through the blazing afternoon
The hand drums talk together like locusts;
The flute pours out its endless, thin stream,
Threading it in and out the clatter of sticks upon
    wood-blocks.
Drums and bells exchange handfuls of bright coins,
Drums and bells scatter their music, like pennies, all
    over the air,
And see, the lutanist's thin hand
Rapidly picks the spangling notes off from his wires
And throws them about like drops of water.

Behind the bamboo blinds,
Behind the palms,
In the green, sundappled apartments of her palace
Redslippered Ariadne, with a tiny yawn,
Tosses a ball upon her roulette wheel.

Suddenly, dead north,
A Greek ship leaps over the horizon, skips like a colt,
    paws the foam.
The ship courses through the pasture of bright
    amethysts
And whinnies at the jetty.
The whole city runs to see:

Quick as closing your hand
The racing sail's down.
Then the drums are stunned, and the crowd, exalted, cries:
O Theseus! O Grecian hero!

Like a thought through the mind
Ariadne moves to the window.
Arrows of light, in every direction,
Leap from the armor of the black-eyed captain.
Arrows of light
Resound within her like the strings of a guitar.

THE ORACLE

The girls with eyes of wicks of lights,
Thin as the rushes, and as many,
Make in their minds uncertain shapes of music,
And slyly string their phony harps with twine.

The girls with eyes of drops of water,
Thin as the fires, and as frightened,
Bring pennies and their empty zodiacs.
Horses, loose on a plain, drum
The secret dance their thought does now!

Come up and light your harmless questions.
Burn them to the Brazen Face,
And wait, in terror, for the Brazen Voice.

   "You girls with eyes of wicks of lights,
   Shake me: I ring like a bank.
   I shout like the assembly: 'Go, be presidents!'
   You shall all marry rectangles!"

"But you with eyes of drops of water,
Punch my brass eyes with your little fists;
I am a box, my voice is only electric.
So keep your pennies for the poor;
Sew, in your houses, and cry."

But already, down the far, fast ladders of light
The stern, astounding angel
Starts with a truer message,
Carrying a lily.

TROPICS

At noon the sky goes off like a gun.

Guards, on the Penal Island,
Converging, mad as murder, in the swearing cane,
Arrest the four footed wind.

But the chained and numbered men
Do not cease their labor:
Building a cage for the devouring sun.

At six o'clock, exactly,
The day explodes like a bomb,
And it is night.

Instantly, the guards
Hide in the jungle, build a boat
And escape.

But the prisoners of the state
Do not cease their labor:
Collecting the asphalt fragments of the night.

FUGITIVE

Out in the green sun-dancing cane a mad half-Spaniard
Hiding, like a robber, from a coffee-drinking Judas,
Fears the newspaper owners
And the millionaires.

Planted, like bulbs, in the wet earth of sleep
His eyes had started to sprout:
Sea-changing in his murk of dreaming blood,
And shining in his fathoms of ambition,
Bones had begun to turn to money.

But now with secret agents out of mind
And mad sunstorm of parrots out of memory,
Beyond two miles of jungle,
He only sees the sweetly drumming sun.

And yet his waking memory, a murderous rooster,
Crested with a rag of meat,
Whirls its spurs in a cloud of magic feathers,
Braving the bread-colored dust.

But bamboo trees click in the wind like rosaries.
Charmed with watchfulness and thirst
His paper mask plays, (always), dead.

And in the priestly darkness of his love
Twenty prayers at once, to Saint Lazare
Talk with tongues of candle-flame,

And one by one are folded up
The treacherous, fly-catching flowers of his will.

ASH WEDNESDAY

The naked traveller,
Stretching, against the iron dawn, the bowstrings of
    his eyes,
Starves on the mad sierra.

But the sleepers,
Prisoners in a lovely world of weeds,
Make a small, red cry,
And change their dreams.

Proud as the mane of the whinnying air,
Yet humble as the flakes of water
Or the chips of the stone sun, the traveller
Is nailed to the hill by the light of March's razor;

And when the desert barks, in a rage of love
For the noon of the eclipse,
He lies with his throat cut, in a frozen crater.

Then the sleepers,
Prisoners of a moonward power of tides,
Slain by the stillness of their own reflections,
Sit up, in their graves, with a white cry,
And die of terror at the traveller's murder.

SONG

Come where the grieving rivers of the night
Copy the speeches of the sea:
And hear how this devouring weather
Steals our music.

Under a tent of branches
Our harps can grow.

In the flowering of our windless morning
We should be slow-paced watchmen,
Crossing, on our ecliptics, with a cry of planets,
Homesick, at the sharp rim
Of our Jerusalem, the day.

Weep where the splendid armies of the sky
Copy the prisoner's visions:
Keep the arrows of your eyes unquivered.
Light more watch fires:

Because the thieving stars may come
And steal our lives.

SOME BLOODY MUTINY

Some bloody mutiny opens up our earth
With bitten furrow, and the share's deep drive;
And in the breezy glitter of the sod,
We're sown, like snapshots, by the sun.

Tackle of nerve and vein
Sews tight the soul to our experimental flesh:
Blood and lymph, the body's tailors,
Display their zebra natures in our zoo of skin.

See where the pretty children curse the sea,
Trading their pennies for the sun,
Ripping the rind of Eden, monkey-handed!

Grown murderers rewind
The manners of the firmament to fit
Tricks of our clockwork treachery.
We time our Easters by the rumpus
In our dancehall arteries.

"The world's my photograph.
The tick in my heart is not my brother's keeper."
Says the radio in the throat:
"The war's my mirror, and there's no Good Friday."

Yet heaven is given
To ingrow in this flimsy cage of structures,
Battle the ravage of our ordinary marrow,
And flower for us
Upon the bonebranch we made dead.

CRUSOE

Sometimes the sun beats up the rocks of capes
And robs the green world with a clangor of banks.

Then the citizens
Come out to stone the sky; and with their guns
Mean to shoot the highpowered spheres to pieces:
At dawn, the laws, in the yards of all the prisons,
Propose to hang the robber, the breeder of life.

What if no more men will learn to turn again
And run to the rainy world's boundaries?
What if no more men will learn to atone
By hard, horseplay of shipwreck in the drench of
    Magellan,
And still steer by the stars' unending Lent?

What if the last man
Will no more learn, and run
The stern, foundering ocean, north of the line,
Where crew and cargo drown in the thrash of the wreck,
The day he's driven to his Penal Island,
His own rich acre of island, like the wiseguy Crusoe!

DIRGE

Some one who hears the bugle neigh will know
How cold it is when sentries die by starlight.

But none who love to hear the hammering drum
Will look, when the betrayer
Laughs in the desert like a broken monument,
Ringing his tongue in the red bell of his head,
Gesturing like a flag.

The air that quivered after the earthquake
(When God died like a thief)
Still plays the ancient forums like pianos;
The treacherous wind, lover of the demented,
Will harp forever in the haunted temples.

What speeches do the birds make
With their beaks, to the desolate dead?
And yet we love those carsick amphitheaters,
Nor hear our Messenger come home from hell
With hands shot full of blood.

No one who loves the fleering fife will feel
The light of morning stab his flesh,

But some who hear the trumpet's raving, in the
    ruined sky,
Will dread the burnished helmet of the sun,
Whose anger goes before the King.

A SONG

When it was day, we heard the panes of windows
Clash like tin
When they were blinded by the sun.
And, walking by the walls of silent houses,
We were deafened by the spring.

O, it was then we said we heard the queen of Carthage
Sing in her window,
And saw the armor of Aeneas
Come crowding through the flowerbeds,
To glitter in the jangling shadows of her door.

O it was then we said we saw the sun
Ride like a piker through the flowering tree,
When all those branches rippled in a cloud of ribbons!
He came parading through the city's cheering bullring.
Riding between the houses,
And the branches' curtains,
Like a shower.

But now, slow steps of walkers in the evening
Walk on the stones like the precise, loud
Ominous talk of fretful waterclocks,
And wear away the waning light.

Forget the flashing aspens, how they rang, this morning,
In the mimic rivers of the wind,
For all are silent.

One by one, come home, my pretty children;
Put away the choiring day for it is done;
And in the stillness of the tree, the sunset's solemn 'cellos
One by one begin to play,
While evening fills the city's avenues
With all her quiet pianos.

APRIL

April, like a leopard in the windy woods,
Sports with the javelins of the weather;

And the hunters,
Eye-level with the world's clean brim,
Sight their strings, in masking rocks not moving,
And shower with arrows
The innocent, immortal season.

Hear how like lights these following releases
Of sharpened shaft-flights sing across the air,
And play right through, unwounding, clearest windworks—

To disappear, unpublished, in the reeds.

Where their words are quenched, the world is quickened:
The lean air suddenly flowers,
The little voices of the rivers change;

So that the hunters put away their silver quivers,
Die to the level of river and rockbrim,
And are translated, homeward,
To the other, solemn, world.

THE GREEK WOMEN

The ladies in red capes and golden bracelets
Walk like reeds and talk like rivers,
And sigh, like Vichy water, in the doorways;

And looks run down the land like colts,
Race with the wind, (the mares, their mothers', lover)
Down to the empty harbor.

All spine and sandal stand the willow women;
They shake their silver bangles
In the olive-light of clouds and windows,
Talking, among themselves, like violins;

And, opening their eyes wide as horizons,
Seem to await the navy home from Troy.

No longer stand together, widow women!
Give your gold ornaments to the poor,
Make run the waterspeech of beads between your fingers:
For Troy is burned, and Greece is cursed,
The plague comes like a cloud.
All your men are sleeping in the alien earth,

But one.
And Clytemnestra, walking like a willow, stares.

Beads and bracelets gently knifeclash all about her,
Because the conqueror, the homecome hero,
The soldier, Agamemnon,
Bleeds in her conscience, twisting like a root.

CALYPSO'S ISLAND

See with how little motion, now, the noon wind
Fills the woods' eyes with flirting oleanders,
While perpendicular sun lets fall
Nickels and dimes on the deep harbor.

Fair cries of divers fly in the air
Amid the rigging of the newcome schooner,
And the white ship
Rides like a petal on the purple water
And flings her clangorous anchor in the quiet deeps,
And wrecks the waving waterlights.

Then Queen Calypso
Wakes from a dreaming lifetime in her house of wicker,
Sees all at once the shadows on the matting
Coming and going like a leopard;
Hears for the first time the flame-feathered birds
Shout their litany in the savage tree;

And slowly tastes the red red wound
Of the sweet pomegranate,

And lifts her eyelids like the lids of treasures.

THE PRIDE OF THE DEAD

The doors are down before the ancient tombs
And wind dies in the empty gate.
The paper souls of famous generals
Complain, as dry as leaves, among the stones of Thebes.

The jars of gravel that was one time corn,
The wineskins that the mourners left them,
They know will all be dry forever,
These tired emperors, stitched up for good,
As black as leather.

So we are startled by the leaf-speech of some skinny Alexander:
"Strike from the harpstrings of the rain
Bars of a dirge.
Pacify the ancient dead
For fear they be allowed to love the thin, salt smell of life,
And drift across the rims of graves
Like smoke across a crater,
And loiter in your windless squares,
And scare the living, hiding in the rubble of the
    ruined treasuries."

The paper souls of emperors,
Frisk on the stones as sharp as leaves, and sing:
"Draw back upon our night some windless morning,
And hang it like a shroud upon your burning country,
And strike us, from the tinny harpstrings of the rain
Bars of a dirge."

THE BOMBARDED CITY

Now let no man abide
In the lunar wood
The place of blood.

Let no man abide here,
Not even in a dream,
Not in the lunar forest of this undersea.

Oh you who can a living shadow show
Grieving in the broken street,
Fear, fear the drowners,
Fear the dead!
But if you swagger like the warring Leader
Fear far more
What curse rides down the starlit air,
Curse of the little children killed!
Curse of the little children killed!

Then let no living man, or dead, abide
In this lunar wood,
No, not even in a dream.

For when the houses lean along the night
Like broken tombs,
And shout, with silent windows,
Naked and windy as the mouths of masks,
They still pour down
(As conch-shells, from their curling sleep, the sea)
The air raid's perished roar.

But do not look aside at what you hear.
Fear where you tread,
And be aware of danger growing like a nightshade
Through the openings of the stone.
But mostly fear the forum,
Where, in the midst, an arch and pediment,
Space out, in honor of the guilty Warlord,
A starlit area
Much like the white geometry of peace:

O dread that silent place!
For even when field flowers shall spring
Out of the Leader's lips, and open eyes,
And even while the quiet root
Shall ravel his murdering brain,
Let no one, even on that holiday,
Forget the never-sleeping curse.
And even when the grass grows in his groin,
And golden-rod works in his rib,
And in his teeth the ragweed grins,
As furious as ambition's diligence:
And when, in wind,
His greedy belly waves, kneedeep in weeds,
O dread the childish voices even then,
Still scratching near him like a leaf,
And fear the following feet
That are laid down like little blades,
Nor face the curses of the innocent
That mew behind you like a silver hinge.

For even in the dream of peace
All men will flee the weedy street,
The forum fallen down,
The cursed arenas full of blood,
Hearing the wind creep in the crannied stone:

Oh, no man can remain,
Hearing those souls weep in the hollow ruin.

For there no life is possible,
Because the eyes of soldiers, blind, destroyed,
Lurk like Medusas of despair,
Lay for the living in the lunar door,
Ready to stare outside
And freeze the little leaping nerves
Behind the emperor's sight.

And there no life is possible
Because a weeping childvoice, thin
Unbodied as the sky,
Rings like an echo in the empty window:
And thence its sound
Flies out to feel, with fingers sharp as scalpels,
The little bones inside the politician's ear.

Oh let no man abide
In the lunar wood,
The place of blood.
Let no man abide there, no,
Not even in a dream.

THE STORM AT NIGHT

All night the wind sings like a surf
Filling our windows with the flailing hailstorm.
The fearful prisoner lies bound
In blankets and bodily sleep:
Morning will come, the wind will die away, and he will see,
What argosies lie drawn and quartered, on the sand
    and boulders
Of his Tierra del Fuego:
What cargoes foundered off the Greenland of his icy dream,
His Labradors of greed and grief.

How many men have rock and flood undone,
Who never tried to cry, in the welter of the deadly weather:
"Oh save us, in the dark tornadoes of Genesareth!"

But see, how through the waterthrash of surf and reef
The mind fights homeward to the beach,

Works loose, half dead, from the huge seas,
And lets its poor, mute mask be lifted to the light,
So sleep can leak away, and leave the water-dazzled eyes
To wake and wonder!

For morning works a miracle of sun and silence,
And light drowns in the trees.

THE OHIO RIVER—LOUISVILLE

No one can hear the loud voice of the city
Because of the tremendous silence
Of this slow-moving river, quiet as space.

Not the towering bridge, the crawling train,
Not the knives of pylons
Clashing in the sun,
And not the sky-swung cables;
Not the outboard boat
Swearing in the fiery distance like a locust,
Not the iron cries of men:
Nothing is heard,
Only the immense and silent movement of the river.

The trains go through the summer quiet as paper,
And, in the powerhouse, the singing dynamos
Make no more noise than cotton.
All life is quieter than the weeds
On which lies lightly sprawling,
Like white birds shot to death,
The bathers' clothing.

But only where the swimmers float like alligators,
And with their eyes as dark as creosote
Scrutinize the murderous heat,
Only there is anything heard:
The thin, salt voice of violence,
That whines, like a mosquito, in their simmering blood.

THE DREAMING TRADER

Blacker and whiter than the pages of his ledger
The dreaming trader turns to stone
Because he hears the wind's voice sing this song:
"You shall set sail from the steps of the Exchange
And not be seen until the word returns: 'Lost with all hands.'
You shall set sail from the steps of the Sub-Treasury
And pass Grand Central at the fall of night
And never be heard of again."

The banker and the shipwright and the craven trader
Can spread their plans, and talk their mathematics
Among the ladders and the stanchions of the skinny ships;
(The cargoliners, in a leafless forest, on their ways).
But when the steel trees sing like harpstrings in the
        winter windstorm,
Their minds roll up like blueprints,
And they blow away.

Blacker and whiter than the pages of his ledger
The dreaming trader turns to stone:
"You shall set sail from the steps of the Exchange:
And not be seen until the word returns: 'Lost with all hands.'
You shall set sail from the steps of the Sub-Treasury

And pass Grand Central at the fall of night
And founder in the dark Sargassos of your own
    intolerable dream
And never be heard of again."

THE HOUSE OF CAIPHAS

Somewhere, inside the wintry colonnade,
Stands, like a churchdoor statue, God's Apostle,
Good St. Peter, by the brazier,
With his back turned to the trail.

As scared and violent as flocks of birds of prey,
The testimonies of the holy beggars
Fly from the stones, and scatter in the windy shadows.

The accusations of the holy judge
Rise, in succession, dignified as rockets,
Soar out of silence to their towering explosions
And, with their meteors, raid the earth.

And the gates of night fall shut with the clangor of arms.

The crafty eyes of witnesses, set free to riot,
Now shine as sharp as needles at the carved Apostle's mantle.
Voices begin to rise, like water, in the colonnade;
Fingers accuse him like a herd of cattle.

Then the Apostle, white as marble, weak as tin
Cries out upon the crowd:
And, no less artificial than the radios of his voice,
He flees into the freezing night.

And all the constellations vanish out of heaven
With a glassy cry;
Cocks crow as sharp as steel in the terrible, clear east,

And the gates of night fall shut with the thunder of Massbells.

AUBADE—HARLEM

for Baroness C. de Hueck

Across the cages of the keyless aviaries,
The lines and wires, the gallows of the broken kites,
Crucify, against the fearful light,
The ragged dresses of the little children.
Soon, in the sterile jungles of the waterpipes and ladders,
The bleeding sun, a bird of prey, will terrify the poor,
These will forget the unbelievable moon.

But in the cells of whiter buildings,
Where the glass dawn is brighter than the knives of surgeons,
Paler than alcohol or ether, shinier than money,
The white men's wives, like Pilate's,
Cry in the peril of their frozen dreams:

"Daylight has driven iron spikes,
Into the flesh of Jesus' hands and feet:
Four flowers of blood have nailed Him to the walls of Harlem."

Along the white halls of the clinics and the hospitals
Pilate evaporates with a cry:
They have cut down two hundred Judases,
Hanged by the neck in the opera houses and the museum.

82

Across the cages of the keyless aviaries,
The lines and wires, the gallows of the broken kites,
Crucify, against the fearful light,
The ragged dresses of the little children.

AUBADE—THE ANNUNCIATION

When the dim light, at Lauds, comes strike her window,
Bellsong falls out of Heaven with a sound of glass.

Prayers fly in the mind like larks,
Thoughts hide in the height like hawks:
And while the country churches tell their blessings to
     the distance,
Her slow words move,
(Like summer winds the wheat) her innocent love:
Desires glitter in her mind
Like morning stars:

Until her name is suddenly spoken
Like a meteor falling.

She can no longer hear shrill day
Sing in the east,
Nor see the lovely woods begin to toss their manes.
The rivers have begun to sing.
The little clouds shine in the sky like girls:
She has no eyes to see their faces.

Speech of an angel shines in the waters of her thought
     like diamonds,
Rides like a sunburst on the hillsides of her heart,

And is brought home like harvests,
Hid in her house, and stored
Like the sweet summer's riches in our peaceful barns.

But in the world of March outside her dwelling,
The farmers and the planters
Fear to begin their sowing, and its lengthy labor,
Where, on the brown, bare furrows,
The winter wind still croons as dumb as pain.

DIRGE FOR A TOWN IN FRANCE

Up among the stucco pears, the iron vines,
Mute as their watered roses, their mimosas,
The wives gaze down among the traceries
Of balconies: the one-time finery
Of iron, suburban balconies.

Down in the shadowy doors,
Men fold their arms,
And hearken after the departing day
That somewhere sings more softly
Than merry-go-rounds in distant fairs.

O, it is not those first, faint stars
Whose fair light, falling, whispers in the river;
And it is not the dusty wind,
Waving the waterskirts of the shy-talking fountain,

That wakes the wooden horses' orchestra,
The fifing goldfinch, and the phony flute,
And the steam robins and electric nightingales

That blurred the ding of cymbals,
That other time, when childhood turned and turned
As grave as sculpture in a zodiac.

And yet the mystery comes on
Spontaneous as the street-lights, in the plane trees:
The trees, whose paint falls off in flakes,
Elaborate as the arches
Of a deserted opera!

The roses and mimosas in the windows
Adore the night they breathe, not understanding;
The women dream of bread and chocolate
In their aquariums
Of traceries, and lace, and cherubim;

But the men die, down in the shadowy doors,
The way their thoughts die in their eyes,
To see those sad and funny children
Run down the colonnade of trees
Where the carnival doesn't exist:
Those children, who are lost too soon,
With fading laughter, on the road along the river:
Gone, like the slowing cavalcade, the homeward horses.

AUBADE—THE CITY

Now that the clouds have come like cattle
To the cold waters of the city's river,
All the windows turn their scandalized expression
Toward the tide's tin dazzle,

And question, with their weak-eyed stare,
The riotous sun.

From several places at a time
Cries of defiance,
As delicate as frost, as sharp as glass,
Rise from the porcelain buildings
And break in the blue sky.

Then, falling swiftly from the air,
The fragments of this fragile indignation
Ring on the echoing streets
No louder than a shower of pins.

But suddenly the bridges' choiring cables
Jangle gently in the wind
And play like quiet piano-strings.

All down the faces of the buildings
Windows begin to close
Like figures in a long division.

Those whose eyes all night have simulated sleep,
Suddenly stare, from where they lie, like wolves,
Tied in the tangle of the bedding,

And listen for the waking blood
To flood the apprehensive silence of their flesh.
They fear the heart that now lies quenched may quicken,
And start to romp against the rib,
Soft and insistent as a secret bell.

They also fear the light will grow
Into the windows of their hiding places, like a tree

Of tropical flowers
And put them, one by one, to flight.

Then life will have to begin.
Pieces of paper, lying in the streets,
Will start up, in the twisting wind,
And fly like idiot birds before the faces of the crowds.
And in the roaring buildings
Elevator doors will have begun
To clash like swords.

THE PERIL

When anger comes to the coast of our desolate country
And the sky is the color of armor,
We listen, in the silence of the cliffs and bays as still as steel,
For the cry that terrifies the sentinel.
And if it sound, oh! suddener than Java dancers
Face us all the swords we fear.
Well, we have arms: we will put them to trial.

But even as we wait, in hiding, for the unknown signal,
It is the Bridegroom comes like lightning where we
      never looked!
His eyes are angels, armed in smiles of fire.
His Word puts out the spark of every other sun
Faster than sunlight ever hid the cities
Of the fire-crowded universe!
How shall I stand such light, being dim as my fear?

Rob me, and make me poor enough to bear my
    priceless ransom;

Lock me and dower me in the gifts and jails of tribulation:
Stab me and save me with the five lights of Your Crucifixion!

And I'll become as strong as wax, as weak as diamonds,
And read Your speeches deeper than the sea
And, like the sky, fair!

ADVENT

Charm with your stainlessness these winter nights,
Skies, and be perfect!
Fly vivider in the fiery dark, you quiet meteors,
And disappear.
You moon, be slow to go down,
This is your full!

The four white roads make off in silence
Towards the four parts of the starry universe.
Time falls like manna at the corners of the wintry earth.
We have become more humble than the rocks,
More wakeful than the patient hills.

Charm with your stainlessness these nights in Advent,
     holy spheres,
While minds, as meek as beasts,
Stay close at home in the sweet hay;
And intellects are quieter than the flocks that feed by starlight.

Oh pour your darkness and your brightness over all our
     solemn valleys,
You skies: and travel like the gentle Virgin,
Toward the planets' stately setting,

Oh white full moon as quiet as Bethlehem!

CAROL

Flocks feed by darkness with a noise of whispers,
In the dry grass of pastures,
And lull the solemn night with their weak bells.

The little towns upon the rocky hills
Look down as meek as children:
Because they have seen come this holy time.

God's glory, now, is kindled gentler than low candlelight
Under the rafters of a barn:
Eternal Peace is sleeping in the hay,
And Wisdom's born in secret in a straw-roofed stable.

And O! Make holy music in the stars, you happy angels.
You shepherds, gather on the hill.
Look up, you timid flocks, where the three kings
Are coming through the wintry trees;

While we unnumbered children of the wicked centuries
Come after with our penances and prayers,
And lay them down in the sweet-smelling hay
Beside the wise men's golden jars.

HOW LONG WE WAIT

How long we wait, with minds as quiet as time,
Like sentries on a tower.
How long we watch, by night, like the astronomers.

Heaven, when will we hear you sing,
Arising from our grassy hills,

And say: "The dark is done, and Day
Laughs like a Bridegroom in His tent, the lovely sun,
His tent the sun, His tent the smiling sky!"

How long we wait with minds as dim as ponds
While stars swim slowly homeward in the water of
      our west!
Heaven, when will we hear you sing?

How long we listened to the silence of our vineyards
And heard no bird stir in the rising barley.
The stars go home behind the shaggy trees.
Our minds are grey as rivers.

O earth, when will you wake in the green wheat,
And all our Trappist cedars sing:
"Bright land, lift up your leafy gates!
You abbey steeple, sing with bells!
For look, our Sun rejoices like a dancer
On the rim of our hills."

In the blue west the moon is uttered like the word:
      "Farewell."

A LETTER TO MY FRIENDS

On entering the Monastery of Our Lady of Gethsemani, 1941

This holy House of God,
Nazareth, where Christ lived as a boy,

These sheds and cloisters,
The very stones and beams are all befriended
By cleaner sun, by rarer birds, by lovelier flowers.

Lost in the tigers' and the lions' wilderness,
More than we fear, we love these holy stones,
These thorns, the phoenix's sweet and spikey tree.

More than we fear, we love the holy desert,
Where separate strangers, hid in their disguises,
Have come to meet, by night, the quiet Christ.

We who have some time wandered in those crowded
    ruins,
(Farewell, you woebegone, sad towns)
We who have wandered like (the ones I hear) the
    moaning trains,
(Begone, sad towns!)
We'll live it over for you here.

Here all your ruins are rebuilt as fast as you destroy
    yourselves,
In your unlucky wisdom,
Here in the House of God
And on the holy hill,
Where fields are the friends of plenteous heaven,
While starlight feeds, as bright as manna,
All our rough earth with wakeful grace.

And look, the ruins have become Jerusalems,
And the sick cities re-arise, like shining Sions!
Jerusalems, these walls and rooves,
These bowers and fragrant sheds,

Our desert's wooden door,
The arches, and the windows, and the tower!

THE CANDLEMAS PROCESSION

Lumen
Ad revelationem gentium.

Look kindly, Jesus, where we come,
New Simeons, to kindle,
Each at Your infant sacrifice his own life's candle.

And when Your flame turns into many tongues,
See how the One is multiplied, among us, hundreds!
And goes among the humble, and consoles our
    sinful kindred.

It is for this we come,
And, kneeling, each receive one flame:
Ad revelationem gentium.

Our lives, like candles, spell this simple symbol:

Weep like our bodily life, sweet work of bees,
Sweeten the world, with your slow sacrifice.
And this shall be our praise:
That by our glad expense, our Father's will
Burned and consumed us for a parable.

Nor burn we now with brown and smoky flames, but bright
Until our sacrifice is done,
(By which not we, but You are known)

And then, returning to our Father, one by one,
Give back our lives like wise and waxen lights.

CANA

"This beginning of miracles did Jesus in Cana of Galilee."

Once when our eyes were clean as noon, our rooms
Filled with the joys of Cana's feast:
For Jesus came, and His disciples, and His Mother,
And after them the singers
And some men with violins.

Once when our minds were Galilees,
And clean as skies our faces,
Our simple rooms were charmed with sun.

Our thoughts went in and out in whiter coats than
    God's disciples',
In Cana's crowded rooms, at Cana's tables.

Nor did we seem to fear the wine would fail:
For ready, in a row, to fill with water and a miracle,
We saw our earthen vessels, waiting empty.
What wine those humble waterjars foretell!

Wine for the ones who, bended to the dirty earth,
Have feared, since lovely Eden, the sun's fire,
Yet hardly mumble, in their dusty mouths, one prayer.

Wine for old Adam, digging in the briars!

THE WIDOW OF NAIM

The men that cut their graves in the grey rocks
Go down more slowly than the sun upon their dusty country:
White as the wall, the weepers leave the town,
To be the friends of grief, and follow
To the new tomb a widow's sorrow.

The men with hands as hard as rope,
(Some smell of harvests, some of nets,) the strangers,
Come up the hill more slowly than the seasons of the year.

"Why do you walk in funerals, you men of Naim,
Why go you down to graves, with eyes like winters,
And your cold faces clean as cliffs?
See how we come, our brows are full of sun,
Our smiles are fairer than the wheat and hay,
Our eyes are saner than the sea.
Lay down your burden at our four-roads' crossing,
And learn a wonder from the Christ, our Traveller."

    (Oh, you will say that those old times
    Are all dried up like water,
    Since the great God went walking on a road to
        Naim,
    How many hundred years has slept again in death
    That widow's son, after the marvel of his miracle:
    He did not rise for long, and sleeps forever.
    And what of the men of the town?
    What have the desert winds done to the dust
    Of the poor weepers, and the widow's friends?)

The men that cut their graves in the grey rocks
Spoke to the sons of God upon the four cross roads:

"Men of Genesareth, who climb our hill as slow as
　　spring or summer,
Christ is your Master, and we see His eyes are Jordans,
His hands and feet are wounded, and His words are wine.
He has let death baptize the one who stirs and wakens
In the bier we carry,
That we may read the Cross and Easter in this rising,
And learn the endless heaven
Promised to all the widow-Church's risen children."

ST. PAUL

When I was Saul, and sat among the cloaks,
My eyes were stones, I saw no sight of heaven,
Open to take the spirit of the twisting Stephen.
When I was Saul, and sat among the rocks,
I locked my eyes, and made my brain my tomb,
Sealed with what boulders rolled across my reason!

When I was Saul and walked upon the blazing desert
My road was quiet as a trap.
I feared what word would split high noon with light
And lock my life, and try to drive me mad:
And thus I saw the Voice that struck me dead.

Tie up my breath, and wind me in white sheets of anguish,
And lay me in my three days' sepulchre
Until I find my Easter in a vision.

Oh Christ! Give back my life, go, cross Damascus,
Find out my Ananias in that other room:
Command him, as you do, in this my dream;

He knows my locks, and owns my ransom,
Waits for Your word to take his keys and come.

TRAPPISTS, WORKING

Now all our saws sing holy sonnets in this world of timber
Where oaks go off like guns, and fall like cataracts,
Pouring their roar into the wood's green well.

Walk to us, Jesus, through the wall of trees,
And find us still adorers in these airy churches,
Singing our other Office with our saws and axes.
Still teach Your children in the busy forest,
And let some little sunlight reach us, in our mental
      shades, and leafy studies.

When time has turned the country white with grain
And filled our regions with the thrashing sun,
Walk to us, Jesus, through the walls of wheat
When our two tractors come to cut them down:
Sow some light winds upon the acres of our spirit,
And cool the regions where our prayers are reapers,
And slake us, Heaven, with Your living rivers.

THE SNARE

for St. Benedict, in thanksgiving

Once when, like birds, we feared the hunter's gun
Yet saw no enemy anywhere,
Lord, was our neck not in the hunter's snare?

How can we count the times we nearly died
By trickery, in the peaceful trees?
We played in places made for our destruction,
Flew in and out the little windows set, we thought,
To be our special, safe resort.
We planned our fortunes in an open trap.
Led by our recklessness into the nets,
Taking the bait, and slipping through the strings,
Who saved us, in the places that we thought were safe?

Oh, though you'll seem to lose all sight of hiding thongs,
Poor blindness rest, and weakness smile:
For while, yourselves, you'd never find them,
Fold up your fear of them in heavenly Communion!

Then we'll be free of all the knots that try to tie us.
The sliding loop, the flying spring catch us no more than air.
We shall have died to them before they ever thought of us,
So fast our feet, now clumsy, and most full of clay,
Become when Jesus' grace has made them heavenly.

AN INVOCATION TO ST. LUCY

Lucy, whose day is in our darkest season,
(Although your name is full of light,)
We walkers in the murk and rain of flesh and sense,
Lost in the midnight of our dead world's winter solstice
Look for the fogs to open on your friendly star.

We have long since cut down the summer of our history;
Our cheerful towns have all gone out like fireflies in October.
The fields are flooded and the vine is bare:
How have our long days dwindled, now the world is frozen!

Locked in the cold jails of our stubborn will,
Oh hear the shovels growling in the gravel.
This is the way they'll make our beds for ever,
Ours, whose Decembers have put out the sun:
Doors of whose souls are shut against the summertime!

Martyr, whose short day sees our winter and our Calvary,
Show us some light, who seem forsaken by the sky:
We have so dwelt in darkness that our eyes are screened
    and dim,
And all but blinded by the weakest ray.

Hallow the vespers and December of our life, O
    martyred Lucy:
Console our solstice with your friendly day.

ST. THOMAS AQUINAS

The stars put out their pale opinions, one by one,
While the black-friar breaks the Truth, his Host,
Among his friends the simple Substances:
For thus he fathered minds to reason's peace,
And fed the children of the Kingdom
With the Person in the intellectual Bread.

His mind had never smarted with the bitter reek
Of the world's night, the flesh's smoke:
His eyes were always cradles for the Word of God:
His intellect His Bethlehem.

Better than Jacob's dream,
He saw how all created essences go up and down

Upon their Jacob's ladder,
Finding their own degree of likeness
To the Pure Act and Perfect Essence.

When matter lay as light as snow
On the strong Apennine of form,
And morning rose upon the church of Fossanova,
All creation lay transparent, as serene as water,
Full of the Child Who consecrates the universe,
Informing all with power and meaning, like a
    Sacrament.

But oh, the day that sings upon the ridge
Steals from the stars the brittle fire of their analogies:
They vanish in the single intuition
Of the rising sun:
And the grey monks' Cistercian *"Subvenite"*
Follows Aquinas in his ransomed flight,
And loses him amid the cheering cherubim.

ST. ALBERIC

When your loud axe's echo on the ponds, at early
    morning,
Scared the shy mallard from the shallows grey as tin,
The glades gave back your hammers' antiphons—
The din of nails that shamed the lazy spring.
Striving, like Adam, with the barren wildwood,
And with the desolation of the brake,
You builded, in a reedy place
A cloister and a Ladychurch.

But when the stones and clean-hewn beams
Heard no more sounds but of the bees, your thoughtful eyes
Were always full of exile,
Though peaceful with the peace of pilgrims, and
    with happiness
That shamed, in the deep wood, the sentimental doves.

When in the church your canticles were done,
Even your silences were better than the birds, whose song
Still fell, like fountains, from the forest to your sunny cloister.
And when, in the high-noon of contemplation,
    reason died by blindness,
Your faith escaped, and found the flowering Cross—
Loving, in Christ, the agony of Adam:
Body and Spirit tilled and gardened with our
    penances and death.

And from the flowers of that frightful Paradise,
(The wounds that heal the loving mind)
Your diligence could draw such excellence
As shamed the bees at work in the wild rock.

Then did you fill the cloisters of your intellect,
The tabernacles in the secret churches of your will.
Slowly you built sweet counsel, like a honeycomb,
And fed your life with living Wisdom, Heaven's essence.

THE IMAGE OF TRUE LOVERS' DEATH

It happened when they came to find our brother,
The men from the police,
And knocked at his five doors

With stern, accusing face:
"Come out, unprofitable monk,
And view our spurious badges,
While we convince you of sin:
(The mess your garden's in.)"

Before they cleared their iron throats
Or knocked or rang again,
Our brother was off to the hills,
Leaving his body in this position.

Inquire no more, stern aliens,
He is no longer in this place.
He has absconded through another exit.
He vanished when he heard your steps.
If you had never come,
Would he have made his escape?

But he has left us by the windows of his attic,
Dying the image of true lovers' death.
Follow him, if you think you can,
The birds point out his path:
But no, you cannot see him where he everywhere appears
In all kinds of disguises.
The beadles pass him by, and never know,
Nor think to see him in his brothers' faces.

* * *

And thus the day begins.
The false detectives vanish with a cry.
The bells for sweet Communion fall like dew among
    the shepherds.
The land sings softly with the waking sky:

"No longer seek your brother in his rational flesh,
For he has thrown his five wise wits away,

And gone to hide his whole delight
In somebody else's joy.

"Shepherd, he'll make your gladness a disguise to clothe
    his laughter.
Look to the substance of your best desires,
And you will find him praying there.

"The grace in your elated heart
Will be that loving sinner's glad abode.
The peace in your clean breast,
Is where he sits, with God, and takes his rest.

"And in your deepest happiness
He hides and keeps his holy house,
And bleeds there, on a daily Cross,
With Christ, in the strong joys of your Eucharist."

THE FALL OF NIGHT

When the eleventh hour
Unbars the burning west,
And all the clouds go home like flocks,
The pines upon our barrier,
Stand in the gates of night, like laborers,
And wait their pay.

A shepherd scans the white accounting of the evening star,
And moonlight fires a brittle spear
Into the windows of the cottager:
To the red west, the homeward farmers sing:
"We bring these heavy wagons full of hay to
    make Your bed,

O Mercy, born between the animals.
Here in our harvest rest Your friendless head.
Kill, with Your smiles, our cruel sins,
While lights lean down to drink
The waters of Your look.
The lances of Your loving voice
Are sharper than the sabres of the Seraphim."

"The tree of Jesse growing in our garden,
With branches spread against the noonward wall,
Once sacrificed, in May, a cloudy choir of blossoms—
Flowers that died of pity for the burden of the
        virgin summer:
But see the August apples, red as blood.
Father, forget the arbors where we hid, in Eden:
And let these cross-branch fruits transfigure us
And make us gods."

The shepherd on the solemn hill,
Shot through the shoulder by a rising planet,
Views the disaster of the burning west:
—The fiery doors of Jacob's tents,
The blazing armor of the Cherubim.

For the low walls of the western world are
        burning down,
The woods go up to meet
The white battalions of the rising night.

Oh skies, fly slowly with your heavy freight,
And moon, unlock the Judge's gate:
Here are the wagons of the final harvest.
Oh see the hallows, crowding to their window-sills,
And the high houses where the angels wait.

The rivers hide, because their eyes are wet.

THE BIOGRAPHY

Oh read the verses of the loaded scourges,
And what is written in their terrible remarks:
"The Blood runs down the walls of Cambridge town,
As useless as the waters of the narrow river—
While pub and alley gamble for His vesture."

Although my life is written on Christ's Body like
    a map,
The nails have printed in those open hands
More than the abstract names of sins,
More than the countries and the towns,
The names of streets, the numbers of the houses,
The record of the days and nights,
When I have murdered Him in every square and street.

Lance and thorn, and scourge and nail
Have more than made His Flesh my chronicle.
My journeys more than bite His bleeding feet.

Christ, from my cradle, I had known You everywhere,
And even though I sinned, I walked in You, and knew
    You were my world:
You were my France and England,
My seas and my America:
You were my life and air, and yet I would not own You.

Oh, when I loved You, even while I hated You,
Loving and yet refusing You in all the glories of
    Your universe

It was Your living Flesh I tore and trampled, not the
    air and earth:

Not that You feel us, in created things,
But knowing You, in them, made every sin a sacrilege;
And every act of greed became a desecration,
Spoiled and dishonored You as in Your Eucharist.

And yet with every wound You robbed me of a crime,
And as each blow was paid with Blood,
You paid me also each great sin with greater graces.
For even as I killed You,
You made Yourself a greater thief than any in Your
        company,
Stealing my sins into Your dying life,
Robbing me even of my death.

Where, on what cross my agony will come
I do not ask You:
For it is written and accomplished here,
On every Crucifix, on every altar.
It is my narrative that drowns and is forgotten
In Your five open Jordans,
Your voice that cries my: *"Consummatum est."*

If on Your Cross Your life and death and mine are one,
Love teaches me to read, in You, the rest of a new history.
I trace my days back to another childhood,
Exchanging, as I go,
New York and Cuba for Your Galilee,
And Cambridge for Your Nazareth,
Until I come again to my beginning,
And find a manger, star and straw,
A pair of animals, some simple men,
And thus I learn that I was born,
Now not in France, but Bethlehem.

THE BETRAYAL

The sense that sits in the thin skins of lips
Was waiting with a traitor's kiss that made You sweat
    with death,
When envy, in the Lenten night,
Shone sharp as lightnings: and we came with blades.

What hate, what worlds of wormwood did our tongues distil!
We cried with voices dry as shot,
In Pilate's yard where pride of life
And love of glory laced Your brows in Blood.

What were our curses, dark as vinegar,
We swore, with tongues as sharp as thongs,
On Golgotha, where pride of life,
With easy slanders nailed You to the wood!

And all we uttered, all, was nails and gall,
With our desires cruel as steel.
We digged Your hands, and filled them full of Blood.
With little smiles as dry as dice
We whipped and killed You for Your lovely world.

You died, and paid Your traitors with a prayer
And cured our swearing darkness with Your wounds'
    five lights.
Eyes see Your holy hands, and, in them, flowers.
You let the doubter's finger feel the sun in Your side,
Ears have Your words, and tongues believe You wheat:
You feed with life the lips that kissed You dead!

RAHAB'S HOUSE

Now the lean children of the God of armies
(Their feet command the quaking earth)
Rise in the desert, and divide old Jordan
To crown this city with a ring of drums.
(But see the signal, like a crimson scar
Bleeding on Rahab's window-sill,
Spelling her safety with the red of our Redemption.)

The trumpets scare the valley with their sudden anger,
And thunderheads lean down to understand the
          nodding ark,
While Joshua's friend, the frowning sun,
Rises to burn the drunken houses with his look.
(But far more red upon the wall
Is Rahab's rescue than his scarlet threat.)

The clarions bind the bastions with their silver treble,
Shiver the city with their golden shout:
(Wells dry up, and stars fly back,
The eyes of Jericho go out,)
The drums around the reeling ark
Shatter the ramparts with a ring of thunder.

The kings that sat
On gilded chairs,
The princes and the great
Are dead.
Only a harlot and her fearful kindred
Fly like sparrows from that sudden grin of fire.

It is the flowers that will one day rise from Rahab's earth,
That have redeemed them from the hell of Jericho.

A rod will grow
From Jesse's tree,
Among her sons, the lords of Bethlehem,
And flower into Paradise.

Look at the gentle irises admiring one another by
    the water,
Under the leafy shadows of the Virgin's mercy,
And all the primroses and laughing flags
Bowing before Our Lady Mary in the Eden of her intercession,
And praising her, because they see the generations
Fly like a hundred thousand swallows into heaven,
Out of the jaws of Jericho,
Because it was the Son of God
Whose crimson signal wounded Rahab's wall,
Uttered our rescue in a figure of His Blood.

AFTER THE NIGHT OFFICE—
GETHSEMANI ABBEY

It is not yet the grey and frosty time
When barns ride out of the night like ships:
We do not see the Brothers, bearing lanterns,
Sink in the quiet mist,
As various as the spirits who, with lamps, are sent
To search our souls' Jerusalems
Until our houses are at rest
And minds enfold the Word, our Guest.

Praises and canticles anticipate
Each day the singing bells that wake the sun,
But now our psalmody is done.
Our hasting souls outstrip the day:

Now, before dawn, they have their noon.
The Truth that transsubstantiates the body's night
Has made our minds His temple-tent:
Open the secret eye of faith
And drink these deeps of invisible light.

The weak walls
Of the world fall
And heaven, in floods, comes pouring in:
Sink from your shallows, soul, into eternity,
And slake your wonder at that deep-lake spring.
We touch the rays we cannot see,
We feel the light that seems to sing.

Go back to bed, red sun, you are too late,
And hide behind Mount Olivet—
For like the flying moon, held prisoner,
Within the branches of a juniper,
So in the cages of consciousness
The Dove of God is prisoner yet:
Unruly sun, go back to bed.

But now the lances of the morning
Fire all their gold against the steeple and the water-tower.
Returning to the windows of our deep abode of peace,
Emerging at our conscious doors
We find our souls all soaked in grace, like Gideon's fleece.

SONG FOR THE BLESSED SACRAMENT

The Child is sleeping in His golden house
Not to our Lent unknown,

Or to the windy meadows where the morning cries:
    "Rejoice!"
A thousand flowers think of Him, and raise their heads,
And wake Him with the echoes of their tiny shout.

But oh, the Child is weeping in a tender cloud.
Let the repentant deserts of the mind,
Our sandy wills, their barren rocks,
(Where we have dreaded death by dryness
Or an arrow in the night,
Or something hiding in the lion's cavern)
Sudden astonish us with reed and rush,
And streams enchant us with their dancing lights.

Oh charm the belfries of the budding wood,
Brown thrush and cardinal,
Blackbird and oriole,
Pouring upon the land your golden din.
And when you wild Cistercians tune your praises
To our Latin, with your native liturgy,
We'll come and cultivate our sacrifice of corn and apples
And grow our hay and barley,
Wheat and wine.

And now the Child is laughing in His sunny door,
For all our atmosphere, alive with light,
And full of heaven, like an intellect,
Raises, before the faces of the flowering hills,
(And with no hands but those of spirit and of miracle)
The glorious Christ, as light as grace,
And flies Him homeward to His Father's house.

The Child is singing in His tent of stars.

THE WORD—A RESPONSORY

"Eructavit cor meum verbum bonum."

My heart hath uttered ...
 Whom we desire to see,
 Whose thoughts are worlds,
 And Whose delights
 Shine like perfections in the universe:
 Whose admirable joy
 Burns in the bosom of the triple Light:
My heart hath uttered a good Word.

 Who drives across the stormy hill
 His flocks of flying sun:
 In Whom our admiration falls and dies
 Like the sown seed alighting from the travels of
  the wind,
 To rise again when we receive our rain
 And shoot the earth of April with the blades of
  greenest praises.
My heart hath uttered ...
 The vital sap
 And blood of every growth,
 Nodding and talking in the rushes
 To the water, to the way-farer:
Verbum bonum!
 Whose keyless news
 Unlocks the secret places
 Of the peace-enfolded soul:
 Whose exultation
 Rifles the hidden riches of the will,
Oh be our glory! Never die!

My heart hath uttered a good Word,
 Whose Name is: "Sent"
 Whom we desire to love:

Strong, in the fathoms of the heart, unseen,
Spending us heaven silent as a spring,
O perfect Word!
O Verbum bonum!

Whose Name is: "Savior,"
Whom we desire to hold;
Burn in our hearts, burn in our living marrow, own
    our being,
Hide us and heal us in the hug of Thy delight,
Whose admirable might
Sings in the furnace of the Triple Glory!

Eructavit cor meum verbum bonum.

THE DARK ENCOUNTER

O night of admiration, full of choirs,
O night of deepest praise,
And darkness full of triumph:
What secret and intrepid Visitor
Has come to crack our sepulchre?
He softly springs the locks of death
In the foretold encounter!

O silence with no syllable for weapon,
Drunk with valor,
Whose speechless wonder solves the knots of flesh our captor:
Dower desires with your eloquence!

O darkness full of warning and abandon,
(Disarming every enemy,
Slaying the meaning of the mind's alarums)

Why do our steps still hesitate
Upon the threshold of incredible possession,
The sill of the tremendous rest,
Reading the riddle of His unexpected question?

O silence full of exclamation!
It is the time of the attack.
Our eyes are wider than the word: "Aware."
O darkness full of vision, vivid night,
Defying the frontier.

O silence full of execution,
All intuiton and desire lie destroyed
When Substance is our Conqueror.
O midnight full of victory,
And silence of the wonderful acclaim,
And darkness full of sweet delight.

O night of admiration, full of choirs,
O night of deepest praise,
And darkness full of sweet delight!
What secret and intrepid Visitor
Has come to raise us from the dead?
He softly springs the locks of time, our sepulchre,
In the foretold encounter.

THE VICTORY

Sing your new song in the winepress where these
    bloody pence
Weep from the skin of our Gethsemani,
Knowing that we must die to break the seed our prison

And spring like wheat from the wet earth
Of who knows what arena:
Sing when the grinding locks
Break up our little cages,
Casting our exultation in those mills of teeth
To praise God with the great Ignatius Martyr.

Smile in the white eyes of the angry mist
For we have heard the thunder of the thousand harpers
Outside a blinded window,
There on the silent cobblestones,
Ring from the hobnails of a firing-squad
Hard by the russet, russet wall.

Shall we not love You, Christ,
Best in a shuttered house,
Although the silver windows sweat with dread?
Shall we not praise You, Savior,
Now at the rising of the sickle moon, our murderess,
When dawn is colder than a knife
Between the marrow and the flesh?

This is the word You utter
To search our being to its roots:
This is the judgement and the question
And the joy we suffer:
This is our trial, this the weight of gladness that we
      cannot bear,
But turn to water and to blood.

For some have gone, with bands, to die in battle,
Some die, with glory, in the sea:
Some with speeches, some by guns,
But we, like Peter, upside down.

Pride cannot jail us in the newsreels
For a death so humble.
That is the gladness that unlocks our chrysalis:
We have no grandeur and no name.
For who shall try to pay us money for our blinded faces,
And our broken gait:
Or who shall praise us, falling all the way to Calvary?

The customs never catch us
With the stars our contraband
The day we hear the quiet gravel
Suddenly swearing at the steps of the Gestapo!

Then shall our hearts not sing
With vision and with victory
Because our eyes are full of blood?
Shall we not love you better, Brothers,
Wearing beneath the rags of our disguise
The Christ Who died for us?

Look up, you captives, crowding to the water,
Look up, Ezechiel, and see the open heavens
Salute you with the vision of the winged Evangelists.
You with your ankles in the water and your garments white,
Lift up your heads, begin to sing:
And let your sights, exulting, rise and meet
The miracle of living creatures
In their burning, frowning flight.
The message of their lamps and fires
Warns you: make ready for the Face that speaks
    like lightning,
Uttering the new name of your exultation
Deep in the vitals of your soul.
Make ready for the Christ, Whose smile, like lightning,
Sets free the song of everlasting glory
That now sleeps, in your paper flesh, like dynamite.

THE TRAPPIST CEMETERY—GETHSEMANI

Brothers, the curving grasses and their daughters
Will never print your praises:
The trees our sisters, in their summer dresses,
Guard your fame in these green cradles:
The simple crosses are content to hide your characters.

Oh do not fear
The birds that bicker in the lonely belfry
Will ever give away your legends.
Yet when the sun, exulting like a dying martyr,
Canonizes, with his splendid fire, the sombre hills,
Your graves all smile like little children,
And your wise crosses trust the mothering night
That folds them in the Sanctuary's wings.

You need not hear the momentary rumors of the road
Where cities pass and vanish in a single car
Filling the cut beside the mill
With roar and radio,
Hurling the air into the wayside branches
Leaving the leaves alive with panic.

See, the kind universe,
Wheeling in love about the abbey steeple,
Lights up your sleepy nursery with stars.
                    *   *   *
God, in your bodily life,
Untied the snares of anger and desire,
Hid your flesh from envy by these country altars,
Beneath these holy eaves where even sparrows have
        their houses.
But oh, how like the swallows and the chimney swifts
Do your free souls in glory play!

116

And with a cleaner flight,
Keener, more graceful circles,
Rarer and finer arcs
Then all these innocent attacks that skim our steeple!
How like these children of the summer evening
Do your rejoicing spirits
Deride the dry earth with their aviation!

But now the treble harps of night begin to play in the
	deep wood,
To praise your holy sleep,
And all the frogs along the creek
Chant in the moony waters to the Queen of Peace.
And we, the mariners, and travellers,
The wide-eyed immigrants,
Praying and sweating in our steerage cabins,
Lie still and count with love the measured bells
That tell the deep-sea leagues until your harbor.

Already on this working earth you knew what
	nameless love
Adorns the heart with peace by night,
Hearing, adoring all the dark arrivals of eternity.
Oh, here on earth you knew what secret thirst
Arming the mind with instinct,
Answers the challenges of God with garrisons
Of unified desire
And facing Him in His new wars
Is slain at last in an exchange of lives.

Teach us, Cistercian Fathers, how to wear
Silence, our humble armor.
Pray us a torrent of the seven spirits
That are our wine and stamina:
Because your work is not yet done.

But look: the valleys shine with promises,
And every burning morning is a prophecy of Christ
Coming to raise and vindicate
Even our sorry flesh.

Then will your graves, Gethsemani, give up their angels,
Return them to their souls to learn
The songs and attitudes of glory.
Then will creation rise again like gold
Clean, from the furnace of your litanies:
The beasts and trees shall share your resurrection,
And a new world be born from these green tombs.

A WHITSUN CANTICLE

Olivet, Olivet! Where heaven robbed us
And stole our Christ, and sailed Him to the sky!
Oh, on that day His garments fluttered like a thousand flags
To see His feet command the sunny air.
You did not weep, Jerusalem: your towers and domes
Surprised the firmament with smiles of bronze.

Oh, could you not console us, you applauding acres
Better than the angels and their white command
Who packed and shuttered us, in utter beggary,
Behind the thin doors of the Cenacle?

But blindness falls more lightly than a shell
And look, our newborn eyes, as keen as children,
Knowing no splash or smear of too much light,
Laugh in the sharpest wonder of their vision
And drink the oceanic pressure of their sudden glory.

Father, Father, Whom we thought so hidden
Somewhere behind the jealous walls of Mars,
Oh how You visit us, at the deep roots of life,
With glad reprisals.
Oh drown us in the compound fortunes of these ten
    days' usury,
Reproach our lamentation with these fiery tongues:
Pay all our ransoms with a flock of notes
New-minted in Your golden furnaces.
Astound our nature with the wealth of Your revenge
For all our fear, and our concern.
Then pour us from the Cenacle into the sunny streets
And we will go evangelize the continents.

Minds, minds, sing like spring
To see the hills that fling their hands into the air:
To see the trees all yield their gladness to the tender
    winds
And open wide their treasuries:
Behold the birds, released like angels, from those leafy
    palaces,
With fire and blue and red-gold splashing in their
    painted wings,
Each one proclaiming part of the Apocalypse.
They aim their flights at all the four horizons
And fire their arrows of tremendous news.

World, world, sing like spring
To hear the harvests praising Heaven with a
    thousand voices:
Behold the fertile clouds, in golden fleets,
Like flying frigates, full of gifts.
Behold the clouds, with loads of Gospel,
Splendid and simple as Apostles, in their outward flight!
The waters of the sea all flash with laughter,

Leaping as if to kiss those high, high galleons,
That ride the heavens, full of freight.

But who shall tell the blazes and exchanges
The hidden lightning and the smiles of blinding night,
The kiss and vanish of the sudden invitation,
The game and promise of espousal?

O Holy Spirit, hear, we call Your Name aloud,
We speak You plain and humble in the terms of prayer,
Whatever talk You grant us:
One day we run among the rocks as lithe as lions,
But it is better that, the next, You tame our jubilee,
And prune our praises lean as supplication:
Make us believe You better in the crazy desert,
And seek You better in the skipping heat,
Follow Your messages until we beat our heads
Against the jazz of the horizon.
We'll find You there as much as in the caves of shade,
The grass and springs of the oasis:
But only wring us always, at the center of our inward earth,
Artesian secrets for the roots of love.

But if we walk up to the waist
In the green exultation of the growing harvest,
And if, in the ripe days, the sheaves and increase,
Springing to life on the off-beat of the tractor's congas
Bound from the bouncing binder light as lambs:
Or if we fly, like doves, to the blue woods and consolations
Of the peaceful August,
And in high hiding ring our muffled bells:
Forgive us, always, if our clumsy wills,
Reeling with the possession of so pure a pleasure,
Stumble and break the bottles of our Pentecost.

Beloved Spirit, You are all the prudence and the power
That change our dust and nothing into fields and fruits:
Enfold our lives forever in the compass of Your
      peaceful hills.
Build us a monastery, yes, forever,
(Stones of our cloister lofty as transparent air
And wonderful as light)
In the full fields of gentle Heaven.
Build us our cells forever in Your Mercy's woods:
Then tell Orion and Andromeda our hearts are heavens
And that our eyes are light-years deep,
Sounding Your will, Your peace, in its unbounded fathoms:
Oh balance all our turning orbits, till that morning,
Upon the center and the level of Your holy love:
Then lock our souls forever in the nucleus of its Law.

ODE TO THE PRESENT CENTURY

What heartbeats, lisping like a lizard in a broken cistern,
Tell you, my prudent citizen, that you are nearly dead?
We heard your pains revolving on the axis of a shout:
The cops and doctors view the winter of your knifelong blood.

They chart the reeling of your clockwise reason
Flying in spirals to escape philosophy,
While life's ecliptic, drives you like an arrow
To the pit of pain.
And one by one your wars break up the arctic
Of your faultless logic,
And wills retreat upon themselves until the final seizure:

Your frozen understanding separates
And dies in floes.

Oh how you plot the crowflight of that cunning thief,
        your appetite,
But never see what fortunes
Turn to poison in your blood.
How have you hammered all your senses into curses,
Forever twisting in your memory
The nails of sensuality and death.
Have we not seen you stand, full-armed,
And miss the heavens with the aimless rifles of your fear?
When are you going to unclench
The whited nerve of your rapacity, you cannibal:
Or draw one breath in truth and faith,
You son of Cain?

But if you are in love with fortunes, or with forgery,
Oh, learn to mint you golden courage
With the image of all Mercy's Sovereign,
Turn all your hunger to humility and to forgiveness,
Forsake your deserts of centrifugal desire:
Then ride in peaceful circles to the depths of life,
And hide you from your burning noon-day devil
Where clean rock-water dropwise spends, and dies in rings.

ST. JOHN BAPTIST

I

When, for the fifteenth year, Tiberius Caesar
Cursed, with his reign, the Roman world,
Sharing the Near-East with a tribe of tetrarchs,

The Word of God was made in far-off province:
Deliverance from the herd of armored cattle,
When, from the desert, John came down to Jordan.

But his prophetic messages
Were worded in a code the scribes were not prepared
    to understand.
Where, in their lexicons, was written: "Brood of vipers,"
Applied, that is, to them?

"Who is this Lamb, Whose love
Shall fall upon His people like an army:
Who is this Savior, Whose sandal-latchet
This furious Precursor is afraid to loose?"

His words of mercy and of patience shall be flails
Appointed for the separation of the wheat and chaff.
But who shall fear the violence
And crisis of His threshing-floor
Except the envious and selfish heart?
Choose to be chaff, and fear the Winnower,
For then you never will abide His Baptism of Fire and Spirit.
You proud and strong,
You confident in judgment and in understanding,
You who have weighed and measured every sin
And have so clearly analyzed the prophecies
As to be blinded on the day of their fulfilment:
Your might shall crumble and fall down before Him
    like a wall,
And all the needy and the poor shall enter in,
Pass through your ruins, and possess your kingdom.

This is the day that you shall hear and hate
The voice of His beloved servant.
This is the day your scrutiny shall fear
A terrible and peaceful angel, dressed in skins,

Knowing it is your greedy eyes, not his, that die of hunger.
For God has known and loved him, from his mother's womb,
Remembering his name, filling his life with grace,
Teaching him prophecy and wisdom,
To burn before the Face of Christ,
Name Him and vanish, like a proclamation.

II

Tell us, Prophet, Whom you met upon the far frontier
At the defended bridge, the guarded outpost.

"I passed the guards and sentries,
Their lances did not stay me, or the gate of spikes

Or the abysses of the empty night.
I walked on darkness

To the place of the appointed meeting:
I took my sealed instructions,
But did not wait
For compliment or for congratulation from my
        hidden Captain.
Even at my return
I passed unseen beside the stern defenders
In their nests of guns,
And while the spies were trying to decode some secret
In my plain, true name.
I left them like the night wind."

What did you learn on the wild mountain
When hell came dancing on the noon-day rocks?

"I learned my hands could hold
Rivers of water
And spend them like an everlasting treasure.

124

I learned to see the waking desert
Smiling to behold me with the springs her ransom,
Open her clear eyes in a miracle of transformation,
And the dry wilderness
Suddenly dressed in meadows,
All garlanded with an embroidery of flowering orchards
Sang with a virgin's voice,
Descending to her wedding in these waters
With the Prince of Life.
All barrenness and death lie drowned
Here in the fountains He has sanctified,
And the deep harps of Jordan
Play to the contrite world as sweet as heaven."

But did your eyes buy wrath and imprecation
In the red cinemas of the mirage?

"My eyes did not consult the heat or the horizon:
I did not imitate the spurious intrepidity
Of that mad light full of revenge.
God did not hide me in the desert to instruct my soul
In the fascism of an asp or scorpion.
The sun that burned me to an Arab taught me nothing:
My mind is not in my skin.
I went into the desert to receive
The keys of my deliverance
From image and from concept and from desire.
I learned not wrath but love,
Waiting in darkness for the secret stranger
Who, like an inward fire,
Would try me in the crucibles of His unconquerable Law:
His heat, more searching than the breath of the Simoon,
Separates love from hunger
And peace from satiation,
Burning, destroying all the matrices of anger and revenge.

It is because my love, as strong as steel, is armed against
    all hate
That those who hate their own lives fear me like a sabre."

III

St. John, strong Baptist,
Angel before the face of the Messiah
Desert-dweller, knowing the solitudes that lie
Beyond anxiety and doubt,
Eagle whose flight is higher than our atmosphere
Of hesitation and surmise,
You are the first Cistercian and the greatest Trappist:
Never abandon us, your few but faithful children,
For we remember your amazing life,
Where you laid down for us the form and pattern of
Our love for Christ,
Being so close to Him you were His twin.
Oh buy us, by your intercession, in your mighty heaven,
Not your great name, St. John, or ministry,
But oh, your solitude and death:
And most of all, gain us your great command of graces,
Making our poor hands also fountains full of life
    and wonder
Spending, in endless rivers, to the universe,
Christ, in secret, and His Father, and His sanctifying Spirit.

CLAIRVAUX

I

"Hidden in this heaven-harbor
Wood-cradle valley, narrow and away from men,

Bernard built me, model of all solitudes,
Picture of contemplation and of love, the figure of all prayer
Clairvaux cloister."

Abbey, whose back is to the hills whose backs are to the world,
Your inward look is ever resting
Upon your central garth and garden, full of sun,
Your catch-light cloister.
In-turning, Peace-finding, living in a mirror that attracts
        the noon
You look at deep all-heaven in the pool: your heart,
Down-looking, down, not up, within, not out,
Downdrawing all the sky into your quiet
Well or pool or mirror-lake of clear humility.

Holy, immense, the arching air,
The vaulted heaven, full of liberty,
That never even notices the continents,
Passing them forever by, in fleets of light,
Sees you, Clairvaux, and is astounded by the confidence
        of your expectancy,
Leans down into your loving and wide-open heart
And loves you, who have kept yourself for the blue sky alone,
And know no other landscape, and no other view.
O white, O modest cloister,
Shy cloister, Heaven is your prisoner.
He comes to earth and hides His image in your heart
Where He may rest unseen by the grey, grasping,
Jealous, double-dealing world:
The day that flies the complicated alleys
And the blind yards, and covered squares, and
        wall-eyed markets
Fills your clean court with seas of peace.

But oh, how all the light-and-shaded bays are garlanded
        with life,

With brotherlife, slow growing in the fruitful silence,
In this tender sun,
Clinging in strength to these safe walls, and one another,
All interlacing, in the light, as close as vines:
Godlove in all their ways and gestures flowering
And God's peace giving firstfruits in their quietude.

O holy Bernard, wise in brotherlove,
Vintner who train and grow, and prune and tie us
Fast, trim us in sure and perfect arbors of stability and rule:
You have forseen what vintages the Holy Spirit,
Ripening, in our concord, as in vine-vein the strong sun,
Will trample in His press, His charity, in the due day,
To barrel us, His Burgundy.

II

These arches live together
Like psalm and antiphon,
And spend the light across our pavements
Spilling on warm stone all the sweet, drawn day:

Pouring in sun through rib and leaf and flower of
        foliate window
Gardening the ground with shadow-light, with day and night
In every lovely interplay.

My brothers, do you see these arches' stones, how much
        they weigh,
Yet how the leaning stress of charity
Sports with weight, and laughs at height,
Destroying with light life all heaviness,
Forgetting gravity in flight,
Flying up bravely, arching over, poised in high hover,
Never fear, almost forever!

Nature is so transfigured by their stress on one another
That these square stones are angels: Oh, but Brothers,
Only by leaning on their key,
Who is their Christ and Father, their superior:
He is no greater or more mighty stone,
Still less the architect, or engineer:
And yet he bears the clearest image of the Builder's meaning
Both for himself and all the rest:
He is the center of the Maker's mind and plan,
The clue to all their marvelous flight,
Their keystone, lord, abbot and head.

III

Now fall, time, slow bells spending,
Spilling the hours, oh, the night-song, day-song,
All the intervals, work's end
Into the deep wood and farthest forest, vale's heart,
    glade and bottom
Home-call sending grange and sheepfold wheat
    and rye-field,
Prayerword telling, home to be in cloister-court,
Under the arches, reading by the door-sill,
Praying in uncarven choir-stall,
By plain altars, cowled adorers, where Christ hangs
    and hides in golden dove,
Dwells in the air above our heads
And overshadows all our prayer with His tabernacle wings.

Oh peal your quiet unpretension and succession, time,
    your seasons
No-hurrying us to our sweet, certain, everlasting home;
And pour the news of these our slow progressions into
    the deep,

Down-falling with little echo into (peace) our garth-well,
Paying your bells like Christ our price, oh, yes, like
      Peace-blood's
Ransom into our hearts:
Our everlasting priceblood hour by hour you distil,
Spilling us grace like gold, our Christ like gold,
Grace-blood into our peace you send,
Christ-blood, rich without end,

Spending us God to buy our silence and our holy cloister,
And keep us in His wounds, our walls, sure and secure:
Oh pay us, beg us, bells, our daily Christ,
As every midnight, noon and evening
Dawns our glorious rescue
In hymn and antiphon and psalm.

LA SALETTE

It is a hundred years since your shy feet
Ventured to stand upon the pasture grass of the high Alps,
Coming no deeper in our smoky atmosphere
Than these blue skies, the mountain eyes
Of the two shepherd children, young as flowers,
Born to be dazzled by no mortal snow.

Lady, it is a hundred years
Since those fair, terrible tears
Reproved, with their amazing grief
All the proud candor of those altitudes:
Crowning the flowers at your feet
With diamonds, that seized upon, transfigured into nails
      of light
The rays of the mountain sun!—

And by their news,
(Which came with cowbells to the evening village
And to the world with church-bells
After not too many days,)
And by their news

We thought the walls of all hard hearts
Had broken down, and given in,
Poured out their dirty garrisons of sin,
And washed the streets with our own blood, if need be—
—Only to have them clean!

And though we did not understand
The weight and import of so great a sorrow,
We never thought so soon to have seen
The loss of its undying memory,
Passing from the black world without a word,
Without a funeral!
For while our teeth were battling in the meat of miracles
        and favors,
Your words, your prophecies, were all forgotten!

Now, one by one,
The things you said
Have come to be fulfilled.

John, in the might of his Apocalypse, could not foretell
Half of the story of our monstrous century,
In which the arm of your inexorable Son,
Bound, by His Truth, to disavow your intercession
For this wolf-world, this craven zoo,
Has bombed the doors of hell clean off their hinges,
And burst the cage of antichrist,
Starting, with two great thunderbolts,
The chariots of Armageddon.

FIGURES FOR AN APOCALYPSE
(1947)

"And at midnight there was a cry made: Behold, the Bridegroom cometh, go ye forth to meet Him."

FIGURES FOR AN APOCALYPSE

I

Come down, come down Beloved
And make the brazen waters burn beneath Thy feet.

The mountains shine like wax,
And the cliffs, for fear of Thy look,
Gleam like sweet wax.
Thine eyes are furnaces;
The fireproof rocks unbar their adamantine banks
And weep like wax,
Spilling their diamonds and their emeralds.

Come down, come down Beloved
From the towers of Thy abode.

The waters shine like tin
In the alarming light.
The seas all ring their bells of steel
Beneath Thy terrible feet,
And the mountains quiver like rubber
To the drums of Thy tread.

For, from the beginning of the world,
How few of us have heard the silver of Thy creed
Or paid our hearts for hours of emptiness
With gold of Thy belief?

The eyes that will not coin Thy Incarnation
Figured in every field and flowering tree—
How shall they pay for the drink of those last lights
Poured out on them that expect Thee?

Splitting the seven countries
With the prism of Thy smile,
Confound all augury:
Sever the center of our continents
And through that unpredictable gate lead in
The world's last night,
Clad in the wrath of Armageddon
And in Thy fires arrayed.

Light, then, Thy way to us between the kindled cities
And wake us with Thy trumpet's nine-mile cry,
Forging our minds with the too clear,
Too sudden "BRIDEGROOM!" bright as iron.

And Thou, in the armor of Thy creed's most solemn
    articles,
Rising tremendous in the black gates of death's empty
    Senegal,
Lead out Thy Bride still breathless with dazzle of release,
Still fluttering with the ribbons of the cities' mile-long
    flames
And we, (oh glad!)
Find we our kept, our tended lamps,
Secret amid the dinning herds of the alarum;
While Sidon and the walls of Tyre
Wet as the wax backs of the hog-hundreds, once, among
    the Gadarenes,
Fall down and drown in foaming seas.

II

Come to your windows, rich women,
Rise up in your rooms
And come to your windows, queens!

"We have walked up and down the splendid marble
Strict as compasses,
And viewed our shadows along the dining rooms,
Upon the clean, expensive stone."

Come to your doors, rich women.
Weep in the doors of your treasuries,
You thin, unprofitable queens:
Weep for the bangles on your jeweled bones.

"We have stood in the late light
Of the most lonely afternoons,
And counted all the hours that accused us
Cutting to the division of the marrow and the spine."

How long has silence flourished
In the houses of their joy?
See, now, the broken window panes
Sing to them in their years without harvest
Keener than a violin!

"Why do you still wear
The dead gauds of your Mardi-Gras,
Crabbing in the unquiet noises of the dawn,
Grey, artificial Shebas, spurious queens?"

"We had not planned to have so great a Lent
Bind us and bite us with its heavy chain!"

Shall the Spirit be poured out upon this land?
Shall ever life swell up again in the drained veins,
As wild as wine?

Come to your windows, rich women;
Die in the doors of your need, you starving queens:
"For the vintage is at an end,
The gathering shall come no more."

III

(*Advice to my Friends Robert Lax and Edward Rice, to get
away while they still can.*)

Down at the Hotel Sherlock Holmes,
The walls being full of ears,
We sit with eyes as bright as milk
Writing our snow-white messages
To the lords of the bloody prison:
How shall we bargain a reprieve,
Win pity for the poor pilgrims,
Or forge a paper to Paradise
From the gates of the smouldering jail?
Shall they condemn all joy to die
In the jaws of this cat-and-dog harbor?

Down at the Fauntleroy Bar
With brimstone in our sorry drink,
We sit with eyes as sharp as stones
Writing our names in code—
Fearing to look where the windows ache
With the sight of the Babylon beast.
The skylights of our intellect
Have gone as grey as frost,

While the dawn makes ready, with coated tongue,
To mutter the last alarm:
We'd ask the man for a time-table
But the time-tables are all gone:
And so we sit with eyes like towers
In the hour of the final train.

Down at the Hotel Wonderland
With eyes as mad as rocks,
We swear at the wine as blue as fire
In the glass of our phony grail.
Oh, the despot touts are ripping their collars,
Cursing the atmosphere.
It is too late to fly away
From the city full of sulphur,
From the wide walks where antichrist
Slips us his cruel snare.
The dawn bides like a basilisk
In the doors of the Frankenstein building,
And the cops come down the street in fours
With clubs as loud as bells.

Time, time to go to the terminal
And make the escaping train
With eyes as bright as palaces
And thoughts like nightingales.
It is the hour to fly without passports
From Juda to the mountains,
And hide while cities turn to butter
For fear of the secret bomb.
We'll arm for our own invisible battle
In the wells of the pathless wood
Wounding our limbs with prayers and Lent,
Shooting the traitor memory
And throwing away our guns—

And learning to fight like Gedeon's men,
Hiding our lights in jugs.

IV

(*Cf. Apoc.* XIV, 14.)

Look in the night, look, look in the night:
Heaven stands open like a little temple,
With a man in the door
Having a sickle in his hand.

The steel is cleaner than ice,
The blade is sharper than thought:
The curve is like an intellect, neat!
He lifts up the sickle, and the stars cry out in alarm.
Look in the night, look, look in the night:
The man in the silver garment
Steps down from heaven's temple door.
The seas of the dark world
Boil to the brim with fear.
He raises the sickle. The blade flashes like a cry.

He thrusts in the sickle
And it begins to sing like wind
In the most quiet harvest of the midnight world.

Fly, fly to the mountains!
The temple door is full of angels.
Fly, fly to the hills!
The men on the red horses wait with guns
Along the blue world's burning brim!

The sickle rings like breezes
In harvesting this sleepy world,
Flashing and falling light as music.
There are a thousand angels standing in the gateway of
      the heaven-temple,
Viewing this voiceless harvesting.

Then, suddenly, comes the real dread, the real sound.
From out the empty universe,
Beyond the infinite air, the high star-spirals,
Out of the core of some far furious trumpet
The first wild note begins to spring,
And fires its anger, in an instant, through the ranks
Of the attending angels,
And bites my soul with lightnings live as steel!

V

Landscape, Prophet and Wild-dog

The trees stand like figures in a theatre.
Then suddenly there comes a prophet, running for his life,
And the wild-dog behind him.
And now the wild-dog has him by the ankle
And the man goes down.

"Oh prophet, when it was afternoon you told us:
'Tonight is the millenium,
The withering-away of the state.
The skies, in smiles, shall fold upon the world,
Melting all injustice in the rigors of their breezy love.'
And all night long we waited at the desert's edge,
Hearing this wild-dog, only, on the far mountain,
Watching the white moon giggle in the stream!"

The two trees stand like Masters of Arts
And observe the wild-dog
Nailing his knives into the prophet's shoulder.

"Oh prophet, when it was night you came and told us:
'Tomorrow is the millenium,
The golden age!
The human race will wake up
And find dollars growing out of the palms of their hands,
And the whole world will die of brotherly love
Because the factories jig like drums
And furnaces feed themselves,
And all men lie in idleness upon the quilted pastures,
Tuning their friendly radios and dreaming in the sun!"

"But when the grey day dawned
What flame flared in the jaws of the avenging mills!
We heard the clash of hell within the gates of the
    embattled Factory
And thousands died in the teeth of those sarcastic fires!"

"And now the rivers are poisoned,
The skies rain blood
And all the springs are brackish with the taste
Of these your prophecies.
Oh prophet, tell us plainly, at last:
When is the day of our success?"

But there is no answer in the dead jaws.
And the air is full of wings.
The crows come down and sit like senators
On the arms of the two trees.

At the edge of the salt-lands
In the dry-blue clay

The wild-dog, with a red claw scuffs out a little hollow,
Burying the prophet's meatless shin.

VI

In the Ruins of New York

The moon is paler than an actress.
We have beheld her mourning in the brown ivy
Of the dendric bridges,—
In the brown, broken ivy
That loves but a span of air.

The moon is paler than an actress, and weeps for you,
      New York,
Seeking to see you through the tattered bridges,
Leaning down to catch the sham brass
Of your sophisticated voice,
Whose songs are heard no more!

Oh how quiet it is after the black night
When flames out of the clouds burned down your
         cariated teeth,
And when those lightnings,
Lancing the black boils of Harlem and the Bronx,
Spilled the remaining prisoners,
(The tens and twenties of the living)
Into the trees of Jersey,
To the green farms, to find their liberty.

How are they down, how have they fallen down
Those great strong towers of ice and steel,
And melted by what terror and what miracle?
What fires and lights tore down,

With the white anger of their sudden accusation,
Those towers of silver and of steel?

You whose streets grew up on trellises
With roots in Bowling Green and tap-roots in the
    Upper Bay:
How are you stripped, now, to your skeleton:
What has become of your live and dead flesh:
Where is the shimmer of your bawdy leaves?
Oh, where your children in the evening of your final Sunday
Gunned after one another in the shadows of the Paramount,
The ashes of the leveled towers still curl with tufts of smoke
Veiling your obsequies in their incinerating haze
They write, in embers, this your epitaph:

   "This was a city
   That dressed herself in paper money.
   She lived four hundred years
   With nickles running in her veins.
   She loved the waters of the seven purple seas,
   And burned on her own green harbor
   Higher and whiter than ever any Tyre.
   She was as callous as a taxi;
   Her high-heeled eyes were sometimes blue as gin,
   And she nailed them, all the days of her life,
   Through the hearts of her six million poor.
   Now she has died in the terrors of a sudden
      contemplation
   —Drowned in the waters of her own, her
      poisoned well."

Can we console you, stars,
For the so long survival of such wickedness?
Tomorrow and the day after

Grasses and flowers will grow
Upon the bosom of Manhattan.
And soon the branches of the hickory and sycamore
Will wave where all those dirty windows were—
Ivy and the wild-grape vine
Will tear those weak walls down,
Burying the brownstone fronts in freshness and
    fragrant flowers;
And the wild-rose and the crab-apple tree
Will bloom in all those silent mid-town dells.

There shall be doves' nests, and hives of bees
In the cliffs of the ancient apartments,
And birds shall sing in the sunny hawthorns
Where was once Park Avenue.
And where Grand Central was, shall be a little hill
Clustered with sweet, dark pine.

Will there be some farmer, think you,
Clearing a place in the woods,
Planting an acre of bannering corn
On the heights above Harlem forest?
Will hunters come explore
The virgin glades of Broadway for the lynx and deer?
Or will some hermit, hiding in the birches, build himself
    a cell
With the stones of the city hall,
When all the caved-in subways turn to streams
And creeks of fish,
Flowing in sun and silence to the reedy Battery?

But now the moon is paler than a statue.
She reaches out and hangs her lamp
In the iron trees of this destroyed Hesperides.
And by that light, under the caves that once were banks
    and theaters,

The hairy ones come out to play—
And we believe we hear the singing of the manticores
Echo along the rocks of Wall and Pine

And we are full of fear, and muter than the
        upside-down stars
That limp in the lame waters,
Muter than the mother moon who, white as death,
Flies and escapes across the wastes of Jersey.

VII

Landscape: Beast

Yonder, by the eastward sea
Where smoke melts in a saucer of extinguished cities,
The last men stand, in delegations,
Waiting to see the seven-headed business
Promised us, from those unpublished deeps:
Waiting to see those horns and diadems
And hear the seven voices of the final blasphemy.

And westward, where the other waters are as slick as silk
And slide, in the grey evening, with uncertain lights,
(Screened by the smoke of the extinguished studios)
The last men wait to see the seven-headed thing.
They stand around the radios
Wearing their regalia on their thin excited breasts,
Waving the signals of their masonry.
What will happen, when they see those heads, those horns
Dishevel the flickering sea?

How will they bare their foreheads, and put forth their hands
And wince with the last indelible brand,
And wear the dolour of that animal's number,
And evermore be burned with her disgusting name?

Inland in the lazy distance, where a dozen planes still play
As loud as horseflies, round the ruins of an average town,
A blue-green medium dragon, swimming in the river,
Emerges from the muddy waters, comes to romp awhile
    upon the land.
She rises on the pathless shore,
And goes to roll in the ashes of the ravaged country.
But no man turns to see and be surprised
Where those grey flanks flash palely in the sun.
Who shall gather to see an ordinary dragon, in this day
    of anger,
Or wonder at those scales as usual as sin?

Meanwhile, upon the broken mountains of the south
No one observes the angels passing to and fro:
And no one sees the fire that shoots beneath the hoofs
Of all the white, impatient horses.

And no one hears or fears the music of those blazing swords.

(Northward, northward, what lies there to see?
Who shall recount the terror of those ruined streets?

And who shall dare to look where all the birds with
    golden beaks
Stab at the blue eyes of the murdered saints?)

VIII

The Heavenly City

City, when we see you coming down,
Coming down from God
To be the new world's crown:
How shall they sing, the fresh, unsalted seas
Hearing your harmonies!

For there is no more death,
No need to cure those waters, now, with any brine;
Their shores give them no dead,
Rivers no blood, no rot to stain them.

Because the cruel algebra of war
Is now no more.
And the steel circle of time, inexorable,
Bites like a padlock shut, forever,
In the smoke of the last bomb:
And in that trap the murderers and sorcerers and
    crooked leaders
Go rolling home to hell.
And history is done.

Shine with your lamb-light, shine upon the world:
You are the new creation's sun.
And standing on their twelve foundations,
Lo, the twelve gates that are One Christ are wide as canticles:
And Oh! Begin to hear the thunder of the songs within
    the crystal Towers,
While all the saints rise from their earth with feet like light
And fly to tread the quick-gold of those streets,

Oh City, when we see you sailing down,
Sailing down from God,
Dressed in the glory of the Trinity, and angel-crowned
In nine white diadems of liturgy.

LANDSCAPE: WHEATFIELDS

Frown there like Cressy or like Agincourt,
You fierce and bearded shocks and sheaves

And shake your grain-spears,
And know no tremor in your vigilant
Your stern array, my summer chevaliers!

Although the wagons,
(Hear how the battle of those wheels,
Worrying the loose wood with their momentary thunder
Leaves us to guess some trestle, there, behind the sycamores,)
Although the empty wagons come,

Rise up, like kings out of the pages of a chronicle
And cry your courage in your golden beards;
For now the summer-time is half-way done,
Gliding to a dramatic crisis
Sure as the deep waters to the sedentary mill.

Arise like kings and prophets from the pages of an
        ancient Bible,
And blind us with the burnish of your message in our June:
Then raise your hands and bless us
And depart, like old Melchisedech, and find your
        proper Salem.

The slow hours crowd upon us.
Our days slide evenly toward the term of all our liturgy,
And all our weeks are after Pentecost.

Summer divides his garrisons,
Surrenders up his strongest forts,
Strikes all his russet banners one by one.
And while these ancient men of war
Casting us in the teeth with the reproof of their surrender
(By which their fruitfulness is all fulfilled,)
Throw down their arms,

Face we the day when we go up to stake our graces
Against unconquerable God:
Try, with our trivial increase, in that time of harvest
To stem the army of His attributes!

Oh pray us full of marrow, Queen of Heaven,
For those mills, His truth, our glory!
Crown us with alleluias on that day of fight!

(Light falls as fair as lyres, beamy between the branches,
Plays like an angel on the mill-dam, where the lazy stream
Suddenly turns to clouds of song and rain,)
Oh pray us, Lady, full of faith and graces,
Arm us with fruits against that contest and comparison,
Arm us with ripeness for the wagons of our Christ!

TWO STATES OF PRAYER

In wild October when the low hills lie
With open eye
And own the land like lions,

Our prayer is like the thousands in the far, forgotten stadiums,
Building its exultation like a tower of fire,
Until the marvelous woods spring to their feet
And raid the skies with their red-headed shout:

This is the way our hearts take flame
And burn us down, on pyres of prayer, with too much glory.

But when the trees have all torn up their programs,
Scattering the pathos of immense migrations to the
     open-handed winds,

Clouding and saddening the dusky valley,
Sorrow begins to bully the bare bars
Of those forsaken cages
As thought lies slaughtered in the broken doors.

But by the light of our December mornings,
Though words stand frozen in the voice's well
And all the country pumps are dumb,
Look where the landscape, like a white Cistercian,
Puts on the ample winter like a cowl
And so conceals, beneath the drifts as deep as quietude,
The ragged fences and the ravaged field.

The hills lie still, the woods their Sabbath keep.
The farms, half buried in their winter coats
Are warm as sheep.
When was there ever greater than this penitential peace
Outshining all the songs of June with radiant silences?

November analyzed our bankruptcies, but now
His observations lie knee-deep beneath our
    Christmas mercies,
While folded in the buried seed
The virtual summer lives and sleeps;
And every acre keeps its treasure like a kingly secret.

A LETTER TO AMERICA

America, when you were born, and when the plains
Spelled out their miles of praises in the sun
What glory and what history
The rivers seemed to prepare.

We hear them, now, in the Kentucky summer,
While all the locusts drown our forests in their iron prayer:
And we dream of you, beloved, sleeping in your leafy bosom.

How long are we to wake
With eyes that turn to wells of blood
Seeing the hell that gets you from us
With his treacherous embrace!

The bands that raced our flesh
With smiles as raw as scars,
Can kill you, Kansas, with their high-powered thirst.
Have you not heard the vast Missouri sing
To drown them with those billion gallon silences?

But when the day is quieter
Than your primeval cradle
All our green woods fill, once again, with wishful lies:
Maybe the cities, (sing the birds, our travellers)
Maybe the cities have begun to heal,
And stanched their smoky hemorrhage:
Maybe they have begun to mend their cauteries,
Parsing the muteness of so many dead.

Down where the movies grit
Their white electric teeth,
Maybe the glorious children have rebelled
And rinsed their mental slums
In the clean drench of an incalculable grief.

Maybe their penitence has torn the phony sunset
To view their devil dressed in laudanum,
And scotched his crazy spectre,
And learned the liberty of the unfathomable stars,
Within the doors of their confessionals,
Their new, more lasting Lexingtons!

But oh! the flowering cancers of that love
That eats your earth with roots of steel!
No few fast hours can drain your flesh
Of all those seas of candied poison,

Until our long Gregorian cry
Bows down the stars' Samaritan
To rue the pity of so cruel a murder.

THREE POSTCARDS FROM THE MONASTERY

I

The pilgrim passes swiftly.
All the strange towns,
Wrapped in their double cloaks
(Of rain and of non-entity)
Veil their elusive faces.

The pale world, white as plaster,
(Its doors are dumb, its windows far too blind for
    lamentation)
Dies like problematical news.

We have receded from the things
You printed on those unidentified facades.
We barely dream about the frontispiece
Of your collapsing palaces.
We can refuse your tin.

The smoky choirs
Of those far five-o'clock trombones
Have blown away. Our eyes
Are clean as the September night.
Our minds, (our silences) are light years deep.

Who shall amaze us with the noise of your discovery,
    America?
Who shall make known to us your new, true name,
Instead of knocking at our gates,
Bidding us look again upon that blank and pictured
    concentration?

Because the ticker-tapes are dead,
The radios are all shot:
But we have gone up to buy you Andromeda.

II

It is because the sun
Shines on the shallows like a cannonade
That we have come inland.

It is because the cloudy sea
Hailing the cliffs as loud as promises,
Saluting all the continent with foaming orchestras,

Raided the shore with tons of silver
That we have fled to the penniless hills,
Hidden in the poor, laborious fields.

We stood one moment by the bridgehead of those
    fatal fortunes:
Days that offered to fill our hands with gold,
Surfs that crowded the grey rocks with ballyhoo.

Shall I speak plain against the sun?
Or sing together with the comic-operas of the sea?
We have refused the reward,
We have abandoned the man-hunt.

But when the contest is over
We shall inherit the world.

III

Once were begotten
In the wombs of the deep mountains:
Born over and over in the play of penitential tunnels.
Such was our birth and resurrection from the freezing east
The night we cleared you, Pittsburgh, in a maze of lights.

Our lives were suddenly weaned in strange Ohio,
(Whose towns made little love to us, in their green requiems)
Weaned from the land and atmosphere of men.

Have you ever heard this music
Sung over and over by night,
How we will live in *loco pascuae?*
Or the assuring voices of those inward violins
Play: "Going to Gethsemani?"

(We were begotten in the tunnels of December rain,
Born from the wombs of news and tribulation,
By night, by wakeful rosary:
Such was my birth, my resurrection from the freezing east,
The night we cleared you, Cincinnati, in a maze of lights.)

ON THE ANNIVERSARY OF MY BAPTISM

Certain waters are as blue as metal
Or as salt as sorrow.

Others wince like brass in the hammering sun,
Or stammer all over with tremors of shadow
That die as fast as the light winds
Whose flights surprise the promontories
And the marble bay.

Some are crowded everywhere, off-shore, with purple coral
Between the fleets of light that founder in the sand.
Others are full of yawls, or loud with launches,
Or sadder than the bitter smoke
Of tug and trawler, tramp and collier,

Or as grey as battle.

Oh! Since I was a baby in the Pyrenees,
When old St. Martin marked me for the cloister from
        high Canigou,

How many deeps, how many wicked seas
Went to befriend me with a flash of white-caps
Louder than laughter in the wind and sun,
Or sluggered all our brown bows gunwale-under
In their rowdy thunder—
Only to return me to the land.

Do you suppose that if the green Atlantic
Had ever cracked our brittle shell
And rifled all the cabins for their fruit of drunken passengers,
Do you suppose my sins,
Once we were sorted and disposed forever
Along the shelves of that profound, unvisited museum,
Would there have been immune,
Or learned to keep their coats of unreality
From the deep sea's most patient candying?

156

The day You made the waters,
And dragged them down from the dividing islands
And made them spring with fish,
You planned to bless the brine out of the seas
That were to be my death.

And this is the ninth November since my world's end and
        my Genesis,
When, with the sting of salt in my dry mouth,
Cross-crowned with water by the priest,
Stunned at the execution of my old companion, death,
And with the murder of my savage history,
You drowned me in the shallow font.

My eyes, swimming in unexpected infancy,
Were far too frail for such a favor:
They still close-kept the stone shell of their empty sepulchre:
But, though they saw none, guessed the new-come Trinity
That charged my sinews with His secret life.

SONG: CONTEMPLATION

O land alive with miracles!
O clad in streams,
Countering the silver summer's pleasant arrows
And beating them with the kind armor
Of your enkindled water-vesture,

Lift your blue trees into the early sun!

O country wild with talent
Is there an hour in you that does not rouse our mind
        with songs?

The boughs that bend in the weak wind
Open us momentary windows, here and there,
Into those deep and purple galleries,
Disclosing us the birds your genius;

And yet the earth is loud
With more than this their timid vaudeville.

O brilliant wood!
Yours is the voice of a new world;
And all the hills burn with such blinding art

That Christ and angels walk among us, everywhere.
These are their ways, their fiery footsteps,
That flash and vanish, smile and pass;
—By those bright passengers our groves are all inspired.
Lo, we have seen you, we have seized you, wonder,
Caught you, half held you in the larch and lighted birch:
But in that capture you have sailed us half-mile-high into
    the air
To taste the silences of the inimitable hawk:

Nor do we swing upon the wind
To scan the flattened barns as brown as blood
Growing into the surface of the wounded earth,
Or learn the white roads, livid as a whipcut scar.
For suddenly we have forgotten your geography,
Old nature, and your map of prey,
And know no more the low world scourged with travelling.

The genuine steps, the obvious degrees
The measured cart-ways and the fields we trod all day
And the tunes of the clattering shops,
Even the songs that crowned the highest hill
Find us no longer beggars for their petty coin.

158

We've left the stations of the mendicants
And the ways of the workaday saints.

But in the dazzled, high and unelectric air
Seized in the talons of the terrible Dove,
The huge, unwounding Spirit,
We suddenly escape the drag of earth
Fly from the dizzy paw of gravity
And swimming in the wind that lies beyond the track
Of thought and genius and of desire,

Trample the white, appalling stratosphere.

A MYSTERIOUS SONG IN THE SPRING OF THE YEAR

In April, when our land last died
And secrecy rebelled against the sun,
And hidden heaven mocked the visible systems
With white untouchable flowers,

Old Duty, sitting at his beggarpost,
Counted the changes of the sun-and-water season:
All spattered, there, behind the willow's greening shower.
Now it was he who tried to woo us to the purchase
Of accurate annals of our state,
Waking, upon our passage, with a musical cry.
But we refused his all too faithful history.

What exorcist
Had stilled you, five commercial senses,
And locked away your lion-light
And saved our capture from those bleeding paws?

Or into what division had we slipped,
Figured in what oblique escape,
Sidelong into eternity, between the angular hour?

The bells were ever at their belfry-place,
Quarter by quarter rang us to our busy death,
Reckoning-up our obligations
In the high tower's teller-cages:

But we with work too suddenly done
And locked in a trice to the unexpected Cross
Had died and gone our way, ten, twenty years ahead
    of the appointed time.

Oh, life, put down your organ-grinder's cup,
Tax us no more, greyfellow, for our ears are shuttered:
Our eyes are dark, but we are not asleep:
Our hands are folded where we work, in state, *in requie.*

Oh happy death, where life and fright,
Where love and loss are drawn apart
And stand, forever, separate,
While one by one the fragments of a century
Disintegrate and fall in silence all about us:
And these are news of peace, but not dismay,

For heaven is builded deeper and stronger everywhere
From the collapse of our neglected history.

CANTICLE FOR THE BLESSED VIRGIN

I

Die, Boreas,
And drown your ruins in the gaudy sea,

December, clash your cymbals once again
And put them away.
The crops come thronging from the ground.
The land is green with strength.
The harvests sing like confidence
In the ascetic earth.
Let there be no more patience
With your iron music, death:
Stand, continents, and wear the spring your crown!

The ox-eyed land,
The muted lakes,
The cloudy groves that praise you, Lady, with their blooms,
Fuse and destroy their lights
And burn them into gold for you, great Virgin,
Coining your honor in the glorious sun.

The skies speed up to meet you, and the seas
Swim you the silver of their crests.
If you delay to come, we'll see the meteors, by night,
Skimming before your way,
Lighting the time of death's dismay
In lights as lithe as animals.
And God will blaze your pathway with the incandescent stars.

But oh! Queen of all grace and counsel,
Cause of our joy, Oh Clement Virgin, come:
Show us those eyes as chaste as lightning,
Kinder than June and true as Scripture.
Heal with your looks the poisons of the universe,
And claim your Son's regenerate world!

Because your Christ disposed Orion and Andromeda
And ordered the clean spheres,
And interplayed the chiming suns to be your toy,

Charm you with antiphon and psalmody
And canticle, and countersong;

Because your Christ
Fired the fair stars with argent for your raiment,
And charged the sinner's tears
With clean repentent lights—
(As on the day you found me in the dens of libraries
And crushed the jeweled head of heresy)—
He gave you every one of the redeemed to be your dowry
And angels for your crown.

Come from the compass quarter where the thunder sleeps
And let the pity of those eyes
Rout all the armies of our million dangers
Here where we lie in siege:
For you unlock the treasures of the bleeding Wood.
You hold the Mass-keys, and the locks of Calvary,
And All-grace springs in the founts of your demand.

II

Lady, whose smiles are full of counsel and theology,
Never have you withheld those seas of light
Whose surf confounds the keenest eye.
Grace me to be the soldier of your Scotus,
Arming my actions with the news
Of your Immaculate command.

You, who have saved me from the ones about to break me
On the iron wheels of sin,

And bought me from the torturer
With all the florins of the Parasceve:
If Christ will burn me clean
Of my red-handed perjuries,
Win me His Blood again, and blazon me His priest.

But if my hands that one time wore the stench of death
Are too unworthy of the Liturgy
That speaks our deathless Pasch in veils of Bread,
Make me, until my death, His priest in secret
Offering Mass in all-day's sacrifice.

Teach me to take all grace
And spring it into blades of act,
Grow spears and sheaves of charity,
While each new instant, (new eternity)
Flowering with clean and individual circumstance,
Speaks me the whisper of His consecrating Spirit.
Then will obedience bring forth new Incarnations
Shining to God with the features of His Christ.

ENVOI:

Tower, stars, and oh! you sun in Aries,
Shatter a way for her through the embattled weather,
Until the hills
Tidy their fields, and fill them full of flowers
For those Annunciations:

And hell shall melt his onsets
Faster than January's brawling clouds
Doomed by the music of her chariot.

DUNS SCOTUS

Striking like lightning to the quick of the real world
Scotus has mined all ranges to their deepest veins:
But where, oh, on what blazing mountain of theology
And in what Sinai's furnace
Did God refine that gold?

Who ruled those arguments in their triumphant order
And armed them with their strict celestial light?
See the lance-lightning, blade-glitter, banner-progress
As love advances, company by company
In sunlit teams his clean embattled reasons,

Until the firmament, with high heavenly marvel
Views in our crystal souls her blue embodiment,
Unfurls a thousand flags above our heads—
It is the music of Our Lady's army!

For Scotus is her theologian,
Nor has there ever been a braver chivalry than his precision.
His thoughts are skies of cloudless peace
Bright as the vesture of her grand aurora
Filled with the rising Christ.

But we, a weak, suspicious generation,
Loving emotion, hating prayer,
We are not worthy of his wisdom.
Creeping like beasts between the mountain's feet
We look for laws in the Arabian dust.
We have no notion of his freedom

Whose acts despise the chains of choice and passion.
We have no love for his beatitude
Whose act renounces motion:

Whose love flies home forever
As silver as felicity,
Working and quiet in the dancelight of an everlasting arrow.

Lady, the image of whose heaven
Sings in the might of Scotus' reasoning:
There is no line of his that has not blazed your glory in
the schools,
Though in the dark words, without romance,
Calling us to swear you our liege.

Language was far too puny for his great theology:
But, oh! His thought strode through those words
Bright as the conquering Christ
Between the clouds His enemies:
And in the clearing storm, and Sinai's dying thunder
Scotus comes out, and shakes his golden locks
And sings like the African sun.

TWO DESERT FATHERS

I

St. Jerome

The light that rises on Jehosaphat
Greyer than the rocks
On which the Baptist stood and preached,
Showed you the coming of the solemn Christ.
You heard His speech proceeding like an army
Before Whose tread all understanding shall succumb
Knowing no way of withstanding the weight of
His language

Or the keen, bright, two-way sword-measure
Of that Judgment.

The light that sank upon the valley of the final settlement
Showed you over and over the wreckage of the universe
Boiling like wine out of the faucets of that ruined stadium
Far bloodier than the vintage of those evenings in the
    trampled west.

Jerome! Jerome!
What is this voice comes down to us
Down the far tunnels from the heaven of your solitude?
You who have died hard by the caves of Bethlehem
Forgotten by the barren world, the hater of the Incarnation,
Oh, now, how suddenly risen again
You chide us with that language loud with fight:
Language of one who had to wrestle in the long
    night's wilderness
With the wild angel, Revelation.

Words were not made to dress such lightning
And thought cracks under the pressure of that thunder
When your most learned, mad
And immaculate indignation

Sunders with its meteors the darkness of our classic
    intellection,
Severs our midnight like a streak of flying pullmans
And challenges our black unhappiness
Lord as the lights of an express.

II

St. Paul the Hermit

When Egypt dies behind a hundred miles of heat
And the low Nile is long, long lost in leagues of rock

What silences begin to weigh upon the world as heavy as
     a mountain,
Towering to the high frown of the sky-blue equator
Whereon the giant sun
Drums on the noon and stuns the wide
Imaginary ocean with his cannonade,
Where shall we find the road to you?
This is the central pole of desolation
Where all the ways lie lost.
Yet here is where you one day came,
Ages ago, a cockle-pilgrim or a fugitive,
Barefoot and poor, or sandalled only
In peacefulness and Gospel-shoon.

How can we make our way to where you are
Facing all day the innocent terror
That shadows us behind this cliff?
What eyes we seem to feel
Reaching toward our backs as frail as tentacles:
Eyes that we turn to face, and never see!
And worse than they:
Who are these mopping legendary creatures,
Smiling and beckoning with hoof and fin:
The centaurs, and their fabled colloquy!
How shall we bear the mewing of these fauns,
Or trust such hairy messengers?

But no, here is no hell-spy.
Here in these white-hot solitudes
We have outstripped the level of deception;
We are beyond the doors of devil-trap.

Therefore we cross the invisible frontier
And come upon your paradise, Father of anchorites,
And your simplicity.

Thus did the great St. Anthony
Make your discovery
Saint, who of all great saints, oh! I most envy!

Alone, alone
In the den by the date tree,
The years told you their numbers one by one
And made more than a century:
But you had forgotten them all.
They were no longer than a quarter hour.

Because God, God
The One I hunt and never capture,
Opened His door, and lo, His loneliness invaded you.

Alone, alone
Sitting in the sunny den-door
Under that date tree,
Wounded from head to foot by His most isolated Trinity,
Asking no more questions,
Forgetting how to spell the thought of scrutiny
And wanting no secret
You died to the world of concept
Upon the cross of your humility.

And then your agonizing wounds
Endowed you, in the lair of the forgotten forgers;
Your dark unutterable wounds
Endowed you like a millionaire.

The years went shining by
And there you dwelled,
Grander and wealthier than a fountain,
Quieter and nobler than that old oasis
Of the first, the sinless world.

And the fair springs of your interminable, wordless prayer
Went out in secret to transfigure distant cities
With the picture of your charity,
While here the lions came, and bowed their huge ferocity,
Gambolled and played to please your gentle gaze
And swept the dust before your den with their great manes.

Alone, under the companion and untalking tree
And having lost the key of every mystery
And strayed from the ways of enquiry
You fell upon my God where I and all men
Fear to go walking on such lack of evidence:
But you, slain in the center of your wits,
Passed through the obvious door
Too real for us to find.

And now, old Father of the alone,
Pray us into your stillness,
Into the glory of that faith where you were fed by ravens:

Because our minds, lovers of map and line
Charting the way to heaven with a peck of compasses,
Plotting to catch our Christ between some numbered parallels,
Trick us with too much logic to the waters
Of the iron Nile
And draw us down to old magnetic Thebes
And to the harlot crowned in martyr-murder,
Throned on the money-colored sea.

SPRING: MONASTERY FARM

When it is spring,
When the huge bulls roam in their pens
And sing like trains;

When the white orchards dream in the noon
And all those trees are dens of light
And boom with honey bees,

The blue-eyed streams
No longer lock their mirth among the icy shales
But run to meet the sun with faces clean.

When Aries
Stands at the crossed ecliptic with a golden cry,
We'll sing the grain that dies and triumphs in the
        secret ground.
Though in our labor and our rational Lent we bend our heads
And glaze the dark earth with a shining ploughshare,
Our minds more ardent, hearts insatiable
Than all the amber bees that wrestle in the daffodils,
Sing in the flowers of Your theology.

For, in the sap and music of the region's spring
We hear the picture of Your voice, Creator,
And in our heartspeace answer You
And offer You the world.

For, for all these, their spring is their necessity:
But we have traded April for our ransom and our
        Hundredfold.
Our songs complete those deep, uncomprehending choirs.

For, for all these, their spring is their necessity,
Which, by Your Cross and grace, is made our glory and
        our Sacrament:
As every golden instant mints the Christ Who keeps us free.

ST. JOHN'S NIGHT

Now where the hills of Languedoc are blue with vineyards
Swimming to the brows of the low ridges brown as shells,
A thousand villages begin to name your night with fires.

The flames that wake as wide as faith,
Opening their fierce and innocent eyes from hill to hill
In the midsummer nightfall,
Burn at the ageless cross-roads these their
Pagan and converted fires.

And the dark shocks of the fair summer's harvest
Rise up in the deep fields
Where for two thousand years, St. John,
Your fires are young among us;
They cry there, loud as was your desert testimony,
Out by the grey olive groves,
Out at the crossing of the vineyard roads
Where once the wheat sheaves wept with blood
In warning to the sickles of the manichees.

And in our hearts, here in another nation
Is made your deep midsummer night.
It is a night of other fires,

Wherein all thoughts, all wreckage of the noisy world
Swim out of ken like leaves, or smoke upon the pools of wind.

Oh, listen to that darkness, listen to that deep darkness,
Listen to those seas of darkness on whose shores we stand
     and die.
Now can we have you, peace, now can we sleep in Your will,
     sweet God of peace?

Now can we have Your Word and in Him rest?

Prophet and hermit, great John-Baptist,
You who have brought us to the door-sill of your wilderness,
You who have won for us
The first faint savor of the world's desertion:
When shall we have to eat the things that we have
     barely tasted?
When shall we have your own vast loneliness's
     holy honeycomb?

You hold in your two hands, lo! more than Baptism:
The fruits and the three virtues and the seven presents.
We wait upon your intercession:
Or die we without mercy on the rim of those
     impossible shores?

Kindle, kindle in this wilderness
The tracks of those wonderful fires:
Clean us and lead us in the new night, with the power of Elias
And find us out the summits of the love and prayer
That Wisdom wants of us, oh Bridegroom's Friend!

And take us to the secret tents,
The sacred, unimaginable tabernacles
Burning upon the hills of our desire!

THE SONG OF THE TRAVELLER

How light the heavy world becomes, when with
     transparent waters
All the shy elms and wakeful appletrees are dressed!
How the sun shouts, and spins his wheel of flame

And shoots the whole land full of diamonds
Enriching every flower's watery vesture with his praise,
O green spring mornings when we hear creation singing!

The stones between our steps are radium and platinum
When, on this sacred day, sweet Christ, we climb Your hill;
And all the hours, our steps,
Pray us our way to the high top with silent music from
    the clouds
As each new bench-mark builds us to a quieter altitude,
Promising those holy heights where the low world will die.

Shall we look back out of this airy treasury
And spill the plenty that we have already in our hands
To view you, cities full of sorcery,
And count the regiments deployed on your grey plain
Where you lie boiling in your smoky wars?

For lo! the music of your treachery
Still plagues us with a sullen rumor in this sinless sun,
And your coarse voice still reaches us.
Sandpapering the silence of our atmosphere.
Shall we turn back to hear those far, far fragile trumpets play?

Let us but lean one moment to the witchery of your
    thin clarions
And all our flowery mountain will be tattered with a coat
    of weeds;
And the bright sun, our friend, turning to a prodigious
    enemy,
Will burn our way with curses,
Hardening our hesitation, in that instant, to a
    solid weight,

To bake us white as monuments, like Mistress Lot,
Saltpillars planted on the stony road from Sodom.

EVENING: ZERO WEATHER

Now the lone world is streaky as a wall of marble
With veins of clear and frozen snow.
There is no bird-song there, no hare's track
No badger working in the russet grass:
All the bare fields are silent as eternity.

And the whole herd is home in the long barn.
The brothers come, with hoods about their faces,
Following their plumes of breath
Lugging the gleaming buckets one by one.

This was a day when shovels would have struck
Full flakes of fire out of the land like rock:
And ground cries out like iron beneath our boots

When all the monks come in with eyes as clean as the cold sky
And axes under their arms,
Still paying out *Ave Marias*
With rosaries between their bleeding fingers.

We shake the chips out of our robes outside the door
And go to hide in cowls as deep as clouds,
Bowing our shoulders in the church's shadow, lean
        and whipped,
To wait upon your Vespers, Mother of God!

And we have eyes no more for the dark pillars or the
        freezing windows,
Ears for the rumorous cloister or the chimes of time
        above our heads:
For we are sunken in the summer of our adoration,
And plunge, down, down into the fathoms of our secret joy
That swims with indefinable fire.

And we will never see the copper sunset
Linger a moment, like an echo, on the frozen hill
Then suddenly die an hour before the Angelus.

For we have found our Christ, our August
Here in the zero days before Lent—
We are already binding up our sheaves of harvest
Beating the lazy liturgy, going up with exultation
Even on the eve of our Ash Wednesday,
And entering our blazing heaven by the doors of
    the Assumption!

THE TRANSFORMATION:
FOR THE SACRED HEART

Heart, in the ardor of Whose holy day
The June is blazing on our world of fruit and wheat,
Smile on our lives, and sanctify them with a new
    love's vintage
And with Your fires vivify our veins.

Lo, the whole humble earth
Bows and is broken with Your loads of bounty, and the trees
Fail and give way as we besiege them with a score of ladders.
We have no time to turn and hear the tiger-lilies all
    along the field,
Whose outcry warns the world of Love's immense invasion
Coming to crowd our continent with full-armed shocks.
And look! Those regiments are all around us!
How shall we flee you? You will 'siege us in our
    bursting barns
And force us to a parley in our vines and garden.

Lord, in this splendid season
When all the things that grow extend their arms and show
    the world Your love,

Shall the free wills of men alone
Bide in their January ice
And keep the stubborn winter of their fruitlessness?

Why are we all afraid of love?
Why should we, who are far greater than the grain
Fear to fall in the ground and die?
Have You not planned for minds and wills
Their own more subtle biochemistry?

This is the end of my old ways, dear Christ!
Now I will hear Your voice at last
And leave the frosts (that is: the fears) of my December.
And though You kill me, (as You must) more, more I'll trust
    in you.
For though the darkness and the furious waters of
    that planting
Seep down and eat my life away
Yet my dark night both eats and feeds me,
'Til I begin to know what new life, green life springs within
    my bones.

Heart, in the long, daily buryings of anguish and of prayer,
Or when I seem to die on the dry burning stone, among
    the thorns,
It is no longer I, but You Who work and grow:
It is your life, not mine that makes these new green blades
In the transforming of my soul.
Oh, long before the June, if I but could
I would begin to count my loads of grain,
Hailing the hundreds of the heaven-harvests.

But though they are not yet for man's accounting,
Still in the planted earth I'll hold these hills of gold
Between the blade and the green ear.

RIEVAULX: ST. AILRED

Once when the white clouds praised you, Yorkshire,
Flying before the sun, flying before the eastern wind,
What greenness grew along the waters,
Flowering in the valleys of the purple moor.

Once when the strong sun blessed you, kind as Christ
Slaying the winter mist, delivering the blinded fells,
Banking a million treasures in the waters of the Rye,
Who were the saints who came to claim your peacefulness
And build a valley's silence into bowers of permanent stone?

The viewless wind came walking on the land like a Messiah
Spending the thin scent of the russet heather,
Lauding the flowering gorse and the green broom:
Because this was your spring.
The sky had new-discovered you, and looked and loved you
Began to teach you songs to sing upon the day of
        your espousal.
So Rievaulx raised her white cathedral in the wilderness
Arising in her strength and newness beautiful as Judith.

By night, by night the lamps of York go to and fro
Searching the city with their bleeding eyes
To find where Holofernes lies.
St. Ailred, did you know the dead Assyrian
Whom the new Ladychurch has slain?

Court-craft and pride of heart lie dead
With heads struck off, in Scotland, where were once
    your palace premises.
Go where the tender branches bend and swing
Because the lark and thrush are jeweling the April with
    their hymns,
And spy, between the sunny coppices
The new roof-beams, and smell the curling bake-house smoke
And see the barns and ordered yards
And hear the harmony of their various work.

The sun that plays in the amazing church
Melts all the rigor of those cowls as grey as stone—
Or in the evening gloom that clouds them through those
    tintless panes,
The choirs fall down in tidal waves
And thunder on the darkened forms in a white surf
    of *Glorias*:
And thence we see the tribes, the tribes go up
To their Jerusalem
Out of the quiet tumult of their fierce Gregorian death!

And thence we see the tribes, the tribes go up
And find their Christ, adore Him in His blazing Sion
While the great psalms are flowering along the vaulted stones.

Oh, who shall tell the glory and the grace-price and the
    everlasting power
Of what was once the Grey Monks' sacrifice,
When with the slow and ending canticle they broke
    their choirs
And bent them to the ground:

What were your names, you hundred thousand cross-cowled
    nameless saints?

Burning before the Lord upon the altar of your poverty
    and love,
You there destroyed before the face of His great Majesty
All the world's armies and her kingdoms and her centuries of
    blood and fire,
And all her palaces and all her treasuries
And the glory of her crowns.

THEORY OF PRAYER

Not in the streets, not in the white streets
Nor in the crowded porticoes
Shall we catch You in our words,
Or lock You in the lenses of our cameras,
You Who escaped the subtle Aristotle,
Blinding us by Your evidence,
Your too clear evidence, Your everywhere.

Not in the groves, not in the flowering green groves
Where the pretty idols dwell
Shall we find the path to Your pavilion
Tented in clouds and fire:—
We are only following the echo
Of our own lyres.

The wise man's blood
Freezes in every vein and artery
With the blue poison of his own indelible prudence.
And the lover,
Caught in the loop of his own lie
Strangles like a hare:
While the singers are suddenly killed,
Slain by the blades of their own song—

The words that clash like razors in the throat
Severing the tender strings.

For the things that we utter turn and betray us,
Writing the names of our sins on flesh and bone
In lights as hard as diamonds.
And the things we think have sold us to the enemy
Writing the names of our sins on the raw marrow
In lights as sharp as glass.
And our desires,
Uncovering their faces one by one
Are seen to be our murderers!
How did you break your jails, you black assassins?
How did you find us out, you numbered men?

Logic has ruined us,
Theorems have flung their folly at us,
Economy has left us full of swords
And all our blood is gone:
Oh, how like a death, now, is our prayer become!
We lie and wait upon the unknown Savior
Waking and waking in the guarded tomb. . . .

But the armed ocean of peace,
The full-armed ocean is suddenly within us.
Where, where, peace, did you get in?
And the armed ocean of quiet,
The full armed ocean, stands within us:
Where, from what wells, hid in the middle of our essence,
You silences, did you come pouring in?

But all our thoughts lie still, and in this shipwreck
We'll learn the theory of prayer:
"How many hate their own safe death,
Their cell, their submarine!"

"How many hate Your Cross, Your Key, the only one
To beat that last invincible door
That will surprise us, Peace, with Your invasion
And let us in those soundless fathoms where You dwell."

CLAIRVAUX PRISON

It is a year of strategy.

The bureaucrats, wiping the blood off their fingers
In the gates of the Temple of Reason,
Have voted to poison the enemy's well.

They know their danger.
They need to throw some dead thing
Into the living waters that were once Clairvaux,
And kill the too clean image
In the heart of such a spring.

Nine or a dozen murderers
And a hundred others with the grime of knavery upon them
Go colonize the ancient cloister
On the morrow of the Constitution:
And in the shadows of the broken church,
Each dead soul starts to blossom in his sepulchre
Cursing the comfortable sun.

Heaven, with a strange impassivity,
Shows no particular horror for this grim cartoon:
Lets each new sphinx
Crouch in his iron hermitage
Musing the means to end this leprous noviceship.

And no fire falls.
No brimstone buries these absinthial silences
Or purifies the poisoned sanctuary to a pile of ash.

God is holding you as evidence, Clairvaux;
Saving you, with a most terrifying Providence,
Because you are so true an image of a world
That was untrue to Him.
You are too good a mirror to be broken and destroyed.

Your faithful glass,
Patient of all the grime and blood of the late centuries
Suffers the face of the new liberty,
Frames out the new fraternity for all to contemplate:
Receives equality and holds it fast
With a firm hug of locks,

That those who have never forgotten
The days of Bernard and the first Cistercians
May read the terror of those messages
And fly to keep their freedom in the servitude of grace.

NATURAL HISTORY

There is a grey wall, in places overhung
With the abundant surf of honeysuckle:
It is a place of shelter, full of sun.

There, in the middle of September, in the vintner's workdays
When the skies begin to change,
Putting away the steams of August 'til the air is loud with blue,
The creeping things, in the wise diligence of an ascetic season,

Have worked their small momentous wonder,
Prepared their winter's sleep.

O Savior! How we learn Your mercy and Your Providence,
Seeing these creatures in their tiny and tremendous labor:
Each one diligent and alone
Furling and arming himself in a grey case, the color
    of the wall.

Who told these six or seven creepers how to hasten to
    this place, this safety,
This warm home-haven, better than a Riviera,
And to these stones that will, all winter, never know
    the wind?
Or who has brought them here together,
With no time-table and no calendar,
On this particular day?
Measure the quality of the obedience
With which their natures hear Your thought and come,
Each worm hastening as best he can
To die here in this patch of sun.

Leaving all leaves and grasses and the smaller flowers
And all their haunts unseen and summer pastures
They do not stay to study Your command, Your mystery,
That this, the only thing they know, must cease
And they must seal themselves in silences and sleep.
See with what zeal they wrestle off their ancient, tawny life
And fight with all their might to end their private histories
And lock their days in the cocoon.

Walk we and ponder on this miracle
And on the way Your creatures love Your will,
While we, with all our minds and light, how slow
Hard-hearted in our faithlessness, and stubborn as the
    coldest stone!

It was Your St. Theresa struck the deeps
Of this astounding parable—
For all creation teaches us some way of prayer.

Here on the Trappist wall, beside the cemetery,
Two figures, death and contemplation,
Write themselves out before us in the easy sun
Where everything that moves is full of mystical theology.

Shall we still fear the fight that wrests our way
Free from the vesture of our ancient days,
Killing the prisoner, Adam, in us,
And laying us away to sleep a space, in the transforming
    Christ?

Oh, we, who know from faith and Scripture
All the scope and end of metamorphosis,
Run we like these creatures in their glad alacrity
To our far sweeter figurative death,

When we can learn such ways to God from creeping things
And sanctity from a black and russet worm!

A CHRISTMAS CARD

When the white stars talk together like sisters
And when the winter hills
Raise their grand semblance in the freezing night,
Somewhere one window
Bleeds like the brown eye of an open forge.

Hills, stars,
White stars that stand above the eastern stable,

Look down and offer Him
The dim adoring light of your belief,
Whose small Heart bleeds with infinite fire.

Shall not this Child
(When we shall hear the bells of His amazing voice)
Conquer the winter of our hateful century?

And when His Lady Mother leans upon the crib,
Lo, with what rapiers
Those two loves fence and flame their brilliancy!

Here in this straw lie planned the fires
That will melt all our sufferings:
He is our Lamb, our holocaust!

And one by one the shepherds, with their snowy feet,
Stamp and shake out their hats upon the stable dirt,
And one by one kneel down to look upon their Life.

WINTER AFTERNOON

Who shall bridle the winds, in their seven directions,
(Now from the north, now from the livid east)
Worrying again these birdless branches,
Storming our forests from the dark south, or the west?

We are within the wild doors of another winter
And the black cedars, bowing in the sleet
Sigh all their incoherent music to the tuneless country
Waking the deep wood's muffled antiphons.
Walking among the sleepless, iron cemetery crosses,
We praise you, winter, from the deck
Of this our lonely Abbey like an anchored battleship:

While the Kentucky forest
Pouring upon our prows her rumorous seas
Wakes our wordless prayers with the soft din of an Atlantic.

And we look up and praise you, winter,
And think of time and the uncertain centuries
Flying before your armies like the coward sky.

And oh! From some far rock some echo of your iron,
    December,
Halts our slow steps, and calls us to the armored parapet
Searching the flying skyline for some glare of prophecy.

We thought we heard John-Baptist or Elias, there, on
    the dark hill
Or else the angel with the trumpet of the Judgement.

FREEDOM AS EXPERIENCE

When, as the captive of Your own invincible consent,
You love the image of Your endless Love,
Three-Personed God, what intellect
Shall take the measure of that liberty?

Compared with Love, Your Triune Law,
All the inexorable stars are anarchists:
Yet they are bound by Love and Love is infinitely free.

Minds cannot understand, nor systems imitate
The scope of such simplicity.
All the desires and hungers that defy Your Law
Wither to fears, and perish in imprisonment:

And all the hopes that seem to founder in the shadows
    of a cross
Wake from a momentary sepulchre, and they are blinded
    by their freedom!

Because our natures poise and point towards You
Our loves revolve about You as the planets swing upon
    the sun
And all suns sing together in their gravitational worlds.

And so, some days in prayer Your Love,
Prisoning us in darkness from the values of Your universe,
Delivers us from measure and from time,
Melts all the barriers that stop our passage to eternity
And solves the hours our chains.

And then, as fires like jewels germinate
Deep in the stone heart of a Kaffir mountain,
So now our gravity, our new-created deep desire
Burns in our life's mine like an undiscovered diamond.

Locked in that strength we stay and stay
And cannot go away
For You have given us our liberty.

Imprisoned in the fortunes of Your adamant
We can no longer move, for we are free.

THE SOWING OF MEANINGS

See the high birds! Is their's the song
That flies among the wood-light
Wounding the listener with such bright arrows?

Or do they play in wheeling silences
Defining in the perfect sky
The bounds of (here below) our solitude,

Where spring has generated lights of green
To glow in clouds upon the sombre branches?

Ponds full of sky and stillnesses
What heavy summer songs still sleep
Under the tawny rushes at your brim?

More than a season will be born here, nature,
In your world of gravid mirrors!
The quiet air awaits one note,
One light, one ray and it will be the angels' spring:
One flash, one glance upon the shiny pond, and then
Asperges me! sweet wilderness, and lo! we are redeemed!

For, like a grain of fire
Smouldering in the heart of every living essence
God plants His undivided power—
Buries His thought too vast for worlds
In seed and root and blade and flower,

Until, in the amazing shadowlights
Of windy, cloudy April,
Surcharging the religious silence of the spring
Creation finds the pressure of its everlasting secret
Too terrible to bear.

Then every way we look, lo! rocks and trees
Pastures and hills and streams and birds and firmament
And our own souls within us flash, and shower us with light,
While the wild countryside, unknown, unvisited of men,
Bears sheaves of clean, transforming fire.

188

And then, oh then the written image, schooled in sacrifice,
The deep united threeness printed in our deepest being,
Shot by the brilliant syllable of such an intuition, turns within,
And plants that light far down into the heart of darkness
    and oblivion
And plunges after to discover flame.

PILGRIMS' SONG

We who have lived too long among your wicked children,
The flint-eyed brats who own your splendid streets,
We give you back Stepmother city, to your grey and
    ailing earth!
The millionaires
(Whose limousines sneak to your side as mute as gluttons)
The millionaires can have you, Egypt, with your
    onion-breath!

Wait we no longer in the taxi-music of your broken gate
Questioning the night our stranger
For maps to measure as a distance from your jeweled lights.
Darkness is our delivery. Now die we to your areas of grief,
Pointing the arrows of our secret flight
To the wide-open winds of the horizon.

Do your forgotten movies still distil those tears of ice?
Fasten no more these pilgrims to your clock-work heart
Nor press them to the beats that tick behind your
    scribbled walls
Where all your sombre ways are a dead-end!
You cannot hold us with your imitation arms!

Breathe us no more the measles of your candy kiss
Unlovely relative! We'll lose you by our stratagem
In the amazing dusk: by the safe way that you ignore:—
We are in love with your antagonist.

And the appalling Cross
The nails that are our liberty become your consternation,
'Til we are bled from death to life, and find your rival:
And our escaping feet
(That love has fledged with the true wings
Of no imaginary Mercury)
Dance on the air, and run upon the surface of the sea

And climb us out of your dark atmosphere to face the
        blinding east
And conquer all skies with hell-harrowing Christ.

THE LANDFALL

We are beyond the ways of the far ships
Here in this coral port,
Farther than the ways of fliers,
Because our destinies have suddenly transported us
Beyond the brim of the enamel world.

O Mariner, what is the name of this uncharted Land?
On these clean shores shall stand what sinless voyager,
What angel breathe the music of this atmosphere?

Look where the thin flamingoes
Burning upon the purple shallows with their rare, pale flames,
Stand silent as our thought, although the birds in the high rock

Rinse our new senses with no mortal note,
What are these wings whose silks amaze the traveller?

The flowering palms charm all the strand
With their supernal scent.
The oleander and the wild hibiscus paint
The land with blood, and unknown blooms
Open to us the Gospel of their five wild wounds.

And the deep ferns sing this epithalame:
"Go up, go up! this desert is the door of heaven!
And it shall prove your frail soul's miracle!
Climb the safe mountain,

Disarm your labored flesh, and taste the treasure of
    these silences
In the high coral hermitage,
While the clean winds bemuse you in the clefted rock;
Or find you there some leafy Crusoe-castle: dwell in trees!

Take down the flagons of the blue and crimson fruits
And reap the everlasting wheat that no man's hand
    has sown,
And strike the rock that runs with waters strong as wine
To fill you with their fortitude:
Because this island is your Christ, your might, your fort,
    your paradise.

And lo! dumb time's grey, smoky argosies
Will never anchor in this emerald harbor
Or find this world of amber,
Spoil the fair music of the silver sea
Or foul these chiming amethysts:
Nor comes there any serpent near this isle trenched in
    deep ocean
And walled with innocent, flowering vines.

But from beyond the cotton clouds,
Between those lovely, white cathedrals full of sun,
The angels study beauty with their steps
And tread like notes of music down the beamy air
To gain this new world's virgin shore:
While from the ocean's jeweled floor
The long-lost divers, rising one by one,
Smile and throw down their dripping fortunes on the sand,

And sing us the strange tale
Of the drowned king (our nature), his return!

THE POET, TO HIS BOOK

Now is the day of our farewell in fear, lean pages:
And shall I leave some blessing on the half of me you
    have devoured?
Were you, in clean obedience, my Cross,
Sent to exchange my life for Christ's in labor?
How shall the seeds upon those furrowed papers flower?
Or have I only bled to sow you full of stones and thorns,
Feeding my minutes to my own dead will?

Or will your little shadow fatten in my life's last hour
And darken for a space my gate to white eternity?

And will I wear you once again, in Purgatory,
Around my mad ribs like a shirt of flame?
Or bear you on my shoulders for a sorry jubilee
My Sinbad's burden?
Is that the way you'd make me both-ways' loser,
Paying the prayers and joys you stole of me,
You thirsty traitor, in my Trappist mornings!

Go, stubborn talker,
Find you a station on the loud world's corners,
And try there, (if your hands be clean) your length
    of patience:
Use there the rhythms that upset my silences,
And spend your pennyworth of prayer
There in the clamor of the Christless avenues:

And try to ransom some one prisoner
Out of those walls of traffic, out of the wheels of
    that unhappiness!

THE TEARS OF THE BLIND LIONS
(1949)

For Jacques Maritain

"When those who love God try to talk about Him, their words are blind lions looking for springs in the desert."

Léon Bloy

SONG

When rain, (sings light) rain has devoured my house
And wind wades through my trees,
The cedars fawn upon the storm with their huge paws.
Silence is louder than a cyclone
In the rude door, my shelter.
And there I eat my air alone
With pure and solitary songs

While others sit in conference.
Their windows grieve, and soon frown
And glass begins to wrinkle with a multitude of water
Till I no longer see their speech
And they no longer know my theater.

Rivers clothe their houses
And hide their naked wisdom.
Their conversations
Go down into the deep like submarines:
Submerge them, with their pale expressions, in my storm.

But I drink rain, drink wind
Distinguish poems
Boiling up out of the cold forest:
Lift to the wind my eyes full of water,
My face and mind, to take their free refreshment.

Thus I live on my own land, on my own island
And speak to God, my God, under the doorway
When rain, (sings light) rain has devoured my house
And winds wade through my trees.

HYMN FOR THE FEAST OF DUNS SCOTUS

On a day in fall, when high winds trouble the country
I visit the borders of my world, and see the colored hills.
And while I walk upon their coasts
The woods and grasses tumble like a sea:
Their waters run after the dry shores
Of the path made for my feet.
And I open the book of Duns Scotus,
To learn the reason for theology.

This is the book whose vision is not its own end,
Whose words are the ways of love, whose term is Trinity:
Three Who is One Who is Love.

One, because One is the reason for loving
And the One Love loved. But Three
Are the Three Lovers Who love and are loved
And are Love.

One is the Love we love, and love for:
But Three are those we love and
One our Three Lovers, loving One another.
Their One Love for One another is their Love for us,
And One is our Love for all Three and all One
And for us, on earth, brothers, one another!

One God is the One Love *propter quam amatur*
And Three Persons of the One Love are *quae amantur*.
So to love One alone is little better
Than loving none.
But to love Three is to love One.

Now today, while these Three
Love One another in me,
Loving me, and I love them,
Suddenly I can no longer live in mortal flesh,

Because your book, O Scotus, burns me like a branding iron!
If I could only breathe I would cry out, if I could cry,
To tell someone what Voices robbed me of my being!

For the sound of my Beloved,
The voice of the sound of my Three Beloved
(One of my Three of my One Beloved)
Comes down out of the heavenly depths
And hits my heart like thunder:
And lo! I am alive and dead
With heart held fast in that Three-Personed Love.

And lo! God, my God!
Look! Look! I travel in Thy strength
I swing in the grasp of Thy Love, Thy great Love's One
    Strength,
I run Thy swift ways, Thy straightest rails
Until my life becomes Thy Life and sails or rides like an
    express!

Word, the whole universe swells with Thy wide-open speed,
Father, the world bursts, breaks, huge Spirit, with Thy might
Then land, sea and wind swing
And roll from my forgotten feet
While God sings victory, sings victory
In the blind day of that defeat.

THE QUICKENING OF ST. JOHN THE BAPTIST

On the Contemplative Vocation

Why do you fly from the drowned shores of Galilee,
From the sands and the lavender water?
Why do you leave the ordinary world, Virgin of Nazareth,

The yellow fishing boats, the farms,
The winesmelling yards and low cellars
Or the oilpress, and the women by the well?
Why do you fly those markets,
Those suburban gardens,
The trumpets of the jealous lilies,
Leaving them all, lovely among the lemon trees?

You have trusted no town
With the news behind your eyes.
You have drowned Gabriel's word in thoughts like seas
And turned toward the stone mountain
To the treeless places.
Virgin of God, why are your clothes like sails?

The day Our Lady, full of Christ,
Entered the dooryard of her relative
Did not her steps, light steps, lay on the paving leaves
    like gold?
Did not her eyes as grey as doves
Alight like the peace of a new world upon that house, upon
    miraculous Elizabeth?

Her salutation
Sings in the stone valley like a Charterhouse bell:
And the unborn saint John
Wakes in his mother's body,
Bounds with the echoes of discovery.

Sing in your cell, small anchorite!
How did you see her in the eyeless dark?
What secret syllable
Woke your young faith to the mad truth
That an unborn baby could be washed in the Spirit of God?
Oh burning joy!

200

What seas of life were planted by that voice!
With what new sense
Did your wise heart receive her Sacrament,
And know her cloistered Christ?

You need no eloquence, wild bairn,
Exulting in your hermitage.
Your ecstasy is your apostolate,
For whom to kick is *contemplata tradere*.
Your joy is the vocation
Of Mother Church's hidden children—
Those who by vow lie buried in the cloister or the hermitage:
The speechless Trappist, or the grey, granite Carthusian,
The quiet Carmelite, the barefoot Clare,
Planted in the night of contemplation,
Sealed in the dark and waiting to be born.

Night is our diocese and silence is our ministry
Poverty our charity and helplessness our tongue-tied
        sermon.
Beyond the scope of sight or sound we dwell upon the air
Seeking the world's gain in an unthinkable experience.
We are exiles in the far end of solitude, living as listeners
With hearts attending to the skies we cannot understand:
Waiting upon the first far drums of Christ the Conqueror,
Planted like sentinels upon the world's frontier.

But in the days, rare days, when our Theotocos
Flying the prosperous world
Appears upon our mountain with her clothes like sails,
Then, like the wise, wild baby,
The unborn John who could not see a thing
We wake and know the Virgin Presence
Receive her Christ into our night
With stabs of an intelligence as white as lightning.

Cooled in the flame of God's dark fire
Washed in His gladness like a vesture of new flame
We burn like eagles in His invincible awareness
And bound and bounce with happiness,
Leap in the womb, our cloud, our faith, our element,
Our contemplation, our anticipated heaven
Till Mother Church sings like an Evangelist.

THE READER

Lord, when the clock strikes
Telling the time with cold tin
And I sit hooded in this lectern

Waiting for the monks to come,
I see the red cheeses, and bowls
All smile with milk in ranks upon their tables.

Light fills my proper globe
(I have won light to read by
With a little, tinkling chain)

And the monks come down the cloister
With robes as voluble as water.
I do not see them but I hear their waves.

It is winter, and my hands prepare
To turn the pages of the saints:
And to the trees Thy moon has frozen on the windows
My tongue shall sing Thy Scripture.

Then the monks pause upon the step
(With me here in this lectern
And Thee there on Thy crucifix)

And gather little pearls of water on their fingers' ends
Smaller than this my psalm.

FROM THE LEGEND OF ST. CLEMENT

I have seen the sun
Spilling its copper petals on the Black Sea
By the base of the prisoners' cliff
Where, from the acts of martyrs,
Tall poems grow up like buildings.

Deep in the wall of the wounded mountain
(Where seas no longer frown)
The songs of the martyrs come up like cities or buildings.
Their chains shine with hymns
And their hands cut down the giant blocks of stone.

Poetry, psalms
Flower with a huge architecture
Raising their grandeur on the gashed cape.
Words of God blaze like a disaster
In the windows of their prophetic cathedral.
But the sighs of the deep multitude
Grow out of the mountain's heart as clean as vines.

O martyrs! O tremendous prisoners!
Burying your murder in this marble hill!
The Lamb shall soon stand
White as a shout against the sky:
His feet shall soon strike rainbows from the rock.
The cliffs give up their buried streams.
Throw down the chains of your wrists, prisoners!
Drink, and swim!

The winds have carried your last sentences
Across Ukraine.
Your poetry shall grow in distant places.
Asia, Greece, Egypt, England know your name.
Your hymns shall stand like vineyards
And swing with fruit in other worlds, in other centuries.

And your ecstasy shall make shade,
Foliage for summers unforeseen
To cover travellers in continents you have not known
When the temples have fallen,
The theaters cemented in your blood have long ago fallen.

Your joy echoes across the carved ridge
Plays across mountains
Stands like fleets or islands
Sailing the seas to Greece,
And after twenty times one hundred
Years of repercussion
Your waters shatter the land at my feet with seas forever
    young.

ON A DAY IN AUGUST

These woods are too impersonal.
The deaf-and-dumb fields, waiting to be shaved of hay
Suffer the hours like an unexpected sea
While locusts fry their music in the sycamores.

But from the curdled places of the sky
(Where a brown wing hovers for carrion)
We have not seen the heaven-people come.

The clean, white saints, have they forgotten us?
Here we lie upon the earth
In the air of our dead grove
Dreaming some wind may come and kiss ourselves in the
    red eyes
With a pennyworth of mercy for our pepper shoulders.
And so we take into our hands the ruins
Of the words our minds have rent.

It is enough.
Our souls are trying to crawl out of our pores.
Our lives are seeping through each part of us like vinegar.
A sad sour death is eating the roots of our hair.

Yet doors of sanitary winds lie open in the clouds
To vistas of those laundries where the clean saints dwell:
If we could only view them from our slum!
But our dream has wandered away
And drowned in the din of the crickets' disconnected prayer.

Thus the grasses and the unemployed goldenrod
Go revel through our farm, and dance around the field.
The blue-black lights come shimmering upon the tar
Where kids made footprints in the melting way to Louisville.
And spooks come out of the road and walk the jagged heat
Like the time we found that drunkard lying still as murder
In the ditch behind the mill.

But you, Saint Clare,
We have been looking up your stairs all afternoon
Wanting to see you walking down some nimbus with your
    gentle friends.

Very well, clouds,
Open your purple bottles,

Cozen us never more with blowsy cotton:
But organize,
Summon the punishing lightning:
Spring those sudden gorgeous trees against the dark
Curtain of apocalypse you'll hang to earth, from heaven:
Let five white branches scourge the land with fire!
And when the first fat drops
Spatter upon the tin top of our church like silver dollars
And thoughts come bathing back to mind with a new life,
Prayer will become our new discovery

When God and His bad earth once more make friends.

CHRISTOPHER COLUMBUS

There was a great Captain with Mary in his sails
Who did not discover Harlem or the East Side
Or Sing Sing or the dead men on the island.
But his heart was like the high mountains.
And when the king gave him money
To go and discover a country
And fixed him up with robes of gold

He threw down all those pesos and stripped to his
        champion skin
And waded into the waters of the sea.
The surf boiled white about his knees
And the tides folded behind him
When he caught the furthest caravels and passed them by.
"There goes Columbus! There he goes!" the sailors cried,
Still he is head and shoulders above the horizon
Leaving us like the pillars of Hercules

Standing westward on the way to the Azores!
What land will he find to believe in, now he knows the world
    is round?

Forest upon forest, mile upon empty mile
The undiscovered continent lies, rock upon rock:
The lakes awake, or move in their mute sleep.
Huge rivers wander where the plains
Are cloudy or dark with seas of buffalo.
Frail waterbirds sing in the weeds of Florida.
Northward, grey seas stir
In sight of the unconscious hills.
There are no prints in the thin snows of Maine.

Suddenly the great Christ-bearing Columbus rises in the sea
Spilling the green Atlantic from his shoulders
And sees America through a veil of waters.
Steam things low like cattle all around him in the rivers.
Towers stand like churches on the rock, in a garden of boats;
Citizens look up like snap-dragons
Crowding the streets and galleries and saluting heaven with
    their songs.
Music comes cascading down the stones until all walls
Are singing the feasts of the saints in the light of processions.

Then the discoverer, rising from the harbor,
Taking the river in his stride
Overtops all tall palaces.
The people cheer their noon-day sun, their giant Gospel
And calm Columbus reaches down to the citizens
The golden fruits of which his arms are full.

All over the new land woods retire to the hills.
Indians come out of the brake with corn and melons
And he blesses the bronze gentry sitting in the air of the
    arcade:

Thousands of Franciscans go through the fields with
    Sacraments
And towns, towns, towns rise out of the ground.

Then the Americans, wearing the new names of saints
Look up and sing into the face of their tall Father
While he is lifted from the earth, blesses his continent.
Birds fly like language from the cloud, his beard.

His smiles are quickly muffled in the sky.
His gestures mild, they melt and disappear.
Waving, waving the little ones have wept him out of sight.

When it is evening, in America's vespers
Feathers of imperfect incense spend themselves
Marking his memory on steeples.
As fast as dark comes down towns, cities,
Returning to the virgin air
Restore these shores to silences.
Woods crawl back into the gulf.
Shadows of Franciscans die in tangled wilds
And there is just one smoke upon the plain
And just one Indian hunter.

What will you do tomorrow, America
Found and lost so soon?
Your Christ has died and gone to Spain
Bearing a precious cross upon his shoulder
And there your story lies in chains.

But the devils are sailing for your harbors
Launching their false doves into the air to fly for your sands.
They bend over their tillers with little fox faces,
Grin like dollars through their fur,
And their meat-eating sails fly down and fold upon your
    shore.

Suddenly the silences of the deep continent
Die in a tornado of guitars.
Our own America tears down her mask of trees
Hailing each pirate with sarcastic towns.
Break open a dozen cities! Let traffic bleed upon the land
And hug your hundred and twenty million paupers in a vice
    without escape
While they are mapped and verified
Plotted, printed, catalogued, numbered and categoried
And sold to the doctors of your sham discovery.

                *   *   *

And now the cities' eyes are tight as ice
When the long cars stream home in nights of autumn.
(The bells Columbus heard are dumb.)
The city's rivers are as still as liquor.
Bars and factories pool their lights
In Michigan's or Erie's mirrors, now, on the night of the
    game.
(But the bells Columbus heard are dumb.)
The city's face is frozen like a screen of silver
When the universities turn in
And winter sings in the bridges
Tearing the grand harps down.

But the children sing no hymn for the feast of Saint
    Columbus.
They watch the long, long armies drifting home.

ST. MALACHY

In November, in the days to remember the dead
When air smells cold as earth,

St. Malachy, who is very old, gets up,
Parts the thin curtain of trees and dawns upon our land.

His coat is filled with drops of rain, and he is bearded
With all the seas of Poseidon.
(Is it a crozier, or a trident in his hand?)
He weeps against the gothic window, and the empty cloister
Mourns like an ocean shell.

Two bells in the steeple
Talk faintly to the old stranger
And the tower considers his waters.
"I have been sent to see my festival," (his cavern speaks!)
"For I am the saint of the day.
Shall I shake the drops from my locks and stand in your
        transept,
Or, leaving you, rest in the silence of my history?"

So the bells rang and we opened the antiphoners
And the wrens and larks flew up out of the pages.
Our thoughts became lambs. Our hearts swam like seas.
One monk believed that we should sing to him
Some stone-age hymn
Or something in the giant language.
So we played to him in the plainsong of the giant Gregory:
Oceans of Scripture sang upon bony Eire.

Then the last salvage of flowers
(Fostered under glass after the gardens foundered)
Held up their little lamps on Malachy's altar
To peer into his wooden eyes before the Mass began.

Rain sighed down the sides of the stone church.
Storms sailed by all day in battle fleets.

At five o'clock, when we tried to see the sun, the
    speechless visitor
Sighed and arose and shook the humus from his feet
And with his trident stirred our trees
And left down-wood, shaking some drops upon the ground.

Thus copper flames fall, tongues of fire fall
The leaves in hundreds fall upon his passing
While night sends down her dreadnought darkness
Upon this spurious Pentecost.

And the Melchisedec of our year's end
Who came without a parent, leaves without a trace,
And rain comes rattling down upon our forest
Like the doors of a country jail.

THE CAPTIVES—A PSALM

Quomodo cantabimus canticum Domini in terra aliena?

Somewhere a king walks in his gallery
Owning the gorges of a fiery city.
Brass traffic shakes the walls. The windows shiver with
    business.
It is the bulls' day. The citizens
Build themselves each hour another god
And fry a fatter idol out of mud.

They cut themselves a crooked idiom
To the winged animals, upon their houses.
Prayers are made of money, songs of numbers,
Hymns of the blood of the killed.

Old ladies are treasured in sugar.
Young ones rot in wine.
The flesh of the fat organizers smiles with oil.

Blessed is the army that will one day crush you, city,
Like a golden spider.
Blest are they that hate you. Blest are they
That dash your brats against the stones.
The children of God have died, O Babylon,
Of thy wild algebra.

Days, days are the journey
From wall to wall. And miles
Miles of houses shelter terror.
And we lie chained to their dry roots, O Israel!

Our bodies are greyer than mud.
There, butterflies are born to be dancers
And fly in black and blue along the drunken river
Where, in the willow trees, Assyria lynched our song!

May my bones burn and ravens eat my flesh
If I forget thee, contemplation!
May language perish from my tongue
If I do not remember thee, O Sion, city of vision,
Whose heights have windows finer than the firmament
When night pours down her canticles
And peace sings on thy watchtowers like the stars of Job.

THE CITY AFTER NOON

What if the wild confinement were empty
And the felons were free to come home?

I saw Ohio, whom I love,
I saw the wide river between buildings
My big brown lady, going west.

What if the wild confinement were empty
And the policies were all gone!
If they could wash the stains of avarice
From faces, lust from the little houses,
And let some respiration through the satin sky!
What if the wild confinement were empty
And the lunatic pigeons were once again sane!

What a universe my tears betray
On St. Clare's Day, on St. Clare's Day!
Where the children of heaven are not yet born
And the fathers of destitution run
With horse, bottle and gun
To burn my river with their rum.
What a deluge my tears betray
On St. Clare's Day
When the Little One dies of hunger in His manger.
Is there none to entertain my daughter's stranger
Or take my old man's wager?
With horse, bottle and feathers
They have set fire to the most holy weather!

What if the wild contentments were full
And the furlongs were free to go farming!
I saw the river's daughters overwhelm a hill.
Water made all places plain.

There is a green wonder up and down Ohio:
Oh woods and woods, across my dangerous mother!
What if the wild contentment were full
And there were nothing left in the world

But fields, water and sun
And space went on forever to eternity, without a rim?

What if the wild confinement were empty
And the sheriffs were free to go home!

IN THE RAIN AND THE SUN

Watch out for this peeled doorlight!
Here, without rain, without shame
My noonday dusk made spots upon the walk:
Tall drops pelted the concrete with their jewelry
Belonging to the old world's bones.

Owning this view, in the air of a hermit's weather,
I count the fragmentary rain
In drops as blue as coal
Until I plumb the shadows full of thunder.
My prayers supervise the atmosphere
Till storms call all hounds home.

Out of the towers of water
Four or five mountains come walking
To see the little monks' graves.
Flying the neutral stones I dwell between cedars
And see the countries sleeping in their beds:
Lands of the watermen, where poplars bend.
Wild seas amuse the world with water:
No end to all the surfs that charm our shores
Fattening the sands with their old foam and their old roar.

Thus in the boom of waves' advantage
Dogs and lions come to my tame home

Won by the bells of my Cistercian jungle.
O love the livid fringes
In which their robes are drenched!

Songs of the lions and whales!
With my pen between my fingers
Making the waterworld sing!
Sweet Christ, discover diamonds
And sapphires in my verse
While I burn the sap of my pine house
For praise of the ocean sun.

I have walked upon the whole days' surf
Rinsing Thy bays with hymns.
My eyes have swept horizons clean
Of ships and rain.
Upon the lacquered swells my feet no longer run.
Sliding all over the sea I come
To the hap of a slippery harbor.

Dogs have gone back to their ghosts
And the many lions, home.
But words fling wide the windows of their houses—
Adam and Eve walk down my coast
Praising the tears of the treasurer sun:
I hang Thy rubies on these autumn trees,
On the bones of the homegoing thunder.

DRY PLACES

No cars go by
Where dogs are barking at the desert.

Yet it is not twenty years since many lamps
Shed their juices in this one time town
And stores grew big lights, like oranges and pears.

Now not one lame miner
Sits on the rotten verandah,
Works in the irons where
Judas' shadow dwells.
Yet I could hew a city
From the side of their hill.

O deep stone covert where the dusk
Is full of lighted beasts
And the mad stars preach wars without end:
Whose bushes and grasses live without water,

There the skinny father of hate rolls in his dust
And if the wind should shift one leaf
The dead jump up and bark for their ghosts:
Their dry bones want our penniless souls.

Bones, go back to your baskets.
Get your fingers out of my clean skin.
Rest in your rainless death until your own souls
Come back in the appointed way and sort you out from
    your remains.

We who are still alive will wring a few green blades
From the floor of this valley
Though ploughs abhor your metal and your clay.
Rather than starve with you in rocks without oasis,
We will get up and work your loam
Until some prayer or some lean sentence
Bleeds like the quickest root they ever cut.

For we cannot forget the legend of the world's childhood
Or the track to the dogwood valley
And Adam our Father's old grass farm
Wherein they gave the animals names
And knew Christ was promised first without scars
When all God's larks called out to Him
In their wild orchard.

JE CROIS EN L'AMOUR *

Je crois en l'Amour
Qui dort et vit, caché dans les semences,

Et lorsque je respire mon printemps
Dans la fraicheur des sommets liturgiques
En voyant tous les arbres et les blés verts,
L'émoi s'éveille au plus profond
De mon être mortel: et l'adoration
Sonne comme les cloches légendaires
Qui entonnent leurs chants sourds au sein de l'océan.

Et quand le soleil géant de mon été
A frappé l'or de toutes mes gerbes
Je fais fortune: c'est là mon chant, mon capital,
Ma louange de Notre Dame!

O frères, venez me rejoindre,
Buvez le vin de Melchisédec
Tandis que tous ces monts régenérés
Chantent la paix, vêtus des vignes d'Isaïe:

* For the English translation, by William Davis, see below, p. 825.

Car c'est ainsi que naissent les poëmes
Dans le creux de mon coeur d'homme
Et dans le sein de mon rocher fendu!

TO THE IMMACULATE VIRGIN,
ON A WINTER NIGHT

Lady, the night is falling and the dark
Steals all the blood from the scarred west.
The stars come out and freeze my heart
With drops of untouchable music, frail as ice
And bitter as the new year's cross.

Where in the world has any voice
Prayed to you, Lady, for the peace that's in your power?
In a day of blood and many beatings
I see the governments rise up, behind the steel horizon,
And take their weapons and begin to kill.

Where in the world has any city trusted you?
Out where the soldiers camp the guns begin to thump
And another winter time comes down
To seal our years in ice.
The last train cries out
And runs in terror from this farmers' valley
Where all the little birds are dead.

The roads are white, the fields are mute
There are no voices in the wood
And trees make gallows up against the sharp-eyed stars.
Oh where will Christ be killed again
In the land of these dead men?

Lady, the night has got us by the heart
And the whole world is tumbling down.
Words turn to ice in my dry throat
Praying for a land without prayer,

Walking to you on water all winter
In a year that wants more war.

A RESPONSORY, 1948

Suppose the dead could crown their wit
With some intemperate exercise,
Spring wine from their ivory
Or roses from their eyes?

Or if the wise could understand
And the world without heart
That the dead are not yet dead
And that the living live apart

And the wounded are healing,
Though in a place of flame.
The sick in a great ship
Are riding. They are riding home.

Suppose the dead could crown their wit
With some intemperate exercise,
Spring wine from their ivory
Or roses from their eyes?

Two cities sailed together
For many thousand years.

And now they drift asunder.
The tides of new wars

Sweep the sad heavens,
Divide the massed stars,
The black and white universe
The booming spheres.

Down, down, down
The white armies fall
Moving their ordered snows
Toward the jaws of hell.

Suppose the dead could crown their wit
With some intemperate exercise,
Spring wine from their ivory
Or roses from their eyes?

A PSALM

When psalms surprise me with their music
And antiphons turn to rum
The Spirit sings: the bottom drops out of my soul

And from the center of my cellar, Love, louder than thunder
Opens a heaven of naked air.

New eyes awaken.
I send Love's name into the world with wings
And songs grow up around me like a jungle.
Choirs of all creatures sing the tunes
Your Spirit played in Eden.

Zebras and antelopes and birds of paradise
Shine on the face of the abyss
And I am drunk with the great wilderness
Of the sixth day in Genesis.

But sound is never half so fair
As when that music turns to air
And the universe dies of excellence.

Sun, moon and stars
Fall from their heavenly towers.
Joys walk no longer down the blue world's shore.

Though fires loiter, lights still fly on the air of the gulf,
All fear another wind, another thunder:
Then one more voice
Snuffs all their flares in one gust.

And I go forth with no more wine and no more stars
And no more buds and no more Eden
And no more animals and no more sea:
While God sings by Himself in acres of night
And walls fall down, that guarded Paradise.

SENESCENTE MUNDO

Senescente mundo, when the hot globe
Shrivels and cracks
And uninhibited atoms resolve
Earth and water, fruit and flower, body and animal soul,
All the blue stars come tumbling down.
Beauty and ugliness and love and hate
Wisdom and politics are all alike undone.

Toward that fiery day we run like crabs
With our bad-tempered armor on.
"With blood and carpets, oranges and ashes,
Rubber and limes and bones,"
(So sing the children on the Avenue)
"With cardboard and dirty water and a few flames for
    the Peacelover's ghost,
We know where the dead bodies are
Studying the ceiling from the floors of their homes,
With smoke and roses, slate and wire
And crushed fruit and much fire."

Yet in the middle of this murderous season
Great Christ, my fingers touch Thy wheat
And hold Thee hidden in the compass of Thy paper sun.
There is no war will not obey this cup of Blood,
This wine in which I sink Thy words, in the anonymous
    dawn!
I hear a Sovereign talking in my arteries
Reversing, with His Promises, all things
That now go on with fire and thunder.
His Truth is greater than disaster.
His Peace imposes silence on the evidence against us.

And though the world, at last, has swallowed her own
    solemn laughter
And has condemned herself to hell:
Suppose a whole new universe, a great clean Kingdom
Were to rise up like an Atlantis in the East,
Surprise this earth, this cinder, with new holiness!

Here in my hands I hold that secret Easter.
Tomorrow, this will be my Mass's answer,
Because of my companions whom the wilderness has eaten,
Crying like Jonas in the belly of our whale.

THE STRANGE ISLANDS
(1957)

For Mark and Dorothy Van Doren

PART ONE

HOW TO ENTER A BIG CITY

I

Swing by starwhite bones and
Lights tick in the middle.
Blue and white steel
Black and white
People hurrying along the wall.
"Here you are, bury my dead bones."

Curve behind the sun again
Towers full of ice. Rich
Glass houses, "Here,
Have a little of my blood,"
Rich people!"

Wheat in towers. Meat on ice.
Cattlecars. Miles of wide-open walls.
Baseball between these sudden tracks.
Yell past the red street—
Have you any water to drink, City?
Rich glass buildings, give us milk!
Give us coffee! Give us rum!

There are huge clouds all over the sky.
River smells of gasoline.
Cars after cars after cars, and then
A little yellow street goes by without a murmur.

There came a man
("Those are radios, that were his eyes")
Who offered to sell us his bones.

Swing by starwhite buildings and
Lights come to life with a sound
Of bugs under the dead rib.

Miles of it. Still the same city.

II

Do you know where you are going?
Do you know whom you must meet?

Fortune, perhaps, or good news
Or the doctor, or the ladies
In the long bookstore,
The angry man in the milkbar
The drunkard under the clock.
Fortune, perhaps, or wonder
Or, perhaps, death.

In any case, our tracks
Are aimed at a working horizon.
The buildings, turning twice about the sun,
Settle in their respective positions.
Centered in its own incurable discontent, the City
Consents to be recognized.

III

Then people come out into the light of afternoon,
Covered all over with black powder,

And begin to attack one another with statements
Or to ignore one another with horror.
Customs have not changed.
Young men full of coffee and
Old women with medicine under their skin
Are all approaching death at twenty miles an hour.

Everywhere there is optimism without love
And pessimism without understanding,
They who have new clothes, and smell of haircuts
Cannot agree to be at peace
With their own images, shadowing them in windows
From store to store.

IV

Until the lights come on with a swagger of frauds
And savage ferns,
The brown-eyed daughters of ravens,
Sing in the lucky doors
While night comes down the street like the millennium
Wrapping the houses in dark feathers
Soothing the town with a sign
Healing the strong wings of sunstroke.
Then the wind of an easy river wipes the flies
Off my Kentucky collarbone.

The claws of the treacherous stars
Renegade drums of wood
Endure the heavenward protest.
Their music heaves and hides.
Rain and foam and oil
Make sabbaths for our wounds.
(Come, come, let all come home!)

The summer sighs, and runs.
My broken bird is under the whole town,
My cross is for the gypsies I am leaving
And there are real fountains under the floor.

V

Branches baptize our faces with silver
Where the sweet silent avenue escapes into the hills.
Winds at last possess our empty country
There, there under the moon
In parabolas of milk and iron
The ghosts of historical men
(Figures of sorrow and dust)
Weep along the hills like turpentine.
And seas of flowering tobacco
Surround the drowning sons of Daniel Boone.

THE GUNS OF FORT KNOX

Guns at the camp (I hear them suddenly)
Guns make the little houses jump. I feel
Explosions in my feet, through boards.
Wars work under the floor. Wars
Dance in the foundations. Trees
Must also feel the guns they do not want
Even in their core.
As each charge bumps the shocked earth
They shudder from the root.

Shock the hills, you guns! They are
Not too firm even without dynamite.

These Chinese clayfoot hills
Founded in their own shale
Shift their feet in friable stone.

Such ruins cannot
Keep the armies of the dead
From starting up again.
They'll hear these guns tonight
Tomorrow or some other time.
They'll wake. They'll rise
Through the stunned rocks, form
Regiments and do death's work once more.

Guns, I say, this is not
The right resurrection. All day long
You punch the doors of death to wake
A slain generation. Let them lie
Still. Let them sleep on,
O Guns. Shake no more
(But leave the locks secure)
Hell's door.

NOCTURNE

Night has a sea which quenches the machine
Or part of it. Night has tides of rain
And sources which go on
Washing our houses when we turn to dream.

Night has, for flesh and ghost, a weak-eyed sun
Whose light the anxious living fear. Shapes of the dead
Make legends with the rest of us: that all

Must miss some train, be late at school,
Found without money in the strange hotel.

O night, whose golden spark in the safe mind
Explores all countries where the soul has gone,
Explain the colored shapes whose hundreds
Fly in the wind from every broken pod.

O one-eyed night, whose wisdom sails from God
By deep canals to heave and change our falls.
Your choirs amaze the thoughtful heart.
What were the notes, then, of your sacred tone
Uttering, while thought was stopped,
The one prophetic question?

If I could answer you, your tides and histories
Would end, or would begin all storms.

SPRING STORM

When in their ignorance and haste the skies must fall
Upon our white-eyed home, and blindly turn
Feeling the four long limits of the wall,

How unsubstantial is our present state
In the clean blowing of those elements
Whose study is our problem and our fate?

The intellects go mumbling in the snow,
And find the blurred, incredible sun (and moon)
Jammed in the white door, and the troubled straits
The dugout where the fallen sky lies down.

A mess of secret trumpets, with their weight
Of portents, veil the bluntness where we run.

How true a passion has this hour begun!
The sky melts on my patient animal
(My pointless self, the hunter of my home),
My breath burns in the open like a ton
In the blue waking of those elements
Whose study is our quibble and our doom.

O watch the woolen hundreds on the run!

WHETHER THERE IS ENJOYMENT IN BITTERNESS

This afternoon, let me
Be a sad person. Am I not
Permitted (like other men)
To be sick of myself?

Am I not allowed to be hollow,
Or fall in the hole
Or break my bones (within me)
In the trap set by my own
Lie to myself? O my friend,
I too must sin and sin.

I too must hurt other people and
(Since I am no exception)
I must be hated by them.

Do not forbid me, therefore,
To taste the same bitter poison,

And drink the gall that love
(Love most of all) so easily becomes.

Do not forbid me (once again) to be
Angry, bitter, disillusioned,
Wishing I could die.

While life and death
Are killing one another in my flesh,
Leave me in peace. I can enjoy,
Even as other men, this agony.

Only (whoever you may be)
Pray for my soul. Speak my name
To Him, for in my bitterness
I hardly speak to Him: and He
While He is busy killing me
Refuses to listen.

SPORTS WITHOUT BLOOD
—A LETTER TO DYLAN THOMAS (1948)

I

In old King George's June
When evening drowned and sang in the peeled water,
Hate took place in Cambridge, and a cricketer's death
Under the tents of Chesterton.

It was to be a night without religion.
The houses rumpled their ancient skins:
The century still thundered at their doors.

"Now here they come, down the abiding sky
Lovers of many monies under the sun.
Crosscolored bodies, in which is vanity.
Hush-hush waters cripple the world that's upside down,
And lives are flights on the face of motherofpearl heaven
Until old crossbones get their skulls in greysize capture.
The race is over. Life and death are even."

In this same night of ales
I was uprooted by my own ghost
Not without fury and
Not without cost.
The rivers mummed, grandfathers
Grumbled at my door.
War in the water and war on the grass,
War in the belly and feet and face,
(Crosscolored bodies in which is vomiting)
The war in the river was, perhaps, worse:
The upside down were last and first.

"Thus did the oarsmen feel the waters of their fen
(With dog-drunk gasbodies winning under the tank)
Scattering the shadows of a railway bridge
And seven willow women mad as trees:
They smashed the gas river over and under,
The blue-brown river, bad as drink."
Their smiles have shivered all that order
And boats slide down their oil on an army of wrinkles
While blades replace the upside down cathedrals
With a wallop of bells.

In old King George's attic
When everything went black in the piled city
Pain took place in colleges, and bloodless sports
Under the tents of Chesterton.

II

Old Joe and Rosa's martyr
Seven principal oarsmen and Jack-John the lad of the lawns
Planted a relic of our spotting biograph
Here, in a spell between two bombs.
And here we bloom, amid the marigolds
Sad, with the central doll of an old photo,
The treeless grills, and the pelouse.

Oh, the bald lawns, and the enclosure
The green we had to smell!
What subtle matter for an effigy
Between the door and the wall:
And there the old, whose airless voice
Fell from our England's winding sheet,
Withdrew their leaves, let George and Dragon
Drown in the porter's little room.
All the bodies dangle in a garden of bowls.

But you proceeded to the burial.
Night by night in Camden Town
Up and down the furry buildings,
In and out the boxing alleys, dark as tea
You walked with murder in your music box
And played the pieces of blind England all around the down.

Thus the men lay down to sleep in the pavilion
With a whisper of flannel and leather;
The ladies all arranged themselves upon the ground
With a wuthering of old fowls:
And now from their ten million pots and pipes
Their dreams crept out and fumed at the wet night,
While they slept in the cloud without Christ.
Then angels ploughed them under the ground

234

With little songs as sharp as needles
And words that shone by night as bright as omens.

III

Blind northern friends, whose hopeless manor
Fox and grouse have come to own,
Bred hand in glove with pestilence
The ivy eats your castle down.

The horns of thunder drown and die
When evenings sing their frittered song.
The sonnets of my tearless eye
Shine on the city's second string.

Cling to the city's second rung
While oarsmen feel their frozen fen:
And boat by boat their tocsins ring
And house by house their walls cave in.

Then the blue pleasures are destroyed
Whose seas concern the oarsman's blade.
The halls are severed, bridges bleed
And the drowned world is animate,

Til the brown boats, devouring all,
Wipe out the city's second spring,
Sail on, while the cathedrals fall
And feel what rain the bellnotes bring.

Before the formal racers come
And puzzles are once more unfurled,
Come, let us drink our poisoned home
And swim in the face of a glass world!

All the world's waters whimper and cry
And evils eat body and soul.
The times have carried love away.
And tides have swallowed charity.

Bound, bound, my fens, whose soundless song
Both verse and prose have come to end.
It is the everlasting wrong:
Our cities vanish in the wind.

IV

They have given the cricketer a grass heart
And a dry purse like a leaf, Look!
Look! The little butterflies come out!
He was wounded, he was wounded in the wars
Where the roots our umpires are.
It is a funny death, when flowers undermine castles.
O Listen to their calls
Listen to their wooden calls.
"Chop-chop," says bats (or blocks):
But we shall drive in another direction,
Leaving this people to its own calm,
And turn again to waters brown, whose underlights,
Whose manners are insane
With the oars of the young man trained
To separate a mirror into riddles.

Come, let us die in some other direction
Sooner than the houses in the river quiver and begin
    their dance
And fall in the terrible frown.

EXPLOITS OF A MACHINE AGE

For Robert Lax

Once again they were dismayed
By their own thin faces in the morning. They

Hoped they would not die today either.
They hoped for some light
Breakfast and a steady hand.

To the protected work
They fled, to the unsafe machinery
They lived by. "It will go better this time,
We have arranged, at last,
To succeed. Better luck
This time."

So they went to the
Guarded plant, muttering, "Better luck,
Better luck,"
(Till the clowns in the sun cried,
"Then He struck!").

But no! Nothing was felt or heard.
Once again the explosion was
Purely mental. It shook them, though,
And they went pale around noon.
The machines were safe. Nothing
At all had happened.
Literally nothing.

Exhausted by this nothing, they
Came home, faced the steadfast apartment,

Globes, windows, and even moon.
And they made up their minds.

They climbed into their dwellings, grim
As yesterday, and always muttering,
"Better luck tomorrow!"

THE ANATOMY OF MELANCHOLY

There was a man, born like
Other men, but he had a
Different name. He always

Took himself seriously
And kept his head before it was too late,
Because his nurse had
Struck him in the cradle.

Wherever he went he kept his
Eye on the clock. His heart was not
On his sleeve, but his tongue was ready
With a civil answer.

One day he could not find his feet.
He lost his balance and began to sing:
When he sang, they paid him to shut up,
He was no longer happy when he smiled.

He tried to walk and they
Put him in jail. He spoke
And showed a broken tooth.
When he sat down he lost face.

It was a long night before he woke up
And was found beside himself when he
Came to his senses.
No one cared to have him around
Though his heart was in the right place
Clucking like a hen.

No one remembered but the business men
Who entered brandishing a bill.
They greeted him and smiled as they sat.
"You have," they said (as he lost his voice)
"A serious problem."
So they took away his house.
The cops went off
With his sister and daughter.
He kept a stiff upper lip but no
Money and no social standing.

"What shall I do?" he cried, "drink or gamble?"
He left in no direction, followed by his dog
(The dog is man's best friend), and

Puritans had them arrested
For romping as they walked
And barking as they spoke.

ELIAS—VARIATIONS ON A THEME

I

Under the blunt pine
In the winter sun

The pathway dies
And the wilds begin.
Here the bird abides
Where the ground is warm
And sings alone.

Listen, Elias,
To the southern wind
Where the grass is brown,
Live beneath this pine
In wind and rain.
Listen to the woods,
Listen to the ground.

O listen, Elias
(Where the bird abides
And sings alone),
The sun grows pale
Where passes One
Who bends no blade, no fern.
Listen to His word.

*"Where the fields end
Thou shalt be My friend.
Where the bird is gone
Thou shalt be My son."*

How the pine burns
In the furious sun
When the prophets come
To Jerusalem.
(Listen, Elias,
To the covering wing?)
To Jerusalem
Where the knife is drawn.

(Do her children run
To the covering wing?)
Look, look, My son,
At the smashed wood
At the bloody stone.

Where the fields end
And the stars begin
Listen, Elias,
To the winter rain.
For the seed sleeps
By the sleeping stone.
But the seed has life
While the stone has none.

   "Where the fields end
   Thou shalt be My friend.
   Where the bird is gone
   Thou shalt be My son."

II

There were supposed to be
Not birds but spirits of flame
Around the old wagon.
("Bring me my chariot")
There were supposed
To be fiery devices,
Grand machines, all flame,
With supernatural wings
Beyond the full creek.
("Bring me my chariot of fire")
All flame, beyond the rotten tree!
Flame? This old wagon

With the wet, smashed wheels
Is better. ("My chariot")
This derelict is better.
("Of fire.") It abides
(Swifter) in the brown ferns
And burns nothing. Bring me ("Of fire")
Better still the old trailer ("My chariot")
With the dead stove in it, and the rain
Comes down the pipe and covers the floor.
Bring me my chariot of rain. Bring me
My old chariot of broken-down rain.
Bring, bring my old fire, my old storm,
My old trailer; faster and faster it stands still,
Faster and faster it stays where it has always been,
Behind the felled oaks, faster, burning nothing.
Broken and perfect, facing south,
Facing the sound of distant guns,
Facing the wall of distance where blue hills
Hide in the fading rain.

Where the woods are cut down the punished
Trailer stands alone and becomes
(Against all the better intentions of the owners)
The House of God
The Gate of Heaven.
("My chariot of fire")

III

The seed, as I have said,
Hides in the frozen sod.
Stones, shaped by rivers they will
Never care about or feel,
Cover the cultivated soil.

The seed, by nature, waits to grow and bear
Fruit. Therefore it is not alone
As stones, or inanimate things are:
That is to say, alone by nature,
Or alone forever.

Where do so many waters come from on an empty hill?
Rain we had despaired of, rain
Which is sent from somewhere else, descended
To fix an exhausted mountain.
Listen to the waters, if possible,
And discern the words "False prophet"
False prophet! "So much better is the water's message,
So much more confident than our own. It is quite sure
You are a false prophet, so 'Go back'
(You have not had the patience of a rock or tree)
Go back into the cities. They want to receive you
Because you are not sent to them. You are a false prophet."

Go back where everyone, in heavy hours,
Is of a different mind, and each is his own burden,
And each mind is its own division
With sickness for diversion and war for
Business reasons. Go where the divided
Cannot stand to be too well. For then they would be held
Responsible for their own misery.

And I have been a man without silence,
A man without patience, with too many
Questions. I have blamed God
Thinking to blame only men
And defend Him Who does not need to be defended.
I have blamed ("defended") Him for Whom the wise stones
(Stones I lately condemned)
Waited in the patient
Creek that is now wet and clean of all ruins.

So now, if I were to return
To my own city (yes my own city), I would be
Neither accepted nor rejected.
For I have no message,
I would be lost together with the others.

IV

Under the blunt pine
I who am not sent
Remain. The pathway dies,
The journey has begun.
Here the bird abides
And sings on top of the forgotten
Storm. The ground is warm.
He sings no particular message.
His hymn has one pattern, no more planned,
No less perfectly planned
And no more arbitrary
Than the pattern in the seed, the salt,
The snow, the cell, the drop of rain.

   (Snow says: I have my own pattern;
   Rain says: no arbitrary plan!
   River says: I go my own way.
   Bird says: I am the same.
   The pine tree says also:
   Not compulsion plants me in my place,
   No, not compulsion!)

The free man is not alone as busy men are
But as birds are. The free man sings
Alone as universes do. Built
Upon his own inscrutable pattern

Clear, unmistakable, not invented by himself alone
Or for himself, but for the universe also.

Nor does he make it his business to be recognized
Or care to have himself found out
As if some special subterfuge were needed
To get himself known for who he is.

The free man does not float
On the tides of his own expedition
Nor is he sent on ventures as busy men are,
Bound to an inexorable result:
But like the birds or lilies
He seeks first the Kingdom, without care.
Nor need the free man remember
Any street or city, or keep campaigns
In his head, or countries for that matter
Or any other economy.

                    Under the blunt pine
Elias becomes his own geography
(Supposing geography to be necessary at all),
Elias becomes his own wild bird, with God in the center,
His own wide field which nobody owns,
His own pattern, surrounding the Spirit
By which he is himself surrounded:

For the free man's road has neither beginning nor end.

PART TWO

THE TOWER OF BABEL

A Morality

The whole earth used the same language and the same speech. While men were migrating eastward, they discovered a valley in the land of Sennaar and settled there. They said to one another, "Come, let us make bricks and bake them." They used bricks for stone and bitumen for mortar. Then they said, "Let us build ourselves a city and a tower with its top in the heavens; let us make a name for ourselves lest we be scattered all over the earth." The LORD came down to see the city and the tower which men had built. And the LORD said, "Truly they are one people and they all have the same language. This is the beginning of what they will do. Let us go down, and there confuse their language so that they will not understand one another's speech." So the LORD scattered them from that place all over the earth; and they stopped building the city. For this reason it was called Babel, because there the LORD confused the speech of all the earth.—GENESIS 11:1–9.

Two kinds of love have created two Cities: the earthly city is created by the love of self to the point of contempt for GOD: the heavenly city by love of GOD to the point of self-contempt. The earthly city glories in herself only, the heavenly glories in the LORD. The earthly city seeks her glory from men, the heavenly, through the witness of a good conscience, finds GOD *in herself as her supreme glory. The earthly city loves her own power, but the heavenly turns to* GOD *and says "I will love Thee, o* GOD *my strength!"* . . .—St. Augustine, THE CITY OF GOD, xiv, 28.

And a mighty angel took up a stone, as it were a great millstone and cast it into the sea saying: with such violence as this shall Babylon that great city be thrown down and shall be found no more at all. . . . For all nations have been deceived by her enchantments, and in her was found the blood of prophets and of saints and of all that were slain upon the earth.— APOCALYPSE 18:21,23–24.

PART ONE—THE LEGEND OF THE TOWER

Scene One—The Building of the Tower

RAPHAEL, THOMAS, FIRST BUILDER, SECOND BUILDER, LEADER, CAPTAIN, CHORUS

[*Musical Prelude—the building of the Tower. Enter* RAPHAEL *and* THOMAS.]

THOMAS: Ought we, Raphael, to join
The builders of this city?
We can quickly learn
Their language and their ambition.
RAPHAEL: No, we must stand apart.
If we learn their language
We will no longer understand
What is being said.

248

If we imitate their zeal
We will lose all sense of what is to be done.
    THOMAS: They are clear-minded men
Of one purpose.
    RAPHAEL: No. They only appear
To know what they are building.
They think it is a tower
That will reach heaven.
They think they speak the same
Language, that they are of one
Mind.
                    Presently
We shall discover that they are
Only of one voice. Many minds,
Many thoughts signifying nothing.
Many words, many plans
Without purpose. Divided hearts,
Weak hands. Hearts that will be
Closed to one another. Hands
Armed against one another.
There is no agreement.
There can be no tower.
    FIRST BUILDER: I believe in the tower.
Therefore I will work longer hours.
    SECOND BUILDER: I believe in the Leader.
Therefore I will sacrifice myself
To build this tower.
    FIRST BUILDER: I believe in our common language,
Therefore I will serve the Leader.
    SECOND BUILDER: I believe in labor without reward.
The Tower is reward enough.
    FIRST BUILDER: I believe in work without food and sleep
Although it is not yet possible.
    SECOND BUILDER: The Leader will make it possible.

FIRST BUILDER: Everyone knows that the Leader
Will make everything possible.
SECOND BUILDER: It is good that we agree brother.
Let us never stop working;
Let us build this Tower for the Leader who loves war.
FIRST BUILDER: Yet, it is good that we agree. Let us
Build this Tower for the Leader who loves peace.
CAPTAIN: Silence! Stop work. Listen to the Leader.
LEADER: The Tower is nearly finished.
It is the greatest of all Towers, in fact
It is the only perfect and eternal Tower. There has never been
And never will be another such Tower.
The Tower is inviolable. It will
Be attacked by invisible powers
From above and from below by agents of social corruption.
Are you tired of work, my people?
Then, when the Tower is built,
We shall have war. But the Tower is impregnable.
Do your duty. Soon you will
Taste the excitement of war.
CAPTAIN: Back to work. The Tower must be finished by
nightfall.
CHORUS: Grow Babylon, grow,
Great Babylon, touch the stars.
What if the Lord should see you, now?
Grow, Babylon, Grow!
RAPHAEL [*The dialogue continues against the background of
the* CHORUS]: They suppose that if they build a high tower very
quickly, they will be nearly as strong as God, Whom they
imagine to be only a little stronger than themselves. And if the
highest part of the tower is level with the lowest part of
heaven, man and God will have to discuss everything on
equal terms.

THOMAS: It is therefore a religious tower, and they are men
of faith.

250

RAPHAEL: No, it is a tower of unbelief.

THOMAS: What have they failed to believe in?

RAPHAEL: Two things: First they do not believe in themselves, and because of this they do not believe in God. Because they do not believe in themselves or in God, they cannot believe in unity. Consequently they cannot be united. Therefore they cannot finish the tower which they imagine they are building.

THOMAS: Nevertheless they are very busy with whatever they think they are doing.

RAPHAEL: That is a pretense. Activity is their substitute for faith. Instead of believing in themselves, they seek to convince themselves, by their activity, that they exist. And their activity pretends to direct itself against God, in order that they may reassure themselves that He does not exist.

THOMAS: Why so?

RAPHAEL: Because if He does not exist, then they do not have to be troubled with the problem of their own existence either. For if they admit they exist they will have to love one another, and this they find insupportable.

THOMAS: But surely they love one another! Otherwise how could they unite in a common endeavor? Surely, they are united, and their union has brought them success.

RAPHAEL: No, they have only united in their common, though hidden, desire to fail. Their ambition is only the occasion for a failure they certainly seek. But they require that this failure come upon them, as it were, out of the stars. They want to blame their ruin on fate, and still have the secret satisfaction of ruining themselves.

THOMAS: Why should they do so much work in order to fail?

RAPHAEL: Their hearts seek disaster as a relief from the tedium of an unsatisfactory existence. Ruin will at least divide them from one another. They will be able to scatter, to run away, to put barricades against one another. Since they cannot stand the pretense of unity, they must seek the open avowal of their enmity.

FIRST BUILDER: What is this thing called war which has been promised us as our reward for finishing the tower?

SECOND BUILDER: It is another work invented by the Leader, more glorious than this one as well as more exhausting.

CAPTAIN: Silence. Stop work! The Leader will ascend to the garden he has planted on the summit of the Tower he has built. He will walk and sing under the exotic trees upon whose branches he will presently hang the heads of our common enemies.

LEADER: Already I see that the skies are as full of words as they are of stars. Each word becomes an instrument of war. Words of the clocks and devils. Words of the wheels and machines. Steel words stronger than flesh or spirit. Secret words which divide the essences of things. Last of all, the one word which strikes at the heart of creation, and dissolves it into its original nothingness. Give me possession of this one word, and I will forget every other.

CHORUS: Fear! Fear!
Feel the business that springs
Out of the dark. Feel fear pass cold
Hands (like wind) over your skin!
Fear talks out of the thundercloud.
Ships fold their wings. The almond trees
Grow pale before the storm.

[CHORUS *continues as background to following dialogue.*]

THOMAS: Raphael, I am scared, I see the tower nodding against the moon. I see the great cranes bending under the cloud.

RAPHAEL: Look at the little boats, Thomas, how they fly down the river. See how the carts topple off the side of the road!

THOMAS: O Raphael, that cloud first came up out of the desert no bigger than a man's fist. Then at once it stood

252

over the tower like a man's arm. Then suddenly the burly dark filled the whole sky. Can you still hear me in this wind?

RAPHAEL: Wind with a thousand fingers pulls away the scaffolding. With a thousand invisible fists the wind beats on the battlements of the great Tower.

FIRST WATCHMAN: Blow the trumpets! Blow the storm-warning trumpet!

VOICE: It is too late, the storm is already upon us.

WATCHMAN: Blow the fire trumpet, blow the fire trumpet!

VOICE: It is too late, Fire has sprouted from a hole in the Tower!

CHORUS: Hide us from the fall, hide us from the fall!
Hide us in the catacomb, hide us in the well!
Hide us in the ground, hide us from the sky!
Hide us from the Tower's fall!

WATCHMAN: Blow the poison trumpet, blow the poison trumpet!

VOICE: Too late! The captains have already taken poison.

WATCHMAN: Then blow the trumpet of division.

VOICE: Blow the trumpet of division!

THOMAS: This is Babylon's end!

RAPHAEL: No, it is Babylon's beginning!

CHORUS: Now blow upon this plain you winds of heaven.
Blow, blow, you winds of God, upon the sands.
Scatter the seeds of war to the world's end.

Scene Two—The Trial

RAPHAEL, THOMAS, SOLDIERS, CAPTAIN, LEADER, PROFESSOR, PROPAGANDA, FALSEHOOD, LANGUAGE, CHORUS

[SCENE—*Square in a half-ruined city*. RAPHAEL *and* THOMAS.]

RAPHAEL: Everywhere the great machines of war
Stand face to face. The hunters in the sky

Bargain with life and death.
Babylon, like a great star wandering from its orbit,
Unsettles the universe, dragging nations down into chaos.
    THOMAS: Is this the same city? All the cities in the world
Begin to look like the same city.
Wagons come down to the water
Where the crowds stand
After flags have fallen. Angry men
Stand without speech,
Wait for the conquering army.
    SOLDIERS [*enter, singing marching song*]:
The bar snake and the zigzag snake
Will bite each other in the head
And drown each other in the river:
Who will reign when both are dead?
The fire bird and the water bird
Have brought good luck to Babylon
But who will reign when both are dead?
    CAPTAIN: Gather the citizens in the square
And fill the whole city
With the sound of one voice.
There shall be no other voice. For peace,
Peace is this: only a giant voice.
There shall be one Babylon, fearing the orator.
There shall be one Babylon, hating itself.
    [*Enter* LEADER, PROFESSOR, LAWYERS.]
    LEADER: Now we must settle the question of guilt.
The Tower fell. Babylon was dishonored.
Our armies, though everywhere victorious,
Are full of traitors. Sabotage
Halts the production of new weapons.
Who is responsible?
    CHORUS: Nothing is light, nothing is dark,
Nothing is defined. Sunlight and darkness
Both bring forth new fear.

Things are beginning to lose their names,
Persons their character. All
Wear the look of death, and become terrible.
    CAPTAIN: Silence! Traitors. Salute the Leader!
He brings you life, salvation,
Prosperity, peace. Can you not see that despair,
Unhappiness, will presently cease to exist?
    LEADER: Who has taught these people the lies they utter?
What enemy has poisoned their minds?
    CAPTAIN: We know the traitor's name,
One who was at first our best friend, one who was
Our most capable officer. One we thought
Would not fail us.
    LEADER: Who is it then?
    CAPTAIN: Language! He and his regiments, the words,
Have sold out to the enemy.
    LEADER: Impossible.
Words have always been our best soldiers.
They have defeated meaning in every engagement
And have almost made an end of reality.
    CAPTAIN: No, Majesty. They are in league with sense,
Order and even silence. They are in the pay
Of thought and of communication.
    LEADER: Then they have betrayed their sacred trust
For theirs is a mission of division and destruction.
    CAPTAIN: Our first witness will explain the functions of
language.
    PROFESSOR: History is a dialogue
Between forward and backward
Going inevitably forward by the abuse of thought
And the gradual destruction of intelligence.
Now the function of the word is
To designate: first the machine,
Then what the machine produces,
And finally what the machine destroys.

Words have no other function.
They belong by right to the political process:
Doing, making, destroying. Or rather
Being done, being made, being destroyed.
Such is history.

CAPTAIN: This witness can prove that language is the
enemy of history and should therefore be abolished.

LEADER: Let him proceed.

PROFESSOR: The word is a means of locomotion
Forward and backward
Along the infinite horizontal plane
Created by the history
Which words themselves destroy
(Substituting what *ought* to have happened
For what actually happened).

LEADER: But if that is the case, Language is the fulfilment of
history. Why then should it be destroyed?

PROFESSOR: The machine must always destroy
The maker of the machine, for this proves
That the machine is greater than the one who made it
Just as man is more important than God.
Words reflect this principle, in their relation to history.
Words create history. But they, in turn,
Must be destroyed by the history they have created.
The word supersedes the event, as light emerges from
          darkness,
Transforming the event into something it was not.
But the event, in turn, supersedes its interpretation as
          darkness
Replaces light, and in the end it is darkness that wins.
And the words of the historian are forgotten.

LEADER: Which then is real? The light, or the darkness?

PROFESSOR: Words create reality as fast as they are eaten by it,
And they destroy reality as fast as they themselves

Come back to life, out of the minds of men.
This is the movement of history:
The backward, forward working of the web;
The plunge forward, into the web,
The struggle backward, but not out of the web.

LEADER: Words, then, are the ultimate reality! Let there never again be any silence. Let tongues never be still. For if there be silence, our history will instantly be unmade, and if we stop talking we will cease to exist. Words, therefore, are acquitted. Let Silence be called to the stand.

CAPTAIN: One moment! It is not so simple. There are three kinds of language. There is true language, there is falsehood, and there is propaganda. Let us call all three to the stand, beginning with the most dangerous.

LEADER: Call Truth to the stand!

CLERK: Truth, tell us your name.

TRUTH: My name is Truth.

CLERK: Where do you live?

TRUTH: In things as they are, in minds that see things as they are, in wills that conform to things as they are.

LAWYER: Truth, you are the enemy of the Mammoth State.
You have pretended to serve us, and you have
All the while poisoned the minds of the people
With enemy doctrines. You refuse
To conform your declarations to the pure
Slogans of our Leader. You are therefore
Insubordinate, a saboteur, a spy,
A tool of the enemy.
How many murders, bombings, acts
Of open or hidden violence have you
Not committed against us? You are
The worst of enemies. You are
The destroyer of the Tower.

VOICES: To the salt mines! To the salt mines!

TRUTH: You are your own enemies. You destroyed your
own Tower.

VOICES: Put him to death.
Shoot him! Down with him!
Kill him. He is the People's enemy.

SECOND PHILOSOPHER: I can defend Truth.

CAPTAIN: Shall we hear his witness?

LEADER: Give him one minute, not more.

SECOND PHILOSOPHER: There is no need to put Truth to death.
Truth has never existed, there is no Truth.
Everything is vague. The world, O Leader,
Which only seems to exist,
Needs to be expressed in words which seem to exist.
Actually, nothing has real being.
Seeming is existing. Everything that seems,
Is. It is what it wants to be.
It has no being, only wanting.
Truth, then, may seem to exist.
But what is it? If we look too close
We see right through the seeming.
Leader, there is no Truth.

VOICES: He is right! There is no truth!

OTHER VOICES: He is a liar! Truth exists, but it is not true.

LEADER: Truth or no Truth, words are agents of the traitor:
Meaning. Let them be put to death.

VOICES: Death, death, death,
Let words be put to death!

CAPTAIN: One moment!
Not all words claim to be true.
The pure, holy, divine words of the Leader,
What are they? Are they true?

[*Awkward silence, broken by the* LEADER.]

LEADER: Send this witness to the salt mines.
I have words of my own. Call Propaganda to the stand!

258

CLERK: Do you swear to conceal the truth, the whole truth and to confuse nothing but the issue?

PROPAGANDA: I do.

LEADER: What is your name?

PROPAGANDA: Legion.

LEADER: Where do you live?

PROPAGANDA: In the heads of the people.

LEADER: What do the people look like?

PROPAGANDA: Zombies.

LEADER: How long have they looked like zombies?

PROPAGANDA: Since we got inside.

LEADER: How did you get inside?

PROPAGANDA: By shots in the arm, by beatings over the head, noises in the ear and all the right kind of medicines.

LEADER: Who destroyed the Tower?

PROPAGANDA: The religious warmongers, the clergy, the free-masons, the Pope, the millionaires, the Elders of Zion, the Young Men's Christian Association, the Jesuits and the Legion of Mary.

LEADER: You are a faithful guardian of the Mammoth Democracy, you shall be decorated with the order of the Tower and you shall possess exclusive freedom of speech and worship in every part of the world. Go forth and form the minds of the young. [*Turning to* CLERK] Call Falsehood to the stand.

[*Solemn music—enter* FALSEHOOD.]

VOICE: This must be one of the gods.

LEADER: Sir, who are you?

FALSEHOOD: Why, I am Truth.

LEADER: Ah, yes. We should have known.

FALSEHOOD: I built the Tower.

VOICE: The builder of the Tower, the builder of the Tower!

LEADER: Your worship, will you be so kind as to tell us the function of language, and indicate whether or not words had anything to do with the ruin of the tower? Are words faithful to our cause, or should they be done away with? Can our empire subsist without language?

FALSEHOOD: I am your strength. Without me you fall. I will give you the only words that will serve your purpose. You should never have listened to anyone but me. Your city is made in my image and likeness. I penetrate reality by destroying it. Those who follow me will be split in half and each one, instead of being one man, will become two angels. If you follow me and listen to my words, you will find this out for yourself.

CAPTAIN: This must be the voice of our creator.

LEADER: Tell us, Majesty, who destroyed the Tower?

FALSEHOOD: The Tower has never been destroyed. Just as I am immortal, the Tower is indestructible. The Tower is a spiritual reality and so am I. The Tower is everywhere. What you call the fall of the Tower was only its beginning, its passage into a new, more active phase of existence. The Tower is not a building but an influence, a mentality, an invisible power. The Tower stands, and I am the King who lives on the summit of the Tower. And because I am everywhere, everywhere is the Tower of Babel.

LEADER: Divine and omnipresent Majesty, forgive us for not having recognized you. What shall we do with the people who resist your authority?

FALSEHOOD: Let all men serve me in chains.

CHORUS: Grow, Babylon, grow,
Serve your Lord in chains.
Chains will be your liberty.
Grow, Babylon, grow!

CLERK: There is one more witness!

LEADER: Who is he?

CAPTAIN: His name is Silence.

LEADER: Useless! Throw him out! Let silence be crucified!
[*Music, an all-out crucifixion of silence.*]

PART TWO—THE CITY OF GOD

Scene One—Zodiac

[SCENE—*A river bank.*]

RAPHAEL, THOMAS, PROPHET, CHILDREN

RAPHAEL: Once there was a city where these marshes are,
Ships at dockside, barrels on the quay,
Children running between the wheels
Watching the foreigner's sandal
Fearing the unknown words of the men with scars.
THOMAS: Now all is sand, and grass, and water
Where the rank marsh draws down one crooked gull.
Men have gone from this place. There is
Neither cursing, nor praying, nor dancing.
Neither living nor dying, buying nor selling.
No more traffic on the water front
No more pianos in the cabaret.
PROPHET: The city under the sand
Lives everywhere. It is not a buried city.
The westward ships will soon discover
The old city, on another continent
Young and new. The southward ships
Will find that the city was never destroyed.
The northward plane soon sees the sun
Shine on the towers of the same Babylon.
RAPHAEL: The stars pursue their prey.
Across the edge of the sky
Time moves east and west
Covering the land with light and darkness,
Life and death, truth and illusion.
The hills stand where they were before,
The stars pass by.

CHILDREN: Washed in winter's rivers
Ancient seasons come:
Cancer and Orion,
The Bear and Capricorn.

PROPHET: Men were made to be the mirror of God. They were meant to be one mirror filled with His one light. When will the pieces be brought together again, and receive the divine image?

CHILDREN: Washed in silent streams
The Lion and the Twins
Come crowned in diadems
With weapons in their hands.

RAPHAEL: Words once contained the silences beyond the stars. Words given us by God, bound minds in agreement, and in agreement made them strong. Because they were strong, men became free. They were free because they thought the same thing. They were strong because they knew the same truth and lived by it, working together.

CHILDREN: The Beast stands in the sky
With poison in his thorn.
The Archer bides his time
And death hangs on his arm.

PROPHET: But the languages of men have become empty
    palaces
Where the winds blow in every room.
Strange spirits sing in them. The ruined houses are
Hiding-places for men at arms.

CHILDREN: Washed in splendid rain
The Bull, the fishes come,
The Crab, the Waterman,
And put their packages down.

PROPHET: The Word of God, coming from afar,
Is always near: Near in the stillness of the thing that moves,
Near in the silence of the thing that speaks.
Near, not dead, even in the heart of one that lies.

His silence is always near. His Word is near.
We cannot listen. We turn away fearing an accuser.

CHILDREN: Washed in silent peace
The Swan and Sirius come,
The Virgin with the Scales,
The wind, and the bone moon.

PROPHET: In the last days the Word, wise without omen, strong without armies, will come to the crossroads of the broken universe. Then Truth will speak to the dead. Then God will awaken them from oblivion with His Word, and they shall sit up in their tombs, and look upon the Word Whom they have slain, and recognize His eyes like wine.

CHILDREN: Storms and tides of spring
Divide their chains and come.
The ram rides in their brine
Stronger than the sun.

PROPHET: Do not think the destroyed city is entirely evil. As a symbol is destroyed to give place to a reality, so the shadow of Babylon will be destroyed to give place to the light which it might have contained. Men will indeed be of one tongue, and they will indeed build a city that will reach from earth to heaven. This new city will not be the tower of sin, but the City of God. Not the wisdom of men shall build this city, nor their machines, not their power. But the great city shall be built without hands, without labor, without money and without plans. It will be a perfect city, built on eternal foundations, and it shall stand forever, because it is built by the thought and the silence and the wisdom and the power of God. But you, my brothers, and I are stones in the wall of this city. Let us run to find our places. Though we may run in the dark, our destiny is full of glory.

THE ANCIENT, PROPHET, RAPHAEL, THOMAS, DANCERS, FIRST VIL-
LAGER, SECOND VILLAGER, EXILES, CHORUS

[SCENE—*A village on a river.*]

THE ANCIENT: By the ever changing waters
We sit down and weep
As if we had some other home.
  CHORUS: Lord, when the skies fall down to hell
Who will stop the giant wheel
Who will break the strict machine
Who will save us from the mill?
  RAPHAEL: Exiles, where have you come from,
Where are you going?
  CHORUS: We found no man to lead us into our own land
Because we found no man to tell us of our own land.
We have forgotten where we came from. How can we tell
Where we might be going?
  THE ANCIENT: As long as I can remember we have wandered
    by these rivers
We have wept by these waters
As if we had some other home.
  CHORUS: Who will define movement and rest,
Who will distinguish strength and fear,
Give us a name that tells the mind
More than an echo in the ear?
  THE ANCIENT: I have heard my Fathers say that we came
from another country.
  FIRST EXILE: One by one we lost our names.
Men gave us numbers.
  SECOND EXILE: Words were poured over us like water.
Sentences ran down our necks
Like sand. Sand and water,

Good and evil, truth and lies
All were the same.

FIRST EXILE: There are no actions
Only explanations.
Men give us numbers.

THE ANCIENT: For years there has been found
No man to teach us.

SECOND EXILE: No word to wash our wounded minds.

FIRST EXILE: The words of this land
Are interminable signals of their own emptiness,
Signs without meaning.

SECOND EXILE: Our speeches have ended in exhaustion.

CHORUS: Lord, when the pieces of the world
Melt in the enfolding flame
Who will raise our bones from death,
Who will call us back again?
How shall we hear and understand
A word that we have never learned
A name that we were never told
A cry that man has never made?

PROPHET: If you have not heard your name, it is not because
it has not been spoken. The Lord, Who names you, lives
within you. You live by the name he utters in secret. This is
the hope that you are rooted in.

FIRST EXILE: Is there then hope within us?

SECOND EXILE: Are we rooted in something?

PROPHET: If you exist, you exist in hope. To cease hoping is
to cease existing. To hope, and to exist, is to have roots in God.
But one can hope and yet be hopeless: that is, one can exist
without believing in one's existence. The man who does
not believe in his own existence is rooted in despair. But he
could not despair if he were not able to hope. Your exis-
tence, though you despair, is rooted in hope.

FIRST EXILE: Why must we despair?

SECOND EXILE: Why must we live in fear,

As if our life were cursed by stars,
As if the wheel of the sky would, without fail,
Drag us to a bad end?

RAPHAEL: Stars are too wise to think of you,
Too innocent to harm you.

THOMAS: They are the signals of the Christ,
Who holds them in His hand.

THOMAS: You will wait for their light in winter
Learning discipline.
You will work until they come in summertime
When the words of God will be planted among you,
Growing in work and patience.

FIRST EXILE: Is there work for us, somewhere, without
slavery?

SECOND EXILE: Is there a discipline that will give us peace?

PROPHET: Christ's mercy heals the regions of the mind.
Blessed by Him our acts are free.
Heard by Him
Our silences bear fruit. All our words become true.

THE ANCIENT: Ah, yes, I have heard in the past that words
could be true.

RAPHAEL: They are meant to bind minds together in the
joy of truth.

THOMAS: You must discover new words reborn out of an
old time
Like new seeds from an old harvest
If you would bless the world with rest and labor,
With speech and silence
And crown your peace with timeless blossoms
When the strong Child climbs quietly to His throne.

THE ANCIENT: Our Fathers told us that before we were made
captives we lived in our own villages and worked the land,
worshipped together, held festivals. There were marriages.
There were harvests. Children were born and the old people
were laid to rest in the Church's shadow. Men spoke to one

another quietly in the market place, and one man could agree
with another.

RAPHAEL: Villages are slow to forget
The silences of ancient years.
Houses and churches cling together
Fastened by the words of older generations
And by the silences of the dead Fathers.
So windows stare together at the sun.
Smokes of separate houses
Climb the morning sky together.
Meals are made together.
The same swallows twitter together
Under the shutters of the houses.
One clear bell tells all times,
One same small bell
Recalls the silence of the blessed Fathers.

THE ANCIENT: Look, here is a village! Here is a festival!

FIRST EXILE: Houses see their faces in the water,
Dressed in flags and vines. Boats and wagons
Gather. Flowering wagons and crowned oxen!

SECOND EXILE: There are blue and yellow canopies
For flute, fiddle and drum.

RAPHAEL: Singing together, dancing together
Signify that the people are one.

DANCERS: Once a body had a soul
They were in agreement.
Said the body to the soul,
I will be your raiment.
Said the spirit to the flesh
Now we are a person.

RAPHAEL: When hills are dressed in vines and fruit
And houses see their faces in the water,
They send their boats into the noonday sun.

FIRST VILLAGER: Music and dancing signify
That we are one.

So we laugh in the decorated square,
Dancing around the fiddlers under the awning.

SECOND VILLAGER: Those who sing in the boats, trailing their
 fingers
In the water, echo the dancers on the shore.

DANCERS: Once a person had a friend
They were in agreement.
Said the person to his friend,
Take my heart and keep it.
You and I will live alike
As a single person.

THOMAS: Look, there are two villages. One, on the shore, is the real village. The other, upside down in the water, is the image of the first. The houses of the real village are solid, the houses in the water are destroyed by the movements in the water, but recreate their image in the stillness that follows.

RAPHAEL: So it is with our world. The city of men, on earth, is the inverted reflection of another city. What is eternal and unchanging stands reflected in the restless waters of time, and many of the events of our history are simply movements in the water that destroy the temporal shadow of eternity. We who are obsessed with movement, measure the importance of events by their power to unsettle our world. We look for meaning only in the cataclysms which obscure the image of reality. But all the things pass away, and the picture of the real city returns, although there may be no one left to recognize it, or to understand.

FIRST VILLAGER: In the gray hours before dawn
When horses stir in the stable,
Swallows twitter outside the shutter,
The streets smell of fresh bread,
And when the churchdoor opens
One can see the lighted candles in the shadows,
And listen to the sacring bell.

SECOND VILLAGER: Before the sun was up

We had already milked the cows,
Watered the horses, hitched up the teams.
We worked together in one another's fields,
Bringing home the hay.
Everybody's grapes will redden the gutters
When we make wine together, in September.

FIRST VILLAGER: And now we all unite
To celebrate a wedding. In this festival
We dance together because we are glad
To be living together. We have heard
The same songs before, at other weddings.
That is why we play them now.
We find ourselves made new
In singing what was sung before.

DANCERS: Once a person had a friend
They were in agreement.
Said the person to his friend
Take my heart and keep it.
You and I will live alike
As a single person.

THE ANCIENT: These people do not sit together by the waters and weep, as we are accustomed to. Why is it that they are happy, while we have always lived in sorrow?

PROPHET: These are the men who have never been conquered by the builders of the ancient tower. Because they do not kill with the sword, they do not fear death. Because they do not live by the machine, they fear no insecurity. Since they say what they mean, they are able to love another, and since they live mostly in silence they know what is the beginning of life, and its meaning and its end. For they are the children of God.

THE ANCIENT: How is it that the whole world is not like this?

RAPHAEL: It shall be so, for Babylon has fallen.

[*Sound of a distant trumpet.*]

THOMAS: Listen, I hear a trumpet
From beyond the hills.

RAPHAEL: It announces the great messenger.

VOICE [*slowly, out of the distance*]: "I will destroy the name
of Babylon, and the remains, and the bud, and the offspring,
saith the Lord."

THOMAS: Whose voice was that?

RAPHAEL: *Dicit Leo—*
It was the Loin of Isaias,
Waking on the watchtower.
The desert-thrasher,
Seeing beyond mountains,
Whole nights upon his tower.

CHORUS: It was the Lion
Who sees in the dark
Who hunts upon the mountains:
By whom the enemy lies killed.

[*Trumpets. Sounds of a storm and of a distant battle.*]

PROPHET: Now is the time when the great city must at last
    fall
By the power of its own curse. Cursed by God
Because its builders cursed themselves,
They hated peace, refused the blessing.
They hated to be themselves, hated to be men.
Wanting to be gods, they were made less than themselves.
They might have become gods
If they had deigned to remain men.

CHORUS: In one hour, O Babylon,
In one night hour, after so many years,
After so much blood, and so much power,
In one small hour you lie destroyed.

RAPHAEL: Yours was a long hot day that burned the earth,
    and now
Your sun goes down in fire and rain

270

Not without glory. But it is not your glory,
Babylon: destroyed in one hour,
You shall be forgotten forever.
  VOICE [*out of the distance*]: Babylon the great is fallen, is
    fallen
And is become the house of emptiness
And is carried away by the night birds.
The kings have seen her, drowning in the sea.
  CHORUS: Fire can quench water
Flame can stand upon foam
Blood lies on the rock
When the sea goes home.
Nails can give back thunder
Fire can leap from wood
And mercy from the Heart of Man
Though that Heart be dead.
  [RAPHAEL *and* THOMAS *speak against the background of the*
    CHORUS.]
  THOMAS: I hear the voices of the islands. What do they sing?
  RAPHAEL: They sing that Babylon has fallen.
  THOMAS: I hear the voices of the hills. What do they sing?
  RAPHAEL: They say there shall be no more war.
  THOMAS: I hear the voices of the Cities. What do they sing?
  RAPHAEL: There is no more despair!
  CHORUS: We know the Word of God is spoken
Never to be forgotten.
Not to be echoed in the ear,
Printed upon a piece of paper
And forgotten.
  THOMAS: How was Babylon destroyed?
  CHORUS: By one Word uttered in silence
Babylon is destroyed.
  THOMAS: But by what one word was Babylon destroyed?
  RAPHAEL: By the One Word Who is in the beginning, and

Who sustains all things, and Who shall be in the end. He was, and He is, and He shall be. He Who Is has only to be mentioned, and all He knows not is no longer known.

THOMAS: Who is the Word, the Beginning and the End?

RAPHAEL: He is the King of Glory!

CHORUS: *In Principio.*

PROPHET: The Word of God on high
Is the fountain of wisdom.
His ways are eternal commandments.

CHORUS: *Erat Verbum.*
Et Verbum erat apud Deum.

PROPHET: The Word leaped down in darkness men could
touch
Nor did the dark deliver them.

CHORUS: *Et Deus erat Verbum.*

RAPHAEL: The Word held open the divided sea
Until the tide drowned kings.
The Word spoke on the Mountain.

CHORUS: *Et Deus erat Verbum.*

PROPHET: Men who were bitten in the desert
Grew well, remembering the Word
Or seeing His mysterious sign.

CHORUS: *Verbum caro factum,*
Verbum sanctum!

THOMAS: Flesh did not understand
The Word made flesh.
Those who feared the voice of thunder
Scorned to eat the Word made Bread.

CHORUS: *Verbum crucis,*
Verbum sanctum.

THOMAS: Not wheat, nor meat
Nor meal, nor bread:
The Word was given in the desert
Where snow endured the force of fire.
The Word came down upon the wilderness

Touching the tongues of men in crystal morsels.

CHORUS: *Verbum crucis,*
Verbum pacis.

PROPHET: Those who have taken peace upon their tongue
Have eaten heaven:
They have made heaven in the midst of us,
Jerusalem in Babylon.

CHORUS: *Verbum crucis.*

RAPHAEL: This is the Word the prophet saw:
This is the tender plant
The bleeding root in his despised report:
The Word who would not speak when He was wounded.

CHORUS: *Verbum sanctum.*

PROPHET: Give rest, give rest, O Lord,
To the slain souls who sing beneath the altar.
Give the robes and rest and thrones to the white martyrs
Who swore and signed with their own blood:
"Thy words are true!"

CHORUS: *Adorate verbum sanctum in aeternum.*

ALL: Lo the Word and the white horse
With eyes of flame to judge and fight
Power and meekness in His hand
Mercy in His look like wine.
He alone can break the seal
And tell the conquerors His Name.

ADOREMUS DOMINUM!

PART THREE

BIRDCAGE WALK

1

One royal afternoon
When I was young and easily surprised
By uncles coming from the park
At the command of nurses and of guards,

I wondered, over trees and ponds,
At the sorry, rude walls
And the white windows of the apartments.

"These," said my uncle, "are the tallest houses."

2

Yes, in the spring of my joy
When I was visibly affected by a gaitered bishop,
Large and unsteady in the flagged yard,
Guards, dogs and blackbirds fled on every hand.

"He is an old one," said uncle,
"The gaiters are real."

3

Rippled, fistfed windows of your
Dun high houses! Then
Come cages made of pretty willows
Where they put the palace girls!
Green ducks wade slowly from the marble water.
One swan reproves a saucy daughter.

I consider my own true pond,
Look for the beginning and the end.
I lead the bishop down lanes and islands.

4

Yes, in the windows of my first existence
Before my yawns became seasons,
When nurses and uncles were sure,
Chinese fowl fought the frosty water
Startled by this old pontifex.

"No bridge" (He smiled
Between the budding branches),
"No crossing to the cage
Of the paradise bird!"

Astounded by the sermons in the leaves
I cried, "No! No! The stars have higher houses!"

Kicking the robins and ganders
From the floor of his insular world
The magic bishop leaned his blessing on the children.

5

That was the bold day when
Moved by the unexpected summons
I opened all the palace aviaries
As by a king's representative
I was appointed fowler.

LANDSCAPE

1

A Personage is seen
Leaning upon a cushion
Printed with cornflowers.

A Child appears
Holding up a pencil.

"This is a picture
(Says the Child to the Personage)
Of the vortex."

"Draw it your own way,"
Says the Personage.

(Music is heard
Pure in the island windows,
Sea-music on the Child's
Interminable shore, his coral home.)

Behind a blue mountain
Covered with chickenfoot trees,
The molten sun appears,
A heavy, painted flower.

A Personage is seen
Leaning upon the mountain
With the sun in one hand
And a pencil in the other.

"This is a picture
(Says the Personage to the Child)
Of the beginning of the world."

"Or of its end!" cries the Child
Hiding himself in the cushions.

2

A Woman appears
Leaning upon the Child's shoulder.
He looks up again.

"This is my Mother
(Says the Child to the Personage)
Older than the moon."

(Grecian horses are heard
Returning from the foam
Of the pure island's windows,
And the Child's horizons.)

"My Mother is a world
(Says the Child to the Personage)
Printed with gillyflowers."

"Paint her your own way"
(Says the Personage to the Child).
And, lifting up his pencil,
He crosses out the sun.

WISDOM

I studied it and it taught me nothing.
I learned it and soon forgot everything else:
Having forgotten, I was burdened with knowledge—
The insupportable knowledge of nothing.

How sweet my life would be, if I were wise!
Wisdom is well known
When it is no longer seen or thought of.
Only then is understanding bearable.

"WHEN IN THE SOUL
OF THE SERENE DISCIPLE . . ."

When in the soul of the serene disciple
With no more Fathers to imitate
Poverty is a success,
It is a small thing to say the roof is gone:
He has not even a house.

Stars, as well as friends,
Are angry with the noble ruin.
Saints depart in several directions.

Be still:
There is no longer any need of comment.

It was a lucky wind
That blew away his halo with his cares,
A lucky sea that drowned his reputation.

Here you will find
Neither a proverb nor a memorandum.
There are no ways,
No methods to admire
Where poverty is no achievement.
His God lives in his emptiness like an affliction.

What choice remains?
Well, to be ordinary is not a choice:
It is the usual freedom
Of men without visions.

IN SILENCE

Be still
Listen to the stones of the wall.
Be silent, they try
To speak your

Name.
Listen
To the living walls.
Who are you?
Who
Are you? Whose
Silence are you?

Who (be quiet)
Are you (as these stones

Are quiet). Do not
Think of what you are
Still less of
What you may one day be.
Rather
Be what you are (but who?) be
The unthinkable one
You do not know.

O be still, while
You are still alive,
And all things live around you
Speaking (I do not hear)
To your own being,
Speaking by the Unknown
That is in you and in themselves.

"I will try, like them
To be my own silence:
And this is difficult. The whole
World is secretly on fire. The stones
Burn, even the stones
They burn me. How can a man be still or
Listen to all things burning? How can he dare
To sit with them when
All their silence
Is on fire?"

EARLY MASS

(St. Joseph Infirmary—Louisville)

There is a Bread which You and I propose.
It is Your truth. And more: it is ourselves.

There was a wickedness whose end is blessing.
Come, people, to the Cross and Wedding!

His are the mysteries which I expound
And mine the children whom His stars befriend.
Our Christ has cleanly built His sacred town.

What do the windows of His city say?
His innocence is written on your sky!
Because we think His Latin we are part of one another,
Together when I am away.

Come to the ark and stone
Come to the Holies where His work is done,
Dear hasty doves, transparent in His sun!

Gather us God in honeycombs,
My Israel, in the Ohio valley!
For brightness falls upon our dark.

Death owns a wasted kingdom.
Bless and restore the blind, straighten the broken limb.
These mended stones shall build Jerusalem.

Come to the golden fence with folded hands
And see your Bird, kneel to your white Beloved.
Here is your Father at my finger's end!

The clouds are torn. Summon the winds of fall.
On street and water, track and river, shine, November!
Open the doors and own the avenue
For see: we are the makers of a risen world, the brothers
        of a new
Brown universe whose liturgy
Sweetly consumes my bones.

A PRELUDE:
FOR THE FEAST OF ST. AGNES

O small St. Agnes, dressed in gold
With fire and rainbows round about your face:
Sing with the martyrs in my Mass's Canon!

Come home, come home, old centuries
Whose soundless islands ring me from within,
Whose saints walk down a winter morning's iris,
Wait upon this altar stone
(Some of them holding palms
But others hyacinths!).

I speak your name with wine upon my lips
Drowned in the singing of the quiet catacomb.
My feet upon forget-me-nots
I sink this little frigate in the Blood of silence
And put my pall upon the cup
Working the mystery of peace, whose mercies must
Run down and find us, Saint, by Saint John's stairs.

No lines, no globes,
No compasses, no staring fires
No candle's cup to swing upon
My night's dark ocean.

There the pretended horns of time grow dim.
No tunes, no signals claim us any more.
The cities cry, perhaps, like peacocks.
But the cloud has come.

I kneel in this stone corner having blood upon my wrist
And blood upon my breast,
O small St. Agnes, dressed in martyrdom
With fire and water waving in your hair.

THE ANNUNCIATION

Ashes of paper, ashes of a world
Wandering, when fire is done:
We argue with the drops of rain!

Until One comes Who walks unseen
Even in elements we have destroyed.
Deeper than any nerve
He enters flesh and bone.
Planting His truth, He puts our substance on.
Air, earth and rain
Rework the frame that fire has ruined.
What was dead is waiting for His Flame.
Sparks of His Spirit spend their seeds, and hide
To grow like irises, born before summertime.
These blue things bud in Israel.

The girl prays by the bare wall
Between the lamp and the chair.
(Framed with an angel in our galleries
She has a richer painted room, sometimes a crown.
Yet seven pillars of obscurity
Build her to Wisdom's house, and Ark, and Tower.
She is the Secret of another Testament
She owns their manna in her jar.)

Fifteen years old—
The flowers printed on her dress
Cease moving in the middle of her prayer
When God, Who sends the messenger,
Meets His messenger in her Heart.
Her answer, between breath and breath,
Wrings from her innocence our Sacrament!
In her white body God becomes our Bread.

It is her tenderness
Heats the dead world like David on his bed.
Times that were too soon criminal
And never wanted to be normal
Evade the beast that has pursued
You, me and Adam out of Eden's wood.
Suddenly we find ourselves assembled
Cured and recollected under several green trees.

Her prudence wrestled with the Dove
To hide us in His cloud of steel and silver:
These are the mysteries of her Son.
And here my heart, a purchased outlaw,
Prays in her possession
Until her Jesus makes my heart
Smile like a flower in her blameless hand.

SINCERITY

Omnis homo mendax

As for the liar, fear him less
Than one who thinks himself sincere,
Who, having deceived himself,
Can deceive you with a good conscience.

One who doubts his own truth
May mistrust another less:

Knowing in his own heart,
That all men are liars
He will be less outraged
When he is deceived by another.

So, too, will he sooner believe
In the sincerity of God.

The sincerity of God! Who never justifies
His actions to men! Who makes no bargains
With any other sincerity, because He knows
There is no other! Who does what He pleases
And never protests His innocence!

Which of us can stand the sincerity of God?

Which of us can bear a Lord
Who is neither guilty nor innocent
(Who cannot be innocent because He cannot be guilty)?

What has our sincerity to do with His
Whose truth is no approval of our truth
And is not judged by anyone,
Even by Himself?

(Yet if I think myself sincere
I will approve the purity of God
Convinced that my own purity
Is approved by Him.)

So, when the Lord speaks, we go to sleep
Or turn quickly to some more congenial business
Since, as every liar knows,
No man can bear such sincerity.

TO A SEVERE NUN

I know, Sister, that solitude
Will never dismay you. You have chosen

A path too steep for others to follow.
I take it you prefer to go without them.

You will not complain that others are fickle
When they abandon you, renouncing the contest.
After all, they have not understood
That love is a contest, and that the love you demand
Is a match, in which you overcome your friends
After a long agony.

Thus you have no visible companions. Yet, drive on,
Drive on: do not consider your despair! Imagine rather
That there are many saints around you in the same
        desperation,
Violent, without contact, without responsibility,
Except of course to their own just souls
And to the God Who cannot blame them.

You know where you are going. You alone
In the whole convent know what bitter comfort
Eludes the malcontents who travel this unusual desert,
Seeking the impossible, and not the Absolute—
Sustained always by the same hate.

Do not be disconcerted, Sister, if in spite of your effort
The impertinent truth shows up weakness at least in others
And distracts you with their suffering.
Do not be humbled if, for an instant,
Christ seems glad to suffer in another.

Forget this scandal. Do not look at them
Or you may lose your nerve, and come to admit
That violence is your evasion and that you,
You most of all, are weak.

ELEGY FOR THE MONASTERY BARN

As though an aged person were to wear
Too gay a dress
And walk about the neighborhood
Announcing the hour of her death,

So now, one summer day's end,
At suppertime, when wheels are still,
The long barn suddenly puts on the traitor, beauty,
And hails us with a dangerous cry,
For: "Look!" she calls to the country,
"Look how fast I dress myself in fire!"

Had we half guessed how long her spacious shadows
Harbored a woman's vanity
We would be less surprised to see her now
So loved, and so attended, and so feared.

She, in whose airless heart
We burst our veins to fill her full of hay,
Now stands apart.
She will not have us near her. Terribly,
Sweet Christ, how terribly her beauty burns us now!

And yet she has another legacy,
More delicate, to leave us, and more rare.

Who knew her solitude?
Who heard the peace downstairs
While flames ran whispering among the rafters?
Who felt the silence, there,
The long, hushed gallery
Clean and resigned and waiting for the fire?

Look! They have all come back to speak their summary:
Fifty invisible cattle, the past years
Assume their solemn places one by one.
This is the little minute of their destiny.
Here is their meaning found. Here is their end.

Laved in the flame as in a Sacrament
The brilliant walls are holy
In their first-last hour of joy.

Fly from within the barn! Fly from the silence
Of this creature sanctified by fire!
Let no man stay inside to look upon the Lord!
Let no man wait within and see the Holy
One sitting in the presence of disaster
Thinking upon this barn His gentle doom!

STRANGER

When no one listens
To the quiet trees
When no one notices
The sun in the pool

Where no one feels
The first drop of rain
Or sees the last star

Or hails the first morning
Of a giant world
Where peace begins
And rages end:

One bird sits still
Watching the work of God:
One turning leaf,
Two falling blossoms,
Ten circles upon the pond.

One cloud upon the hillside,
Two shadows in the valley
And the light strikes home.
Now dawn commands the capture
Of the tallest fortune,
The surrender
Of no less marvelous prize!

Closer and clearer
Than any wordy master,
Thou inward Stranger
Whom I have never seen,

Deeper and cleaner
Than the clamorous ocean,
Seize up my silence
Hold me in Thy Hand!

Now act is waste
And suffering undone
Laws become prodigals
Limits are torn down
For envy has no property
And passion is none.

Look, the vast Light stands still
Our cleanest Light is One!

ORIGINAL CHILD BOMB
(1962)

ORIGINAL CHILD BOMB

Points for meditation to be scratched on the walls of a cave

1: In the year 1945 an Original Child was born. The name Original Child was given to it by the Japanese people, who recognized that it was the first of its kind.

2: On April 12th, 1945, Mr. Harry Truman became the President of the United States, which was then fighting the second world war. Mr. Truman was a vice president who became president by accident when his predecessor died of a cerebral hemorrhage. He did not know as much about the war as the president before him did. He knew a lot less about the war than many people did.

About one hour after Mr. Truman became president, his aides told him about a new bomb which was being developed by atomic scientists. They called it the "atomic bomb." They said scientists had been working on it for six years and that it had so far cost two billion dollars. They added that its power was equal to that of twenty thousand tons of TNT. A single bomb could destroy a city. One of those present added, in a reverent tone, that the new explosive might eventually destroy the whole world.

But Admiral Leahy told the President the bomb would never work.

3: President Truman formed a committee of men to tell him if this bomb would work, and if so, what he should do with it. Some members of this committee felt that the bomb would jeopardize the future of civilization. They were against its use. Others wanted it to be used in demonstration on a forest of cryptomeria trees, but not against a civil or military target. Many atomic scientists warned that the use of atomic power in war would be difficult and even impossible to control. The danger would be very great. Finally, there were others who believed that if the bomb were used just once or twice, on one or two Japanese cities, there would be no more war. They believed the new bomb would produce eternal peace.

4: In June 1945 the Japanese government was taking steps to negotiate for peace. On one hand the Japanese ambassador tried to interest the Russian government in acting as a go-between with the United States. On the other hand, an un-official approach was made secretly through Mr. Allen Dulles in Switzerland. The Russians said they were not in-terested and that they would not negotiate. Nothing was done about the other proposal which was not official. The Japanese High Command was not in favor of asking for peace, but wanted to continue the war, even if the Japanese mainland were invaded. The generals believed that the war should continue until everybody was dead. The Japanese gen-erals were professional soldiers.

5: In the same month of June, the President's committee de-cided that the new bomb should be dropped on a Japanese city. This would be a demonstration of the bomb on a civil and military target. As "demonstration" it would be a kind of a "show." "Civilians" all over the world love a good "show." The "destructive" aspect of the bomb would be "military."

6: The same committee also asked if America's friendly ally, the Soviet Union, should be informed of the atomic bomb. Someone suggested that this information would make the Soviet Union even more friendly than it was already. But all finally agreed that the Soviet Union was now friendly enough.

7: There was discussion about which city should be selected as the first target. Some wanted it to be Kyoto, an ancient capital of Japan and a center of the Buddhist religion. Others said no, this would cause bitterness. As a result of a chance conversation, Mr. Stimson, the Secretary of War, had recently read up on the history and beauties of Kyoto. He insisted that this city should be left untouched. Some wanted Tokyo to be the first target, but others argued that Tokyo had already been practically destroyed by fire raids and could no longer be considered a "target." So it was decided Hiroshima was the most opportune target, as it had not yet been bombed at all. Lucky Hiroshima! What others had experienced over a period of four years would happen to Hiroshima in a single day! Much time would be saved, and "time is money!"

8: When they bombed Hiroshima they would put the following out of business: The Ube Nitrogen Fertilizer Company; the Ube Soda Company; the Nippon Motor Oil Company; the Sumitoma Chemical Company; the Sumitoma Aluminum Company; and most of the inhabitants.

9: At this time some atomic scientists protested again, warning that the use of the bomb in war would tend to make the United States unpopular. But the President's committee was by now fully convinced that the bomb had to be used. Its use

295

would arouse the attention of the Japanese military class and give them food for thought.

10: Admiral Leahy renewed his declaration that the bomb would not explode.

11: On the 4th of July, when the United States in displays of fireworks celebrates its independence from British rule, the British and Americans agreed together that the bomb ought to be used against Japan.

12: On July 7th the Emperor of Japan pleaded with the Soviet Government to act as mediator for peace between Japan and the Allies. Molotov said the question would be "studied." In order to facilitate this "study" Soviet troops in Siberia prepared to attack the Japanese. The Allies had, in any case, been urging Russia to join the war against Japan. However, now that the atomic bomb was nearly ready, some thought it would be better if the Russians took a rest.

13: The time was coming for the new bomb to be tested, in the New Mexico desert. A name was chosen to designate this secret operation. It was called "Trinity."

14: At 5:30 A.M. on July 16th, 1945 a plutonium bomb was successfully exploded in the desert at Almagordo, New Mexico. It was suspended from a hundred foot steel tower which evaporated. There was a fireball a mile wide. The great flash could be seen for a radius of 250 miles. A blind woman miles away said she perceived light. There was a cloud of smoke 40,000 feet high. It was shaped like a toadstool.

15: Many who saw the experiment expressed their satisfaction in religious terms. A semi-official report even quoted a religious book—The New Testament, "Lord, I believe, help thou my unbelief." There was an atmosphere of devotion. It was a great act of faith. They believed the explosion was exceptionally powerful.

16: Admiral Leahy, still a "doubting Thomas," said that the bomb would not explode when dropped from a plane over a city. Others may have had "faith," but he had his own variety of "hope."

17: On July 21st a full written report of the explosion reached President Truman at Potsdam. The report was documented by pictures. President Truman read the report and looked at the pictures before starting out for the conference. When he left his mood was jaunty and his step was light.

18: That afternoon Mr. Stimson called on Mr. Churchill, and laid before him a sheet of paper bearing a code message about the successful test. The message read "Babies satisfactorily born." Mr. Churchill was quick to realize that there was more in this than met the eye. Mr. Stimson satisfied his legitimate curiosity.

19: On this same day sixty atomic scientists who knew of the test signed a petition that the bomb should not be used against

Japan without a convincing warning and an opportunity to surrender.

At this time the U.S.S. Indianapolis, which had left San Francisco on the 18th, was sailing toward the Island of Tinian, with some U 235 in a lead bucket. The fissionable material was about the size of a softball, but there was enough for one atomic bomb. Instructions were that if the ship sank, the Uranium was to be saved first, before any life. The mechanism of the bomb was on board the U.S.S. Indianapolis, but it was not yet assembled.

20: On July 26th the Potsdam declaration was issued. An ultimatum was given to Japan: "Surrender unconditionally or be destroyed." Nothing was said about the new bomb. But pamphlets dropped all over Japan threatened "an enormous air bombardment" if the army would not surrender. On July 26th the U.S.S. Indianapolis arrived at Tinian and the bomb was delivered.

21: On July 28th, since the Japanese High Command wished to continue the war, the ultimatum was rejected. A censored version of the ultimatum appeared in the Japanese press with the comment that it was "an attempt to drive a wedge between the military and the Japanese people." But the Emperor continued to hope that the Russians, after "studying" his proposal, would help to negotiate a peace. On July 30th Mr. Stimson revised a draft of the announcement that was to be made after the bomb was dropped on the Japanese target. The statement was much better than the original draft.

22: On August 1st the bomb was assembled in an airconditioned hut on Tinian. Those who handled the bomb referred to it as "Little Boy." Their care for the Original Child was devoted and tender.

23: On August 2nd President Truman was the guest of His Majesty King George VI on board the H.M.S. Renown in Plymouth Harbor. The atomic bomb was praised. Admiral Leahy, who was present, declared that the bomb would not work. His Majesty George VI offered a small wager to the contrary.

24: On August 2nd a special message from the Japanese Foreign Minister was sent to the Japanese Ambassador in Moscow. "It is requested that further efforts be exerted . . . Since the loss of one day may result in a thousand years of regret, it is requested that you immediately have a talk with Molotov." But Molotov did not return from Potsdam until the day the bomb fell.

25: On August 4th the bombing crew on Tinian watched a movie of "Trinity" (the Almagordo Test). August 5th was a Sunday but there was little time for formal worship. They said a quick prayer that the war might end "very soon." On that day, Col. Tibbetts, who was in command of the B–29 that was to drop the bomb, felt that his bomber ought to have a name. He baptized it Enola Gay, after his mother in Iowa. Col. Tibbetts was a well balanced man, and not sentimental. He did not have a nervous breakdown after the bombing, like some of the other members of the crew.

26: On Sunday afternoon "Little Boy" was brought out in procession and devoutly tucked away in the womb of Enola

Gay. That evening few were able to sleep. They were as excited as little boys on Christmas Eve.

27: At 1:37 A.M. August 6th the weather scout plane took off. It was named the Straight Flush, in reference to the mechanical action of a water closet. There was a picture of one, to make this evident.

28: At the last minute before taking off Col. Tibbetts changed the secret radio call sign from "Visitor" to "Dimples." The Bombing Mission would be a kind of flying smile.

29: At 2:45 A.M. Enola Gay got off the ground with difficulty. Over Iwo Jima she met her escort, two more B–29s, one of which was called the Great Artiste. Together they proceeded to Japan.

30: At 6:40 they climbed to 31,000 feet, the bombing altitude. The sky was clear. It was a perfect morning.

31: At 3:09 they reached Hiroshima and started the bomb run. The city was full of sun. The fliers could see the green grass in the gardens. No fighters rose up to meet them. There was no flak. No one in the city bothered to take cover.

32: The bomb exploded within 100 feet of the aiming point. The fireball was 18,000 feet across. The temperature at the center of the fireball was 100,000,000 degrees. The people who were near the center became nothing. The whole city was blown to bits and the ruins all caught fire instantly everywhere, burning briskly. 70,000 people were killed right away or died within a few hours. Those who did not die at once suffered great pain. Few of them were soldiers.

33: The men in the plane perceived that the raid had been successful, but they thought of the people in the city and they were not perfectly happy. Some felt they had done wrong. But in any case they had obeyed orders. "It was war."

34: Over the radio went the code message that the bomb had been successful: "Visible effects greater than Trinity . . . Proceeding to Papacy." Papacy was the code name for Tinian.

35: It took a little while for the rest of Japan to find out what had happened to Hiroshima. Papers were forbidden to publish any news of the new bomb. A four line item said that Hiroshima had been hit by incendiary bombs and added: "It seems that some damage was caused to the city and its vicinity."

36: Then the military governor of the Prefecture of Hiroshima issued a proclamation full of martial spirit. To all the people without hands, without feet, with their faces falling off, with their intestines hanging out, with their whole bodies full of radiation, he declared: "We must not rest a single day in our war effort . . . We must bear in mind that the annihilation of the stubborn enemy is our road to revenge." He was a professional soldier.

37: On August 8th Molotov finally summoned the Japanese Ambassador. At last neutral Russia would give an answer to the Emperor's inquiry. Molotov said coldly that the Soviet Union was declaring war on Japan.

38: On August 9th another bomb was dropped on Nagasaki, though Hiroshima was still burning. On August 11th the Emperor overruled his high command and accepted the peace terms dictated at Potsdam. Yet for three days discussion continued, until on August 14th the surrender was made public and final.

39: Even then the Soviet troops thought they ought to fight in Manchuria "just a little longer." They felt that even though they could not, at this time, be of help in Japan, it would be worth while if they displayed their good will in Manchuria, or even in Korea.

40: As to the Original Child that was now born, President Truman summed up the philosophy of the situation in a few words. "We found the bomb" he said "and we used it."

41: Since that summer many other bombs have been "found." What is going to happen? At the time of writing, after a season of brisk speculation, men seem to be fatigued by the whole question.

EMBLEMS OF A SEASON OF FURY
(1963)

You shall find one Captain Spurio with his cicatrice, an emblem of war, here on his sinister cheek. It was this very sword entrenched it.

Shakespeare: All's Well, II.i.44

Et il n'y aura pas d'acquittement pour les nations
Mais seulement pour les âmes une à une.

Raissa Maritain

WHY SOME LOOK UP TO PLANETS AND HEROES

Brooding and seated at the summit
Of a well-engineered explosion
He prepared his thoughts for fireflies and warnings

Only a tourist only a shy American
Flung into public sky by an ingenious weapon
Prepared for every legend

His space once visited by apes and Russians
No longer perfectly pure
Still proffered virginal joys and free rides
In his barrel of fun
A starspangled somersault
A sky-high Mothers' Day

Four times that day his sun would set
Upon the casual rider
Streaking past the stars
At seventeen thousand miles per hour

Our winning Rover delighted
To remain hung up in cool hours and long trips
Smiling and riding in eternal transports

Even where a dog died in a globe
And still comes round enclosed
In a heaven of Russian wires

Uncle stayed alive
Gone in a globe of light
Ripping around the pretty world of girls and sights

"It will be fun" he thinks
"If by my cunning flight
The ignorant and Africans become convinced"

Convinced of what? Nobody knows
And Major is far out
Four days ahead of his own news

Until at last the shy American smiles
Colliding once again with air fire and lenses
To stand on noisy earth
And engineer consent

Consent to what? Nobody knows
What engine next will dig a moon
What costly uncles stand on Mars

What next device will fill the air with burning dollars
Or else lay out the low down number of some Day

What day? May we consent?
Consent to what? Nobody knows.
Yet the computers are convinced
Fed full of numbers by the True Believers.

THE MOSLEMS' ANGEL OF DEATH

(Algeria 1961)

Like a jeweled peacock he stirs all over
With fireflies. He takes his pleasure in
Lights.

He is a great honeycomb of shining bees
Knowing every dust with sugar in it.
He has a million fueled eyes.

With all his eyes he explores life.

The firefly city stirs all over with knowledge.
His high buildings see too many
Persons: he has found out
Their times and when their windows
Will go out.

He turns the city lights in his fingers like money.

No other angel knows this one's place,
No other sees his phoenix wings, or understands
That he is lord of Death.

(Death was once allowed
To yell at the sky:
"I am death!
I take friend from friend!
I am death!
I leave your room empty!")

O night, O High Towers! No man can ever
Escape you, O night!

He is a miser. His fingers find the money.
He puts the golden lights in his pocket.

There is one red coal left burning
Beneath the ashes of the great vision.
There is one blood-red eye left open
When the city is burnt out.

Azrael! Azrael!
See the end of trouble!

AND SO GOODBYE TO CITIES

Now the official nerve is cauterized
And the love machine, angry,
Dances with a spark.
Hornets in the mind
Hate the weak opinion's fury and luck.
This is the day the calendar must bark.

For cities have grown old in war and fun.
The sick idea runs riot. Man is so limber
He slips under himself
And kisses his last wish.
His light still talks and ticks.
His look prints the same number
On mechanical feats.
The deed melts over again, and the world changes:
All must change, now, while he sweats and creeps.

All changes. Luck is now complete.
All falls together in a grand seizure.
Winners wrestle in the smoke:
This is the day their calendar must choke.

Well, what is left?
A pretty little flame
A gone cloud, the way the sight first came:
And Lot's wife, sleeping at the switch.

The old boy still moves
Still works his drunken feet
Through the suburban ash:
He babbles of a hot mountain
Through his white moustache.

But what is left?
A pretty little grace,
(If one can think that way)
Wine of dragons in a poorly
Lighted, isolated place,

Covered with garbage from the black explosion
Wine of dragons and the warming
Old machine runs loose again,
Starting another city with a new disgrace.

AN ELEGY FOR FIVE OLD LADIES

(Newton, Mass., April 20: Five women ranging in age from 80 to 96 drowned this afternoon when a driverless car rolled across a rest home lawn and sank in Crystal Lake . . . THE NEW YORK TIMES)

Let us forget that it is spring and celebrate the rider-
less will of five victims.
Old companions are sitting silent in the home. Five
of their number have suddenly gone too far, as if
waifs,
As if orphans were to swim without license. Their
ride was not lucky. It took them very far out of
bounds.
Mrs. Watson said she saw them all go at three-forty-
five. Their bell had rung too loud and too late.
It was a season when water is too cold for anyone,
and is especially icy for an old person.
The brazen sedan was not to be trusted. The wheels
went too well for one short and straight journey.
It was the last: the doors did not open.
Dimly and too late they saw themselves on a very
wicked lawn. May God have mercy on their
recreation!

Let us accordingly pay homage to five now legendary
persons, the very chaste daughters of one unlucky
ride.

Let the perversity of a machine become our common
study, while I name loudly five loyal spouses of
death!

SONG: IN THE SHOWS
OF THE ROUND OX

i

In the shows of the round Ox
(O pagan night)
They fought their lucky stars.

Light of a wicked sun
And flying cars.

In the shows of the brass barn
(O fatal sun)
They lost a morning's fortune.

ii

"There is no game like money"
(Cries the man with the hand)
"So sell your brother."

Light of a gambling clock
And trained symbols.
When they win, they drown.

"There is no game like homeward"
Cry the whirlwind trumpeters.

iii

To the shallow water
They are standing on
These waterwalkers owe
No genuine fortune.

Strong ones have their own
Problems and pardons
For the iron ox.

iv

Tell me the name of the brass horn
That makes all the money.
Tell me the day of the wargames
Where gold is won.
The winning day is the day
On my green paper.
The first-last dollar's number
Is my own name.

v

The brass fighting cocks
And bloodred winners

Ask no pardon
And present no problem.

(But there is no game like pardon).

vi

The fight is over. Eyes of the furious Ox
Are brass suns. There is no game like standing on the
     water:

But there is no winner.

Strong ones have their own
Mercies and questions
For brazen fortune.

GLOSS ON THE SIN OF IXION

He saw her: that is, he labored.
He loved sweet business (Juno was success)
He laid eyes always on sweet fat
Energetic trade, and diligence
Made his world steam.

Our world too must steam and flame.
Ours must spin. Effort will break
A bank. Work will run
(Wheels within wheels)
Monopolies.

He'll hold her. Hold her fast
In a quick cloud
Of wrong words
Or dizzy lunches!

"Hold fast, Ixion! Get famous, strong!
Go hug dear mother profit in the dark. Possess earth,
Possess money!"
Yet he missed.
He spilled.

Giants rise
Heavy-set brothers of mess and fight,
Smoky bulldozers!
Wheeling cities burn!
Glass monsters break
Open faces, lit with high money.

Giant mechanical boys:
Their dirty eyes spin.
Smell history at work
And watch overkill.

Heavy war bums
Political wheels and copper generals
Drink nuclear smoke
And lose manhood.
Shameless, unintelligent,
But shrewd enough
To spill sun power,
Spin the planets,
Ravish sacred man!

Up now comes
Out of earth and hell
Giant war Ixion
Rolling and fighting on the red wheel.

AN ELEGY FOR ERNEST HEMINGWAY

Now for the first time on the night of your death your name is mentioned in convents, *ne cadas in obscurum*.

Now with a true bell your story becomes final. Now men in monasteries, men of requiems, familiar with the dead, include you in their offices.

You stand anonymous among thousands, waiting in the dark at great stations on the edge of countries known to prayer alone, where fires are not merciless, we hope, and not without end.

You pass briefly through our midst. Your books and writings have not been consulted. Our prayers are *pro defuncto N.*

Yet some look up, as though among a crowd of prisoners or displaced persons, they recognized a friend once known in a far country. For these the sun also rose after a forgotten war upon an idiom you made great. They have not forgotten you. In their silence you are still famous, no ritual shade.

How slowly this bell tolls in a monastery tower for a whole age, and for the quick death of an unready dynasty, and for that brave illusion: the adventurous self!

For with one shot the whole hunt is ended!

ELEGY FOR JAMES THURBER

Thurber, they have come, the secret bearers,
At the right time, though fools seem to have won.
Business and generals survive you
At least for one brief day.

Humor is now totally abolished.
The great dogs of nineteen sixty-one
Are nothing to laugh at.

Leave us, good friend. Leave our awful celebration
With pity and relief.
You are not called to solemnize with us
Our final madness.

You have not been invited to hear
The last words of everybody.

316

MACARIUS AND THE PONY

People in a village
At the desert's edge
Had a daughter
Who was changed (they thought)
By magic arts
Into a pony.

At first they berated her
"Why do you have to be a horse?"
She could think of no reply.

So they led her out with a halter
Into the hot waste land
Where there was a saint
Called Macarius
Living in a cell.

"Father" they said
"This young mare here
Is, or was, our daughter.
Enemies, wicked men,
Magicians, have made her
The animal you see.
Now by your prayers to God
Change her back
Into the girl she used to be."

"My prayers" said Macarius,
"Will change nothing,

For I see no mare.
Why do you call this good child
An animal?"

But he led her into his cell
With her parents:
There he spoke to God
Anointing the girl with oil;
And when they saw with what love
He placed his hand upon her head
They realized, at once.
She was no animal.
She had never changed.
She had been a girl from the beginning.

"Your own eyes
(Said Macarius)
Are your enemies.
Your own crooked thoughts
(Said the anchorite)
Change people around you
Into birds and animals.
Your own ill-will
(said the clear-eyed one)
Peoples the world with specters."

(Based on Rufinus' *Historia Monachorum*, ch. 28.)

318

MACARIUS THE YOUNGER

I

The place in which he lived
Is called Scete.

In wide open desert
A day and night's journey
From the monasteries at Nitria.

No road, no path,
No land marks
Show the way there.
You must go by the stars.

Scarce is the water:
Where found at all
It smells poisonous as tar
But is safe to drink.

Few live there
Far apart
Out of one another's sight
True men of God:
Such a place
Suffers only those
Who have made up their minds.

There is great love among them
And love for any other
Who can get that far.

If any traveller
Should reach that place
He receives much care:
One who crosses such wastes
Has needs.

2

Now one day someone brought a bunch of grapes
To Macarius at Scete.

He, forgetful of his own thirst, took the grapes to another
Who was unwell.

He in turn, happy and thanking God for so much love
Took the grapes to yet another.

So the grapes went from cell to cell, all around the desert
No one knowing where they first started.

Until at length one came to Macarius, saying: "Here, Father, are good grapes,
Take them, they will refresh you."

Then Macarius was very glad to see the worth of those men
Who lived hidden in the Desert at Scete.

320

3

At another time the two Macarii, both men of God,
Going to visit a brother
Took the boat that crosses the river.

The boat was full of officers, rich brass,
With horses, boys and guards.

One tribune saw the monks like a pair of sacks
Lying in the stern, ragged bums, having nothing,
Free men.

"You" he said, "are the happy ones.
You laugh at life. You need nothing from the world
But a few rags, a crust of bread."

And one Macarius replied: "It is true,
We follow God. We laugh at life.
And we are sorry life laughs at you."

Then the officer saw himself as he was.
He gave away all that he had
And enlisted in the desert army.

A PICTURE OF LEE YING

She wears old clothes she holds a borrowed handker-
chief and her sorrow shows us the papers have bad
news again today Lee Ying only 19 has to return to
China

Days on foot with little or no food the last six days
on water alone now she must turn back

Three hundred thousand like her must turn back to
China there is no room say the officials in Hong
Kong you must go back where you came from

Point of no return is the caption but this is meaning-
less she must return that is the story

She would not weep if she had reached a point of no
return what she wants is not to return

There is no place for her and no point for thousands
like her there is no point

Their flight from bad news to worse news has caused
alarm

Refugees suffer and authorities feel alarm the press
does not take sides

We know all about the sorrow of Lee Ying one
glance is enough we look at something else

She must go back where she came from no more
need be said

Whenever the authorities are alarmed everyone must
return to China

We too know all about sorrow we have seen it in the
movies

You have our sympathy Miss Lee Ying you must go
where we are sorry for your future

Too bad some people get all the rough breaks the au-
thorities regret

Refugees from China have caused alarm

When the authorities are alarmed what can you do

You can return to China

Their alarm is worse than your sorrow

Please do not look only at the dark side in private
life these are kind men

They are only obeying orders

Over there is Red China where you will remain in
future

There also the authorities are alarmed and they too
obey orders

Please do not look only at the dark side

All the newspapers in the free world explain why you return their readers understand how you feel

You have the sympathy of millions

As a tribute to your sorrow we resolve to spend more money on nuclear weapons there is always a bright side

If this were only a movie a boat would be available have you ever seen our movies they end happily

You would lean at the rail with "him" the sun would set on China kiss and fade

You would marry one of the kind authorities

In our movies there is no law higher than love in real life duty is higher

You would not want the authorities to neglect duty

How do you like the image of the free world sorry you cannot stay

This is the first and last time we will see you in our papers

When you are back home remember us we will be having a good time

324

SONG FOR THE DEATH OF AVERROËS

(from Ibn Al Arabi, after the Spanish version of Asin Palacios)

i

My father sent me on an errand to the house of his friend Averroës, one of the cadis of the city, the great one, the wise Averroës, son of Aristotle.

Averroës had manifested a desire to see me and to learn if it were true that God had spoken to me in solitude.

So I came to the house of Averroës, in Cordova. I was still at that season so young that my beard had not grown, but God had spoken to me.

And when I entered the house of Averroës and reached the apartment in which he was engaged in thought,

He rose from the place where he was sitting and came towards me with affection and respect.

He took me in his arms and said in a questioning tone: "Yes?"

I said: "Yes."

My answer increased his joy.
For he saw that I had understood him right away.

But I realized the source of his satisfaction, and I said immediately: "No."

For though I had understood him, he had not understood me.

Then Averroës was overcome with distress. He turned
    pale.
He began at that moment to doubt.
The whole truth of his own teaching was now in
    question.

He asked me, then: "So, you have learned the an-
    swer: but how?
By the Spirit? By His Light? What answer?
Is it perhaps the same answer that we have learned
    from reason?"

I answered: "Yes and No.
Between the 'yes' and the 'no' spirits fly forth from
    matter,
Between 'yes' and 'no'
The living neck bone is set apart from flesh!"

Then Averroës grew very pale, and sat down in the
    grip of fear.
He seemed to be overcome by stupor
As though he had by chance
Caught the gist of my allusions.

326

Averroës, an eminent philosopher, dedicated entirely to a life of thought, study and rational investigation, could not but give thanks to God for having been permitted to live in a time when he might see with his own eyes a human being who had entered, ignorant, into the spiritual sanctuary and who had emerged as Averroës himself,

Without the help of any education, without study, without books, without teacher.

For this reason he exclaimed: "Here now is that spiritual state the existence of which we have long defended with rational proofs, without ever encountering anyone who had experience of it.

"Praise be to God who has made us live in this time when there exists one of those endowed with mystical gifts, one able to unlock His door, and praised be He for granting me, in addition, the favor of seeing one such person with my own eyes."

I desired to meet Averroës again, and by the mercy of God he was shown to me at a time when I was in ecstasy. But I saw him under such a form that there appeared to be between his person and myself a very thin curtain, through which I could observe him without his being able to see me, or to become aware of the place which I occupied.

There he was, in abstraction, thinking deeply within himself.

And I said: "It is true, then. There is no way by which he can be brought into the place where we others are."

iii

I never saw Averroës again until he died.

His death was in the year 595,* in a city of Morocco, and he was translated most solemnly to Cordova, the place of his sepulchre, where he lies today.

When the body of Averroës was brought once more to Spain, and when the people of Cordova were gathered to watch its return to the city of burial,

The coffin containing his remains was mounted on one side of a beast of burden. And on the other side, for counterweight, what did they hang but all the books Averroës had written!

I too was watching, in the company of the scholar Benchobair, and of my disciple, Benazzarach, the copyist.

Turning to us, the young one said: "Do you not observe what it is that hangs as counterweight to the

* of the Hegira

Master Averroës as he rides by? On one side goes the Master, and on the other side his works, that is to say the books which he composed!"

Then Benchobair explained: "No need to point it out, my son, for it is clearly evident! Blessed be thy tongue that has spoken it!"

I took careful note of this word of my disciple, and I set it apart for future meditation, as a reminder of this event.

For this was the word that held the secret of the occasion, the seed of truth, shown to the disciple, at the burial of Averroës:

I planted the seed within myself thus, in two verses:

> "On one side the Master rides: on the other side,
> his books.
> Tell me: his desires, were they at last fulfilled?"

Three of us friends together stood by and saw, when Averroës was brought to Cordova for burial.

Of these three, two are now gone. May God have pardoned them.

GRACE'S HOUSE

On the summit: it stands on a fair summit
Prepared by winds: and solid smoke
Rolls from the chimney like a snow cloud.
Grace's house is secure.

No blade of grass is not counted,
No blade of grass forgotten on this hill.
Twelve flowers make a token garden.
There is no path to the summit—
No path drawn
To Grace's house.

All the curtains are arranged
Not for hiding but for seeing out.
In one window someone looks out and winks.
Two gnarled short
Fortified trees have knotholes
From which animals look out.
From behind a corner of Grace's house
Another creature peeks out.

Important: hidden in the foreground
Most carefully drawn
The dog smiles, his foreleg curled, his eye like an
    aster.
Nose and collar are made with great attention:
This dog is loved by Grace!

And there: the world!
Mailbox number 5

Is full of Valentines for Grace.
There is a name on the box, name of a family
Not yet ready to be written in language.

A spangled arrow there
Points from our Coney Island
To her green sun-hill.

Between our world and hers
Runs a sweet river:
(No, it is not the road,
It is the uncrossed crystal
Water between our ignorance and her truth.)

O paradise, O child's world!
Where all the grass lives
And all the animals are aware!
The huge sun, bigger than the house
Stands and streams with life in the east
While in the west a thunder cloud
Moves away forever.

No blade of grass is not blessed
On this archetypal, cosmic hill,
This womb of mysteries.

I must not omit to mention a rabbit
And two birds, bathing in the stream
Which is no road, because

Alas, there is no road to Grace's house!

THERE HAS TO BE A JAIL FOR LADIES

There has to be a jail where ladies go
When they are poor, without nice things, and with
    their hair down.
When their beauty is taken from them, when their
    hearts are broken
There is a jail where they must go.

There has to be a jail for ladies, says the Government,
When they are ugly because they are wrong.
It is good for them to stay there a long time
Until the wrong is forgotten.

When no one wants to kiss them any more,
Or only wants to kiss them for money
And take their beauty away
It is right for the wrong to be unheard of for a long
    time
Until the ladies are not remembered.

But I remember one favorite song,
And you ladies may not have forgotten:
"Poor broken blossom, poor faded flower," says my
    song.

Poor ladies, you are jailed roses:
When you speak you curse, when you curse
God and Hell are rusted together in one red voice
Coming as sweet as dust out of a little hollow heart.
Is there no child, then, in that empty heart?

Poor ladies, if you ever sang
It would be brown notes and sad, from understand-
    ing too much
No amount of soapsy sudsy supersuds will make you
Dainty again and not guilty
Until the very end, when you are all forgotten.
There is a jail, where guilt is not forgotten.

Not many days, or many years of that stale wall, that
    smell of disinfectant
Trying, without wanting, to kill your sin
Can make you innocent again:
So I come with this sad song
I love you, dusty and sore,
I love you, unhappy ones.

You are jailed buttercups, you are small field flowers,
To me your voice is not brown
Nor is God rusted together with Hell.
Tell me, darlings, can God be in Hell?
You may curse; but He makes your dry voice turn to
    butter
(Though for the policeman it is still brown)
God becomes your heart's prisoner, He will laugh at
    judges.
He will laugh at the jail.
He will make me write this song.

Keep me in your pocket if you have one. Keep me in
    your heart if you have no pocket.

It is not right for your sorrow to be unknown for-
ever.
Therefore I come with these voices:

Poor ladies, do not despair—
God will come to your window with skylarks
And pluck each year like a white rose.

A DREAM AT ARLES ON THE NIGHT
OF THE MISTRAL

Arise, dusty shadow, Mars
Dark commander
To whom barbarians run
Dazed by this wind.

Tonight the heart is cold
And thirsty men must fall
To iron blows.

In moonlit smoke,
O red-eyed presence!
News of fury!

Behind the flying poplars,
Fires and horns,
Two twisting armies
Wound the incurable mind.

334

Through one small door
To get to the express
Away from dogs and wrecks
And spectral commanders:

Through one tight door
From the distracted heart's
Brothel and citadel,

Tonight the road is straight
And dark Sebastian,
(Was he an African soldier?)
Floats to death down wind
Like smoke, over the canals,
Over the cathedral at Narbonne.

AND THE CHILDREN OF BIRMINGHAM

And the children of Birmingham
Walked into the story
Of Grandma's pointed teeth
("Better to love you with")
Reasonable citizens
Rose to exhort them all:
"Return at once to schools of friendship.
Buy in stores of love and law."

(And tales were told
Of man's best friend, the Law.)

And the children of Birmingham
Walked in the shadow
Of Grandma's devil
Smack up against
The singing wall.
Fire and water
Poured over everyone:
"Hymns were extreme,
So there could be no pardon!"

And old Grandma
Began the lesson
Of everybody's skin,
Everybody's fun:
"Liberty may bite
An irresponsible race
Forever singing,"
Grandma said,
"Forever making love:
Look at all the children!"

(And tales were told
Of man's best friend, the Law.)

And the children of Birmingham
Walked into the fury
Of Grandma's hug:
Her friendly cells
("Better to love you with.")
Her friendly officers
And "dooms of love."

Laws had a very long day
And all were weary.

But what the children did that time
Gave their town
A name to be remembered!

(And tales were told
Of man's best friend, the Law.)

SONG FOR NOBODY

A yellow flower
(Light and spirit)
Sings by itself
For nobody.

A golden spirit
(Light and emptiness)
Sings without a word
By itself.

Let no one touch this gentle sun
In whose dark eye
Someone is awake.

(No light, no gold, no name, no color
And no thought:
O, wide awake!)

A golden heaven
Sings by itself
A song to nobody.

ADVICE TO A YOUNG PROPHET

Keep away, son, these lakes are salt. These flowers
Eat insects. Here private lunatics
Yell and skip in a very dry country.

Or where some haywire monument
Some badfaced daddy of fear
Commands an unintelligent rite.

To dance on the unlucky mountain,
To dance they go, and shake the sin
Out of their feet and hands,

Frenzied until the sudden night
Falls very quiet, and magic sin
Creeps, secret, back again.

Badlands echo with omens of ruin:
Seven are very satisfied, regaining possession:
(Bring a little mescaline, you'll get along!)

There's something in your bones,
There's someone dirty in your critical skin,

There's a tradition in your cruel misdirected finger
Which you must obey, and scribble in the hot sand:

"Let everybody come and attend
Where lights and airs are fixed
To teach and entertain. O watch the sandy people
Hopping in the naked bull's-eye,

Shake the wildness out of their limbs,
Try to make peace like John in skins
Elijah in the timid air
or Anthony in tombs:

Pluck the imaginary trigger, brothers.
Shoot the devil: he'll be back again!"

America needs these fatal friends
Of God and country, to grovel in mystical ashes,
Pretty big prophets whose words don't burn,
Fighting the strenuous imago all day long.

Only these lunatics, (O happy chance)
Only these are sent. Only this anaemic thunder
Grumbles on the salt flats, in rainless night:

O go home, brother, go home!
The devil's back again,
And magic Hell is swallowing flies.

SONG: IF YOU SEEK...

If you seek a heavenly light
I, Solitude, am your professor!

I go before you into emptiness,
Raise strange suns for your new mornings,
Opening the windows
Of your innermost apartment.

When I, loneliness, give my special signal
Follow my silence, follow where I beckon!
Fear not, little beast, little spirit
(Thou word and animal)
I, Solitude, am angel
And have prayed in your name.

Look at the empty, wealthy night
The pilgrim moon!
I am the appointed hour,
The "now" that cuts
Time like a blade.

I am the unexpected flash
Beyond "yes," beyond "no,"
The forerunner of the Word of God.

Follow my ways and I will lead you
To golden-haired suns,
Logos and music, blameless joys,
Innocent of questions
And beyond answers:

For I, Solitude, am thine own self:
I, Nothingness, am thy All.
I, Silence, am thy Amen!

SEVEN ARCHAIC IMAGES

I Primordial locutions and ventures:
A procession to the forest
(To Mother Chaos)
With bull-roarers and stone knives.

A procession to the caves
(To the beginning)
Womb of a secret hill
Paradise
Covered inside with animals.

II The magic door
Wide open.
Dance and fire.
Blood.

Yellow smoke goes straight up.

The solemn oath
Then, winds.

The smoke bends
And disappears.

(Talons of eagles
Black and blue thunder:
Desperation.)

III The cauldron.
North, south, east, west,
And in the center
The cauldron
Seething with enemies.

We eat.

IV Night council.
They stand together
Hiding the fire.

Night wind rustles
Their heavy wings
Firelight glitters
On the feathercoats.

The double axe
Shines.

O shapeless heads, (The Ancestors)
O nodding crowns of birds!
A magic answer!

V Winter morning: banners and snow.
They stand upon the monument
Living presences
Of the winged dead.

History begins again
With sacrifice.

Drums,
Banners and snow.

VI Feathered images
Of kings and heroes.
Monsters in pursuit.

Man-eating war
Shakes the land with drums:
The sacred enclosure
The house of omens and weapons.

Bring coins, jewels, women and victims,
Bring sacred whores
To the hieratic city.

O great dishonorable beast, War,
Cockroach and millionaire,
Snake-eyed cousin of pestilence
Why do we dance for you,
Why do we dance to exhaustion?

VII Music
The sadness of laws:
The toys of the gods
Dance.

O SWEET IRRATIONAL WORSHIP

Wind and a bobwhite
And the afternoon sun.

By ceasing to question the sun
I have become light,

Bird and wind.

My leaves sing.

I am earth, earth

All these lighted things
Grow from my heart.

A tall, spare pine
Stands like the initial of my first
Name when I had one.

When I had a spirit,
When I was on fire
When this valley was
Made out of fresh air
You spoke my name
In naming Your silence:
O sweet, irrational worship!

I am earth, earth

My heart's love
Bursts with hay and flowers.
I am a lake of blue air
In which my own appointed place
Field and valley
Stand reflected.

I am earth, earth

Out of my grass heart
Rises the bobwhite.

Out of my nameless weeds
His foolish worship.

CHANT TO BE USED IN PROCESSIONS AROUND A SITE WITH FURNACES

How we made them sleep and purified them

How we perfectly cleaned up the people and worked
a big heater

I was the commander I made improvements and
installed a guaranteed system taking account of hu-
man weakness I purified and I remained decent

How I commanded

I made cleaning appointments and then I made the travellers sleep and after that I made soap

I was born into a Catholic family but as these people were not going to need a priest I did not become a priest I installed a perfectly good machine it gave satisfaction to many

When trains arrived the soiled passengers received appointments for fun in the bathroom they did not guess

It was a very big bathroom for two thousand people it awaited arrival and they arrived safely

There would be an orchestra of merry widows not all the time much art

If they arrived at all they would be given a greeting card to send home taken care of with good jobs wishing you would come to our joke

Another improvement I made was I built the chambers for two thousand invitations at a time the naked votaries were disinfected with Zyklon B

Children of tender age were always invited by reason of their youth they were unable to work they were marked out for play

They were washed like the others and more than the others

346

Very frequently women would hide their children in the piles of clothing but of course when we came to find them we would send the children into the chamber to be bathed

How often I commanded and made improvements and sealed the door on top there were flowers the men came with crystals I guaranteed the crystal parlor

I guaranteed the chamber and it was sealed you could see through portholes

They waited for the shower it was not hot water that came through vents though efficient winds gave full satisfaction portholes showed this

The satisfied all ran together to the doors awaiting arrival it was guaranteed they made ends meet

How I could tell by their cries that love came to a full stop I found the ones I had made clean after about a half hour

Jewish male inmates then worked up nice they had rubber boots in return for adequate food I could not guess their appetite

Those at the door were taken apart out of a fully stopped love by rubber made inmates strategic hair and teeth being used later for defense

347

Then the males removed all clean love rings and made
away with happy gold

How I commanded and made soap 12 lbs fat 10
quarts water 8 oz to a lb of caustic soda but it was
hard to find any fat

A big new firm promoted steel forks operating on a
a cylinder they got the contract and with faultless
workmanship delivered very fast goods

"For transporting the customers we suggest using
light carts on wheels a drawing is submitted"

"We acknowledge four steady furnaces and an emer-
gency guarantee"

"I am a big new commander operating on a cylinder
I elevate the purified materials boil for 2 to 3 hours
and then cool"

For putting them into a test fragrance I suggested an
express elevator operated by the latest cylinder it was
guaranteed

Their love was fully stopped by our perfected ovens
but the love rings were salvaged

Thanks to the satisfaction of male inmates operating
the heaters without need of compensation our guests
were warmed

All the while I had obeyed perfectly

So I was hanged in a commanding position with a
full view of the site plant and grounds

You smile at my career but you would do as I did if
you knew yourself and dared

In my day we worked hard we saw what we did our
self-sacrifice was conscientious and complete our work
was faultless and detailed

Do not think yourself better because you burn up
friends and enemies with long-range missiles without
ever seeing what you have done

A MESSENGER FROM THE HORIZON

Look, a naked runner
A messenger,
Following the wind
From budding hills.

By sweet sunstroke
Wounded and signed,
(He is therefore sacred)
Silence is his way.

Rain is his own
Most private weather.
Amazement is his star.

O stranger, our early hope
Flies fast by,
A mute comet, an empty sun.
Adam is his name!

O primeval angel
Virgin brother of astonishment,
Born of one word, one bare
Inquisitive diamond.

O blessed,
Invulnerable cry,
O unplanned Saturday,
O lucky Father!

Come without warning
A friend of hurricanes,
Lightning in your bones!
We will open to you
The sun-door, the noble eye!

Open to rain, to somersaulting air,
To everything that swims,
To skies that wake,
Flare and applaud.

(It is too late, he flies the other way
Wrapping his honesty in rain.)

* * *

Pardon all runners,
All speechless, alien winds,
All mad waters.

Pardon their impulses,
Their wild attitudes,
Their young flights, their reticence.

When a message has no clothes on
How can it be spoken?

NIGHT-FLOWERING CACTUS

I know my time, which is obscure, silent and brief
For I am present without warning one night only.

When sun rises on the brass valleys I become serpent.

Though I show my true self only in the dark and to
        no man
(For I appear by day as serpent)
I belong neither to night nor day.

351

Sun and city never see my deep white bell
Or know my timeless moment of void:
There is no reply to my munificence.

When I come I lift my sudden Eucharist
Out of the earth's unfathomable joy
Clean and total I obey the world's body
I am intricate and whole, not art but wrought passion
Excellent deep pleasure of essential waters
Holiness of form and mineral mirth:

I am the extreme purity of virginal thirst.

I neither show my truth nor conceal it
My innocence is descried dimly
Only by divine gift
As a white cavern without explanation.

He who sees my purity
Dares not speak of it.
When I open once for all my impeccable bell
No one questions my silence:
The all-knowing bird of night flies out of my mouth.

Have you seen it? Then though my mirth has
    quickly ended
You live forever in its echo:
You will never be the same again.

LOVE WINTER WHEN THE PLANT
SAYS NOTHING

O little forests, meekly
Touch the snow with low branches!
O covered stones
Hide the house of growth!

Secret
Vegetal words,
Unlettered water,
Daily zero.

Pray undistracted
Curled tree
Carved in steel—
Buried zenith!

Fire, turn inward
To your weak fort,
To a burly infant spot,
A house of nothing.

O peace, bless this mad place:
Silence, love this growth.

O silence, golden zero
Unsetting sun

Love winter when the plant says nothing.

THE FALL

There is no where in you a paradise that is no place
    and there
You do not enter except without a story.

To enter there is to become unnameable.

Whoever is there is homeless for he has no door and
    no identity with which to go out and to come in.

Whoever is nowhere is nobody, and therefore cannot
    exist except as unborn:
No disguise will avail him anything

Such a one is neither lost nor found.

But he who has an address is lost.

They fall, they fall into apartments and are securely
    established!

They find themselves in streets. They are licensed
To proceed from place to place
They now know their own names
They can name several friends and know
Their own telephones must some time ring.

If all telephones ring at once, if all names are shouted
    at once and all cars crash at one crossing:
If all cities explode and fly away in dust

Yet identities refuse to be lost. There is a name and
    number for everyone.

There is a definite place for bodies, there are pigeon
    holes for ashes:
Such security can business buy!

Who would dare to go nameless in so secure a uni-
    verse?
Yet, to tell the truth, only the nameless are at home
    in it.

They bear with them in the center of nowhere the
    unborn flower of nothing:
This is the paradise tree. It must remain unseen until
    words end and arguments are silent.

TO ALFONSO CORTES

You stand before the dark
Wet night of leaves
In glasses and a witty hat
With a tropical guitar,
And the white crumpled
Clothes of sugar countries.
So droll, to be the mad
Saint of a hot republic!

You smile in a mist of years
Where your country has placed you
To think about the paper
You hold in your hand:
For critical services
At some unrecorded time
The Nation awards you
This empty room.

Have you noted in cryptograms
Upon the tiny white leaf
Some fortunate index,
Some sign of the age?

Or do you announce
A central tumult
Out of reach of their patrols?

No, you stand still
And you begin to smile
As you read rainbows
On the empty paper.

NEWS FROM THE SCHOOL
AT CHARTRES

I. Remember, master, I asked you
   To take this child Godfrey, my kinsman,
   And teach him in your school.

I asked you, for God's love and mine,
To say yes, and take him.

Your piety received my request
Kindly. You said
You consented to take him.
Not only that, but if necessary
He could read in your own books,

And you would faithfully see
To all his needs.
Now that I am far from there
Word has been brought me: he is shut
Out of your school, and idle.

So I appeal once more
To your heart's kindness:
Do keep your promise—
I beg you to. I beg you.
Farewell.

II. Dearest Father, here is our friend Harry.
Receive him kindly, be good to him.
Our clothes
Are laundered in his house
And his wife
Gives us our haircuts.

III. Sweet mother, get the monks' money
That they owe, and Lord Aymon's too
And send it soon with the monk Helyas.

I am having a psalter made;
I need some ducats.
You too, with what you owe,
Get two dozen sheets of parchment
And send them to me.
And as for you, little brother Jacques,
Come along with Helyas, the monk:
Come to Chartres and learn!

IV. Mother, in the same mail
  With the monks' money and parchment
  If you were also thinking
  Of our winter clothing
  Send some thick lamb skins
  And good parchment to make a psalter
  Also Father's heavy boots. Good-bye.
  Yes; and send chalk, good
  Good chalk.
  The chalk here won't write.

V. We have written little gloses
  And we owe money.
  I made a marvelous coat
  With those lamb skins
  But I owe money
  So you bring it, dear, with you
  When you come
  Or send it at the next fair.

VI. They say deep thoughts
  Cannot be put into words.

And I believe it
I am at such a peak
Of happiness I burst,
And have no words to burst with.
But I break my silence and say—
Dear friend, be well, be every bit as well
As I want you to be.
If you are well, then I am well too.
If you are content, I am content also.
So send me something your Muse
Says, of how you feel:
Send by some clerk's hand
News of your joy at Chartres,
To Chateaudun, to your own friend
And say you too are mine.

VII. Remember, brother,
To do all things wisely
And send to me, Aurelian, your friend
My little books, by this honest messenger.
Have you forgotten? We studied, as one person,
Looking together into the same book of Logic.

WHAT TO THINK WHEN IT
RAINS BLOOD

(After a letter of Fulbert of Chartres to King Robert,—XI Cent.)

I have been instructed by your sacred Majesty to ex-
amine the histories, and see if a rain of blood is

recorded, and to tell your Majesty what such rain portends.

I have found Livy, Valerius, Orosius and several others who relate a portent of this kind. But for the present let it suffice to summon one of them only as witness, Gregory, Bishop of Tours, because of the authority of his religious life.

This same Gregory declares, in the VI book of his histories, and the IV chapter: "In the seventh year of King Childebert, which was also the twenty first of Childeric and Guntran, in the middle of winter there was a summer downpour with lightning and frightful thunder.

Blossoms flowered on the trees. That star which I have before named 'comet' appeared again, having all around itself an inky darkness, so that the comet appeared to be looking out of a hole, glittering amid the shadows and shaking its long hair.

Then there went forth from it a ray of awful magniture which from afar looked like the smoke of a great fire. This was seen in the western sky in the first hour of the night.

Now on the holy day of Easter, in the city of Soissons, the sky was seen to burn, so that there appeared to be two conflagrations, the one greater and the other less. After the space of two hours these were joined together in one, and having been made into a huge signal-light, disappeared.

Then in the region of Paris true blood rained from a cloud and fell upon the garments of many persons, so soiling them that, stricken with horror at their own clothes, they tore them off and threw them away. And at three places within the city this prodigy appeared.

In the territory of Senlis, the house of a certain man, when he got up in the morning, was seen to be spattered all over, inside, with blood. And that year there was a great plague among the people.

Various illnesses, a honey-colored sickness, and also pustules and tumors caused the death of many. But others, who took care, lived.

We have also learned that in that year, in the city of Narbonne, a disease of the private parts raged so furiously that a man knew he was finished as soon as this punishment came upon him." Thus far Gregory of Tours.

It is evident therefore, from this and from the other histories I have mentioned, that a rain of blood foretells that thousands must soon perish in a great disaster.

Now if you have lately heard of this kind of rain falling upon a certain part of your kingdom,

And if you have learned that this blood-rain, falling on stone or on man's flesh, could not be washed away, Yet falling on wood could be washed away with ease: this seems to me to indicate three types of men.
The stones are impious men. Flesh represents fornicators. Wood, which is neither hard like stone nor soft like flesh, indicates those who are neither impious nor fornicators.

And therefore, when there shall descend upon those two kinds of men for whom it is predicted the sword of pestilence, designated by this rain of blood which sticks to them,
If they should be converted they will not be damned, dying for eternity in their blood.

As for those others to whom the blood-rain does not stick, they may well be set altogether free from their bondage by the anguish of death, or by some other means, according to the decision of the most secret and supreme Judge.

Farewell, religious King!

HAGIA SOPHIA

I. *Dawn. The Hour of Lauds.*

There is in all visible things an invisible fecundity, a dimmed light, a meek namelessness, a hidden wholeness. This mysterious Unity and Integrity is Wisdom, the Mother of all, *Natura naturans.* There is in all things an inexhaustible sweetness and purity, a silence that is a fount of action and joy. It rises up in wordless gentleness and flows out to me from the unseen roots of all created being, welcoming me tenderly, saluting me with indescribable humility. This is at once my own being, my own nature, and the Gift of my Creator's Thought and Art within me, speaking as Hagia Sophia, speaking as my sister, Wisdom.

I am awakened, I am born again at the voice of this my Sister, sent to me from the depths of the divine fecundity.

Let us suppose I am a man lying asleep in a hospital. I am indeed this man lying asleep. It is July the second, the Feast of Our Lady's Visitation. A Feast of Wisdom.

At five-thirty in the morning I am dreaming in a very quiet room when a soft voice awakens me from my dream. I am like all mankind awakening from all the dreams that ever were dreamed in all the nights of the world. It is like the One Christ awakening in all the separate selves that ever were separate and isolated and alone in all the lands of the earth. It is like all minds coming back together into awareness from all distractions, cross-purposes and confusions, into unity of love. It is like the first morning of the world (when Adam, at the sweet voice of Wisdom awoke from nonentity and knew her), and like the Last Morning of the world when all the fragments of Adam will return from death at the voice of Hagia Sophia, and will know where they stand.

Such is the awakening of one man, one morning, at the voice of a nurse in the hospital. Awakening out of languor and darkness, out of helplessness, out of sleep, newly confronting reality and finding it to be gentleness.

It is like being awakened by Eve. It is like being awakened by the Blessed Virgin. It is like coming forth from primordial nothingness and standing in clarity, in Paradise.

In the cool hand of the nurse there is the touch of all life, the touch of Spirit.

Thus Wisdom cries out to all who will hear (*Sapientia clamitat in plateis*) and she cries out particularly to the little, to the ignorant and the helpless.

Who is more little, who is more poor than the helpless man who lies asleep in his bed without awareness and without defense? Who is more trusting than he who must entrust himself each night to sleep? What is the reward of his trust? Gentleness comes to him when he is most helpless and awakens him, refreshed, beginning to be made whole. Love takes him by the hand, and opens to him the doors of another life, another day.

(But he who has defended himself, fought for himself in sickness, planned for himself, guarded himself, loved himself alone and watched over his own life all night, is killed at last by exhaustion. For him there is no newness. Everything is stale and old.)

When the helpless one awakens strong at the voice of mercy, it is as if Life his Sister, as if the Blessed Virgin, (his own flesh, his own sister), as if Nature made wise by God's Art and Incarnation were to stand over him and invite him with unutterable sweetness to be awake and to live. This is what it means to recognize Hagia Sophia.

II. *Early Morning. The Hour of Prime.*

O blessed, silent one, who speaks everywhere!

We do not hear the soft voice, the gentle voice, the merciful and feminine.

We do not hear mercy, or yielding love, or non-resistance, or non-reprisal. In her there are no reasons and no answers. Yet she is the candor of God's light, the expression of His simplicity.

We do not hear the uncomplaining pardon that bows down the innocent visages of flowers to the dewy earth. We do not see the Child who is prisoner in all the people, and who says nothing. She smiles, for though they have bound her, she cannot be a prisoner. Not that she is strong, or clever, but simply that she does not understand imprisonment.

The helpless one, abandoned to sweet sleep, him the gentle one will awake: Sophia.

All that is sweet in her tenderness will speak to him on all sides in everything, without ceasing, and he will never be the same again. He will have awakened not to conquest and dark pleasure but to the impeccable pure simplicity of One consciousness in all and through all: one Wisdom, one Child, one Meaning, one Sister.

The stars rejoice in their setting, and in the rising of the Sun. The heavenly lights rejoice in the going forth of one man to make a new world in the morning, because he has come out of the confused primordial dark night into consciousness. He has expressed the clear silence of Sophia in his own heart. He has become eternal.

III. *High Morning. The Hour of Tierce.*

The Sun burns in the sky like the Face of God, but we do not know his countenance as terrible. His light is diffused in the air and the light of God is diffused by Hagia Sophia.

We do not see the Blinding One in black emptiness. He speaks to us gently in ten thousand things, in which His light is one fulness and one Wisdom.

Thus He shines not on them but from within them. Such is the loving-kindness of Wisdom.

All the perfections of created things are also in God; and therefore He is at once Father and Mother. As Father He stands in solitary might surrounded by darkness. As Mother His shining is diffused, embracing all His creatures with merciful tenderness and light. The Diffuse Shining of God is Hagia Sophia. We call her His "glory." In Sophia His power is experienced only as mercy and as love.

(When the recluses of fourteenth-century England heard their Church Bells and looked out upon the wolds and fens under a kind sky, they spoke in their hearts to "Jesus our Mother." It was Sophia that had awakened in their childlike hearts.)

Perhaps in a certain very primitive aspect Sophia is the unknown, the dark, the nameless Ousia. Perhaps she is even the Divine Nature, One in Father, Son and Holy Ghost. And perhaps she is in infinite light unmanifest, not even waiting to be known as Light. This I do not know. Out of the silence Light is spoken. We do not hear it or see it until it is spoken.

In the Nameless Beginning, without Beginning, was the Light. We have not seen this Beginning. I do not know where she is, in this Beginning. I do not speak of her as a Beginning, but as a manifestation.

Now the Wisdom of God, Sophia, comes forth, reaching from "end to end mightily." She wills to be also the unseen pivot of all nature, the center and significance of all the light that is *in* all and *for* all. That which is poorest and humblest, that which is most hidden in all things is nevertheless most obvious in them, and quite manifest, for it is their own self that stands before us, naked and without care.

Sophia, the feminine child, is playing in the world, obvious and unseen, playing at all times before the Creator. Her delights are to be with the children of men. She is their sister. The core of life that exists in all things is tenderness, mercy, virginity, the Light, the Life considered as passive, as received, as given, as taken, as inexhaustibly renewed by the Gift of God. Sophia is Gift, is Spirit, *Donum Dei*. She is God-given and God Himself as Gift. God as all, and God reduced to Nothing: inexhaustible nothingness. *Exinanivit semetipsum*. Humility as the source of unfailing light.

Hagia Sophia in all things is the Divine Life reflected in them, considered as a spontaneous participation, as their invitation to the Wedding Feast.

Sophia is God's sharing of Himself with creatures. His outpouring, and the Love by which He is given, and known, held and loved.

She is in all things like the air receiving the sunlight. In her they prosper. In her they glorify God. In her they rejoice to reflect Him. In her they are united with him. She is the union between them. She is the Love that unites them. She is life as communion, life as thanksgiving, life as praise, life as festival, life as glory.

Because she receives perfectly there is in her no stain. She is love without blemish, and gratitude without self-complacency. All things praise her by being themselves and by sharing in the Wedding Feast. She is the Bride and the Feast and the Wedding.

The feminine principle in the world is the inexhaustible source of creative realizations of the Father's glory. She is His manifestation in radiant splendor! But she remains unseen, glimpsed only by a few. Sometimes there are none who know her at all.

Sophia is the mercy of God in us. She is the tenderness with which the infinitely mysterious power of pardon turns the darkness of our sins into the light of grace. She is the inexhaustible fountain of kindness, and would almost seem to be, in herself, all mercy. So she does in us a greater work than that of Creation: the work of new being in grace, the work of pardon, the work of transformation from brightness to brightness *tamquam a Domini Spiritu*. She is in us the yielding and tender counterpart of the power, justice and creative dynamism of the Father.

IV. *Sunset. The Hour of Compline. Salve Regina.*

Now the Blessed Virgin Mary is the one created being who enacts and shows forth in her life all that is hidden in Sophia. Because of this she can be said to be a personal manifestation of Sophia, Who in God is *Ousia* rather than Person.

Natura in Mary becomes pure Mother. In her, *Natura* is as she was from the origin from her divine birth. In Mary *Natura* is all wise and is manifested as an all-prudent, all-loving, all-pure person: not a Creator, and not a Redeemer, but perfect Creature, perfectly Redeemed, the fruit of all God's great power, the perfect expression of wisdom in mercy.

It is she, it is Mary, Sophia, who in sadness and joy, with the full awareness of what she is doing, sets upon the Second Person, the Logos, a crown which is His Human Nature. Thus her consent opens the door of created nature, of time, of history, to the Word of God.

God enters into His creation. Through her wise answer, through her obedient understanding, through the sweet yielding consent of Sophia, God enters without publicity into the city of rapacious men.

She crowns Him not with what is glorious, but with what is greater than glory: the one thing greater than glory is weakness, nothingness, poverty.

She sends the infinitely Rich and Powerful One forth as poor and helpless, in His mission of inexpressible mercy, to die for us on the Cross.

The shadows fall. The stars appear. The birds begin to sleep. Night embraces the silent half of the earth.

A vagrant, a destitute wanderer with dusty feet, finds his way down a new road. A homeless God, lost in the night, without papers, without identification, without even a number, a frail expendable exile lies down in desolation under the sweet stars of the world and entrusts Himself to sleep.

A LETTER TO PABLO ANTONIO
CUADRA CONCERNING GIANTS

At a moment when all the discordant voices of modern society attempt to exorcize the vertigo of man with scientific clichés or prophetic curses I come to share with you reflections that are neither tragic nor, I hope, fatuous. They are simply the thoughts of one civilized man to another, dictated by a spirit of sobriety and concern, and with no pretensions to exorcize anything. The vertigo of the twentieth century needs no permission of yours or mine to continue. The tornado has not consulted any of us, and will not do so. This does not mean that we are helpless. It only means that our salvation lies in understanding our exact position, not in flattering ourselves that we have brought the whirlwind into being by ourselves, or that we can calm it with a wave of the hand.

It is certainly true that the storm of history has arisen out of our own hearts. It has sprung unbidden out of the emptiness of technological man. It is the genie he has summoned out of the depths of his own confusion, this complacent sorcerer's apprentice who spends billions on weapons of destruction and space rockets when he cannot provide decent meals, shelter and clothing for two thirds of the human race. Is it improper to doubt the intelligence and sincerity of modern man? I know it is not accepted as a sign of progressive thinking to question the enlightenment of the twentieth century barbarian. But I no longer have any desire to be considered enlightened by the standards of the stool pigeons and torturers whose most signal claim to success is that they have built so many extermination camps and operated them to the limit of their capacity.

These glorious characters, revelling in paroxysms of collective paranoia, have now aligned themselves in enormous power blocs of which the most striking feature is that they resemble one another like a pair of twins. I had not clearly understood from Ezekiel that Gog and Magog were to fight one another, although I knew that they were to be overcome. I knew that their ponderous brutality would exhaust itself on the mountains of Israel and provide a feast for the birds of the air. But I had not expected we would all be so intimately involved in their downfall. The truth is that there is a little of Gog and Magog even in the best of us.

We must be wary of ourselves when the worst that is in man becomes objectified in society, approved, acclaimed and deified, when hatred becomes patriotism and murder a holy duty, when spying and delation are called love of truth and the stool pigeon is a public benefactor, when the gnawing and prurient resentments of frustrated bureaucrats become the conscience of the people and the gangster is enthroned in power, then we must fear the voice of our own heart, even when it denounces them. For are we not all tainted with the same poison?

That is why we must not be deceived by the giants, and by their thunderous denunciations of one another, their preparations for mutual destruction. The fact that they are powerful does not mean that they are sane, and the fact that they speak with intense conviction does not mean that they speak the truth. Nor is their size any proof that they possess a metaphysical solidity. Are they not perhaps spectres without essence, emanations from the terrified and puny hearts of politicians, policemen and millionaires?

We live in an age of bad dreams, in which the scientist and engineer possess the power to give external form to the phantasms of man's unconscious. The bright weapons that sing in the atmosphere, ready to pulverize the cities of the world, are the dreams of giants without a center. Their mathematical evolutions are hieratic rites devised by Shamans without belief. One is permitted to wish their dreams had been less sordid!

But perhaps they are also the emanations of our own subliminal self!

2

I have learned that an age in which politicians talk about peace is an age in which everybody expects war: the great men of the earth would not talk of peace so much if they did not secretly believe it possible, with *one more war,* to annihilate their enemies forever. Always, "after just one more war" it will dawn, the new era of love: but first everybody who is hated must be eliminated. For hate, you see, is the mother of their kind of love.

Unfortunately the love that is to be born out of hate will never be born. Hatred is sterile; it breeds

374

nothing but the image of its own empty fury, its own nothingness. Love cannot come of emptiness. It is full of reality. Hatred destroys the real being of man in fighting the fiction which it calls "the enemy." For man is concrete and alive, but "the enemy" is a subjective abstraction. A society that kills real men in order to deliver itself from the phantasm of a paranoid delusion is already possessed by the demon of destructiveness because it has made itself incapable of love. It refuses, *a priori,* to love. It is dedicated not to concrete relations of man with man, but only to abstractions about politics, economics, psychology, and even, sometimes, religion.

Gog is a lover of power, Magog is absorbed in the cult of money: their idols differ, and indeed their faces seem to be dead set against one another, but their madness is the same: they are the two faces of Janus looking inward, and dividing with critical fury the polluted sanctuary of dehumanized man.

Only names matter, to Gog and Magog, only labels, only numbers, symbols, slogans. For the sake of a name, a classification, you can be marched away with your pants off to be shot against a wall. For the sake of a name, a word, you can be gassed in a shower-bath and fed to the furnace to be turned into fertilizer. For the sake of a word or even a number they will tan your skin and make it into lampshades. If you want to get a job, make a living, have a home to live in, eat in restaurants and ride in vehicles with other human beings, you have to have a right classification: depending perhaps on the shape of your nose, the color of your eyes, the kink in your hair, the degree to which you are sunburned, or the social status of your grandfather. Life and death today depend on everything except what you *are*. This is called humanism.

Condemnation or rehabilitation have no connection with what you happen to have done. There is no longer any question of ethical standards. We may have been liberated from idealistic objectivity about "right and wrong." This timely liberation from ethical norms and laws enables us to deal with an ever increasing population of undesirables in much more efficient fashion. Attach to each one an arbitrary label, which requires no action on his part and no effort of thought on the part of the accuser. This enables society to get rid of "criminals" without the latter putting anyone to any kind of inconvenience by committing an actual crime. A much more humane and efficient way of dealing with crime! You benevolently shoot a man for all the crimes he *might* commit before he has a chance to commit them.

3

I write to you today from Magog's country. The fact that Magog is to me more sympathetic than Gog does not, I think, affect my objectivity. Nor does it imply a choice of category, a self-classification. Magog and I seldom agree, which is one reason why I write this letter. I must however admit I feel indebted to Magog for allowing me to exist, which Gog perhaps might not. Perhaps it is not to my credit that I half-trust the strain of idealism in Magog, accepting it uncritically as a sign that, for all his blatant, materialistic gigantism, he is still human. Certainly he tolerates in his clients elements of human poignancy, together with an off-beat frivolity which Gog could never comprehend. (Yet Gog, in the right mood, weeps copiously into his vodka.) Magog, on the whole, is not demanding. A little lip service has been enough at least up to the present. He does not require the exorbitant public confessions which are a prelude to disappearance in the realm of Gog. The pressure of Magog is more subtle, more gently persuasive, but no less universal. Yet disagreement is still tolerated.

Magog is in confusion, an easier prey than Gog to panic and discouragement. He is less crafty as a politician, and he is handicapped by a vague and uncomplicated system of beliefs which everyone can understand. Hence the whole world can easily see discrepancies betwen his ideals and actualities. Magog is more often embarrassed than Gog who entertains no objective ideals but only pays homage to a dialectical process by which anything, however disconcerting, can quickly be justified.

Gog, I believe, is fondly hoping that Magog will be driven to despair and ruin himself in some way before it becomes necessary to destroy him. But in any case he is giving Magog every opportunity to discredit himself in the eyes of the rest of the world, so that if he cannot be persuaded to put his own head in the gas oven, his destruction can be made to appear as no crime but as a benefit conferred on the whole human race.

But let me turn from Gog and Magog to the rest of men. And by "the rest of men" I mean those who have not yet committed themselves to the cause of one or the other of the champions. There are many, even within the power groups, who hate wars and hate the slogans, the systems and the official pronouncements of groups under whose dominance they live. But they seem to be able to do nothing about it. Their instinct to protest is restrained by the awareness that whatever they may say, however true, against one implacable power can be turned to good use by another that is even more inhuman. Even in protest one must be discreet, not only for the sake of saving one's skin, but above all for the sake of protecting the virginity of one's own protest against the salacious advances of the publicist, the agitator, or the political police.

4

Let me abandon my facetiousness, and consider the question of the world's future, if it has one. Gog and Magog are persuaded that it has: Gog thinks that the self-destruction of Magog will usher in the golden age of peace and love. Magog thinks that if he and Gog can somehow shoot the rapids of a cold war waged with the chemically pure threat of nuclear weapons they will both emerge into a future of happiness, the nature and the possibility of which still remain to be explained.

I for my part believe in the very serious possibility that Gog and Magog may wake up one morning to find that they have burned and blasted each other off the map during the night, and nothing will remain but the spasmodic exercise of automatic weapons still in the throes of what has casually been termed over-kill. The superogatory retaliation may quite conceivably affect all the neutrals who have managed to escape the main event, but it is still possible that the southern hemisphere may make a dazed and painful comeback, and discover itself alone in a smaller, emptier, better-radiated but still habitable world.

In this new situation it is conceivable that Indonesia, Latin America, Southern Africa and Australia may find themselves heirs to the opportunities and objectives which Gog and Magog shrugged off with such careless abandon.

The largest, richest and best developed single land-mass south of the Equator is South America. The vast majority of its population is Indian, or of mixed Indian blood. The white minority in South Africa would quite probably disappear. A relic of European stock might survive in Australia and New Zealand. Let us also hopefully assume the partial survival of India and of some Moslem populations in central and northern Africa.

If this should happen it will be an event fraught with a rather extraordinary spiritual significance. It will mean that the more cerebral and mechanistic cultures, those which have tended to live more and more by abstractions and to isolate themselves more and more from the natural world by rationalization, will be succeeded by the sections of the human race which they oppressed and exploited without the slightest appreciation for or understanding for their human reality.

Characteristic of these races is a totally different outlook on life, a spiritual outlook which is not abstract but concrete, not pragmatic but hieratic, intuitive and affective rather than rationalistic and aggressive. The deepest springs of vitality in these races have been sealed up by the Conqueror and Colonizer, where they have not actually been poisoned by him. But if this stone is removed from the spring perhaps its waters will purify themselves by new life and regain their creative, fructifying power. Neither Gog nor Magog can accomplish this for them.

Let me be quite succinct: the greatest sin of the European-Russian-American complex which we call "the West" (and this sin has spread its own way to China), is not only greed and cruelty, not only moral dishonesty and infidelity to truth, but above all *its unmitigated arrogance towards the rest of the human race*. Western civilization is now in full decline into barbarism (a barbarism that springs *from within itself*) because it has been guilty of a twofold disloyalty: to God and to Man. To a Christian who believes in the mystery of the Incarnation, and who by that belief means something more than a pious theory without real humanistic implications, this is not two disloyalties but one. Since the Word was made Flesh, God is in man. God is in *all men*. All men are to be seen and treated as Christ. Failure to do this, the Lord tells us, involves condemnation for disloyalty to the most fundamental of revealed truths. "I was thirsty and you gave me not to drink. I was hungry and you gave me not to eat . . ." (Matthew 25:42). This could be extended in every possible sense: and is meant to be so extended, all over the entire area of human needs, not only for bread, for work, for liberty, for health, but also for truth, for belief, for love, for acceptance, for fellowship and understanding.

One of the great tragedies of the Christian West is the fact that for all the good will of the missionaries and colonizers (they certainly meant well, and behaved humanly, according to their lights which were somewhat brighter than ours), they could not recognize that *the races they conquered were essentially equal to themselves and in some ways superior.*

It was certainly right that Christian Europe should bring Christ to the Indians of Mexico and the Andes, as well as to the Hindus and the Chinese: but where they failed was in their inability to *encounter Christ* already potentially present in the Indians, the Hindus and the Chinese.

Christians have too often forgotten the fact that Christianity found its way into Greek and Roman civilization partly by its spontaneous and creative adaptation of the pre-Christian natural values it found in that civilization. The martyrs rejected all the grossness, the cynicism and falsity of the cult of the state-gods which was simply a cult of secular power, but Clement of Alexandria, Justin and Origen believed that Herakleitos and Socrates had been precursors of Christ. They thought that while God had manifested himself to the Jews through the Law and the Prophets he had also spoken to the Gentiles through their philosophers. Christianity made its way in the world of the first century not by imposing Jewish cultural and social standards on the rest of the world, but by abandoning them, getting free of them so as to be "all things to all men." This was the great drama and the supreme lesson of the Apostolic Age. By the end of the Middle Ages that lesson had been *forgotten*. The preachers of the Gospel to newly discovered continents became preachers and disseminators of European culture and power. They did not enter into dialogue with ancient civilizations: they imposed upon them their own monologue and in preaching Christ they also preached themselves. The very ardor of their self-sacrifice and of their humility enabled them to do this with a clean conscience. But they had omitted to listen to the voice of Christ in the unfamiliar accents of the Indian, as Clement had listened for it in the Pre-Socratics. And now, today, we have a Christianity of Magog.

It is a Christianity of money, of action, of passive crowds, an electronic Christianity of loudspeakers and parades. Magog is himself without belief, cynically tolerant of the athletic yet sentimental Christ devised by some of his clients, because this Christ is profitable to Magog. He is a progressive Christ who does not protest against Pharisees or money changers in the temple. He protests only against Gog.

It is my belief that we should not be too sure of having found Christ in ourselves until we have found him also in the part of humanity that is most remote from our own.

Christ is found not in loud and pompous declarations but in humble and fraternal dialogue. He is found less in a truth that is imposed than in a truth that is shared.

5

If I insist on giving you my truth, and never stop to receive your truth in return, then there can be no truth between us. Christ is present "where two or three are gathered in my name." But to be gathered in the name of Christ is to be gathered in the name of the Word made flesh, of God made man. It is therefore to be gathered in the faith that God has become man and can be seen in man, that he can speak in man and that he can enlighten and inspire love in and through any man I meet. It is true that the visible Church alone has the official mission to sanctify and teach all nations, but no man knows that the stranger he meets coming out of the forest in a new country is not already an invisible member of Christ and perhaps one who has some providential or prophetic message to utter.

Whatever India may have had to say to the West she was forced to remain silent. Whatever China had to say, though some of the first missionaries heard it and understood it, the message was generally ignored as irrelevant. Did anyone pay attention to the voices of the Maya and the Inca, who had deep things to

383

say? By and large their witness was merely suppressed. No one considered that the children of the Sun might, after all, hold in their hearts a spiritual secret. On the contrary, abstract discussions were engaged in to determine whether, in terms of academic philosophy, the Indian was to be considered a rational animal. One shudders at the voice of cerebral Western arrogance even then eviscerated by the rationalism that is ours to-day, judging the living spiritual mystery of primitive man and condemning it to exclusion from the category on which love, friendship, respect, and communion were made to depend.

God speaks, and God is to be heard, not only on Sinai, not only in my own heart, but in the *voice of the stranger*. That is why the peoples of the Orient, and all primitive peoples in general, make so much of the mystery of hospitality.

God must be allowed the right to speak unpredictably. The Holy Spirit, the very voice of Divine Liberty, must always be like the wind in "blowing where he pleases" (John 3:8). In the mystery of the Old Testament there was already a tension between the Law and the Prophets. In the New Testament the Spirit himself is Law, and he is everywhere. He certainly inspires and protects the visible Church, but if we cannot see him unexpectedly in the stranger and the alien, we will not understand him even in the Church. We must find him in our enemy, or we may lose him even in our friend. We must find him in the pagan or we will lose him in our own selves, substituting for his living presence an empty abstraction. How can we

384

reveal to others what we cannot discover in them our-selves? We must, then, see the truth in the stranger, and the truth we see must be a newly living truth, not just a projection of a dead conventional idea of our own—a projection of our own self upon the stranger.

The desecration, de-sacralization of the modern world is manifest above all by the fact that the stranger is of no account. As soon as he is "displaced" he is completely unacceptable. He fits into no familiar category, he is unexplained and therefore a threat to complacency. Everything not easy to account for must be wiped out, and mystery must be wiped out with it. An alien presence interferes with the superficial and faked clarity of our own rationalizations.

6

There is more than one way of morally liquidating the "stranger" and the "alien." It is sufficient to destroy, in some way, that in him which is different and dis-concerting. By pressure, persuasion, or force one can impose on him one's own ideas and attitudes towards life. One can indoctrinate him, brainwash him. He is no longer different. He has been reduced to conform-ity with one's own outlook. Gog, who does nothing if not thoroughly, believes in the thorough liquidation of differences, and the reduction of everyone else to a carbon copy of himself. Magog is somewhat more quixotic: the stranger becomes part of his own screen of fantasies, part of the collective dream life which is manufactured for him on Madison Avenue and in

Hollywood. For all practical purposes, the stranger no longer exists. He is not even seen. He is replaced by a fantastic image. What is seen and approved, in a vague, superficial way, is the stereotype that has been created by the travel agency.

This accounts for the spurious cosmopolitanism of the naive tourist and travelling business man, who wanders everywhere with his camera, his exposure-meter, his spectacles, his sun glasses, his binoculars, and though gazing around him in all directions never sees what is there. He is not capable of doing so. He is too docile to his instructors, to those who have told him everything beforehand. He believes the advertisements of the travel agent at whose suggestion he bought the ticket that landed him wherever he may be. He has been told what he was going to see, and he thinks he is seeing it. Or, failing that, he at least wonders why he is not seeing what he has been led to expect. Under no circumstances does it occur to him to become interested in what is actually there. Still less to enter into a fully human rapport with the human beings who are before him. He has not, of course, questioned their status as rational animals, as the scholastically trained colonists of an earlier age might have done. It just does not occur to him that they might have a life, a spirit, a thought, a culture of their own which has its own peculiar individual character.

He does not know why he is travelling in the first place: indeed he is travelling at somebody else's suggestion. Even at home he is alien from himself. He is doubly alienated when he is out of his own atmosphere. He cannot possibly realize that the stranger has something very valuable, something irreplaceable to give him: something that can never be bought with money, never estimated by publicists, never exploited by political agitators: the spiritual understanding of a friend who belongs to a different culture. The tourist lacks nothing except brothers. For him these do not exist.

The tourist never meets anyone, never encounters anyone, never finds the brother in the stranger. This is his tragedy, and it has been the tragedy of Gog and Magog, especially of Magog, in every part of the world.

If only North Americans had realized, after a hundred and fifty years, that Latin Americans really existed. That they were really people. That they spoke a different language. That they had a culture. That they had more than something to sell! Money has totally corrupted the brotherhood that should have united all the peoples of America. It has destroyed the sense of relationship, the spiritual community that had already begun to flourish in the years of Bolivar. But no! Most North Americans still don't know, and don't care, that Brazil speaks a language other than Spanish, that all Latin Americans do not live for the siesta, that all do not spend their days and nights playing the guitar and making love. They have never awakened to the fact that Latin America is by and large culturally superior to the United States, not only on the level of the wealthy minority which has absorbed more of the sophistication of

Europe, but also among the desperately poor indigenous cultures, some of which are rooted in a past that has never yet been surpassed on this continent.

So the tourist drinks tequila, and thinks it is no good, and waits for the fiesta he has been told to wait for. How should he realize that the Indian who walks down the street with half a house on his head and a hole in his pants, is Christ? All the tourist thinks is that it is odd for so many Indians to be called Jesus.

7

So much for the modern scene: I am no prophet, no one is, for now we have learned to get along without prophets. But I would say that if Gog and Magog are to destroy one another, which they seem quite anxious to do, it would be a great pity if the survivors in the "Third World" attempted to reproduce their collective alienation, horror and insanity, and thus build up another corrupt world to be destroyed by another war. To the whole third world I would say there is one lesson to be learned from the present situation, one lesson of the greatest urgency: be unlike the giants, Gog and Magog. Mark what they do, and act differently. Mark their official pronouncements, their ideologies, and without any difficulty you will find them hollow. Mark their behavior: their bluster, their violence, their blandishments, their hypocrisy: by their fruits you shall know them. In all their boastfulness they have become the victims of their own terror, which is nothing but the emptiness of their own hearts. They claim to be humanists, they claim to know and love man. They have come to liberate man, they say. But they do not know what man is. They are themselves less human than their fathers were, less articulate, less sensitive, less profound, less capable of genuine concern. They are turning into giant insects. Their societies are becoming anthills, without purpose, without meaning, without spirit and joy.

What is wrong with their humanism? It is a humanism of termites, because without God man becomes an insect, a worm in the wood, and even if he can fly, so what? There are flying ants. Even if man flies all over the universe, he is still nothing but a flying ant until he recovers a human center and a human spirit in the depth of his own being.

Karl Marx? Yes, he was a humanist, with a humanist's concerns. He understood the roots of alienation and his understanding even had something spiritual about it. Marx unconsciously built his system on a basically religious pattern, on the Messianism of the Old Testament, and in his own myth Marx was Moses. He understood something of the meaning of liberation, because, he had in his bones the typology of Exodus. To say that he built a "scientific" thought on a foundation of religious symbolism is not to say that he was wrong, but to justify what was basically right about his analysis. Marx did not think only with the top of his head, or reason on the surface of his intelligence. He did not simply verbalize or dogmatize as his followers have done. He was still human. And they?

Ultimately there is no humanism without God. Marx thought that humanism had to be atheistic, and this was because he did not understand God any better than the self-complacent formalists whom he criticized. He thought, as they did, that God was an idea, an abstract essence, forming part of an intellectual superstructure built to justify economic alienation. There is in God nothing abstract. He is not a static entity, an object of thought, a pure essence. The dynamism Marx looked for in history was something that the Bible itself would lead us in some sense to understand and to expect. And liberation from religious alienation was the central theme of the New Testament. But the theme has not been understood. It has too often been forgotten. Yet it is the very heart of the mystery of the Cross.

8

It is not with resignation that I wait for whatever may come, but with an acceptance and an understanding which cannot be confirmed within the limits of pragmatic realism. However meaningless Gog and Magog may be in themselves, the cataclysm they will undoubtedly let loose is full of meaning, full of light. Out of their negation and terror comes certitude and peace for anyone who can fight his way free of their confusion. The worst they can do is bring death upon us and death is of little consequence. Destruction of the body cannot touch the deepest center of life.

When will the bombs fall? Who shall say? Perhaps

Gog and Magog have yet to perfect their policies and their weapons. Perhaps they want to do a neat and masterly job, dropping "clean" bombs, without fallout. It sounds clinical to the point of humanitarian kindness. It is all a lovely, humane piece of surgery. Prompt, efficacious, sterile, pure. That of course was the ideal of the Nazis who conducted the extermination camps twenty years ago: but of course they had not progressed as far as we have. They devoted themselves dutifully to a disgusting job which could never be performed under perfect clinical conditions. Yet they did their best. Gog and Magog will develop the whole thing to its ultimate refinement. I hear they are working on a bomb that will destroy nothing but life. Men, animals, birds, perhaps also vegetation. But it will leave buildings, factories, railways, natural resources. Only one further step, and the weapon will be one of absolute perfection. It should destroy books, works of art, musical instruments, toys, tools and gardens, but not destroy flags, weapons, gallows, electric chairs, gas chambers, instruments of torture or plenty of strait jackets in case someone should accidentally survive. Then the era of love can finally begin. Atheistic humanism can take over.

CABLES TO THE ACE
or
Familiar Liturgies of Misunderstanding
(1968)

For Robert Lax

"La mise en question du monde dans lequel nous sommes ne peut se faire que par la forme et non par une anecdote vaguement sociale ou politique."

A. Robbe-Grillet

PROLOGUE

You, Reader, need no prologue. Do you think these
Horatian Odes are all about you? Far from the new
wine to need a bundle. You are no bundle. Go advertise
yourself.

Why not more pictures? Why not more rhythms, mel-
ody, etc.? All suitable questions to be answered some
other time. The realm of spirit is two doors down the
hall. There you can obtain more soul than you are ready
to cope with, Buster.

The poet has not announced these mosaics on purpose.
Furthermore he has changed his address and his poetics
are on vacation.

He is not roaring in the old tunnel.

Go shake hands with the comics if you demand a preface.
My attitudes are common and my ironies are no less
usual than the bright pages of your favorite magazine.
The soaps, the smells, the liquors, the insurance, the
third, dull, gin-soaked cheer: what more do you want,
Rabble?

Go write your own prologue.

I am the incarnation of everybody and the zones of
    reassurance.

I am the obstetrician of good fortune. I live in the social
    cages of joy.

It is morning, afternoon or evening. Begin.

I too have slept here in my stolen Cadillac.

I too have understudied the Paradise swan.

May 1967

CABLES TO THE ACE

Lament of Ortega. The crowd has revolted. Now there are bathrooms everywhere. Life is exempt from every restriction!

1

Edifying cables can be made musical if played and sung by full-armed societies doomed to an electric war. A heavy imperturbable beat. No indication where to stop. No messages to decode. Cables are never causes. Noises are never values. With the unending vroom vroom vroom of the guitars we will all learn a new kind of obstinacy, together with massive lessons of irony and refusal. We assist once again at the marriage of heaven and hell.

2

A seer interprets the ministry of the stars, the broken gear of a bird. He tests the quality of stone lights, ashen fruits of a fire's forgotten service. He registers their clarity with each new lurch into suspicion. He does not regret for he does not know. He plots the nativity of the pole star, but it neither sets nor rises. Snow melts on the surface of the young brown river, and there are two lids: the petals of sleep. The sayings of the saints are put away in air-conditioned archives.

3

Decoding the looks of opposites. Writing down their silences. Words replaced by moods. Actions punctuated by the hard fall of imperatives. More and more smoke. Since language has become a medium in which we are totally immersed, there is no longer any need to say anything. The saying says itself all around us. No one need attend. Listening is obsolete. So is silence. Each one travels alone in a small blue capsule of indignation. (Some of the better informed have declared war on language.)

4

Letters to a corridor: "Put the whole family out into the hall." (Plato) Now they are outside receiving those hard cosmic cables without interception.
Ideas, productions, answers: sand in the eye. He who has the most sand in his eye thinks he sees everything. It is written: "To see the world in a grain of sand."
Science, Politics, Theology: sandstorms.
Does anybody sing? Some will try the following hymn.

5

Gem notes
Of the examiner
Or terminal declarations:

The Directors
Have engineered a surprise
You will not easily discover:

(Escape in a carload
Of irritated pets
Before the examination)

Come shyly to the main question
There is dishonor in these wires
You will first hesitate then repeat
Then sing louder
To the drivers
Of ironic mechanisms
As they map your political void

You will be approved
By parakeets and lights
For many original
Side-effects
Each nominal conceit
Will be shot down by an electric eye
Your poem is played back to you
From your own trump card

Until all titles are taken away
Events are finally obscure forever
You wake and wonder
Whose case history you composed
As your confessions are filed
In the dialect
Of bureaux and electrons.

6

You taught me language and my profit on't
Is, I know how to curse. The red plague rid you
For learning me your language!

(Caliban)

7

ORIGINAL SIN

(A MEMORIAL ANTHEM FOR FATHER'S DAY)

Weep, weep, little day
For the Father of the lame
Experts are looking
For his name

Weep, weep little day
For your Father's bone
All the expeditions
Dig him one.

He went on one leg
Or maybe four
Science (cautious)
Says "Two or more."

Weep weep little day
For his walking and talking
He walked on two syllables
Or maybe none

Weep little history
For the words he offended
One by one
Beating them grievously
With a shin bone.

8

Write a prayer to a computer? But first of all you have
to find out how It thinks. *Does It dig prayer?* More

important still, does It dig me, and father, mother, etc., etc.? How does one begin: "O Thou great unalarmed and humorless electric sense . . ."? Start out wrong and you give instant offense. You may find yourself shipped off to the camps in a freight car. Prayer is a virtue. But don't begin with the wrong number.

9

"I am doubted, therefore I am. Does this mean that if I insist on making everybody doubt me more, I will become more real? It is enough to doubt them back. By this mutual service we make one another complete. A metaphysic of universal suspicion!" (These words were once heard, uttered by a lonely, disembodied voice, seemingly in a cloud. No one was impressed by them and they were immediately forgotten.)

10

Warm sun. Perhaps these yellow wild-flowers have the minds of little girls. My worship is a blue sky and ten thousand crickets in the deep wet hay of the field. My vow is the silence under their song. I admire the woodpecker and the dove in simple mathematics of flight. Together we study practical norms. The plowed and planted field is red as a brick in the sun and says: *"Now my turn!"* Several of us begin to sing.

11

What do you teach me
Mama my cow?
(My delicate forefathers
Wink in their sleep)

"Seek advancement
Then as now
And never learn to weep!"

What do you want of me
Mama my wit
(While the water runs
And the world spins)
"All the successful
Ride in their Buicks
And grow double chins"

What do you seek of me
Mama my ocean
(While the fire sleeps
In well baked mud)
"Take your shotgun
And put it in the bank
For money is blood."

12

Another sunny birthday. I am tormented by poetry and
loss. The summer morning approaches with shy, tenta-
tive mandibles. There are perhaps better solutions than
to be delicately eaten by an entirely favorable day. But
the day is bright with love and with riches for the un-
concerned. A black butterfly dances on the blond light
of hot cement. My loneliness is nourished by the smell
of freshly cut grass, and the distant complaint of a
freight train. Nine even strokes of the bell fall like a
slowly counted fortune into the far end of my mind
while I walk out at the other end of awareness into a
very new hot morning in which all the symbols have to

be moved. Here is another smiling Jewish New Year
and the myths are about to be changed. We will start up
brand new religious engines in the multiple temples.
Tonight the dark will come alive with fireworks and
age will have scored another minor festival.

13

(THE PLANET OVER EASTERN PARKWAY)

In the region of daffodils
And accurate fears
We seek the layout
The scene of claims

We expect 8 A.M.
With cries of racers
"Here is the entrance
To the start"

And the smart pistol
Glints in the eyes
Of an eternal chief
He sees executives
Begin to run
Over fresh cut graves
The whole civic order
Of salads
Blest and green
By order of the town.

Then the machine
With sterling efforts
Keeps in trim

In tune with oil
Though it needs essential grooves
Say the keepers

And you are always turning it off
Says the owner.

So now it is over
The day of executions
Malfeasances are over and done
In all the books of law

And the cart wheel planet
Goes down in the silos of earth
Whose parkways vanish in the steam
Of ocean feeling
Or the houses of oil-men

Go home go home
And get your picture taken
In a bronze western
An ocean of free admissions
To the houses of night
To the sandy electric stars
And the remaining adventures
Of profiteers.

14

Some may say that the electric world
Is a suspicious village
Or better a jungle where all the howls
Are banal.

NO! The electric jungle is a village
Where howling is not suspicious:
Without it we would be afraid
That fear was usual.

15

They improve their imitable wire
To discover where speech
Is trying to go.

They guess it goes
To the sign of the ear
Talking of portable affairs

Splitting into little mills
Of magnets and seconds
The everlasting carbon vine
A smooth investigation

Paying off into all the vessels and portholes
Of known lawgivers
Who learn the time of the carrier
And the arriver

Relaxed war-gods
Unlock the newest ministry of doors
With capital letters

The seeing line discovers dread
Tracks silvery doom's
Inventive car

Through all electric walks
And expert lights
It commands dawn riders

Lenses discover blue flame
In the mouths
Of fatal children

Parades and takeovers
Follow the parable
Wherever normal.

16

Let choirs of educated men compose
Their shaken elements and present academies of
     electronic renown
With better languages. Knowing health
And marital status first of all they must provide
Automatic spelling devices or moneymaking
Conundrums to program
The next ice-age from end-to-end
In mournful proverbs

Let such choirs intone
More deep insulted shades
That mime the arts of diction
Four-footed metaphors must then parade
Firm resolution or superb command
Of the wrong innuendo

You may indeed be given free of charge
An uninhibited guess
Three pensive norms

But no norm is necessary
For scholars and ages.

Then in the last resort suggestions
Will be wishful and make up erratic formulas
To obtain the best vowel or most
Expensive consonant

If you agree in the end
That in most cases
The best word of all is "ONLY"

17

How it can be done
Without delay

We are seeking ambitious men
Who have captured the sheer fascination
Of Marcus Aurelius
Havelock Ellis and the Marquis de Sade.

We can afford
Top pliable males
Who have always been boys at heart
Drag-racing through darkest Esquire.
Ready to become style leaders
And medium shapes
Hard as nails
Mean as the half-stewed owls we detest

Taking double-breasted advice
On barbells and heart-attacks
With friendliness and sex
At instant command

Able to afford
New areas of mind
With habit frequency and jags
And breathless weekends
Of instant mind-power
For the unusual partner
Or the executive bald on top
But ready to switch
And meet the challenge
Of the next instant
Always looking
Six inches taller.

18

He speaks cautiously to the Tea phone when it invites. He considers the velleities of sixty. He has biblical manners up his sleeve, this Old Master. He will often eat fresh flowers. He is without imperative urges. He worries in his sleep; worries about the code. When he wakes he will have forgotten all his lines. Can such a one have presence of mind? His sons will not be as he is for he is never strange.

19

Studies of man's friendly competitor the rat have shown
That pencils of control can find
Ways out for the withdrawn

Methods are right here says Dr. A for one
(Hiding the sockets in a troubled
Man whose friendly competitor the rat
Is pressing buttons and having fun.)

Man's friendly rat the competitor can prove
Wearing a cap on the vulnerable skull
That the absence of any motive is itself a mover

(*He suddenly looked around*
He spoke out loud
He met and talked with normal
Minds and research

Found fifty persons all with wires in the pleasure center
They were being moved by rats.)

There was more bliss in the tingling doorbell
Of long dead reward
Another man had periodic spells
And even ecstasies
Could he help it if the rat
Kept pressing?
It was a joy
For epileptics to wire
Home to their dead fathers
A long-distance call
Via your own brain
It is like a good feeling but where will it end?

Split second doses of motivation
Keep you in stitches
The potential is enormous
And the pointless smile
Will freeze without delay
An entire parlor

After warning the rat
He worked his own button to death

Back went the fires of ecstasy
And blew the rat sky-high.

Will my rat ever recover?
Will he call again
Ringing the septal region
That earthly
Paradise in the head
Two millimeters away
From my sinus infection?

Political man must learn
To work the pleasure button
And cut off the controlling rat
Science is very near but the morbid
Animal might always win

"It works like a bomb he declared after"

For a split second the competitor beams
All the lighted winners
Suddenly shine together
Like a big city
And at the end of the line stands Santa Claus
With his "Ho-ho" friendly to man

Maybe it could last
If the defender's smile
Were fixed in place by a
Clever surgeon

It can be made to last on rats
Studies of man's friendly competitor the rat

Have shown.

20a

To sons: not to be numb.

Be a lone dog
Little brother
And paddle
Down the crowded street
With sleet in your eye
Killing all the Fathers
With your cigarette.
In the lobbies
And elevators
Be a cloud of hailstones
A visible episode
Or a migrant flame
Feeding on nothing
An anti-prophet
A dry homeless tree
With a knife in your side
And many skinny years to die in
As a life member of the unemployed.

20b

To daughters: to study history.

Finn, Finn
Tribal and double
Wide awake rocks
The fatal craft
Cutlash Finn
To kill time
Before and aft—
Er he sinks his fin
Again in his
Own Wake.

21

Next! The Guards hitch up their belts and look around
for another one who has been lazy, ineffective. Another
one who has shirked duty (and ALL have shirked it).
Political malingerers evading their obligation to believe
in the GREAT MEANING and to work at this belief,
purifying it of personal idiosyncrasy, doubt, guilty reser-
vations, etc. (Some still cultivate attachments and loyal-
ties which are opposed to the GREAT MEANING.)
The Guards hitch up their belts and look around. It is
their duty to teach. They will not hold back or neglect
their work. All their disciplines will *speak!*

22

Twelve smoky gates flame with mass-demonstrations.
Power of Caliban. Mitres of blood and salt. Buildings
     as well-run machines with eyes and teeth (Bosch).
Love the inevitable! Hate alone is perfectly secure in its
     reasons.
Over the door of Hell is written: *"Therefore!"*

23

Rock shot chasms
Promise unplanned flight
Little or no support
Choice is led
Out of bounds
Over the edge:
A slight change
The way is vague
Directions not precise
One method might be
To grow wings in time

And overplay
There is no right
Or wrong way
Here is only theory
The cultivation of air
In all the finals
Results will be awarded
Cheerful names.

24

Bernstein! Can you still hear me? Are you conscious?
(Leaning over ears. Talking to all the cities.)

25

Elastic programs to draft nonspecialist energy and rotate
funds to speedup intake of output: an imperial takeoff!

26

Corporate posture: variables of fat. Move payloads from
room to room. The vulgar replies of the ill tempered
clavicle: imported drinks on a mandatory and immov-
able base. But smiling. Management in the lump is fitted
out for meetings. Roomy handshakes amid displays and
breakthroughs. "We can definitely secure government
aid for Santa Claus!" This way we can be our own
news as well as read it.

27

"Hats off," cried the midget. "Hats off to the human
condition!"

28

The wounded football hero
Is nominated to share
In the human condition
Which he smilingly calls
"Straight fact."

His monumental force
With lovable drives and loads
Now gains at last
A prizewinner's compassion.
The media will name him
Like the name of some big building
Others will call him "Sandy" and
The "Polo King" or just "Mister Charlie"
He will be the leader in handouts
And a high school Socrates
Just as much at home
With the kids on the road
As with the capsule in the stars
Smiling out of all the groggy news prints
In the front seat or in the rumpus room.

And everybody knows
Why they gave him a name
Like some big building
Nominated to share
In the human condition:

*He is coming
To investigate.*

29

Since you and I became engines
Undamaged by blast or heat
Meeting the long curves
With royal welcome and style
We have wandered wherever we went
And filmed the latest effect
Of cartridge rivals

Since we began to be glad
With economy and popular acclaim
We knew sheer action pleasure
Was the nicest thing about owning
Our obsolete
Round-trip invention
Since we gained speed
And turned bright-green in space
We went backstage and met
The legend of air-cooled impulse
In time to regret it

Since when we have become umpires.

30

Morning
The chatter of meats
In jail and color bar
Nine o'clock boil
Traffic and coffee
Funerals in the shade of power
Crowds
Move in cotton mist

And chloroform
Slowly consumes
The energy of motors
An electric goat's head
Turns and smiles
Turns and smiles
Ten stories high
Emerald and gold
But a clergyman goes by
With a placard
"You can still win."
Night sanctuaries
Imaginary refuge
Full of flowers
Dimly lighted bottles
The solemn twittering of news
Names Omens Tunnels
Time to walk
Trustfully
Beside the killer
The image in the magic
Dark tree
The iron voice in the next apartment
Cries NOW
And you flush the toilet.

31

That's the girl in the middle, the one who will show you
her four nude feet any time. Yes, it's swingy tonight in
moongarden ten. But don't blush or run. What is blame
to a scrappy little sweetie like her? Tell 'em hon'. Come
and scud along down with "Bonnie Braes" and beam a
kiss to old vampire Tsars up yonder. You'll swell till

you go down again and it's time to swing out with the
goodest little sonnysmokers and talk hips to this affluent
Monster. Or cool it with a lucky crumb. Someday you'll
see it, though they claim that's not possible: Beach tem-
po fighting the guitars for the dawn cigarette in the gates
of an enemy factory. That's certain. It's all in the full
knowledge of Uncle Sled. Trained lions can tell there's
another heavy-duty load on the way, yes, loaded with
double fun. And Swedes, too, Swedes from the local
cooperation!

32

Don't go unhappy
To the ultraviolet home

You will be met at the next detour
By a squad car
Full of heroes

Now the psycho-
Electric jump
Into spasm:
A ticking spark

Feels great
Kills the snakes
And the odor of heresy

Now meet and kiss
The civic spirit
Marry virtue
In the nearest available alley

Handout
Bluegreen leaflets
Double meanings
A liberal beginning

While the Commander
And all the heroes
Stand around
In good condition.

33

Sartre said Francis Ponge had a moss-complex. Francis
Ponge should have replied that Sartre had a root-com-
plex. But they were not calling each other names. Nor
will I call them names either. We all have the same
anxieties—but we do not use the same words. Sartre
thinks words are saliva. Sartre must have a slobber-
complex. Actually of course all the words are gendarmes
and they stand around us in good condition. But Ponge
delights in his anxiety of cities, seeing them as shells,
skulls, bones, hardened secretions, rarely as pearls. Ang-
kor and Nimes turned out to be shells that were better
than oysters. And what of New York? "Let man," says
Ponge "trim down his words (or shells) to his own size
and do without a monument."

34

The sweetgum avenue leads to a college of charm
Where nubile swimmers learn to value
The exercise of pendulums
And join a long line
Of unreliable dials

For a nominal fee one can confide in a cryphone
With sobs of champagne
Or return from sudden sport to address
The monogag
The telefake
The base undertones of the confessional speaker
Advising trainees
Through cloistered earphones.

Oh the blue electric palaces of polar night
Where the radiograms of hymnody
Get lost in the fan!

The followers of St. Radegund
Rise like one man
On escalators to the new creation
The safe home base of the thunder
The stores of mildest snow
And the liturgical top floor where the future of art
Is revealed to knowers
In corduroy cathedrals.

35

Je vous lis les sonnets d'un capitaine aveugle. Il a les yeux
pleins de beaujolais. Il chante le partage des communions
electriques. L'or et l'argent tintent au sommet du Build-
ing *in extremis*.

C'est l'heure des chars fondus dans le noir de la cité.
Dans les caves, les voix sourdes des taureaux mal rêvés!
l'océan monte dans les couloirs de l'oeil jusqu'à la lu-
mière des matins: et ils sont là, tous les deux: le Soleil
et le Franc-Tireur.

* For the English translation, by William Davis, see below, p. 823.

Poseidon embourbé mange les drapeaux sur la scène des guerres. Il contemple les ruines qu'il aime. Il considère les lois du naufrage. Il médite le commerce des algues. Il entend le son des perles.

Le jour douteux s'embrase à mesure des exhalations. C'est suprême! Le petit feu des argots consume les entretiens. C'est l'escalier orné de questions futiles qui conduit au Magistrat installé sur les étages les plus informes de la pensée. Message féminin! Tu nous attends dans le miroir obscur. Tu nous fais adorer les marchandises des astres, les dynamismes babyloniens.

Descendus de la scène des anges, les mots propres se cherchent parmi les hirondelles.

Platon est là avec les girls. Il les écoute. Il les encourage. Il reste inconnu. L'art devient propice aux cirques d'hiver. Dans la vallée des pleurs, le championnat du smile.

Vers l'abîme: les yeux de fer, les lampes ailées, les fuites autour du pôle. Le soleil brun des antipodes est armé de flèches. Il poursuit l'oiseau candide en fil-de-fer plumé d'orages. C'est l'instant du nerf qui éclate. Le bloc sourd de la sensation. Enfer intime du verbe neutre. L'oiseau se pose enfin sur le dôme des foudres.

Beauté hirsute de l'arsenal réveillé! Le petit barbu, le consul de cuivre, mâche les fumées insondables. Il contemple les arcs-boutants, les ponts navrés, les boucs en folie. Ce sont des enfants du cycle: des marins volages.

419

Il a vu le feu de ses narines, la flamme du socle. Amateur! Il revêt son manteau bordé de sang. Il marche à travers les cibles. Gavé de peines il respire la montée du sel. Il entre dans le traffic des noces. Il y est englouti tout plein de chansons païennes.

La mer Rouge des Pharaons, où le spectacle disparaît dans un chômage de vues, disparition des bien pensants! Les hiéroglyphes essaiment dans les temples du poulpe. Le sacerdoce masqué se promène encore au fond des mers à la recherche d'un Moïse perdu.

Les Mamans. Elles vivent sur les toits. Elles forment les petits oiseaux. Elles ont compris la sagesse de l'oeuf. Elles te proposent la patience et le délire. Elles te sourient au moment de ton choix. Ne choisis pas le neutre. Le front vendu ne te regarde pas O fleurs! signes du plaisir!

La tortue est fière de ses joyaux. Elle étend ses paumes pour les montrer à la pluie.

Fantoche traqué dans la givre voyeuse! Tu nous a embaumés comme des vers à soie. Va-t-on chercher ton Apocalypse dans les souterrains peu connus?

Je m'assieds dans mon champ vert comme un diamant tranquille. J'aborde le domaine bleu de l'air nu. Lumière et somme: la musique est une joie inventée par le silence. Pâquerettes. Toute une géographie de petites filles inconnues dans l'herbe. Charme des monstres enfantins. J'écoute le bourdon rouge des étés, le messager des temps sonores.

Nuage et testament. Je me tais à l'ombre des larmes. Je plains le muscle inutile qui crie: "Moi."

La frontière. Un peu plus loin. Elle est vert-clair. Le sommet. Rien! Les jeunes filles silencieuses entrent dans l'ombre par la porte des élues.

36

Eve moves: golden Mother of baroque lights. She visits a natural supermarket of naked fruits. She wings her perfumes. Le poil humide de ses aisselles. T. S. Eliot is vexed and cannot look.

37

The perfect act is empty. Who can see it? He who forgets form. Out of the formed, the unformed, the empty act proceeds with its own form. Perfect form is momentary. Its perfection vanishes at once. Perfection and emptiness work together for they are the same: the coincidence of momentary form and eternal nothingness. Form: the flash of nothingness. Forget form, and it suddenly appears, ringed and reverberating with its own light, which is nothing. Well, then: stop seeking. Let it all happen. Let it come and go. What? Everything: i.e., nothing.

38

Follow the ways of no man, not even your own. The way that is most yours is no way. For where are you? Unborn! Your way therefore is unborn. Yet you travel. You do not become unborn by stopping a journey you have begun: and you cannot be nowhere by issuing a decree: "I am now nowhere!"

39

"No man can see God except he be blind, or know him except through ignorance, nor understand him except through folly" (Eckhart).

40

Good Morning! Address more inspections to the corporate tunnels. Yours truly.

41

Approved prospect of chairs with visitors to the hero. Temperature is just comfortable for a variety of skins. It is with our skins here that we see each other all around and feel together. We are not overheated, we smell good and we remain smooth. No skin needs to be absolutely private for all are quiet, clean, and cool. The right fragrance is so right it is not noticed. The cool of the whole area is like that of a quiet car and presences. No one is really ailing and no one is quite that tired. See the pictures however for someone elsewhere who is really tired. Hear the sound of the music for someone who is relaxed (with an undercurrent of annoyance). She is glad to be sitting down with her limbs as if her long legs were really hers and really bare. This year the women all worry about their skirts. But she is well arranged. Whether they walk or sit they manage to be well arranged. In any case all is springlike with the scent of very present young women which with all our skin we recognize. Nothing is really private yet each remains alone and each pretends to read a magazine. But each one still smuggles a secret personal question across the frontiers of everybody: the skin of the body and the presence of the scent and the general arrangement. Nothing is out of place or disapproved. One by one each skin will visit the hero.

42

Listen with a tremor to the aero-captain
Who cries: "Try harder!"

And the undaunted martial amputee
Swings in the sky his mountainous limb
For an artificial twelve mile gain
Today, today he is sworn in
As player and caller
Victor and frenzy
By the wild thousands
In their after dinner swoon.

Listen with a tremor to the aero-captain
Who cries: "Do it harder and go further!"

Then will the clever mechanic of haloes
Footprint over again the gameleg ball

By way of exception
The basketface hero
Snores an aero-dream
And hears his own captain exclaim
"I nominate your lost member
This year's leader in profit and loss
In saving common sense
By reason of high flight
Superlative reach
And uncommonly
Spacious habit."

"Strive more imposingly but only at the edges"
Cries the aero-voice!

43

Let us cool your bitter sweet charm with incense and verse
Praising our own comparison with a rich pigment
A new glaze of ours to make you the piquant
Awareness of yourself as enriched with our orchid temper
Mated to our lubricant to melt away
Stubborn little worries known as lines
To restore with magic lanolin our flawless picture of
   YOU
Yes you, our own pity-making sweet charade of oils
We love you with ease on immediate contact
Melting all the tell-tales and sorries
Refuting secret age with our petals of discipline
Our tender departures and unstuck pageantries
And always every day brand new reasons
For not despairing of your own
Fragrant velours.

We will make you into an air-conditioned wishing well
Afloat or abroad we will decorate your
Favorite place with monograms of daring souls
And instant specialists of flavor charm and grace
To win you baroque lawns
And crystal suitings
For your (day off) *Samedi du plaisir.*

44

Future of transgression. It is in the homes of Caliban.
A splendid confusion of cries. Politics of the inflexible
moon-calf. A martial display of bulldozers. Dull energies

in the dust of collapsing walls. Loose minds love the
public muscles of death.

45

(PRAYER TO SAINT ANATOLE)

Anatole Anatole the long jets
String their hungry harps
Across the storm
When everybody cries
In the chemical flame

Anatole Anatole the giant
Fivestar Generals
Riot and War
Bring us in fast cars
To the fire's Republic

To sing their loud
Steel tunes
Those burning blues
For body and soul
Saint Anatole

Anatole Anatole
The fairy bombers
The fatal recorders
The electric lyres.

46

Milton's fiends—Republican, bituminous—begin their
scenarios in the dark stink of burning gasoline. Batman,
the hero of hell, plots the ruin of New York. He has this
advantage: he cannot be consumed by fire.

47

Now the unruly knowing
Weather vane may falter
And be a bad actor
On the encrusted stilt
Of a newly serene
Mind-reading danger

Now the observer tells a lie
Or fixes the marred eye
Of unreflected sin
Inflames the conscious
Bleeding lights
Of so many full freeways
Out of a very ready city

Oh he severely conns
All interested railways
In the heavenly darkness!

He announces the blood-red minute
To go down to get in the earth
To be tightly locked in
As waif and vain hope
In the paddy cellar of fools

Grabbing the snug automatic
Restoratives digests
High fidelity tools
With other vitamin scores and residues

And obsolete information
Like: "No callers
No riders!"

48

Children of large nervous furs
Will grow more pale this morning
In king populations
Where today drug leaders
Will promote an ever increasing traffic
Of irritant colors
Signs of this evident group
Are said to be almost local

Today a small general open space
Was found lodged in the immediate shadow
Of the heavenly pole. It was occupied
Early in the week by Russian force teams
Their symbols are thought
To be unexplained

In New Delhi a fatal sport parade
Involving long mauves and delicate slanders
Was apprehended and constrained at three P.M.
By witnesses with evening gestures
In a menacing place where ten were prohibited
Many others were found missing in colossal purples
And numerous raided halls

All important Washington drolls
Continue today the burning of forbidden customs
Printed joys are rapidly un-deciphered
As from the final page remain
No more than the perfumes
And military shadows
President says the affair must now warn
All the star-secret homespuns and undecided face-makers

Today's top announcement is a frozen society
Publicizing a new sherbet of matrimonial midways
And free family lore all over the front pages
You will meet frank old middle age
With bold acquaintance soon forgotten
In the time sequence
Of an unbearable cycle
So drop the unacquainted
It is marked down
As an illegible name
Too soon for identification.

Atoms are bound to go said Nobel
Prize-waging Physic swinger
In an unpacked science stadium announcement
   Wednesday
He was clapped into recognition
When he was discovered
Suddenly full of crowds.

Martian Doctors recommend a low-cost global enema
To divert the hot civet wave now tending
To swamp nine thousand acres of Mozambique
Our Gemini spores and other space observers note
Small inflammations in the Northern Lights
And remedies beat all aspirin to these same Lights
For further confusion
Consult your ordinary delay
Or wait for the clergy.

A clear-cut daily exercise was taxed out of existence
By Communist thought-control today in a warring
House of votes where Senator Tolling Bell
Announced a bright green apology to wives

428

Deprived by the abolition
But much more fun he decreed
Would soon come of it as fortunately
Only few were present.

You can now win three-cornered advantages in the
    well known
Moon-section of Chicago which is filled since Thursday
With inventions of unprecedented laughter.

49

A lone train alarms the summer silence with a contralto
trident. The old man has won seven nights in formalde-
hyde. He has become a fixture. Go collect the lame tear-
drops of the Dog Star! Who will tell this fine gentleman
his fortunes are wintering? Well, he sings for it!

50

Give me a cunning dollar that tells me no lie
Better informed
Truth-telling twenties
And fifties that understand

I want to carry
Cracking new money
That knows and loves me
And is my intimate all-looking doctor
Old costly whiteheaded
Family friend
I want my money
To know me like whiskey
I want it to forgive
Past present and future

Make me numb
And advertise
My buzzing feedbacking
Business-making mind

O give me a cunning dollar
That tells the right time
It will make me president and sport
And tell me all the secrets
Of the telephone.

I want to know the new combinations
In my pocket I need to possess
Plato's Mother I want
What knows all the scores
And I want my money
To write me business letters
Early every day.

51

Look! The Engineer! He thinks he has caught some-
thing! He wrestles with it in mid-air!

52

Each ant has his appointed task
One to study strategy
And one to teach it
One to cool the frigidaire
And one to heat it.

Each ant has his appointed round
In the technical circuit
All the way to high
One to make it and the other to break it.

And each has his appointed vector
In the mathematical takeoff
In the space-supported dance
The comedy of orders.

And each must know the number of his key
With a key in his eye and an eye for numbers
A number of appointments
A truly legal score:
And each must find his logical apartment.

Each ant has his appointed strategy to heat
To fuse and to fire at the enemy
And cool it down again to ninety-nine
In the right order—
But sometimes with the wrong apparatus.

53

I think poetry must
I think it must
Stay open all night
In beautiful cellars

54

Amid the cries of gang walls and surprises the echoes
come forward. They are nude. A brazen charm expands.
It invests the unguarded senses. Twin stars rise over the
library. Another day lives. It questions the waterworks,
it knows the fevers of Vegas.

55

Outcry. A circus on another planet. The hero does not
trust the evidence of verbs. What evidence? The proof

has very long shores. Hunger. Six o'clock! Stark orations in the terminal. Waiting. Will incense increase in the radiators? The banging old tempest in the rooms of Tenth Street. Leaden echo. The bare tree. The faithless vow. We make the best of bad beginnings and hope the end will do better. Come, Dark-Haired Dawn!

56

On the long road of winding steel
The river road
A messenger comes
With modest anxieties
To seek me in the underworld of waiters.

I sing quietly to the immediate heart
One more wild hope dies of affliction.

The blue girl fumbles with her books and bags. She goes and will never return. That is as it must be every day.

Crowned wells are forming at every table.

A journal of drugged foundations. Sad interludes of rubber weather. Drink Chablis and wait, while crabs crawl backwards into the dumbwaiters. Curtis is in the kitchen troubled with his enemies and all their mean sayings. In his own worried way. A call is issued for nine wreckers to make a long story short in the elevators.

One more wild hope
Dies of affliction

57

Formerly we knew
Years of peaceable system

In which were organized
Chemical wanderings in the paint works
For the civilized and upright
Who could safely view
The rape of Sabines
Secured by Andrew Carnegie
With hat in hand
He surely thinks
Of priceless Flemings

Wandering in secret
Among all his paintings
Uprooted industry follows
A Sabine fortune
Hat in hand
By his presbyterian sense of smell
All his mind
Lost to fortune
All his poems torn.

58

The pencil continues to grieve with long questions in
the same lounge full of sea walkers. All the mailmen
study my friendless state holding back the letters. Be-
hind the curtains placid grooms are looking for scandal.
They won't stay long in this temple of spenders, this
house of grammar and of wine. Will the deceiver wait
longer? In the crowd of beautiful callers one more wild
hope dies of affliction.

59

Our infantry is combing the hideouts
For faults in the enemy's prose
As reported in the extras.

60

Oh, said the discontented check, you will indeed win like
it says in the papers, but first you have to pay.
The bridges burn their builders behind them.

    The colored weepers try their luck with strings.

61

I will get up and go to Marble country
Where deadly smokes grow out of moderate heat
And all the cowboys look for fortunate slogans
Among horses' asses.

62

"Abandon your body and soul into the abundance of
light sent from above and give no thought to enlighten-
ment or illusion. Only sit like a great void of fire.
Breathe quietly. Concern yourself with nothing. . . . Be
like a completely dead man . . . empty of your own will
and of your own ideas. Think of what you cannot think.
In other words, think Nothing." (Dōgen)

All very fine, but his wall is full of cracks. The winds
blow through in every direction. He claims his light is
out and secretly turns it on again to read novels. He
builds a big fire to keep beginners warm: give him
credit for his kindness.

63

Uncle Sam with a knife at his throat
Holds out one hand to shake he promises hell
And he smiles.

Inhabited by a bear
He has to shine he is so eager for joy
And the bear is so thirsty.

Any old animal is secure inside a patriotic bust
Jealous of fresh air the heartbreak world
Is keen on coffee alone and forgets pain.

Ready for night to fall for Ursa Major
To come to light again and extend
A giant claw
Saying "Good Luck mister you can go to hell."

Now with a fortune in weapons and a cowboy riding his
    mind
Uncle Constellation gallops headlong down the sky
To the pure gems of Texas oil and firebird lotteries
And napalm in the magazines and bandits
Come forward eager to be recognized in person
Carried away with implements
To break more bottles with a convivial star
With stallions in the lucky wind
Flaming away like saloons or gone
In the unlucky airborne cars.

64

Note to subversives: Uncle has two extreme right hands
and means business!

65

It was already raining. They discovered all the bags
were empty. They walked slowly toward the gray cars.
They now knew for sure they had lost the same day
twice: once in sand, and once in water.

66

Oh yes it is intelligence
That makes the bubble and weather of "Yes"
To which the self says "No."

Science when the air is right says "Yes"
And all the bubbles in the head repeat "Yes"
Even the corpuscles romp "Yes."

But lowdown
At the bottom of deep water
Deeper than Anna Livia Plurabelle
Or any other river
Some nameless rebel
A Mister Houdini or somebody with fingers
Slips the technical knots
Pops the bubbles in the head
Runs the vote backwards
And turns the bloody cooler
All the way
OFF.

67

This is how to
This is with imperatives
I mean models
If you act
Act HOW.

Do this
When you are missing
Your home address
HUSTLE!

Because ours is a culture of bare-
Faced literal commands:

Go, Buster, GO!

68

(THE PROSPECTS OF NOSTRADAMUS)

In a yoke of steel laughs
Deathloving Jacks
Fly jungle bugs
Their fire loves creeps
They rain down love
On jungle creeps.

Tomorrow the alarm
And Mamas shrilling in the halls
Will play to win
Deathloving Jacks come home
And Mamas win
With green and purple wigs
Their eyes are ringed in lavender
They play for love
When yoked in jungle fun
Their creeps fly home.

In sixty-nine
When leftist moles assay
Our chrome Ideal
And we resist with lucky numbers
And wrong connections
Pocohontas a jungle nun
Returns to win the prize
Outwitting Mamas

And Jacks burn creeps again
In home town fun
That's seventy-one.

In seventy-three
Right-handed Jacks
Skilled in steel techniques
Issue wry alarms
And jokes of fire
The all-star population
Opens in a demon movie
Where cities bubble and pop
I see the champs are creeps
And leftist moles
Play for connections
And play to win
Deathloving Jacks drop their hot cards on living winners
("Thinking of you")
I hear the green-wigged cities
And their jokes of glue.

Seventy-four
Hot yules
London laughs and folds
Capetown swept
Johannesburg is crisp and cold
Where all the creeps have crept
Rio, Caracas, Mexico
Borrow the winning movie for another go
A day of Jacks and cleaners
When love melts Fort Knox Gold

Seventy-six
The gas is getting low

Some cities are out of air
All-star Mamas
Need all the water for their bluegreen hair
A year of frantic moles and drunken doves
Of killer mice and insect winners
Jacks without ammo fight with knives and knucks
A mystic capsule drones
Answer to pop explosion
O fill the empty tank with dooms of love!

The Eighties open with a twotime Easter
Day of a monster clam
No decision and no sound
From the hermetic tomb
No raids or bulletins
Until a simple one-two device
Ignites the champion explosion
And the Giant Mongrel takes over
With a tee-hee combustion
Followed by mists and politicians
In family-sized capsules
Well-provided
Fly for Orion.

Eighty-nine
Day of the grunt
The incision
The killer rat
All the lavender wigs are gone
The last of Jacks and Mamas
Have electronic hospitals on moon.

Two-thousand
Year of the low tone

Berlin:
The bluebottle
Two-thousand
Year of the white bone:
Moscow:
The green fly.
Two-thousand,
The year of the hum:
New York:
The blue sleep
And the champion movie
Smiles at last
Too many creeps have won.

69

(VITAL IMPERATIVES FOR CHESTER)

1. Move that system.
2. Eat more chunks and get young.
3. Own a doll that glows.
4. Swallow cash.
5. Advance and have words with Barbecue.
6. Make noise in bed.
7. Treat yourself to the national experience.
8. Move while stopping and save Bucks.
9. Have bliss in presidential Suburb.
10. Form large bends in those rooms.
11. Have fun with secret radio beams.
12. Open advice space with fatigue piston.
13. Mesh with liberal motives at model home.
14. Desire dermal gloves.
15. Imitate loss of heat needs and sprint.
16. Go drink China Sea.
17. Be a beautiful soul with St. Joseph.

18. Let lucky numbers change your mind.

19. Invite President to defy reality: he fights for YOU.

20. Get with new worlds in nearest Church.

21. Now imitate empty space.

22. Dig good will fronts and phase out.

23. Mulch it.

24. Ape that red trace.

25. Invent giant molars.

26. After the demonstration: bring Catchmouse* to the
    autopsy.

70

DRAMAS OF THE EVENING

Clean-cut pirate meets and befriends priceless stolen owl.

Hidden monument is found living in pleasure-dome
with friend.

Owl and stolen friend co-star in Oliver Twist as portrayed
by select flames.

Beautiful clever custard woman wills free costume in
silent chairs.

Posing space-man compares expert with captive church-
leaders.

Rose woman disguised as science-chief is mistaken for
stolen owl.

Expert hero leaving uptown college becomes survivor of
Trojan war.

Secret outlaw laboratory on burning ranch is scene of
activities:

Owl is shown transforming space-scientists into animals.

* Catchmouse = a famous cat.

Rocket woman teaches available outlaws to operate
   health club in frozen surroundings.
Owl seeks friend who betrayed safety zone with winning
   wrecks.
Keepers, inducing animals to contact invisible author,
   expand trial phones.

Subliminal engineer meets Little Red Riding Hood in
chains and learns love-secrets of best looking fugitives
thru' Thursday.

Artistic duck unmasks owl in underground French
scene: they trace exotic animal forces to latent technique.
Dream interpretation explained as new Funny Girl
comes home with banner exceptions in blindfold plot.
She turns gypsy in visual premises beyond any known
shore. Job's queen reclines forever on a beautiful board.

Sham doctor arrives in flying saucer welcomed by nor-
mal-type kids and gives pain. Wonderful contrived
movement of astrobabes in coptic reservation compound.
Animated clergy storms conceptual void in theo-drama
while Deity groans. Owls and health-buffs take over
haunted network.

Buffs destroy owls with sardonic asides and expert de-
plores incandescence of young ferns.

Riot woman transformed into savings bonds is traced to
unforgettable swans for the entire ruin of one season.

71

Adventure of Giomar: Castilian football
Minding doctrines

442

All night. Fire Harbor
The sky
A cataract. Unforeseen
Borealis
There is nothing left
Send supplies, medicine
And more wine
Cordially.

72

Morning. Good for foliage to resist the faithful wind.
Lean into new light. Listen to well-ordered hills go by,
rank upon rank, in the sun. The heat will soon blaze
blue and white. The long frying of September in the
shallow pan of fields. The sound of the earth goes up to
embrace the constant sky. My own center is the teeming
heart of natural families.

73

Determined to love
Lured by the barbarous fowl
He enters the rusty thicket of wires
Where nothing is tame

He meets his artiste
Who invites him to her ballet
There the swimming head
Makes everybody bleed.

Hanging on the wires
Love is still warm
A breakfast bird:
Eat your winged food!

Eat and go crazy
So crazy you have to fly
It is more than you will ever need!

Dizzy with spectacles
He admires her folly
Her breakfast dance.

He studies each new day's
Article of faith
The engaging records
Of broken heights

The moon is the delight
Of carnival waters
The sun is booming
In cannibal joy

By degrees their liturgy
Becomes rapacious
By degrees
Their careless boat goes down

Determined to love
In the sharp-eyed ocean
He follows all pirates
To the whirlpools.

74

O God do I have to be Wordsworth
Striding on the Blue Fells
With a lake for sale and Lucy
Locked in the hole of my camera?

444

Why do I ruin my whole life
Proclaiming the sorrows of animals
Which I keep in a pack on my shoulder?
Once when I met the Vegetable King
On the way to market
He said something that set me thinking.

"Coleridge," he said, "you bloody fool
Why do you stride over the Blue Fells
Swimming in Walden Pond
In that old football uniform:
Buy yourself an automobile!"

Yet in my heart I knew he had me
Figured for a minister: which is wrong
I am sustained
By ravens only and by the fancies
Of female benefactors.

Better to study the germinating waters of my wood
And know this fever: or die in a distant country
Having become a pure cone
Or turn to my eastern abstinence
With that old inscrutable love cry
And describe a perfect circle.

75

I seek you in the hospital where you work. Will you be
a patch of white moving rapidly across the end of the
next hall? I begin again in every shadow, surrounded by
the sound of scandal and the buzzer calling all doctors
to the presence of alarm.

76

After that we'll meet in some Kingdom they forgot and
there the found will play the songs of the sent. Surely a
big bird with all the shades of light will beat against our
windows. We will then gladly consent to the kindness of
rays and recover the warm knowledge of each other we
once had under those young trees in another May. (It is
a big bird flies right out of the center of the sun.)

77

Angels again
Farmers of the mind
In its flowers and fevers
Fishers in the blue revolutions of oil

They find me always upside down
In these reflected glooms
Lost in the wide rain's
Foundering accelerations

They walk with me
Through the shivering scrap-towns
And clearly show me how to cross
The dubious and elastic
Rail way
To weight weightless
Manuscript burdens

As I become fast freight
A perishing express
To the countries of the dead
In salt water flights
And unprotested weeping
Of old churches

I am an entire sensate parcel
Of registered earth
Working my way through adolescence
To swim dashing storms
Of amusement and attend
The copyrighted tornado
Of sheer sound

Though metal strings
Complain of my mind's eye
Nine fond harmonies
Never leave me alone

Till towns are built bone dry
With vigils and stones
Plate glass music
And oracular houses
Of earth spent calm
Long comas of the propitious time

O heavenly departures
With all the numbered bones
And the perfumes.

78

(THE HARMONIES OF EXCESS)

The hidden lovers in the soil
Become green plants and gardens tomorrow
When they are ordered to re-appear
In the wet sun's poem

Then they force the delighted
Power of buds to laugh louder
They scatter all the cries of light

Like shadow rain and make their bed
Over and over in the hollow flower
The violet bonfire

They spin the senses of the mute morning
In an abandoned river
Love's wreckage is then left to lie
All around the breathless shores
Of my voice
Which on the coasts of larking meadows
Invented all these children and their mischievous noises

So those lovers teach April stars
To riot rebel and follow faithless courses
And it doesn't matter
The seed is not afraid
Of winter or the terrible sweetness
Of the spring's convivial nightmare
Or the hot surprise and dizzy spark
Of their electric promise

For the lovers in the sleeping nerve
Are the hope and the address
Where I send you this burning garden
My talkative morning-glory
My climbing germ of poems.

79

O it is not lazy to be a messenger or to live out of the
shadow of some town. Other masks would be less
trouble. This one is never allowed to be familiar: it is
often the most naked. It is not without risk in a season
of frost. Nothing that is chosen is unbearable.

80

Slowly slowly
Comes Christ through the garden
Speaking to the sacred trees
Their branches bear his light
Without harm

Slowly slowly
Comes Christ through the ruins
Seeking the lost disciple
A timid one
Too literate
To believe words
So he hides

Slowly slowly
Christ rises on the cornfields
It is only the harvest moon
The disciple
Turns over in his sleep
And murmurs:
"My regret!"

The disciple will awaken
When he knows history
But slowly slowly
The Lord of History
Weeps into the fire.

81

Not to be without words in a season of effort. Not to be
without a vow in the summer of harvest. What have the

signs promised on the lonely hill? Word and work have their measure, and so does pain. Look in your own life and see if you find it.

82

It rained dark and cold on the Day of St. Theresa of the
    Heart
For no one yet knew that it was holiday fifteen
It rained like weather in honor of her sacred love
For the notables had built a black stone wall around her
    heart
And the prelates, mayors, and confessors wanted the
    doors closed.
The tongue of her heart, they said, must proffer insults
    to the vision.
So they built four walls of cold rain around the vision.
And the rain came down upon the vision in honor of
    her love.
In the theological cell where she was locked alone with
    the vision
Her heart was pierced by a thousand needles of fire.
Then the mayors, prelates, and confessors all wept to-
    gether in honor of her love.
They went together in procession to the rainy city walls
    and fortified
Their minds, wrapping them in the folds of the black
    storm.
Behind them in the invisible town the jails and convents
    overflowed with flame.
In the smallest window of all St. Theresa
Forgotten by these entranced jokers turned her heart
    into a dove.
The rain ended at that moment.
The dove had flown into the fiery center of the vision.

83

(SOLEMN MUSIC)

Use your numbered line
To describe constellations
Hunter and Capricorn
And heavenly Bears
Amid *Sanctus* sounds
And transports
The golden fury of wires

The lighted years
Of distant space
Are all made human
By modes of music
The questioning *vox humana*
The disciplines of chant

Take your compasses
To measure flight
Expanding silences
And pay attention
To the stillness of the end
Or the beginning
Sanctus
The abyss of brass
The sapphire orchestra

Bear the hot
Well-fired shot
Roaring out
Of the cool dark

And go to meet
In the wet estranged country

The midnight express
Bringing Plato, Prophets, Milton, Blake,
The nine daughters of memory

But use your own numbered line
To go down alone
Into the night sky
Hand over hand
And dig it like a mine.

84

Gelassenheit:
Desert and void. The Uncreated is waste and emptiness
to the creature. Not even sand. Not even stone. Not even
darkness and night. A burning wilderness would at
least be "something." It burns and is wild. But the
Uncreated is no something. Waste. Emptiness. Total
poverty of the Creator: yet from this poverty springs
everything. The waste is inexhaustible. Infinite Zero.
Everything comes from this desert Nothing. Everything
wants to return to it and cannot. For who can return
"nowhere?" But for each of us there is a point of no-
whereness in the middle of movement, a point of noth-
ingness in the midst of being: the incomparable point,
not to be discovered by insight. If you seek it you do not
find it. If you stop seeking, it is there. But you must
not turn to it. Once you become aware of yourself as
seeker, you are lost. But if you are content to be lost you
will be found without knowing it, precisely because
you are lost, for you are, at last, nowhere.

85

The flash of falling metals. The shower of parts,
cameras, guns of experience in the waste heaven of
deadly rays. Cataclysm of designs. Out of the meteor sky

cascades the efficient rage of our team. Down comes
another blazing and dissolute unit melting in mid-air
over a fortunate suburb. A perishing computer blazes
down into a figure of fire and steam. We live under the
rain of stainless leaders. They strike themselves out like
matches and fizz for our conjecture in the streets of
Taurus. Gone is another technical spy in giant and in-
stant heat. Gone is another tested explorer. Gone is
another brilliant intuition of an engineer.

86

"The true word of eternity is spoken only in the spirit of
that man who is himself a wilderness." (Eckhart)
"It is only the shadow of God which enlightened our
inward wilderness: but on the high mountains of the
Promised Land there is no shadow." (Ruysbroeck)

87

I am about to make my home
In the bell's summit
Set my mind a thousand feet high
On the ace of songs
In a mood of needles and random lights
To purify
The quick magnetic sodas of the skin

I will call the deep protectors out of the ground
The givers of wine
The writers of peace and waste
And sundown riddles

The threat of winter gleams in gray-haired windows
And witty mirrors
And fear lies over the sea

But birds fly uncorrected across burnt lands
The surest home is pointless:
We learn by the cables of orioles

I am about to build my nest
In the misdirected and unpaid express
As I walk away from this poem

Hiding the ace of freedoms

88

Finally the public sender of this island shuts down its
trance. The vacation of princes has come to its end. They
all set sail together for the fall of towers.

EPILOGUE

Now leaning over the salt nerve of our wave length we
have decided to send you the frozen exports of a com-
promised musician. You will by your own free choice be
locked in with Jack Sound and his final trumpet. The
name of the day is Doom. But first a word from our
sponsor and his lasting gorgeous lovelorn satisfactions.
Never mind the bugle Miss Daisy. For a dollar ninety-
nine you will have immortal longings here on the front
porch. You will become as slim and lovely as our own
hypnotic phlogiston toothpaste enriched with armpit
deodorant. All you have to do is dance a little and you
will attract the infinite toy attentions of the elite. They
come to you forever in non-stop pullovers and mops of
deep hair. They begin their interminable suggestions.
And now play it Jack! Give it that new-old sound!

(Pourrait être continué)

THE GEOGRAPHY OF LOGRAIRE
(1968)

AUTHOR'S NOTE

This is a purely tentative first draft of a longer work in progress, in which there are, necessarily, many gaps. This is only a beginning of patterns, the first opening up of the dream. A poet spends his life in repeated projects, over and over again attempting to build or to dream the world in which he lives. But more and more he realizes that this world is at once his and everybody's. It cannot be purely private, any more than it can be purely public. It cannot be fully communicated. It grows out of a common participation which is nevertheless recorded in authentically personal images.

In this wide-angle mosaic of poems and dreams I have without scruple mixed what is my own experience with what is almost everybody else's. Thus "Cargo" and "Ghost Dance," for instance, cease to be bizarre anomalies and are experienced as yours and mine as well as "theirs." But for this to be true, what is given of "Cargo" and "Ghost Dance" is most often literal and accurate quotation with slight editing and with of course much personal arrangement. And where more drastic editing is called for by my own dream, well, I have dreamed it.

Much also has been found in the common areas of nightmare to which we are all vulnerable (advertising, news, etc.). The most personally subjective part is perhaps the long meditation on Eros and Thanatos, centering in the New York City Borough of Queens, in the "North" canto.

457

But this dream also reaches out to London and other places in Europe. The focal point is around the gasometers of Elmhurst, the freight yards of Woodside, the crematory in Brooklyn, a Harlem nightclub, the boats in Bayside Bay, the tunnel under the East River leading into Manhattan. This meditation is surrealistic. "Top funnel house" is simply a sort of Hieronymus Bosch building which smokes and looks and is symbolic of death as a presence structured into society itself as guilt, police and undertakers. It is both police station, hospital and crematory which has devoured one by one the bodies of parents, grandparents, etc. Then there is the theme of Famous John as a sort of cloacal Mafia Id. And so on. The "South" canto is more self-evident. "East" and "West," "Cargo" and "Ghost Dance," play out in more universal and primitive myth-dream terms the same struggle of love and death, they enact the common participation of the living and the dead in the work of constructing a world and a viable culture. These poems incidentally are never explicitly theological or even metaphysical. The tactic is on the whole that of an urbane structuralism.

June, 1968

THE GEOGRAPHY OF LOGRAIRE

PROLOGUE: THE ENDLESS INSCRIPTION

1. Long note one wood thrush hear him low in waste pine
   places
   Slow doors all ways of ables open late
   Tarhead unshaven the captain signals
   Should they wait?

2. Down wind and down rain and down mist
   the passenger.

3. In holy ways there is never so much must

4. Should Wales dark Wales slow ways sea coal tar
   Green tar sea stronghold is Wales my grand
   Dark my Wales land father it was green
   With all harps played over and bells
   Should Wales slow Wales dark maps home
   Come go green slow dark maps green late home
   Should long beach death night ever come
   And welcome to dark father-mother land
   Simple white wall house square rock hill
   Green there low water hill rock square
   White home in dark bituminous con-
   Crete ways to plain of fates ways
   Fathers hill and green maps memory plain
   In holy green Wales there is never staying

5. Plain plan is Anglia so must angel father mother **Wales**
    Battle grand opposites in my blood fight hills
    Plains marshes mountains and fight
    Two seas in my self Irish and German
    Celt blood washes in twin seagreen people
    German Tristram is all mates' Grammer
    I had a toy called Tristram and Gurton's
    Needle in another sensitive place
    What Channel bard's boarder house next sweet
    Pub smell on cliff of winds Cliff was
    A welshest player on the rugged green at Clare
    Away next New Wood Forest fool on hunter map
    Ship of forests masts Spain masts in Beaulieu wood
    Minster in the New Wood Minster Frater in the grassy
    Summer sun I lie me down in woods amid the
    Stone borders of bards.

6. In holy walks there is never an order
    Never burden

7. Lay down last burden in green Wales seas end firs
        larches
    Wales all my Wales a ship of green fires
    A wall wails wide beside some other sex
    Gone old stone home on Brecon hill or Tenby harbor
    Where was Grandmother with Welsh Birds
    My family ancestor the Lieutenant in the hated navy
    From the square deck cursed
    Pale eyed Albion without stop.

8. In holy seas there is never so much religion.

9. On a run late hold one won
    Tarhead slaver captain selling the sables
    To Cain and Abel by design

10. Desire desire O sign of ire
    O Ira Dei
    Wrath late will run a rush under the
    Funnel come snow or deadly sign
    Design of ire rather I'd dare it not dare
    It not the ire run late hold strong Wales to a mast
    Young siren sexes of the green sea wash
    Hold captain home to Ithaca in a pattern of getaway
    Hold passion portion siren swinging porter
    Gutt bundle and funk gone
    Down slow mission done as possible
    And another child of Wales
    Is born of sea's Celts
    Won rock weeds dragon designs
    Missions capable defenders

11. In frail pines should they sometimes wait
    Or ponds said one space cotton in captain design
    Trace a dark pine fret way work walks
    In soft South Pine house eroded away
    Sweet smelling Virginia night and mint
    Should they wet those cotton patches
    Wash out a whole town

12. Wash ocean crim cram crimson sea's
    Son Jim's son standing on the frigate
    Jim Son Crow's ocean crosses a span
    Dare heart die Spanish ram or Lamb Son's Blood
    Crimson's well for oceans carnate sin sign
    Ira water Ira will not wash in blood
    Dear slain son lies only capable
    Pain and Abel lay down red designs
    Civil is slain brother sacred wall wood pine

Sacred black brother is beaten to the wall
The other gone down star's spaces home way plain

13. Dahomey pine tar small wood bench bucket
    Under shadow there wait snake
    There coil ire design father of Africa pattern
    Lies all eyes awake eroded night
    Traces gone tire far traces of dawn's fire
    Dead rope hang cotton over captain branch

14. The willing night hides everything
    Wills it tar face fret work wash out all chain
    Saving all one country slave
    Snake and tarheel minister and bat
    And blood and ram and Isaac done in a dare.

15. Plain Savior crosses heaven on a pipe

16. Hay Abraham fennel and grass rain ram under span's
       star
    Red grow the razors in the Spanish hollow

17. Hallow my Savior the workless sparrow
    Closes my old gate on dead tar's ira slam
    Gone far summer too far fret work blood
    Work blood and tire tar under light wood
    Night way plain home to wear death down hard
    Ire hard down on anger heel grind home down
    Wary is smashed cotton-head beaten down mouth
    When will they all go where those white Cains are dead?

18. Sign Redeemer's "R"
    Buys Mars his last war.

SOUTH

I

Will a narrow lane
Save Cain?

The Lamb the killer's friend
Skinned in meetings
Has a raw road and it may rain

WE ALL KNOW CAIN MAY BE THE LONGER RUNNER

High stocks buy Betterman's
Sweet Rosy Country Cross
Captain's a wanted Rosicrucian
Traitor to peevish liquor
Kills a brother in the outside lane

LAMB ADMITS TIES TO CAIN

Flashlight umbrella
Casts blood beam
On Daisy Violet Zinnia
Buttercup Rose
Angry under some steps,
Some rain!

Cain and Daisy lock their golden eyes
We all know Cain
But can a Lamb save Cain the raider?

"Maybe he has two manors one for Sundays
One for weeks anger kicked out nigger
Don't come no more white nigger door
Keep out of here"

Go back sore to wait writing
Where happiness beasts will wait behind a store
A bloody sight for sore eyes
"Top fun for D Tremens above the waist"

HOW WOULD YOU LIKE TO LIVE IN THIS PLACE?

It may be two men met Sunday ten
Wearing their whole wheat hats
Saw Satan with a dark knife cut tobacco
When High Green and Corngod stand together
Over Kentucky's corrugated temper
All wet nightlife to Cain and waif

TEN GUNS ARE OUT OF WORK UP ANGER HOLLOW

Try outsmart Saturday's night air
Tight teller sees city split where
Manmade bloodrains light and chemistry wet
Upon blue grass signs the red flower forever

AND KEEP CAIN OUT OF THAT HOLLOW

"I think we owe you an apology mister part time revolver
Mister tallhat individual smell
All sixfoot fires began on Mars landing Friday
When they found the oilwell"

Light police phone spark starter ten a dollar
All fire marcher explodes an invention
Gates are out a million
Try outstart capricious air
Mister tallhat revolver is everywhere

WHY WILL NOT LAMBS STAY FOREVER WELL IN SKINS?

It may be two men met Sunday ten with a happiness beast
A raw Lamb coming from the hollow
Tied to killer Bishops for the feast

100,000 Negroes most of whom have thin black skin
Tinderfoot passover dry edge light wells away
Blowup a million

TEMPER IS CANDY TO CAIN'S DAISY

In meetings red with Rosy pies
All were had by a good time up Ash's hollow

One narrow lane saved Lamb's friend Paschal Cain

II

1. Roar of red wood racer eats field. Green breakaway go cars light lanes. A robber lends the money. Aluminum gates grand open. Riverchange alongside lights. Mist downstairs. Riverhouse brown: green the riverrace. Mist down stairs. Mist lights. The getaway!

2. Must armyboys craterbodies blown down today tankway? Spill river. Mist. Giant bridge finds way to woman. Silence mimes rivercity. Gate to wettest summers in the South.

3. Roar of red wood rover lights army. Way station all the road to end of one more day. My day. The wandering oculist takes his homework train. Sad red hillside of houses search night. Police begin their shine.

4. Smokeshot low Fort Thomas. Nineteenth century mothers hazel in hell. Push sandy button strike the phone. Soft brazen Sunday hello SUN! It is a sunny day at last through the Hudepohl mist. I am the lonely one whose name is scratched on the plate. I am the lonely photo above giant water. I am the way to Louisville in the end. Doorway sun and the fern. If I went. I am the lonely grey police boat also.

5. I am the crane in stark south flight.

6. Red lover stations all along that road. Riverchance along mist buildings. Silverchange under steel span. Here sun! Here soft smoke siren. Gold plant swings destroyer riverlights up and down. Here examine smoke far down river. Study woman question afraid. Here. Examine the Churches. Wait station. Wait Covington station. Way north. The hazel points of her two visions. Hazel had nine mothers in the same city. Crane has money. Crane opens the aluminum gates. Enters winner.

7. Examine onion Church. Best old copper green spire in German sun. Gone Churches priest examines money book confess detail. Army is here. Churches are here. Gambles omens. Gone Germans. Gone Hudepohl Beer. Here. Sidelights. Riverdays. Wide riverdays. Wide summers. Shock of armies. Lights. Police. All hope destroyed forever. Police aim long light feel bridge. Lightfinger wants detail. Lightfinger love's trigger. Races change.

8. Wet street. Change. Ring Cincinnati. Wake daycolor. Neosubstance comes to life in hospital. She makes wide frightwindows. Haze. Southward goes the sun.

9. Make change. Race electric air. Phone the home. Make every daycolor square indoors very tired. Secure waiting away. Wasting money says hello. Deodorant here today. Stands daycolor change at white desk so sweet. Smell the blonde blushes O. Aim for the lonely waist says Gringo.

10. Green breakaway go all cars light suns. Breakaway change wet stars riverlanes. Night south riverlanes home. Signs spell St. Louis. High power must wire here connect all space. Crosstrack rages seven states. Light runs south

and hello smiles Alabama hello smiles hello. Waiting anyhow says Army Sam. Army waits in vain.

11. Seven states. Now floodlight occupies neo-fleuve. Neon bitch smiles at police racket. High fire spends all night fun. Wasting away without a tremble. Wasting phones hello say seven states. Hello power boats alert river. Traffic never dreamt so wide. Change. Run for the lonely night says Gringo. But we are never alone.

12. Boats alert. City all awake. Carrolton, Louisville, Owensboro, Paducah. Gates open for Victors. Light is neo-strange. Music of lighted copperheads all over town. Wake daycolor neo-sand-storm-stars down city. Orange is awake.

13. Neo-wristwatch kills whitey dead. He was just unlucky.

14. High speed ends connect space. Now speak. Say Fort Knox is home of armor.

15. Maxwell you son of a bitch get off my place.

16. We all made it to the track on a dirty bet. Sorrow has a wet face. A sign: "All losers leave by west gate."

17. Hazel wins. Fresh is the sandwich.

18. Through Knox at nightfall. Armycrater boys face down on the wet table. The grey mistrivers of night. Nightfall lights up houses. Redgrain music beat down houseflats. A ghost dancer walks in a black hat through gates of horn.

III. HYMNS OF LOGRAIRE

1. Nearer my God to rock of eyes
   Or to my chariot of thee
   That is Elias rider of red skies

   Nearer my cherubim
   To the crimson fruit
   In chariot three

   Wishing everybody well
   From now to Monday.

2. Sign on the dome:
   "Expect thy next tread
   Don't tread on the marine."

3. You were sixteen
   My village queen
   Shining in sunpeel paint
   With your strip all recent
   From customary behavior

   You stood alarmed
   O darkeyed think
   Full to the very barrels
   And I wished you cunning
   Glasses and all

Which was the time
We broke the furniture
Trying to get me over
My own wall.

IV. MIAMI YOU ARE ABOUT TO BE SURPRISED

You are going to be pleasantly surprised by this
You will find yourself sweetly insulted
By earphones and you will also
Be pleasantly wet
Where you are going

For you shall make expensive waves
Meeting the answer to women's questions
In a swift novel of suspense

IF YOU HAVE HEART FAILURE WHILE READING THIS
THE POET IS NOT RESPONSIBLE

And you will meet a lot of friends
Falling into hopeless spray
As if that were what you wanted
And limbo dancing (non-lethal)
Will focus the muscles of science
On your waistline
You can't control so many
Wonderful people

When you become exotic bait
For a suburban afternoon
Well you wanted to stay in focus
But did you?

473

ALL NIGHT LONG WHEN YOU CAN'T STAND IT HERE
TAKE IT OR CRACK
WHERE ELSE CAN YOU FIND IT
IN A CAN?

You are going to be warned
By a gourmet with a mouthful of seaweed
Reaching all the way through superb
Armholes

He will try to help you decode
Your own scrambled message
Teach you your own way
As if you wanted that
Will you please try?

And you will be surprised
By Hilton candlelight
With more than the usual bill
(Unless you are pregnant)

Our new method takes you out of the stream
Of cold function
But you have to bend
Like all our other gamebirds
While you are gently made over
All the way down to the jawline
You don't have to be young in years
For the machine to register your secret desires
Which are never secret and always foolish

So you are about to be surprised.

V. TWO MORALITIES

THONGA LAMENT (Africa)

Look the blue oxen
Come down from the altars
To your caverns O Fathers
I stay outside your tunnels
Do you see them coming
The oxen
O Fathers?
Blue oxen into the caverns.
You gave me life O Father
But now you are gone
Now you are secret
Living in famous tunnels
(But where?)
Let us eat together in peace
Let us not disagree
That I and my children
May live long here outside
Out here in the air
Without coughing or swaying
Or losing balance and falling
Into the tunnels
Look O Father
The blue oxen are coming
They will find you
In the caverns.

HARE'S MESSAGE (Hottentot)

One day Moongod wanted to send a message to man. Hare
volunteered to go to man as Moongod's messenger. "Go tell
men," said Moon, "that they shall all rise again the way I
also rise after each dying." But Hare the messenger de-
ceived man, changing the heavenly message to one of earth.
"You must die," he said, "just as I do." Then Moon cursed
Hare. And the Nagama must now never eat Hare's meat.
They do not eat Hare the runner for the runner is death.

VI. A CLEVER STRATAGEM:
OR, HOW TO HANDLE MYSTICS

When I was out in the Nyasaland Missions we held a
meeting of five thousand converts at which religious fervor
naturally mounted to the highest pitch. So much intensity
of religious feeling required to be carefully channeled to
prevent outbursts. Fervor must not be permitted to dissi-
pate itself in wasteful, even riotous disorders. One morning
two of the leading teachers came to report some experiences
they were having. They had been out in the bush all night
praying and they had felt their bodies lifted up from the
earth while bright angelic beings came to meet them as they
ascended. What did this mean? I replied not in word but
in deed. I went to the dispensary, took down the salts, gave
them each a stiff dose and sent them off to bed. The visions
and ascensions immediately ceased, and were replaced by a
sweetly reasonable piety that disturbed no one. A mission-
ary must combine spiritual passion with sound sense. He
must keep an eye on his followers.

VII. NOTES FOR A NEW LITURGY

There's a big Zulu runs the congregation
A woe doctor cherubim chaser
Puts his finger on the chief witch
Has a mind to deter foes
Is by the Star Archangel shown a surprise
Writes his letters in vision mentions his B.A.
From many a college
Has a fan to scatter flies
Receives a penetrating look
From an imaginary visitant in white
Knows all the meanings at once
Knows he is in heaven in rectangles
Of invented saints
Flaming with new degrees and orders every day

"I dreamt this Church I dreamt
Seven precious mitres over my head
My word is final.

"I now General Overseer Concession Registrar
Of Rains and Weather Committeeman
For Pepsi-Cola all over the veldt
Flail of incontinent clergy
Wave my highstrung certificate in times of change
Don't you need a Defender with a medical guarantee?

"You think that I am only a clown-healer from
    the out-district?

Hold this black bag while I lay hands on children
Steady my followers with magic curios
When I sleep I watch you with eyes in my feet
Last night I dreamt of four beds
I must marry again must go get
Another angel-nun
Come holy deaconess we'll ride
Barefoot in yellow busses to Jordan River
Wearing emblems of the common vow

"Subleaders keep telling the message
Like it was new
Confirming my charism as Prime-Mover in Management
I shall continue in office as President
For all time until the earth melt
As all Full-Leaders stand over you wearing their watches
Moulding you by government of thought
And I return a while to the Origin
Ruling through a female medium from an obscure place:

"HOLD THIS MITRE WHILE I STRANGLE CHICKENS
AND THROW THEM IN THE AIR
COVERING THE SACRED STONE WITH BLOODY FEATHERS
(And surround the altar
With lie detectors.)"

VIII. CE XOCHITL: THE SIGN OF FLOWERS
(Mexico)

Men born under Ce Xochitl are cheerful and ingenuous
Inclined to music and pleasure, witty talkers.
The women hard workers and free with their bodies.

(Sahagun)

1. Xochipilli, the Flower Giver:
   They fast in his honor.
   His movable feast: Xochilhuitl.

2. If any man had access to a woman
   Or woman to man in those four fast days
   They spoiled their offering
   Offended the Flower God who would punish
   Their secret parts with boils, buboes,
   Chancres and other rottings.

3. Some ate no chili others at midnight
   Took their corn soup with a flower
   Floating in the middle.
   They call this the "Fast of Flowers."

4. Month nine: in fields and patches
   Of corn gather flowers
   Bring them in armfuls
   To the feasting house
   Keep them overnight
   Then at dawn

Make thick garlands
For the god's yard and day.

5. That same eve the people
Killed hens and little dogs
Plucked hens singed dogs
Made tamales
Up all night
Getting ready

6. Danced on the god's day
Warriors and boys
And public women
Snaking and singing
With no sidestep no turns
No gestures but slow
Solemn composed
In perfect time
Led by those expert in war
With arms around the waists
Of their partners
As though embracing
(Which the other dancers
Were not allowed to do)

7. *Yax Coc Ah Mut*
Feast of the Green Turtle
They dance on tall stilts
Offering the god corn liquor
Peacocks' heads

Dancers come with little clay dogs
And bread.

A dog with black shoulders that is virgin
Is sacrificed.

"Such were the services which their demons commanded
   them."

(Bishop Landa)

IX. THE LADIES OF TLATILCO

1. Effigy vessels shapes of apes
   Men peccaries rabbits coons ducks acrobats and fish
   Long charming little bottlenecks pots bowls
   And inventions:
   > For example
   "when liquid was poured out of the funnel-shaped tail
   the animal's ears whistled softly
   in a double gurgling note."

   (Covarrubias)

2. Mixtec urn: Old man tiger crown holds dog nine.

3. Nine deer effigy coonsong
   Fondest little bowl
   Offered to songstruck dead
   Maize and cactus milk
   Small red beer
   Peppers and chilis in bowls
   Of warm red clay.

   Living acrobats stand in a pyramid.

4. "If they carved wood we shall never know it."

5. Look his brute spear nails placename
   Look he has a glyph
   Stone eye sees conqueror date
   (Too late).

6. The ladies of Tlatilco
   Wore nothing but turbans
   (Skirts only for a dance)
   A lock of hair over the eyes
   Held only by a garland
   Tassels and leaves
   They bleached their black hair
   With lime
   Like the Melanesians.

7. Feminine figurines with two heads or with four eyes
      and ears
   Two noses or doublemouth on the same head
   "Reminiscent of Picasso
   Perhaps connected with idea of twins."

8. A most provocative perfume
   Wicked wicked charms
   Natural spray dispenser
   A special extract
   For four-eyed ladies of fashion
   MY SIN
   "And my most wicked provocative lewd
      dusting-powder excitements."
   (Two noses on the same head)

9. The most thoughtful gift of the year
   With a Queen Anne Rose (Patent No. 3,187,782)
   Budding with terry-loops
   (Two nuns fighting for the same towel)

10. A flowering bath
    Your long-stem skin

Your patent rose
Is all in loops
Is all in tones
Bleach your black hair
With a coat of lime
And dance in your turban.

11. I saw two moons
    In dreadful sweat
    "Fit perfectly under
    A rounded collar jacket"
    I saw two moons
    In shades of toast
    Coming to calm my fright
    Sweet Mother Rose
    Ann Gypsy Nun
    In a new trim
    Toast collar.
    I saw two moons
    Coming from a certain kind of store
    Where the ladies of Tlatilco
    Wear nothing but sweaters
    Bleach their black hair with lime
    Or look like fire clay
    Reddening their hair with dye
    From seeds of achiote.

12. Two ways to tell a primitive bath figurine.
    With an expensive book
    Your skin can tell
    "All her goings graces"
    In taupe or navy
    Cashmere lovat wine

In maize my moons
O so serene
In cardigan charcoal blue
Shetlands hunter green

Two ways to tell a primitive
Nun fighting for
A towel.

13. O patent Gypsy London Rose
    On fire with inventions
    Looking out of a red hood
    Upon acrobats shaved heads
    Wizards and trumpeters

14. O fervent Gypsy Blue we love your diamonds
    We are Boston experts and we understand
    "the whole actively involved female world"
    Which is red
    With achiote seeds
    Rich in naseberries octaniques
    Otaheite apples
    Having great fun in a natural spray
    Dispenser of SIN
    With lime like the Melanesians

    But Picasso
    Was *not* thinking of twins!

X. CHILAM BALAM (Yucatan)

1. "They came to Tísip
   With pepper in their speech
   In 11 Ahau
   Cleared cornfields
   Built a city."

2. They were received like Fathers
   With nodding plumes at the well's edge
   In Itza
   Thus they were called the "Itzaes."

3. Sunrise. New Kingdom.
   Fresh wakes sweet tropic earth!
   Tribute paid in cotton
   For the Four Men
   (North South East West)
   In Chichen.

   Then the Lords
   Rich in cotton
   Meet Gods
   Equal in voice to Gods
   And those whose voices
   Were not equal to Gods' voices
   Were thrown into the well
   To cry louder.

4. Then came Laws
   High pyramids
   Thirteen Itzaes in majesty
   With pepper in their prayers
   Made deals with the Raingods
   In clouds of smoke.

5. "Our Gods have grown bigger" they said
   Then bitter times began
   The plain smoked
   All the way to the sea.

6. Thirteen katuns they ruled.
   Until the treason of Hunac Ceel
   Driven from their cities into jungle
   4 Ahau was the katun
   The wail of lives
   Thirteen katuns of suffering and law
   And they were called in the end
   "The Remnant of Itzaes"
   The last few built Mayapan
   "Maya men"
   Was their new name.

7. Lamentation
   Priests of Xiu
   Slow along the cavern wall
   From altar to altar
   On the well's rim.

8. "The priest asks for green bark. Thirteen times he
   strips all flowers and all leaves off the branches. He
   strips them utterly bare. He binds the stripped branches
   in a bundle. Katuns without hope!"

9. Prayer in the cavern
   For the last time
   Pitch dark well
   Stopping at the altars
   Blind fingers explore the faces
   Of rock signs
   Figures cut in the wall
   Spell: "Justice exists"
   "Heaven exists"
   And the prophet Chilam answers
   Hix binac hix mac
   (Maybe yes maybe no)
   "But now we carry the sons of Itza on our backs like
      boulders."
   And the priests have come to the end of submission.
      The end of desire.
   They are about to destroy themselves because of the
      injuries done to our people.

10. FACE OF THE PRIEST CHILAM WHEN HE IS ON THE POINT OF
    ENTERING THE WELL OF THE CAVERN.

XI. DZULES (Yucatan)

1. "EVERY MOON EVERY YEAR EVERY WIND MUST TRAVEL AND
   PASS ON
   EVERY BLOOD ALSO COMES AT LAST TO ITS PLACE OF REST
   JUST AS IT COMES BRIEFLY TO ITS POWER AND THRONE."

   (Chilam Balam)

2. 11 Ahau signals the landing
   Dzules from the east
   Terror out of the sea
   Withering the flowers

3. "TO MAKE THEIR OWN FLOWER OPEN THEY SACKED AND
   SMASHED THE FLOWER OF OTHERS"

4. 11 Ahau the rising of bearded men
   Who take away the white clothing
   Long gone are the days
   Of the honey-offering

5. They bring down all power smash man to earth make
      green skies
   Weep blood hard and heavy is the maize bread of this
      katun
   Strangled is the flute-hero the painter Yaxal Chuen
      the jeweler
   The Ape Ixkanyultu "Precious Voice"
   His throat is now cut gods driven out
   Singers scattered gone is Kay Nicté

The flower dance around the rock pool
Canta la mujer joven
To call back gone man made gentle as a
Tame animal with dance with charm
To the sweet body lying in the water
Covered with jungle flowers
Dispersados serán por el mundo las mujeres que cantan
Y los hombres que cantan
Y todos los que cantan.

6. AY ENTRISTEZCÁMONOS PORQUE LLEGARON!

7. "You shall feed them" (said the prophecy) "you shall wear their clothing you shall use their hats and you shall talk their language. But their sentences shall speak division."

8. AY ENTRISTEZCÁMONOS PORQUE LLEGARON!

9. "They are destroyed,
   The omens."
   Days and nights
   Show the way
   "Pay heed to the truth which I give you
   In the katun of dishonor."

10. "During five days Ix Haunab, Mother Despair, Ix Huznab, Mother Terror, Ix Kuknab, Mother of Lies, eat from the red-painted bowl, from the white-painted bowl, from the black-painted bowl and from the yellow-painted bowl."

11. MUCHO Y COMPLETO ADULTERIO SERÁ LA OCCUPACIÓN DE TODOS!

12. With brimming tears
    We mourn our lost writings
    The burned books
    The burned men
    The flaming harvests
    Holy maize destroyed
    Teachings of heaven and earth
    Destroyed.

13. The wooden books
    Burned before our eyes
    At the well.

14. We pray the eyes of our sons
    May one day read again
    The stone writings.

15. Silly pigeons
    Pass as men
    Birds to be detested
    They shoot others
    Through the heart.
    Do hummingbirds cheat one another?
    Do they kill one another?

16. No one who travels a bad road
    Ever arrives. The people
    Weigh every word.
    Will lies
    Never end?

17. We have burned sweet copal
    On account of the hangings.

18. *Justitia* = vex Christians.

19. Four katuns
    We ate grass
    Don Antonio Martinez
    Guest of our Nobles
    "Xaul is his name
    As one who aspires to heaven"
    Little by little
    We are degraded
    Wives of our aristocrats
    Take money
    To sleep with enemies

20. "I shall yet prove my name:
    It is Martinez."

21. Do hummingbirds cheat one another?

22. LLEGARON LOS HOMBRES DE DIOS DEL ORIENTE LOS QUE
    TRAYERON EL DOLOR.

23. On a day of 9 Oc
    Arrival of the turkey cocks
    Strutting and gobbling
    Redneck captains with whips
    Fire in their fingers
    Worse than Itzaes
    Friars behind every rock every tree
    Doing business
    Bargaining for our souls
    Book burners and hangmen
    Sling the high rope
    They stretch the necks
    Lift the heads
    Of priest and noble
    Our calendar is lost

Days are forgotten
Words of Hunab Ku
Counterfeit
The world is once again
Controlled by devils
We count the pebbles of the years
In hiding:
Nothing but misfortune.

24. PROTECT THE LIVES OF YOUR POLICE PUT OUT THE SMALL
FIRES WITH FOG OR FOAM MARK THE TROUBLEMAKERS WITH
DYE MOVE THE CROWD WITH WATER-BASED IRRITANTS KEEP
THE CROWDS AWAY FROM THE CAR WITH ELECTRICITY DRIVE
THE SNIPERS OUT OF HIDING WITH TEAR GAS GRENADES
BREAK UP CROWDS WITH SMOKE

25. Memory of the katuns and years swallowed up by
the red moon!
"Then fire devoured the people of Israel and
the prophets."

(Chilam Balam)

A lively business in police helicopters.

26. "One hundred and fifty years later there was an agree-
ment with the foreigners. That is what you are paying
for. There was a war between the whites and the peo-
ple here, the men who used to be great captains of the
nation formerly. That is what you are paying for now."

27. The year fifteen hundred and forty one of the Dzules
1541—day 5 Ik 2 Chen.
*"A high-frequency blower that delivers a banshee howl
beyond the tolerance of human ears."*

494

NORTH

PROLOGUE

WHY I HAVE A WET FOOTPRINT ON TOP
OF MY MIND

To begin a walk
To make an air
Of knowing where to go
To print
Speechless pavements
With secrets in my
Forgotten feet
Or go as I feel
Understand some air
Alone
Around the formerly known
Places
Like going
When going is knowing
(Forgetting)

To have passed there
Walked without a word
To have felt
All my old grounds
Forgotten world
All along
Dream places
Words in my feet

Explain the air of all
Feel it under (me)
Stand
Stand in the unspoken
A cool street
An air of legs
An air of visions

Geography.
I am all (here)
There!

I. QUEENS TUNNEL

1. Top the burning funnel house with watchman's eyes. Pointed otherside reckoning bridge. Courtside Queens paddy wagon. Smoketop funnel house Addy Daddy Wagon. With Sam's Tuna all lighted up. Very funny tunnels of Breughel at Coney. Coney Queen's lights down into sudden tunnel. Spinners. The quick brown bus. Lousdog hit that moon. Gone. Lazy mummies stored in a locked room.
Rivers ever ways light dark down.
Top the burning light everlasting insurance all over this downtown construction.
Woolforth budding up in the light. Look up to it from tunnels. Top the five and ten funnel smoking a little lightly up.
Brookly river sing my orange song: rickety bridge to the funeral parlor.
Life and death are even.
My Lady Mum is all alive in Homer. May might be in love poems or others. Quick into another tunnel.
Van is in the apartments where he used to sing. His girl is kept in a trunk. Food for novel. Baskets of flowers. My Bunny lies over the station. At Queen's Plaza.
They come with baskets of bread. Italian bread. Mafia Geography. Sicily in Queens.
Name one bisquit factory near Woodside. I can. Sunshine before the tunnel.
Tracks all home by boxy meadow come. Manmountain winner. Mafia alp. Name a stadium with a sign for cough medicine. Castoria riverrun coughdrum. Put under a blanket into his tunnel: the Italian champ. Won.

499

The funnel house moves looking all over the then wide
country and down come planes full of Mafia fightfixers.
Tops of the apartments at pillbox hills firing tennis at Jews.
Out of the roars come vendors. It am tutor at Kew to a
tennis. Tennis Latin for the Long Island RR. Backand-
forth to drum drum bubber. Funnel top is watching you.
The kettle moves away from the burners.
A BUILDING SPEAKS: "TURN LEFT FOR THE RACETRACK. THIS IS
THE GEOGRAPHY OF LOGRAIRE."

2. Topsmart cunnels with memorial Chaplin. He went off
pilgrim smart with the collection. Run run the clever cap-
tain all over Queens. Van is in the cunning apartment with
his novel. A flight of pigeons with discipline. I sold my
wagon. I lost my labels in the funny tunnel of scream.

3. Most holy incense burners of Elmhurst save us. Most
Coronas screen us. House of Hungarians feed us. Give us
our Schenley labels from day to day. Give us our public
lessons of love. Swimming grunt lights down to the bot-
tom. Even the Island is long won. Trams to the end. House
of Hungarians spare us. Holy incense burners of Elmhurst
dissolve us. Trains come and gone. Their own hot smell
and passage snuffed entirely under. Save us. *Englouti!*
Periodic swallowing of travel under the East Sound. Then
Hellgate. Dread! Winterdazzle yards of the metropolitan
asshole. Most holy incense burners. Smoking tops. Crowns
of Mafia. Caruso with his boxtops all over the train. Corona.
Then the dumps. Deserve us!

4. Spider track out: spike out some home.
Rattle away to legendary capitals of the Rulers of Lograire.

A land of sandpits here without a single mountain. There go lemons.

Every boy is called Francis.

5. Tracks all home by boxy meadow of champs. Caruso won the top part of the box. He won the whole house. I jeered in the night at fans. I fled from shadowfixers.

6. Lawrence was big and weak with glasses. I despised him at the station. The high sand wall nearby became the place of an apartment. There Lois lived all tiny in a box of candy. I kept her there in case I had a novel. I met her by the lamp. We swam together in ginger ale. The big detective he sat downstairs running the timetables and commanding trains. The dark son of the tugboats married his daughter. The detective told one train after another to circle through Lograire. Dalzell told the tugs and lighters to circle the harbor. Boyer was next door with pictures of his tugboats in the attic. I knew where all the boats came from. I knew all the topdecks of Olympic. Lois and I knew the top of the radio building where I watched. You could not hear ourselves smiling while we trailed together to Sylvania Station. You had to be young then to act foolish in dens. Top funnel house was watching with pointed eyes.

7. It was light week in Lograire and all the phones. Sleepy time under the thickest summers. Insect lights and swings. Mortal tinkle of porches and glasses. Rumrunners call up Edison "inviting you to Charleston." Some sleepy-time man is coming down the island with his saxophone. Uncle Sled laughs across the street on other porches. I am sleepy-time with insects as they hum. The humdrum screen. The lawnmower morning. The hot garden is my hideaway

from the whisperer. I think of clouds. I think alone under the maple.

8.   It was light week in Lograire and all the phones. I am back from Curaçao she said. (They have wires in their voices when they want in Lograire.) When they want you should come by train to the tunnels. Breughel very funny under the city. When they want you should come via Elmhurst (save us the burners) via the gastank via the town. Queens burners defend tunnel.
Ruthie had a friend a big fink from Ohio too big for the apartment. He was too big for that bathroom. He blew down three walls.
Very fast cars in and out the poles under the Woodside elevated.
Name a factory where they make bathrooms: big ones, little ones. Bill worked for the bathrooms.
Head for the funnels into the city of verticals.
Stark hot stacks all night, stacklights, piles, Edisons, orders. The buildings rise full of orders up under lighted planes. Up. I remember. Back from Curaçao she told. Come and see why I have wires in my voice for you now. All of a sudden. I cannot come, I said. I have dead people to attend to. I have to travel the gastanks again to Elmhurst.
The grey-eyed Church is gonna get me I said.
Blue sides in the fishery shop I said, the wines and Mafias of Corona.
I have wires in my voice for you to come she said. I come in very fast cars if I can make it I replied if I can make it past Elmhurst.

9.   It was light week in Lograire. The wine was free. Connie had a bowl. All the boys' names were Frank. He went

all the way to the drugstore to be sick on account of military school. Phones rang. Cops' cars came and went looking at the party.

Anna had a relative in a field and the field had a speakeasy. Connie had an inn called Connie's Inn. Music under the hot tunnels of summer. The cops were in the cellar wanting to do the Charleston with the German maid. Connie had on a wet bathrobe and Frank got sick in the maid's bathroom on account of military school. We went to sleep in a boat that night in the harbor singing in front of fat Tony's. The boats were all beyond the reach of Edison and played their own lights upon the harbor. Several called Frank went all the way. I knew they took him in a copscar from the middle of the Park. I knew Finneran would fall in the middle of Harlem. Some stayed in the boats and others went to Cambridge.

10. All the walls have high grey teeth and tickle the night with signs. All the nights are children of chicken movies. We came home early only to write back to the same movies: "wishing you were here!" The city of verticles. The verses of comicals. The time had come for Auld Lang Syne to forget and for the business to part companies.

11. Don't tromp on the Macaire. Tonton Macoute is in the area. Watch the manholes. Protect the lives of your police. Lively traffic on all the phones. Helicops.

12. Famous John is downstairs under the speakeasy. He is conducting all the spillways. He is the demiurge of all ways out: a devil of a toilet. If you don't know Macaire you can't make it to the subways. But Famous John is sinister: he runs the undertow of a big city. It is all controlled

from under Sugar Hill—the Hill where the diamonds are, where Finneran fell, the diamonds' eyes, Edison's elves, living and loving in nighty coves.

Famous John lives under all the nightspots in an invisible office. He is the city's liver.

If you know Macaire he can fix it for you to get away. But Ruthie has a friend. A big girl from Vassar College. Mum in a tent. Followed by graffiti.

13. Famous John puts a sign on the door: Tonight baby all the Edisons are going to blink.

A message from Sugar Hill: "Famous John is writing his name on your apartment door."

Try to call the Edisons and see if they are still in business. You can't do this anymore. You have to pay Macaire. Tonton sticks his funny head up out of the manholes. Yes, everywhere.

14. Famous John is inviting you to a wondrous trip with his spies. A ride in roofless vans to see tall smokes all over the experience: the smokes of Edison, the spinning winter bridges, the lovelorn whooping crane, the warehouses of Coney's unbeatable fun. Famous John is inviting you to drink at Connie's Inn where the bowl is for everybody. Winedark East River for everybody. And on the winegarbage waters of Spuyten Duyvil we race Big John the New York Central Steamer with our plucky college shell. Insane. Famous John is inviting you to the Catskills for a lightning summer. Observe poetry in a spell. Coney Island with trees and a waterfall.

15. Top the funnel house eyes roving everywhere to watch for Jews and Christians doing it. All the eyes of analysis:

you are counted as you pass through Astoria. All the eyes of the planes coming down. Freightyards of Armageddon. The whole city is full of passengers. It is a seeing city; a singing telephone. Top of funnel house (won by Caruso) is big know-how—counts police helicopters. All the eyes of Jews and Christians are locked in a treasure computer. Top the funnel house eyes tell exactly where you must go. Every way you turn your car it is still there: the electric.

16.   Madmen in a vacant lot bet on a walking kettle. A runner gets his foot caught in the teeth of a field. Cola gardens around the clock intent golf counters win. Never mind. The fight is over furniture, over a bowl, over a lighter, over a burner. The city is observed by invisible buzzards of silk. And a big fat ass from Ohio is a sitter in Elmhurst. Top the funnel house eyes know wherever you go, to the burners, to the houses, to the chapels, to the stores. Who can win? When he raped Kitty in these streets all the people turned away and pretended not to notice.

17.   The sacred books are confiscated by police to keep eyes under sightless dome. Study famous text in court. Sacred words kept shut in horny room. They keep my novels in a box of candy. Shine continental glad warm being in Law. Witness defies sentence structure. Chatterly wins sightless connection in timeworn nickle viewer: hierarchic spectacle. Eyes down everyone. Fold hands, walk aisles, composures, make up for Lawrence in Church. Save famous continental dome from Reds. Extort glad news from Receiver. Famous John will live in hiding with "Roses of Life." Latest sacred arrested books saved up in jealous Senates of memory for more fun until better business. Keep eyes ahead gone dead dome: a shiny bald Church with a hole in the head a

veritable pantheon. Fulltime overwork for Monsignori canonizing randy films. Keep sacred religious motions private. Italian cineasts watch Cardinal taking a bath. Sacred ideas confiscated twice by eminent machine. Good news dame is apprehended and shut up in extended thought. Business reverses blind control and gets better. Cardinal relents and warm room smells great. Author blesses Ruthie's fat friend. Forgiveness all round. Sacred books confined to ecclesiastical pen. Keep ageless roses in cardinal's warm bedroom. Wishing you the wonders of our episcopal garden. Lost his glasses reading books in secret buildings. Never found again. Pantheon doorman saves pleasure dome from detection.

18. See you home under the lamp of lights in guise of protection. Harlem.

19. Sendings: a powder. Stays. Pomade. Twill. Rawhide. Regency Power. Houndstooth. Regal lizard. Amber Rose (code) Send space wines idle while. Send fine lagers ever. Wide unreasonable suit. Whining Mayor (a fake). Transocean signed Captain martyr send Iris signal and help run. Green lemon patron. Help cider. More Scotch. Send universal maroon. Send cricket bats. Junior Navy. Herringbone ten. Aqua fifty-five. Mum's own velvet. Boys' Own Paper. Clips. Flaps. Mumps. Boats. Beds. Too many pink and maroon and magnolia. Signed on China graffito "Joe." Yes, bone China (personal). Oxbone handshake. Glum Mayors. Waders up to the bum. Finnegan's Hall. Byron's Hyde Park roadrunner under the arch. Ship how many freights away Tuesday? Too many. All way back home. Please send tees, shutters, flaxens, needles, tocsins, suds, pumps, raglans, botanicals, turquoise acetate, tire valves,

champagne crepe pantshifts, butter melange, Salem witch house, glyres, bloares, mweers, alps, public gardens. Please send elephant leather chukkas, braised partridge, carryall patch pocket loop-through blendpouch in a variety of stoles. Please send everything: happy roses of life (dames) need instant comfort. Send crocus (for my Japanese juniorette). Yellow pimiento, chili turtleneck for La Vida brava. Send also a message to Carlyle. Solid state. Chef cleft chief ten. Annuity wear poplin top quality premium impact liqueur batiste accelerator tourist accessories and mineral oil. Send. Send. Send send. Sendesend. Send us the other end. Send us all the whiskey.

20. Gryphon rends slipson two piece pioneer. Wave checks a gonerful went. Fully lined savings bake clam tide. Climate is always holy here in Rum. Roses of life come out like flags to welcome police stranger. You can't go wrong with our guard. You add accessories toptop create. Dreamy glassass boats over the ride you fishface. Him boss vanna lighterage. Bovers. Oxers. Beefteas. Stews. Dead hightides climate Duggle Stone Club. Pantry party in the wastelands of Mugg. Up went ten rebels through the viewfinders without flash. Won checks overwhelming barques. Cutty-life still-Sark clambake in editor's home. Much president leads quintet. (Couplet under the bed.) Red forefathers wet the tent. Feeble glare of sportside landing. Why pay extra money for a beach? Deliver big color in sixty flats. $160 model Polaroid second nun. Bishops coming from Cromwell strand. Boston tippety bishop struggles with his finder: doesn't like the view (Poles). Poles apart sighs ace in the cradle. Hot five smokes way over the sea: a five funneled Olympic fights to a draw. Sails over into the mistbergs. Transistorized it makes blackwhite shutterpiece. Shudder

the mudder the fugger under the lugger (seas). Pained spirit of Savoys, meetings, messings, pressings, lavers. MY BONNIE LIES OVER THE OCEAN WITH NEON SCRIPTURES AND SHE IS SENDING PLATES (Mates).
Awright, give it another ten.

21. She is sending me pigeons from Trafalgar panels and stained with colors she is all stranded there. Oh where? Down into the tunnels to find her. Endless are the awaited trains. Gone there. She is sending herself in painted emblems and delicate stained glass. Virgin Mother of lily-light and lost nun of the infirmary nightlight. I go run for the vanished nurse in the subway tunnels of every night.

22. They the cronies are sending spites. Make sure the payers get their plates. Best deliver the bountiful weights to cash songsters. Stripe contours pop colors redsquares and bluestills and greensails. Sweet juleps mend us on our Virginia ways. Sweetmints under the old banktank. Pops out the window and snores a curse over Bank Street: "You come too late and I'll call the police." They the cronies are having a party of twists. Pairs of precious emblems in the windowsights. Why pay extra money for the one on the left? Walking and waking in tropical ranges: two exposure tricolor delivery in the middle of stage. Rectangles and monochromes. Segments and inner faces media mean. Masmass celebrate the wonderful Name. Oils recently placed in sink. Block letouts. Blank letups. Bodyfits under tub.

23. A group of acrylics. Stasis. Sepsis. Cityscapes (cloax, cloax). The bird on the revolving bridge and the watcher on the ravening turntable. Elias with his Polaroid filming the fun. Sit back and stoplooklisten. Under $160. Why pay

more? Gong bundles and secret cameras into uncle tunnel. Down forum drummers into the sun and back into dark next to same cloax. Cloax Max. Circus mum. Palladium hills and the Hippodrum. Vaudeville mums in scanty parallax. All beautiful colors come up in sixty seconds. Still life Dixie postrace march like a mooncolumn advancing into shape. SHE IS SENDING ME ALL HER PAINS and doves her titty posters and contours. Virgins of victory weep their late lights alone lost nights with stills styles and tiny alarms. Waits. The patients liewake lates. Playing the bells until they all vanish down a hole in a carton of smokes.

O RISE AGAIN YOU VACANT SQUARES PIPE TONES
ACROBATIC BARBERS
TAUPES ARE NOW IN ALL THE MOLE GAMES
WINNING THE DIMMEST MIDNIGHT CEERS

Change the flame to number eight. Dreamy glass box will benefit the same. He sleeps wailing for a mate. Famous Tom is drowsing under a weight.

24. Look out mumper lookout to shore. Coonsails! Conmix! Katzenjobber Picnics! Yoyo Silver rushing into the cop-shops. Tonmix riding into places of ownership. Momma Mudder for less than you'd pay. She has a Zeiss under her left and stores information. She has a viewfinder and finds the shapes. Can fashion be considered an investment?

25. THE NORTH AS EVERYBODY KNOWS IS VERY NORD. It is aquilonic.

26. Gare du. Money for Egypt. Mountains of armor way down in Old Cairo where the Virgin blesses Copts and complains about the Holy Spaces. Visit Egypt with Thomas

Mock. Yoyo Lompoc rushing into doubt. They both deliver big. Gare du Garcon. Nasty Nordweapons flame over Suzy Canal.

27. Nordsee chowder. Long shower past Ostende. Shimmer summer. Trawl away over rocking Dutchland. Sick as Dover all over the sea is frailest passenger swooning for the rails. (The missus can't take it.) (Well, keep her under a bed for Class' sake! Keep her under glass for the Sea's sake! Save her glassass for the British viewsem.)

28. Taupes are winning all the cheers this summer. Why pay more for the one that is less? If you add one more accessory you can toptop the funnelbox. You can smell the smokes all the way to Crete. Weeds out of London trawl: Gravesend way. Serious Kent. Reedy showers. Seedy springs. Conrad hunter lives over the beach: hunts editions. Captain Rugby seems unfamiliar at landlubber tea. Major John with a field-size parallax captures the hunter. Funnelhouse sees with twenty eyes. Madmen betting again on the same walking kettle. Kettle's Yard where the paintings are. Funnelhouse meanwhile views with Mafia pot. You can smell the deadly visions all the way to Skete. You can't go wrong in a Skete.

29. North is LNER wending off to Scotch Nero's in the dark. Aberdeen puddings and cobbles. Scotch fisheries. Lake kipperies. The Loch Mess Mumps. The Nordsee haggis. Cuthbert is on his rock warmed by the noses of seals. Hilda on the Hilltower, Bede at his desk, Caedmon in the pub, and Grace sings all her loudest alarms for Old King Cole.

30. Bridgelost. Bridewell. Basewall. Bardbell. Next to St. Andrews. Nord is Forth. Bluegreen aquilons. Walking in a misty season to wink of water. Lighters crafted like jewelry. Pickets like a rave. Cobbles under the castle of a lost queen. Nowhere to assemble in sombre lanes. George comes out briefly in pale sun. He shines on his post. George is sundown's Rex. Crimson boxes of deliverup. Foghorn tempo with gulls. Live whitey, rule the frames. Live whiskey on a thousand clippers.

31. Weeds black sound along gulls foot part waste p︲ce foot way humming iron bridge. Begin again the light of lemons in the little mother doors (Lawrence). Mines are Nord. The mine smokes blue. The minesweeper. Shimmer summer the Nordling tree. Minereader. Coal from under the sea. Offside, you lemon!

32. Speaking of famous drinks there might be a lot more and there is.

33. O bell of blue flame from under the mind. Less than human phones. Celtic masters leave aboard the barcraft. Tell it all to delicate feelers (you ought to see with those ears!) Confessions into the eyes of flowers. Foxgloves and bluebells. Telling it to the elves' eyes, the diamond dews of Uxbridge Foxbridge and Harrow. Sweet blue morning of Harrow (Easter) from the Church and down there is Elaine's house. I confess it to the bluebells. You ought to speak to the elms O browneyed Elaine. We were bluebells to one another on the river. The great grey serious river of Nothing.

34. Speaking of famous words. The Irish singers whirl the gaudy spokes of Bejaysus all over the Isles of Man Skye and Orkney. There Ezechiel comes in a flaming hearse. He rides his own red monument and announces his swords. Wheels, wings of Merkabah. Flaming Ottomans straight out of Dublin. The jeweled teeth of a heavenly contraption. Come ye Evangels to the coasts of Nord.

35. Run run Ezechiel you are on probation!

36. Top the funnel charnel at the police's corner. The spanky wink. The redred. The walky talk. The phenomenon feeler. The top regarder. The bump on the boss. The ozone of gasometers. Eyeshots and droplet pix. Cunning exposures of fun on the run. Nicked in the nakt. Dressing in the Cadillac. Found in the act. Seeming letters and postals of George in the milky sun. Millways. King of the postbus. Comes with a Gainsborough and puts a pillarbox under the tree. I have drops in my eyes and can't see the pictures. Stunsun Newmarket morning. I can't see the starters because I am gated again. Gated in Bridge Street with a pillar of postals. Shred my letters and feed them to the birds. Stunsun Newmarket morning is wide wide all over. Bookies in the lane. Topfunner Newmocker news. Radios and signs. RAF gleamers. Cries of lonely Auden there in the heights. Lincoln fens are for the airmen. I sit alone under the mornings of Cambridge pylons and watch fliers. Icarus falls.

37. Catch forties. The Millways' Tale told to an autobus. Running home from Chesterton by night among the fences. Stunsun and it is another morning. Sunday down by the boatless river. Goldilights of Northmorning see telltale

Maundies colder and older. Gold February tells Millways' boat to spill amid a calm. Tall stands of Twickenham captains. Baroque pieties of a fine Anglican. Loves' labour lost in Twickenham garden.

38. Winner take all Mondays. Climates. Emblem. Surplices. Twinkling garden vision precision eyebeams strung on a string. (Get thee to an eyedoctor.) Excise management pouring·into Pauls with innocent faces cleam. Strike out Mazdas of John Dean oh great dark grinning deathshirt John dumbstruck subway under a guilty city! (The bombers come!)

39. Stained stained to Henley Thames we go to tame the water with our butterflies.

40. Famous John is inventing you a trap with his agents. Old effigy with Anglican sabres. That turning stair goes up to a stone tiger. Tiger burns with his own secret fright. Sinners are betting on a walking kettle of eyes. Tiger tiger burning in the bay escapes double vision. Lettertrap for old Posthumus. (*Eheu fugaces* said our clock in Rye. The clock at Fletcher's.) Oho fliers posthumus oho the airmail letters flip over and glide away. Butterfly papers. Ten a penny prayers. Guarded petitions pouring into Pauls with evident vital claims. Torn out of a lovelorn long summer in Elmhurst (Ruthie had a friend). Simplicissimus (not funny). With a lovesick butterfly (*Fugaces*). Sing it all aloud. Sing sang sung song Cleo to the welkin! The musical Nord is forever aquilonic.

41. Sing a song to Momma Mudder. Winner has all the grey climates. Millways' gone home in the rigging of

misted eyebeams. Baroque summers of hear my song O Thames (flow sweetly til I end). It was light week in Lograire and we saw it in the relatives' field and the way of the world is bent. The Edisons blink. Blink at a cardinal winner out in sportsdale. Make sure the prayers all get to their right place. Stranded in the sun. Sane song sing sang sun! Time tongue tokens of lovelorn trancer. Shimmering Thames by Westminster and under the Savoy. The young hotel is quiet as a nun. Welkin sunstruck welkin sunstruck welkin. Lobsang rivers of Lammermoor. Long-lasting limes. Stained in tunnels claimed by the all seeing master-funnels. Very funny coming into light: sinners all chasing a five legged kettle. Butterfly traffic ten a penny. My prayers are all torn out of the mourning paper. Sing sang song to lucky welkin! Sing sang sun tone (think of a magazine). Suntown Cleotone sang song in downing sun (a Loma) An-cleo-tony. The phone song sung alone at dawn. Prayer is vast (the moaning paper!) the waste blue sky. Gone cleo is my clear tone welkin. I die praising!

42.   Hello Argus yes this is Argus police please I have to report a walking kettle yes every day sinners active in every street. Send agents teargas bazooka mace to slightly broken home of double trouble. Run to our tumble here at Connie's Inn. Signed: Boston.

43.   Voice of a prayer lip stumbles in gross assent.
HELLO AGENTS THIS IS RELIGION CALLING FOR HELP.
Send Argus to command another. Try that second election. Seize another paramilitary chance. Well-meaning prayer lip again fumbles message. IS GOD IN KENT?

44.   Light tower panic in election night view semblance of sheeted type on garden prowl (ten are bit by bats).

Commotion in the mixture. Coonselves permit a dilemma. Loud are the batteries. Favorites all dead. Blossoms insane night with Edison flakes. All red screams Connie in raided bed. Connie Mamma is ahead of dusk (in her sheets). She goes off with lights around her head (the final Regina). Moral redress calls to arms: types explain (rest room in Albuquerque). My Connie lies over the ocean with the doublespread. My Connie is back in the North with pillows under her head. Dramas begin again in Elmhurst. Mum is the laundress.

45. Judge hold hands. Slow door closes in defence. Maladies of innocence! Protect the lives of your local Mafia.

46. When I sat down and wept by Sandy river the city was filled with Mafia passengers landing from the air. O the light came down and wept on the runways. Tiger burning in the weeds escapes double vision. George's geography is all trouble with spies. Nord is the red of Scotland Yard. I stood by the weighing machine in a room so bare so bare. Bare as St. James' Infirmary the room my baby there. My Bonnie was in the far north laid out on a long white table.

47. Mister Justice with frosty eye say too many little legs are going by (the kettle of Hieronymus Bosch). Scary kettle of drugs. Knottypot. Right dress! Squads of drunken bottles all over the yard. Marching vessels. Yes bottles have eyes springs scents visions. Order cubes. Expand senses. Recall movers. Mister Judge with frosty eye view too many senses walking by. Stop that kettle it looks so funny walking at a trot. All the trees walking (like men). The wallpaper has eyes and moves watching. Mister Judge with frosty eye see too many movies going by (on the same

wall). Bottles with hips. Oh mercy, jugs with hands! Little gleamy unkind jars. Phials stick out tongues. A crow flies out of the pitcher. Judge Doublethink condemns an icecube. Restores senses, scents, visions, touches, tastebuds. Stop that kettle walking up the wall on all fours stop those swinging flocks of flocons. STOP THAT PAPER STOP THAT FLASK. STOP ACK ACK STOP FLAK. Too late. Every instrument is moving!

48. Geography is in trouble all over Lograire. Rape of maps by military arm. Judgments fly out of crowsnests all around prison. Points. Pens. Bibbed Parson Calvin bites pot with conviction. Pastor Fingerbone moves jug and troubles the oil. Points to grease foul well name (famous scrambled). Pastor Crowfoot bugs a Delta home. Officer Foulball comes in daddywagon to end Black War of Astoria. Is assailed on Northern Blvd. Pastor Wallpaper does vile sums in the toilets. Father Topknot works for bishops in crowsnest surrounding slum. Performs the deadly operation. Removes another building. All the fractions are in jail being complimented by sermons.

49. Dear Togs. I have chosen electric life with spades. The lines here are almost new. Home is underwater now. Conscience is a bronco well busted. Memory secured by electronic tape. Gunshots on the glassy swamps of night. Uniforms wade under willows calling to the dead.

50. So Christ went down to stay with them Niggers and took his place with them at table. He said to them, "It is very simple much simpler than you imagine." They replied, "You have become a white man and it is not so simple at all."

II

"There is a grain of sand in Lambeth which Satan cannot
    find."
There is a child of God in the sacred cellar undressing
    Louise.
My little brother is climbing all over Catherine.
There is a seed of light in us that cannot be bought
    by Grove Press.
With Pat by the boulders in late afternoon the sailboats did
    not see it.
Tall elms meditate all night and the big dog looks
    into the back seat
The daughters of Schenley approach and withdraw.
They have to giggle.
We sink quietly into naked water where Satan cannot find
    any sand whatever
But where the condoms of others will float in full view
On New Year's morning.

There is a grain of sand in boarding school down
    the long hall
And giant elms cover the cricket field with shadow
I am photographed in an embarrassed collar
My Jerusalem is wide awake with watch fiends
I am searched and investigated by baying bitches
I am a grain of fear in village churches.

There is a pebble of Jerusalem in Ealing
Listens to the everlasting piano in the next home

On spring nights when there is no sleeping
Because the rivers of life are wide awake
And a child must die into manhood
On the cricket field

There is a grain of sand in Lambeth which Satan
        cannot find
While deep in the heart's question a shameless light
Returns no answer.

III. THE RANTERS AND THEIR PLEADS
(London)

1. *Sessions of Gaole delivery held in the Old Bayley the 18, 19, and 20 of this instant January, 1651*
". . . She commends the Organ, Viol, Symbal and Tonges in Charterhouse Lane to be heavenly musick; she tosseth of her glasses freely and comendeth there is no heaven but the pleasures she injoyeth upon earth; she is very familiar at first sight and danceth the Canaries at the sound of a hornpipe."

(*The Routing of the Ranters, 1650*)

2. Met at a tavern
   The David and Harp in Moor Lane
   Sang: "Ram me dam me!"
   And other blasphemies
   To the tune of the Psalms
   Alleged that "Ram"
   Was another name for "God"
   When about to be arrested
   Took up a candle
   Looked in all the corners
   "hunting for his sins"
   And said (so brazen)
   "he found not one."
   Apprehended, examin'd, arraign'd in Old Bayley
   Was sent to Bridewell to beat hemp
   With six companions

Who had danced at supper
Tearing a piece of beef
With damnable opinions
Prancing to the viol
In Adamitic orgies
Calling one another:
"Fellow creature"!

3. GANGRAENA: A CATALOGUE OF ERROURS

"Every creature is an efflux from God
And shall return into God again
As a drop is in the ocean."

"If God be all things then he is sin and wickednesse;
and if he be all things then he is this Dog, this Tobacco
Pipe, he is in me and I am in him, I have heard some
say, blaspheming . . ."

> "... *A deep mystery and great ocean*
> *Where there is no casting anchor*
> *No sounding the bottome.*"

Item: "That there shall be a generall Restauration
wherein all men shall be reconciled to God and saved."
Impious doctrine.

They dishonour and cry downe the Churche!

"I could relate also other errours as that:

IF A MAN WERE STRONGLY MOVED BY THE SPIRIT TO
KILL OR TO COMMIT ADULTERY AND UPON PRAYING

520

AGAINST IT AGAIN AND AGAIN IT CONTINUED AND HE
WAS STILL STRONGLY PRESSED

HE SHOULD DO IT!"

An eye and ear witness
A more true and fuller discovery
Of the Doctrine of those men

4. "Now is the Creature damm'd and ramm'd into its
    only Center
Into the bowels of still Eternity, its Mother's womb
There to dwell forever unknown
This and this only is the 'damnation'
So much terrifying the creature
In its dark apprehensions . . ."

5. GRAND IMPOSTURES ABOMINABLE PRACTISES GROSS DECEITS
LATELY SPREAD ABROAD AND ACTED IN THE COUNTY OF
SOUTHAMPTON.

. . . M. Stubs a late fellow Ranter.

6. Distempered with sickness
Distracted in brain
Thou has left off to read.

". . . and that makes thee to be such a wathercock,
such a well without water, such a wandering star as
thou art, such a cloud tost to and fro with a tempest,
because thou hast no steady rule to steer by or to fix
thee to any one point, but only the whistling, multi-
farious fancies and foolish figments of thine own aiery
brain and inconstant spirit . . ."

"A people so dronish that the whole course of their life is but one SCENE OF SOTTISHNESS."

(The Ranters' Religion)

7. An Abominable Ranter, Jacob Bauthemly, wrote that the Devil and Hell were "the Dark Side of God" and wrote it while in the army. Therefore he was punished by being burned through the tongue. He was afterward found with Quakers and Ranters in Leicestershire spreading his foul sayings and abominations:

"O God what shall I say thou art when thou cans't
      not be named
For if I say I see thee it is nothing but thy seeing
      of thyself . . .

"Nay, I see that God is in all creatures,
Man and Beast, Fish and Fowle,
And every green thing from the highest cedar to the
      ivey on the wall;
And that God is the life and being of them all . . .

"As all things were let out of God:
So shall they all give up their Being, life and
            happiness
Unto God again
Though the clothing dissolve and come to nothing
Yet the inward man still lives . . .

"I find that where God dwells and is come
And hath taken men up and rapt them up
            in the Spirit;
There is a new heaven and a new earth

And my heaven is to have my earthly and dark
Apprehensions of God to cease
And to live no other life than what Christ
Spiritually lives in me . . .

"Sin is the dark side of God but God is not
        the author of sin
Nor does he will it. Sin being a nullity, God cannot
        be the author of it."

8. PROOFS EXAMINATIONS DECLARATIONS
   INDICTMENTS AND CONVICTIONS
   ARRAIGNMENT AND TRYALL
   DAMNABLE AND DIABOLICAL OPINIONS
   DETESTABLE LIVES AND ACTIONS

Late prodigious pranks and unparalleled deportments
Notorious corrupting and disordering of society
"Withal they enjoyned a cursed doctrine of
        LIBERTINISM
Which brought them to all abominable filthiness
        of life:
They say that for a man to be tyed to one woman
Or one woman to one man
Is a fruit of the curse.

SMOKE OF THE BOTTOMLESS PIT
VENTED AND ACTED IN ENGLAND.

9. A Way for Suppression of the obscene licentious and
   impious Practices used by Persons under Pretense of
   Liberty and Religion.

10. They teach that there is neither heaven nor hell
    But what is in man.

    They do not apprehend any wrath
    To be in God.

    I saw a letter that one of them writ to a friend of his
    And at the bottom of the letter he writ thus:
    "From Heaven and Hell or from Deptford
    In the first yeare of my reconciliation to my Selfe."

    Then God does not hate? Not even sin?
    So heaven and hell are in Deptford, Woolwich,
            Battersea and Lambeth?

    Burn him through the tongue!

IV. KANE RELIEF EXPEDITION

1

Morning came at last
The storm over we sighted
Quiet mountains green and
Silver Edens
Walls of an
Empty country—Near?
(We were deceived—30 miles at least)

You can tell when Sunday comes
Everything on shipboard
Quieter
       icebergs like churches
Slow sailing gifts
          visions
A sailor intoned
An Anglican hymn

"One iceberg on our port bow
Resembled a lady dressed in white
Before her shrine"
(Dazzling whiteness
       gemm'd with blue-green)
"In the attitude of prayer"

"As if some magician, etc. . . ."

"Gifts—visions"

A huge berg between us
And the green shore.
"As we were gazing it grounded and the shock caused one
end of it to fall over upon the other and both turned over.
A terrible sight. Crashed like thunder. Spray flew mast-
high"

Then whales came
And played around us all day.

2

Black parapets
Of Disko conjured
Out of cold rain
Something like a sentry box
On a tall summit

A boat shot out
Suddenly produced
From behind that rock
Came for us
With six eskimos
And Lieut. Saxtroph
Of the Danish army.

Our pilot took over
Headed straight for the rock
A crack in the cliff
Ninety yards wide
Secret basin land-
Locked dark
All stone straight up

Two thousand feet
Into the rain
Not a spot of green
I inquir'd where to
Look for the town
He pointed to
Twelve cabins.

Then kayaks all around us
Offered fish for sale
You could obtain
A duck for a bisquit

"The Lieutenant had been in the wars between Denmark
and Schleswig Holstein; he spoke English very well and
during our stay at Lievly done everything in his power to
make our time pass pleasantly. He was a splendid dancer
and sang the national songs of his country with much
spirit."

3

We climbed to a graveyard
High on the wet rock
There bodies sleep in crevices
Covered with light earth then stones
Some were sailors from England
And America
Now asleep
In this black tower
Over Baffin's Bay
Waiting, waiting
In endless winter.

We left them to their sleep
Ran down to meet the living girls.

"I would have given almost anything for a daguerrotype
of that room. Voices soft and clear eyes light blue or hazel.
Not one bad tooth. Their hair is all combed up to the top
of the head and twisted into a knot and tied with ribbons,
red for the unmarried, blue for the married ones. Jumper
or jacket lined with finely dressed deerskin trimmed with
fur and a band of ribbon. The most beautiful part of their
dress is the pantaloons of spotted seal, very soft, with an
embroidered stripe down the front which says: 'ready for
marriage.'"

We called for a Polka. The band
"Struck up Camptown Races we had taught them
The previous night"
Seizing our partners
We all commenced

Better dancing
I never saw at home.

"The space between the pants and boots is filled with a
legging of linen or muslin edged and lined with deerskin.
They were all scrupulously clean."

4

75° N. Melville Bay
July 29.
"A conical island in a bay of ice to starboard. It is the
Sugar Loaf island of whalers. It tells that on rounding

the headland now in sight (Wilcox Point) we shall see the far-famed Devil's Thumb the boundary of dreaded Melville Bay."

July 30.
"Toiling slowly through the leads with plenty of bear tracks around us."

July 31.
"A good lead opening. Towed twelve miles. The much talked of Devil's Thumb is now in sight. It appears to be a huge mass of granite . . . Here begins Melville Bay."

Bay of ice and gales
Grave of whalers
Where "in one disastrous year the whaling fleet
Lost twenty-eight sail."

From the Devil's Thumb northward
Vast glacier
"One of the manufactories
From whence the huge icebergs
Are given off"

Fifty miles wide.

8 days driven to and fro
By masses of ice.
                Waiting
To be crushed
"All provisions on deck
Ready for a run
At a moment's warning."

The bark was thrown over on her beam ends
Our batteau lashed to the bulwark
Was ground to atoms
In a couple of minutes.

"All hands on the qui vive for a smash."

(Must we go 200 miles over ice
Dragging our boats
To Upernavik?)

Finally clear of pack ice on the 13th
We stood for Cape York
Red snow on the rocks. Open water
Finally out
Of Melville Bay!

5

Cape Alexander

Here K. promised to leave a cairn
And a bottle with a clear account of his proceedings
To tell us his intended course
Instead
A small mound
A homeopathic vial containing a mosquito
Covered with cotton
A small piece of cartridge paper
With the letters "OK" written on it
As if with the point of a bullet.

6

78° N. Cape Haterton and Etah

Two Indians on a rock
Like an owl's cry
Signalling

"We landed and found a village of tents in a valley with a
lake of fresh water. A large glacier over the edge of which
a cataract was pouring into the lake. Grass almost knee
deep, full of flowers. Indians in dogskins and the skins of
birds collected around us and examin'd our firearms with
the greatest attention."

"We soon found unmistakable signs of K.'s party having
been there. Knives and cutlery bearing the mark of the
Green River works. Pewter cups and part of a microscope.
Preserved meat and pemmican cans, baking pans, forks,
spoons, a piece of a shirt with the initials H.B., spools of
cotton marked N. York, curtain material, the top rail of a
berth, red velvet and an ivory handled carving knife . . ."

"By signs they gave us to understand that the vessel had
been crushed in the ice. This they done by taking a clay
pipe and crushing it between their hands."

"They pointed to a child and made signs
That K. was a small man
Bald and without whiskers."

O hairless Kane
Lost in ice

How long gone?
They do not understand
Time
But he cured
One of their children.

They catch birds on the rocks by means of nets
Eat the birds raw
Give anything for a knife.

That ivory handled carving knife
Probably stolen.

7

Possession Bay

"Moonlight among the ice presents a scene that none but
those who have sail'd in Arctic regions can form any con-
ception of. It glances from the floe ice with a blinding
glare and gives the icebergs the appearance of mountains
of light.

"Light streaming through a tall archway in a berg
Like scenes in the showy fairy pieces
At the theaters."

8

Pond's Bay

Rookery of loons
"Greatest sight of bird doings"
Cliffs terraced notched every projection
Covered

Thousands
Wheeling over us in moon-
Light so tame
You could knock them down with an oar

Deafening.

"We entered a cave at the foot of the cliff and found it
filled with young loons and gulls."

So we shot 500 weighing 1172 lbs.

9

Sept 4th 1855

Midnight. Gale.

"Get up Dr. we are rushing down on an iceberg."

As I reached the deck
We crashed.

A huge iceberg
Four times as high as the mast
Overhangs our ship
More of the same
Starboard
White mass
Driven head on we
Beat against it
Bows staved in jib

Boom carried away we
Recoil swing star-
Board beam smashes
Into small end of ice-
Berg quarterboat in splinters
All bulwarks driven in
Cathead bumpkins and the rest
Gone
          Wind
Swirling around angle of ice
Like a hurricane
Rush for boats driven back:
"We fired minute guns but the gale was so high the noise
of crashing ice so great the steamer could not hear us . . ."

(The account ends here. Both expeditions reached safety.)

EAST

EAST

LOVE OF THE SULTAN

A SLAVE
CUTS OFF HIS OWN HEAD
AFTER A LONG SPEECH
DECLARING HOW MUCH
HE LOVES THE SULTAN

A QUAINT OLD ASIAN CUSTOM

LOVE
OF
THE
SULTAN!

I. EAST WITH IBN BATTUTA

1. Cairo 1326

Cloisters (khanqahs) of Darvishes
Built by aristocrats
Have silver rings on their doors
The mystics sit down to eat
Each from his private bowl
Each drinks
From his own cup
They are given
Changes of clothing
And a monthly allowance
On Thursday nights
They are given sugar
Soap and oil
For their lamps
And the price of a bath.

In the great cemetery
They build chambers
Pavilions
Hire singers
To chant the *Koran*
Day and night among the tombs
With pleasant voices.

Convent at Dayr at-Tin:
A piece of the Prophet's
Wooden basin with the pencil
With which he applied kohl

The awl
With which he sewed his sandals
Bought by the founder
For a hundred thousand dirhams.

2. *Syria*

Ma'arra and Sarmín: towns
Of abominable Shi'ites
Who hate the Ten Companions
And every person called Omar

In Sarmín (where scented soap
Is made and exported
To Damascus and Cairo)
These heretics so hate the Ten
They will not even say "Ten"
Their brokers at auctions
When they come to "ten"
Say "Nine-plus-one"

One day a faithful Turk
At one of their markets
Heard the broker call "Nine-plus-one"
He went for him with a club, shouting
"You bastard, say TEN!"

"Ten with a club"
Wept the broker.

3. *The Nusayris*

These heretics hate all true believers and when ordered by
        the Sultan
To build mosques build them far from their homes
Keep asses and cattle in them let them fall into disrepair.

If a true believer coming from another country
Stops in a ruined mosque and sings the call to prayer
The infidels say: "Stop braying,
We will bring you a little hay."

Once a stranger came to the Nusayris and told them he was
        the Mahdi
He promised to divide Syria among them
Giving each one a city or a town.
He gave them olive leaves and said:
"These will bring you success. These leaves
Are warrants of your appointment."

They went forth into city and town
And when arrested, each said to the Governor:
"The Imám al-Mahdi has come. He has given me
        this town!"

The Governor would then reply: "Show me your warrant"

Each one then produced his olive leaves
And was flogged.

So the stranger told the heretics to fight:
"Go with myrtle rods," he said
"Instead of swords. The rods
Will turn to swords at the moment of battle."

They entered a town on Friday when the men were
        at the mosque.
They raped the women and the Muslims
Came running out with swords
And cut them to pieces.

News was sent to the capital by carrier pigeon.
      The Governor
Moved out with an army. Twenty thousand heretics
Were slaughtered. The rest hid in the mountains.
They offered one dinar per head if they were spared.
This news went by pigeon to the Sultan
Who said: "Kill them."

But the General
Said these people could be useful
Working on the land
And their lives were spared.

4. Mecca

"The Meccans are very elegant and clean in their dress, and
most of them wear white garments, which you always see
fresh and snowy. They use a great deal of perfume and
kohl and make free use of toothpicks of green arák-wood.

"The Meccan women are extraordinarily beautiful and very
pious and modest. They too make great use of perfumes to
such a degree that they will spend the night hungry in
order to buy perfumes with the price of their food.

"They visit the mosque every Thursday night, wearing
their finest apparel; and the whole sanctuary is saturated
with the smell of their perfume. When one of these women
goes away the odour of the perfume clings to the place
after she has gone."

5. Isfahan

In Isfahan the fair
Surrounded by orchards
(Apricots and quinces
Pears and melons)
The people out-do one another
In banquets
"In the preparation for which
They display all their resources"
One corporation entertained another with viands
Cooked over candles
"The guests returned the invitation
And cooked their viands with silk."

6. Delhi

In the Sultan's apartments
I saw a *Júgí*
Sitting in midair
I fell in a faint
They had to give me a drink
To revive me

And there he was
Still sitting in midair
His companion
Took a sandal from a bag
Beat it on the ground
Til it rose in the air
All by itself and poised
Over the floating one

And it began hitting him
On the back of the neck
Until he floated down
And landed.

"I would tell them to do something else,"
Said the Sultan, "If I did not fear
For your reason."

7. *Calicut*

Chinese vessels at anchor in the harbor
One of the largest in the world. Malabar
Coast of ginger pepper spice
Four decks with cabins saloons
Merchants of Canton Sumatra
Ceylon stay locked in cabins
With wives and slave girls
Sailors bring their boys to sea
Cultivate salads and ginger
In wooden vats

In Calicut I missed my boat
To China and my slave
Girls were all stolen by the King
Of Sumatra and my companions
Were scattered over China
Sumatra and Bengal

When I saw what had happened
I sailed for the Maldives
Where all the inhabitants
Are Muslims

Live on red fish lightly cooked
Or smoked in palmleaf baskets
It tastes like mutton

These natives wear no pants
Only aprons
Bathe twice a day
Use sandalwood and do not fight
Their armor is prayer.

II. EAST WITH MALINOWSKI

We tack into the lagoon
Shipping water I am ready
To throw up

          "Having
The time of my life!"

("He feeling good feeling
Good!" The Filipino giggled
As the passenger
Staggered through the club car
To vomit.)

The time of my life
In a double canoe
With the policeman
And another savage
On the aerial WC
Wrapped in a coxswain's cloak

Kurukuru grass—like rye straw
Golden houses dip their thatch
At high tide

Stimmung—desertion
(Death in Venice)

Dark inside
Bronze bodies appear
At the doors
(Do not shoot
Til you see the whites of their eyes)

"From time to time firm breasts stick out"
(Fear of pointed objects)

Kurukuru stacks (houses)
"Dip their long thatch beards
In the water"
(Morning)
But at night (lowtide)
"I urinated from a height of 13 feet."

Morning again gentle hills
Sprawling spidery trees.
"I evacuated straight into the sea
From a privy above the water"

Then we talked of sun and moon
And the causes of things
On the way to Port Moresby
And McCann's Hotel
Sherry and the gramophone
Icy beer and
                    ". . . that woman
Vulgar beyond endurance."

III. CARGO SONGS

1. Sir William MacGregor
   Representative of Her Majesty the Queen
   Saw the Paramount Chief enthroned
   On a high platform
   Went up and seized him by the hair
   Dragged him to the ground
   Placed himself firmly in the seat of honor:
   "No one shall sit higher in Papua than I."

2. The anthropologist lay low
   Shivered under the hot compress
   Read Bronte and pissed black
   When the wind blew off the sea
   He thought he felt better
   Seemed to hear the bell-charm of St. Martin's
   And Strand traffic humming in his head
   Lay thinking of French chophouses in Soho
   Of anything in fact
   But Trobriand Islanders and coral gardens
   Even his intimate fantasies were far away
   In Russia: Rasputin: a convenient system!
   "How wicked I am," sighed the anthropologist,
   "I need more quinine
   And no one shall sit higher in Trobriand than I."

3. Meanwhile four natives must hang
   Each in a different village
   To impress, the population

The proceedings throughout
Were watched with great interest
By chiefs and a number
Of other natives
All appeared impressed
By the solemnity.

4. Hatedevil missionary has a waxen smell
   Long narrow trousers find their way to hell
   Rams chickens forbidden Kava and the vices
   Of a rivergod seen between trees
   An old man with a forgettable name
   Lights volcano nine.
   The Captain notes odd behavior and shivers.

5. Even though
   The anthropologist is laid low
   There is still nobody higher.

6. After this a native from the North side of Milne Bay
   Possessed by a tree-spirit
   Warned of giant waves
   All must throw away
   Matches, knives, white men's tools
   Destroy houses kill all pigs
   Withdraw inland
   Wearing only long narrow leaves
   "To show entire repudiation of the white man."

7. On the following Sunday the missionary noted with
   surprise that his congregation now consisted only of a
   few children. He learned that the villagers were all in
   the hills, expecting the return of the dead. He pushed

inland without further delay. He found all the men of the village sitting in tense silence. His cordial greeting met with no reply.

8. But the missionary had come prepared:

"I had in my wallet a long thin stick of trade tobacco, a delicacy very much prized by these people, and as I was sitting in the doorway of the Chief's house I took it out and threw it to some men who were sitting behind me in the dark. Almost before they had time to pick it up it came back and struck me in the ear." (*Rev. Abel*)

9. The whites then made for safety moving fast in small groups to the coast. They reached the boats in time. The dead arrived in the village with a cargo of flashlights.

10. Now there is a black King living in the jungle, Iron, with a stone grey skin. Kanaka Shiva, thirty hands, getting ready to shake another mountain. The sky rains magic fire from Black Master. Burning kerosene eats up the villages. Ancestors come with canned meat new suits and plenty of rifles. "A small ring of dancers. Two dancers facing each other with raised drums."

11. But the anthropologist
    Lives with memories
    "The walk with Miss Nussbaum
    In a glacier blue outfit
    The persistent longing
    For mother."

12. *Ein ganz eigentümlich Vorgang.*

Blackfela Catholic Mambu sprinkled their organs with
    holywater
And remained unmarried like a mission sister.
He fed the people with rice that had arrived secretly
    by air.
The church burned down when the Father was home
    in Germany and this was a sign he said.

13. *Ein undankbares, schweres Missionsfeld* said the Father
    on his return.

14. Meanwhile they had eaten everything. The villages
    seemed unnaturally quiet, "full of natives in
    European dress, sitting very still."

They said their ship had now started from Rome
Bringing fountain pens and the removal
Of mystical penalties.

15. "Famous young couple originates new life." Sign on
    this line.
    Be ready for big Blackfela Catholic Steamer:
        Most Sacred Heart of Jesus Ltd
        Turns brown man white
        In a quaking boat
        Full of ancestors
        Speaking in tongues.

But saner elements visited the scientist and told him
    everything.

550

16. Filo a gifted virgin dreamt of God
    Who told her what he thought of white people.

17. The anthropologist suffered a fit of nervous aversion
    for pointed objects.

18. Filo said God had told her he was sending a truckload
    of rifles. One man broke through the fence and nearly
    brained the Father with a sea shell. A mission brother
    slipped away crossed to the other island to bring the
    magistrate and officers. Some rebels got seven years.
    Filo returned under police escort. There was only a
    mild demonstration though everybody knew some to-
    bacco had really fallen from heaven.

19. "I gave them portions of tobacco and they all walked
    away without posing long enough for a time exposure.
    My feelings toward them: exterminate the brutes."
    (*Malinowski*)

20. "Igua massaged me and told me in *delightful* Motu
    about murders of white men as well as his fears of
    what he would do if I died in that way."

21. But a little wire can take a lot of juice and no man
    shall sit higher in Trobriand than I.

IV. PLACE NAMES

Jair son of Manasseh went and seized the encampments
And called them the Encampments of Jair
Nobah went and seized Kenath
With its outlying villages
And called it Nobah
After himself.

> *(Numbers 32: 41-42)*

1827

D'Entrecasteaux enters the bay
Looks it over
Leaves it with name of his ship:
"Astrolabe Bay."

1871-1883

Baron Nikolai Miklouho-Maclay
(Tibud Maclay)
Comes and goes
Exploring
Recording the language
As a reward for hospitality
Leaves the coast with
His own name:
"Maclay Coast"

To further honor
The place where he landed
He called it "Constantine Harbour"
(Grand Duke Constantine
President of the Imperial Russian Geographical Society
Had paid for the trip.)

1878

Australian gold-prospectors
Put in at Bongu
In the good ship *Dove*
But leave at once
Forgetting to name the place
"Dove Harbor"
But there is a "Dove Point"
A hundred miles up the coast.

1884

Herr Finsch
Representing the Neu Guinea Kompagnie
Hoists the German flag
Over "Bismarck (naturally)
Archipelago" "Kaiser
(Of course) Wilhelmsland"
And last but not least
"Finschhafen."

V. TIBUD MACLAY

Tibud Maclay
Came from the moon in a white ship
Stood without weapons
In a shower of arrows
Sat in a bungalow
Full of remedies cameras optical
Instruments and presents
Walked in the night
With his blue lamp

Tibud Maclay
A culture hero
From the land of figureheads
Inventor of nails mirrors
Melons and paint
Whose servant flew away
Over the horizon
Without wings

Tibud Maclay
With a Swede and an Islander
Blue as a god or ancestor
Warned them there would be
Two kinds of white man
Arriving later
A few good
The rest very bad
Hostile deities

Djamans with firearms
Would rob them of land
Work them under whips
Shoot them if they
Ran away

The people
Took this warning to heart
But could not understand

Soon came Herr Finsch
A decent *Djaman*
Saying he was the brother
Of Tibud Maclay
So they received him gladly
He hoisted his flag over their villages
While they celebrated his coming

Then all the others
Began to arrive
They gave the people two axes
Some paint and matches
And then went into business
Taking over the country.

News travelled all over the islands:
"No end of visitors!
Get ready to entertain!"

VI. SEWENDE (Seven Day)

1. Seven Day is an unknown country where aspirins
    come from
And pants and axes and corned beef in cans
It is far beyond the green sea, the white sea, the blue sea
Past Tokyo North America and Germany
But in the same general direction
Far far beyond other countries
No one has seen this blessed land

In the center of snow-night-day
Is a more hidden place
Even more unknown than Sewende
The front door of Big Belong
Who got up very old
Out of Himself in the beginning
Left His endless bed in the morning
And started the Cargo Company
In which we now offer shares
To True Believers.

2. Then the dreamer said we must build a large warehouse
in the bush. We must do everything he said and then
wait: in a short time the warehouse would be filled with
cans of meat, aspirins, hydrogen peroxide, soap, razor
blades, rice, pants, flashlights and everything.

Then we built the warehouse together. And after that
the dreamer said we must wash away all our impurities.
We all drew water and heated it and washed together.

We went in silence to the burial ground. Nobody sang
or danced or said anything. We just sat very still in the
dark waiting for the signal.

At the signal the women took theirs off and we took
ours off and we all began. It was all collected in a bot-
tle with water and poured over the burial place to bring
Cargo.

When the Administration heard about it we had to tear
down the warehouse and carry all the timbers eighteen
miles and throw them in the sea.

3. PRAYER OF KAUM

written in Whiteman's jail
where he was killed and went to Paradise
To see with his own eyes
Ancestors making Cargo
To be shipped to the islands
And see with his own eyes
Whiteman changing all the labels:

"O Father Consel you are so sorry
You are so sorry for us Kanakas.
You can help us we have nothing no planes
No jeeps no ships not even hammers not even pants
Nothing at all because Whiteman
Steals everything and you are so sorry
O Father Consel
Now you send
Something."

(So sorry!)

VII. CARGO CATECHISM

1. Here is how it all began. Old Anut made him some man and woman along flowers animals trees fish putem in a garden belong plenty canned beef ricebags (polished) instant coffee, tobacco matches and candybars. Old man and woman no pants and lots of whiskey. Baimbai plenty pekato mekim plenty trabel. Nogut. Old Anut took away all the canned food before they could even find the canopener. Quick lockup garden and hide all the whiskey. You wantem inferno Ol Man Adam? "Suppose you spik: I no got inferno, baimbai you go along IN."

2. Noah was a gutfela so Old Anut showed him how to build a steamer. Make him strongfela talk: get along steamer with plenty Cargo along all animals quick I make him rain longtime no can finish. Noah had a peaked cap white shirt shorts stockings and shoes. The rain came down and Noah rang the bell and off went the steamer with all the animals that's all. Steamer belong plenty canned beef ricebags (polished) instant coffee tobacco matches and candybars. No whiskey. Old Noah always properly dressed. Nix pekato. Nix trabel.

3. Baimbai rain stops and steamer lands in Australia. Old Noah finds a bottle of whiskey lying around Sydney. Bad news for everybody that's all. Noah want'em one drink work him trouble no can finish. One drink takes off shoes. Two drinks takes off the socks. Son Ham belongs Noah watches and laughs when old boy takes off his pants.

For this Ham is deprived of cargo, canned meat, razorblades etc and sent to New Guinea to be a black man. Shem and Japheth remain white, keep the Cargo and remain in Sydney.

4. Ham belong longtime taro gardens in New Guinea without Cargo canned meat razorblades etc but surrounded by friendly satans who produce good crop. Satans promote much dancing and although there is no whiskey they can work pretty good love magic. Plenty trabel but could be a lot worse (inferno). Food however too simple nothing but roots and pig meat none of it canned and no instant coffee, candybars, polished rice, cocacola, etc. Suppose you wanem canned food you better get rid of Satans. HERAUS! RAUSIM SATAN!

5. Whitefellow come along from Sydney to help *rausim satans,* with less dancing and more work also bibles. Trouble with Bible: is *incomplete.* All the instructions about Cargo torn out. Best parts all missing, rewritten by Jews.

6. Correct information. The ancestors are alive and well in the sky immediately above Sydney Australia. Taught and supervised by the God of the Catholics they are putting meat into cans and sending it to New Guinea correctly labelled for the natives. Also flashlights, razorblades, hammers, etc. Plenty for everybody, black and white alike. While the Cargo is at sea the white crew spends all its time changing the labels and readdressing the natives' shipments to planters, missionaries, government officials and policemen. The problem now is how to get Cargo direct without recourse to ships and planes belonging to white men?

7.   Jesus Christ is now in Sydney waiting to deliver Cargo to natives without the intervention of white men. He has a steamer and it is all loaded. But he does not yet have the proper clothing. Jesus Christ is waiting in a hotel room for someone to bring him a suit.

8.   Word travels fast down the coast. Large gatherings are dispersed by the police. Families are arrested and put in jail because they have arranged bouquets of flowers for the coming of Jesus with the Cargo.

9.   In 1940 amid rumors of distant war a local leader in Madang, after two hours of silent prayer, stood up and announced that the King was coming to take over. Another declared that he was the Apostle Paul and had a radio like the Australians.

The one who announced the Advent of the King was immediately arrested but he was released when, after questioning, it became clear that he was not referring to the Germans.

But the people understood why he had been arrested! Henceforth his message was taken very seriously. Flowers were on display everywhere. When those who displayed flowers were arrested, bouquets were made in secret and hidden under baskets. As soon as Jesus appeared with Cargo they would lift up the baskets. Their world would be all flowers.

VIII. JOHN THE VOLCANO

1

I John Frum—Volcano ancestor—Karaperamun
"My Brother here is Joe
Everything is near to me
See us two Joe-Captain: Cockle Shell."

My three sons come down out of my sky
In long robes and jackets
They are invisible to women
Except to Gladys a little girl
My three sons show themselves under the banyan tree
Giving orders to boys and girls who do not understand.

"If you put a sack of stones
Under the banyan tree
The divine children
Will come down."

My three sons are Isac, Jacob
And Lastuan ("Last One")
Isac does all the talking
Gladys aged twelve
Does the translating
"You boys and girls
Are ropes of John Frum
You live together in a witty cabin
And the night is for dancing."

Tell the other people
These are my desires:
"Bathe together in the lake
Look calm
Heavy buying in the stores
Days of rest: Friday, Monday
Other days: recreation.

"My planes are coming
With prefab houses for all
With radios salaries
For teachers
Means of conveyance."

2

I Neloiag
Am John Frum King
I level the mountain
Where my planes will come
I am King of American Flyers
I can arrest the British
With my telegraph
Though they declare me insane.

I am the Instigator
Just one of the ropes
But Isac the Voice
Speaks to me direct
In secret bushes
Banning colors
On Thursdays only

(Red yellow and blue
Strictly forbidden
Since red is blood
Blue is sickness
Yellow is death.)

3

Isac commanded with a man's voice. "Pull the tickets." We went together to the store. We moved the people out of our way. We climbed over the counters. We carried out all the instructions. Tore off the price tags ("tickets"). With tags all gone the store was cleaner. And it had to be made cleaner. A preparation. Now John Frum can come with his army and Cargo.

(The action was defined by police as "The affair of the tickets." "The defendants entered a European store at White Sands, leapt over the counters and pulled the tickets off the goods.")

I am only
One of the ropes
I communicate instructions
Isac is the one who commands
Sundown Thursday
With a man's voice
"Armies
Cargoes
Coming by jet-plane."

4

Then there appeared to be another uprising by these fanatics. Those who had been exiled to Malekula sent a lot of coconuts back to their home village. These were to be carefully planted on the site of their houses.

The Presbyterian Missionary (disturbed and looking for trouble) saw in this act a symbolic message. Others said this was very doubtful. The agent ordered the coconuts to be dug up. The natives said it was simply a matter of introducing a new variety of nut.

REPORT: "Police measures reasonably effective in spite of coconuts. Leaders however continue propagating ideas in new place of residence. Reunions held near (French) district office. No manifestations. Ropes of John Frum reported north of Port Sandwich and across Straits at Ambrym. Ropes bring message to Presbyterian village. Exiles not fully responsible for what happens after that. Village organized by native militia. Daily drill under capts and lieuts. Change trousers at each meeting. Former Presbyterian natives declare they have no further need of missionaries who can go home at earliest convenience. Boys resume contact with ancestor Volcano Deity by telephone. Woman sees light on crag and hears bell. Moonlight procession to crag with guitars and dancing. Sound of ancestor bell is heard (somewhat muffled and uncertain). They wait. As no further communication is forthcoming from Volcano voice, woman suggests slaughter of cats. This is done. People pay all debts in stores and throw remaining money into the sea.

Baimbai money belong me he come
Face belong you fella King
Take 'em, he go back!

5

And the white ship
Of the Messageries
Came as the voice said
Watchers day and night
Saw it appear
Newly painted white
Plenty of Cargo
Unloaded in the usual place.

"The Chief went to ask the missionary if he were really
sure the goods were for him."

6

Kumala O
We are yams
From Craig Cove to Ambrym
We are potatoes
All over the Islands
Kumala O

It is known that gold pounds were thrown into the sea at
Ranmuhu and Fanu and the bell of Likon rang in the bush
for the night meeting.
Then the missionary
Took his departure.

7

"The movement reached Paama, a wholly Presbyterian
island, where the natives began to rid themselves of all
money and to kill the pigs." It spread to Epi and Pente-
cost. Many visited the defendants at Port Sandwich. "The
exiles had great prestige."

8

Everything in the world has a cause and aim. So Jonfroom mvt. has procedures of its own.

Two main rules: 1. People will stop going to Church
                 2. People will drink a lot of kava.
These rules are still strongly carried out at present.

9

Dear Father Somo,

I am Joe. I forgot something I had to tell you I say to you Somo and Sam Nako that I come here to Vila. The government at Tanna tied you up but that is nothing. Do not forget the tobacco which came to me from John Frum and Nauka. John Frum wanted Nauka to show him the road to come out. Nauka did not know the road so he sent the tobacco to me, to you Somo and to Sam Nako. I made the road so that all the chiefs could go and shake hands with John Frum because I was not there but Karaua softened his heart and showed the chiefs John Frum. John Frum only spoke to them because he did not see me with them. He asked Karaua where I was and Karaua told him I was in Vila.

John Frum and I were together and we arranged that all the others should come to Vila. We talked together about them (the chiefs) and we arranged that the chiefs should follow us when they came out of jail.

John Frum and I came to Sidni [mission village near Lenakel] to look for a place for a house. John Frum pointed where his house was to stand just alongside mine but he did not describe what kind of house. So listen well you Somo and Sam Nako; Nako will provide three men, Natoga will provide three men: Bangor will send three men to build the house and Sidni will provide the food for the workers. You are not to say that the house is for John Frum or for me but just say it is a company or a communal house.

We two are only waiting for the chiefs to go back to Tanna and when the house is ready you will send word to us and John Frum and I will come to the house you will have prepared at Sidni. Then John Frum will gather the white men and talk to them. He will send his son to America to bring the king. You must not be afraid. He showed me aeroplanes at Lonopina [name for Tukosmeru, the highest mountain in Tanna] as thick as the bush.

You two must conceal the contents of this letter. This is not my letter, John Frum is sitting by me as I write.

This is the end of my letter but John Frum's is underneath.

john the great
my brother here is joe: my name is karaperamun
every thing is near to me
see us two joe captain cockle shell.

I am joe. I am saying to you two brothers and father that this spirit writing speaks to you these four lines only which you see. See how his writing has not capital letters. He says cockle shell. The meaning of this is that we two fit like the two halves of a cockle shell. Everything will come from Sidni Jonfrum wants you to answer this letter by the Morinda.

IX. DIALOG WITH MISTER CLAPCOTT

Letter to Mr. Clapcott sir you sonofabitch you notice we
      have now cut down your coconut trees
You have messed with all our women and when this was
      pointed out you have not desisted
And now we are going to fix you Clapcott five men
Will come and you will not hear them come
Since you are deaf
You will be shot and parts will be cut off
Parts also eaten
Because of which
Our dead shall rise
Black shall be white
Cargo shall come to Santo
Ancestors come home in white ship
From where you sent them you sonofabitch
With all your papers.

We will unload the Cargo in our new store
Sharing it among all who have paid their dues.

We sing this nightletter against you Mr. Clapcott
      and tomorrow
All the bodies riding on the winds of resurrection
Shall have white skins because you are gone
So for you Mr. Clapcott we sing this message
Five special delivery bullets in the chest tomorrow
And then our ship will come from America
Where there is no more death

Repeat nightletter Mr. Clapcott sir you sonofabitch
     you notice
Ghost wind has blown down your coconut trees
And your beach is very red.

X. AND A FEW MORE CARGO SONGS

1. When Sir Harry asked Government Agent Nicol "who that woman" was the Agent took her by the hair, pulled her head back and opened her mouth inspecting her teeth and replied: "Oh, that's Rosie."

2. John the Broom is a big man with shining buttons
   He is hidden from women
   (Except Gladys a little girl)
   He will provide the money.

3. Nicol came with twenty police and tied John Frum
        to a tree
   But everyone said it was not the real John Frum
   For John the True
   Had gone to America
   To confer with Rusefel
   To get a Black American Army
   And Liberator Planes
   All flown by Blacks
   And full of dollars
   To let out every man
   In Nicol's prison.

4. *Players Cigarettes:*
   A prophetic interpretation
   Of the ikon.

"Jake Navy he is player and smoker
Good fella seen in vision
By the faithful
Lives in a beard and a battleship lifebelt
He will send his delegate
(Noah's avatar)
To take the place
Of Agent Nicol"
Is everybody happy?

5. Ghost wind come O Brother
Sell me the shivering
For a little piece of paper
Sell me the shivering
For a little piece of Whiteman Times
To roll my cigarette
To blow my Whiteman smoke
In Ghostwind good feeling
O sell me the shivering brother
Give me a ticket to the happy dark
Trade me a houseful of rifles
For a new white skin
In Dark Ghost Wind
Sell me the shivering, Brother,
For Whiteman good times!

WEST

I. DAY SIX O'HARE TELEPHANE

Comes a big slow fish with tailfins erect in light smog
And one other leaves earth
Go trains of insect machines
Thirtynine generals signal eight
Contact barrier four

A United leaves earth
Square silver bug moves into shade under wing building
Standby train three black bugs indifferent
A week after he got sick
A long beetle called Shell
On a firm United basis
Long heavy-assed American dolphin touches earth
Please come to the counter
Where we have your camera
Eastern Airlines has your camera
And two others drink coffee
Out of yellow paper cups

Big Salvador not cooled off yet
From sky silver but
Hotel Fenway takes off at once
To become Charles' Wain

"The wise man who has acquired mental vacuity is not
concerned with contemplation or its absence"

Forty stories of window seats available
Watcher stands on turntable ensemble
Counts passing generals
In curtains and spaces leaving earth
Two bugs like trucks
With airplane's noses
Ride our fables
Armored with earmuffs
Racing alone across asphalt sound
Armored against desert
All members
Not numbered yet

All clear neons come to the confession
The racing numbers
Are not remembered

Big Panam leaves earth
Gets Tax Man started into death
I'll get the teachers expanded
Turn your hat
Over your breath
Small dapper North Central is green for woods
And arrives safe
Flight information requires Queen
All green Braniff leaves earth for Pole
And big United Doppelganger slides very close
Seeking the armed savers

It points at us all and it is named:
"PHILIP."

It swings. Body No. 7204 U
In case of mountain death
Discovers Teacher Jackson
Wins Colorado team maybe
In the snow
In the rare acts

Check tables for Vance Cooper
Advance with boarding arts
The glide area has now won and
Boy you got a lotta SPREAD

Hello say the mignonnes
You can go to bed
You can go to the gorgeous
Community period and

"Though appearing to act he does not engage in action."

Muffled the vice of Lou'ville smoke
The front
Hello money got to go pump earnings
Into bug MM2 for Derby Dad
Telling arrival is a copperhead
Big Mafia sits with mainlining blonde
Regular Bounder Marlo
Come meet world muffin at ticket counter
Ticket country
Mr. Kelsey
Mr. Kelsey
You are now wanted
In ticket country

"It is not distant and it is not the object of attainment."

Come we will pump our money into dogs
And lift our gorgeous raids sky high
Over the sunlit periods
Bending aluminum angels and Tax Man
And giddy grey girls
Over the suburban highschools
Our glide has won
Our teacher has dropped out
Our giant vocal captains are taking off
Whooping and plunging like world police
On distant outside funnels
Stainless diagrams sink
Into muddy air
We leave earth and act
Going to San
Patterns slide down we go for clear
Sanitation heaven
Combing the murky
Surface of profit
San Franciscan wing over abstract
Whorls wide sandpits watershapes
Forms and prints and grids

Invent a name for a town
Any town
"Sewage Town."
And day six is a climbing sun
A day of memory.

"Having finally recognized that the Self is Brahman and
that existence and non-existence are imagined, what should
such a one, free of desires, know, say or do?"

Should he look out of the windows
Seeking Self-Town?
Should the dance of Shivashapes
All over flooded prairies
Make hosts of (soon) Christ-Wheat
Self-bread which could also be
Squares of Buddha-Rice
Or Square Maize about those pyramids
Same green
Same brown, same square
Same is the Ziggurat of everywhere
I am one same burned Indian
Purple of my rivers is the same shed blood
All is flooded
All is my Vietnam charred
Charred by my co-stars
The flying generals.

"He who sees reality in the universe may try to negate it."

To deny linoleum badges
Deride the false tile field floor
Of the great Illinois bathroom
Lettered all over
With busy-signals

To view the many branches of the Shiva-cakes
The veined paddies or pastries
The burned trays of the Ming prairie
Or the porcelain edges
Of the giant Mother Mississippi

"His actions in this world are appearances only."

Appearances of a city
And disappearances
Dubuque dragging its handkerchiefs
Into a lake of cirrus
(Gap with one long leg of extended highway)
Compasses
Veiled
Valed
Vale!

"Not seeing, he appears to see."

A lake of cottons
Iowa needs names

High above this milk
There is a race-leader or power passenger
At odds with the white rest
The cloud captains
An individual safe
A strong-box enclosed self
A much more jealous reason
One among many
Who will have his way
A logical black provider
For only one family
Flying with a fortune in stamps
He stands in line with the others
Outside the highest toilet in the world
To establish a record in rights
High above the torment
Of milling wind and storms

We are All High Police Thors
Holding our own weapons
Into the milk mist each alone
As our battering ram
Fires us all into Franciscan West
As strangers in the same line
United in indifferent skies
Where nobody needs any anger.

    Not seeing he is thought to be over Sioux Falls
    Getting hungry
    Not seeing he is thought to see
    Saying "It is there"
    The family combination shelter and fun
    Room where all is possible.

Sinbad returning from the vines of wire
Makes his savage muffled voice
With playboy accents
To entertain the momentary mignonnes
As if he meant it all in fun

Sinbad returning from Arab voices
With his own best news for everybody boy
Says: "Wellfed cities
Are all below
Standing in line
Beneath enormous gas
Waiting to catch our baseball."

Sinbad the voyager makes his muscles of utterance
Soundless lips entertain the merveilles

Merveilles les vignes
De fil de fer
Hongrie
Les vagues barbares de l'est
Get ready for your invasion baby
Dr. Farges awaits you with his syringe
And Tom Swift rides by below
On his invisible mammoth mountains of art
The granite sides of Rushmore
Now showing four Walt Whitmans
Who once entrusted the nation to rafts

   Four secret presidents
   With stone ideas
   Who mumble under gas
   Our only government
   Has provided free and says:
   "This mildly toxic invention can harm none
   But the enemy."

Merveilles! Secrets! Deadly plans for distant places!
And all high males are flying far west
In a unanimous supermarket of beliefs
Seeking one only motto
For "L'imagination heureuse":
WHY NOT TRY EVERYTHING?

II. AT THIS PRECISE MOMENT OF HISTORY

1. At this precise moment of history
   With Goody-two-shoes running for Congress
   We are testing supersonic engines
   To keep God safe in the cherry tree.
   When I said so in this space last Thursday
   I meant what I said: power struggles.

2. You would never dream of such corn. The colonials in
   sandalwood like running wide open and available for
   protection. You can throw them away without a refund.

3. Dr. Hanfstaengel who was not called Putzi except by
   those who did not know him is taped in the national
   archives. J. Edgar Hoover he ought to know
   And *does* know.

   But calls Dr. Hanfstaengel Putzi nevertheless
   Somewhere on tape in the
   Archives.

   He (Dr. H.) is not a silly man.
   He left in disgust
   About the same time Shirley Temple
   Sat on Roosevelt's knee
   An accomplished pianist
   A remembered personality
   He (Dr. H.) began to teach
   Immortal anecdotes

To his mother a Queen Bee
In the American colony.

4. What is your attitude toward historical subjects?
   —Perhaps it's their size!

5. When I said this in space you would never believe
   Corn Colonel was so expatriated.
   —If you think you know,
   Take this wheel
   And become standard.

6. She is my only living mother
   This bee of the bloody arts
   Bandaging victims of Saturday's dance
   Like a veritable sphinx
   In a totally new combination.

7. The Queen Mother is an enduring vignette
       at an early age.
   Now she ought to be kept in submersible
       decompression chambers

   For a while.

8. What is your attitude toward historical subjects
   Like Queen Colonies?
   —They are permanently fortified
   For shape retention.

9. Solid shades
   Seven zippered pockets
   Close to my old place

Waiting by the road
Big disk brakes
Spinoff
Zoom
Long lights stabbing at the
Two together piggyback
In a stark sports roadster

Regretting his previous outburst
Al loads his. Cadillac
With lovenests.

10. She is my only living investment
    She examines the housing industry
    Counts 3.5 million postwar children
    Turning twenty-one
    And draws her own conclusion
    In the commercial fishing field.

11. Voice of little sexy ventriloquist mignonne:
    "Well I think all of us are agreed and sincerely I my-
    self believe that honest people on both sides have got
    it all on tape. Governor Reagan thinks that nuclear
    wampums are a last resort that ought not to be re-
    sorted." (But little mignonne went right to the point
    with: "We have a commitment to fulfill and we better
    do it quick." No dupe she!)

All historians die of the same events at least twice.

13. I feel that I ought to open this case with an apology.
    Dr. H. certainly has a beautiful voice. He is not a silly
    man. He is misunderstood even by Presidents.

14. You people are criticizing the Church but what are you going to put in her place? Sometime sit down with a pencil and paper and ask yourself what you've got that the Church hasn't.

15. Nothing to add
But the big voice of a detective
Using the wrong first names
In national archives.

16. She sat in shocking pink with an industrial zipper specially designed for sitting on the knees of presidents in broad daylight. She spoke the president's mind. "We have a last resort to be resorted and we better do it quick." He wondered at what he had just said.

17. It was all like running wideopen in a loose gown
Without slippers
At least someplace.

III. GHOST DANCE: Prologue

AMERICAN HORSE FAST THUNDER SPOTTED
HORSE PRETTY BACK GOOD LANCE PRESENT
NOV 27 1890

We were made many promises by the Commissioners but
we never heard from them since.
They talked nice to us and after we signed they took our
land cut down our rations.
They made us believe we would get full sacks if we signed
but instead our sacks are empty.
Our chickens were all stolen our cattle were killed our
crops were entirely lost because we were absent talking
with the Commission.
We are told if we do as white men do we will be better off
but we are getting worse off every year.

When we were in Washington the President
The Secretary the Commissioner promised
We would get back a million lbs. of beef
Taken from us and the Bill
Passed Congress
But the Commissioner
Refused
To give us
Any meat.

IV. GHOST DANCE

1. ALL THE OLD TIME PROPHECIES ABOUT THE WHITES COMING TO THIS COUNTRY AND ABOUT GUNS HAVE COME TRUE SO WHAT WE HAVE DREAMED ABOUT THE END IS PROBABLY TRUE AS WELL.

2. Dr. Sam said Wodziwob was the real Starter. Four Paiute men from Surprise went to hear him. He was around Reno. Four Paiute men went from Surprise to Reno to hear the Starter. Was he telling the Truth?

3. Wodziwob said: "There are a lot of people telling the news but they are not telling it right. What I said was: 'A train is coming' and my real dream was about that train. People made it out different. What Wodziwob said was correct. It was then 1869 and a train was on its way to Hollywood.
What Dr. Sam said was also correct. Wodziwob was the Starter.

4. Wodziwob first gave out news the dead were coming. They were all coming with cups in their hands to drink from. When would they arrive? In about four years.

5. It was announced that the dead were not coming by train.

6. Zonchen reported that he had seen the dead coming. They were on their way. I saw Zonchen when he was down in Reno fifty years ago. I don't know whether he was just a chief or whether he dreamed these things himself.

7. The Starter said the dead were on their way with the Supreme Ruler. They were all coming in a group. No distinction would exist any more between races.

8. He preached at Pyramid Lake: "Our Fathers are coming. Our Mothers are coming. Dance without stopping. Every morning, swim, wash, paint. Paint yourselves black, white, red. Don't stop dancing. Be always happy."

9. They danced five nights without bells, a fire in the center. There was no preaching against the whites. The songs were all new brought by dreamers from the Land of the Dead. Many dancers fainted.

10. Minnie Jo said: "There were Washo doctors who spoke with the dead before the Paiute miracle men and they still do. Our doctors were always talking with the dead. If they say the dead will return, we believe them."

11. The State Capitol Building at Carson City was finished but there was not yet a fence around it. Weneyuga came to the Washo and said he was Dr. Frank. He gave dances and said dead relatives were about to return from the South. "As the dead draw near, put your hands in front of your faces and spread the fingers. Look through the fingers and you will recognize your own relatives."

12. Dr. Frank said that when the dead returned all the white people would disappear and halfbreed children would drop dead. There would be no more race conflict.

13. Dr. Frank said that if he dipped his hands in a stream and roiled the water, the water would then become poison-

ous to white people. But he added that he never did this. He also made red pigment form on the stones of the State Capitol Building. He used this pigment on converts.

14.   He had a staff with red and white rings around it and an eagle feather on top. He planted it by his head when he lay down to sleep. He did not tell what it was for but he believed in it. Sometimes where he planted the stick in the ground he would dig up gold watches military buttons silver chains and insignia.

15.   A very serious dance was held at Reno. It lasted five nights. There were no fun steps. Children had trances. Dr. Frank rubbed his body with phosphorous from old Chinese matches to make it shine in the dark. The song he dreamed and sang this time was: "Indian Father sitting place sound of the wind."

16.   He drew a line on the ground. Everybody who stepped over the line would meet a dead relative.

17.   The Washo doctors said Dr. Frank was an imposter. He headed north with one disciple.

18.   Dr. George gave this rule: "Whenever you dream, paint your face red and white and do what your dream tells you. Otherwise you will turn to stone."

19.   Dr. George came to the mouth of Lost River where he found Captain Jack and the people. He came in winter when no grass was growing. He said that when the grass was eight inches high the dead would return. The deer and

all the animals would return. "The whites will burn up and vanish without leaving any ashes. Dance or you will be turned to stone."

20. Then everybody danced and jumped in the river. They came out of the water with ice in their hair. They told what the coming-back-people wanted us to do.

21. Dr. George stretched a rope around the dance ground and said: "Anyone who tries to molest me will turn to stone as soon as he steps over the rope." The Superintendent came and stepped over the rope. He did not turn to stone. He arrested Dr. George for making the people crazy.

22. Bogus Tom wanted to take the songs about the dead to Oregon but the white people said anyone who sang or danced in Oregon would go to jail. Bogus Tom then showed them papers he had got from a lawyer in Oregon and they allowed him to give a dance. But it was just like church. No drunken people were allowed in.

23. *Cornwallis* (Oregon) *Gazette*, Jan. 4, 1873: "Scarcely an Indian on the Siletz Agency does not express perfect confidence in the prophecies. They are gathering upon the reservations. They are nightly engaged in war dances and decorating themselves with paint and feathers. They are governed by messengers and spies from other tribes. Whites were warned of this last summer by friendly squaws who said the dead would come to life, war would be waged on whites, Indians would take possession of their former hunting grounds and peaceful homes."

24. The Superintendent of the Siletz Reservation denied that the dancing had a warlike character. He said: "I presume two thirds of those who engaged in these dances did so for mere amusement." He was not believed. He said the dances were "less harmful than gambling." The white people did not agree.

25. Old Chocolate Hat was head dreamer for Captain Dick. He stayed with us until he died just lately. He used to shake all over when he told of those days.

26. Baptiste was coming home from the Warm House Dance. He saw a black and white hound run under his house. Then he saw his daughter who had been dead for years go into his house. He was happy because the dead had now started to return. He planned what he would say when he went into his house and found his daughter sitting there alive. When he went in he looked all around and found no one.

27. John Watchino said he would not go to Bogus Tom's Warm House Dance. He added that the dead relatives were not coming back either. He said: "Our God gave us the Indian religion and there was nothing in it about Warm House. Our old religion said the world would change but it never said we would live to see it."

28. Dr. Charlie was asked to get in a trance and find out if the dead were really on the way. Dr. Charlie said his spirit person, Meadowlark, met not one dead person coming from spirit land. This news shook the faith of many dancers.

29. Bogus Tom said: "You dance this. It is a good word. It is like church."

30. Annie Peterson said Coquille Charlie carried the dance around only to make money. He did not say the dead would return or tell what would happen to the whites. Nobody had any visions at Charlie's dance.

31. After a while the dreaming stopped and the Dream Dance turned into a Feather Dance. It was just a fun dance. It was mostly a white man's show.

NOTES ON SOURCES

Publisher's Note: Before he left Our Lady of Gethsemani Monastery in Kentucky in the summer of 1968, setting out on the first stages of the Asian journey from which he did not return, Thomas Merton sent me the typescript of this first book of *The Geography of Lograire*. In his letters he said he hoped to extend the poem, that he envisaged it as a "work in progress" of considerable length, but that this first section could stand by itself and was ready for publication except for proof corrections.

In preparing the typescript for the printer, Barbara Harr, Associate Editor at New Directions, and I made few changes. The inconsistent punctuation was altered only in a few lines where necessary for clarity (once Merton had chided me for wanting to put periods at the end of every stanza in an earlier book) and only obvious misspellings were corrected. It was possible to correct a half dozen small typing errors by checking back to an earlier typed version, which probably dates from Spring, 1968, and to the holograph notebook in which the greater part of the poem appears first to have been composed. This notebook is now a part of the archive at The Thomas Merton Room of Bellarmine-Ursuline College Library, Louisville. It runs to about 160 written pages. The first page is inscribed: "THE NEWSNATCH INVENTION by Thomas Merton 1967," with an epigraph from Gaston Bachelard below: "Rendre imprévisible la parole n'est-il pas un apprentissage de la liberté?" However, I am not certain whether "The Newsnatch Invention" was Merton's first choice of title for *The Geography of Lograire* because the first eleven pages of the notebook contain drafts of short poems that were not incorporated in *Lograire*. A draft of the present prologue begins on the twelfth page of the notebook. From that point onward most of the pages have notes, or quotations from his reading,

595

or drafts that found their way into the final version. There is fairly drastic revision of phrasing between the lines in the notebook and those in the first typescript as well as many additions of amplifying details and even new ideas. "The Geography of Lograire" is written at the head of the twenty-third page above the first draft of the section now called "Queens Tunnel." Sister M. Thérèse, a friend of the poet, has kindly supplied a note which explains the genesis of the name "Lograire."

In the Author's Note (page 457) which accompanied the final typescript Merton tells how he drew on his reading for material: "In this wide-angle mosaic of poems and dreams I have without scruple mixed what is my own experience with what is almost everybody else's. . . . what is given [from other books] is most often literal and accurate quotation with slight editing and with of course much personal arrangement. And where more drastic editing is called for by my own dream, well, I have dreamed it." Merton had prepared a few footnotes, acknowledging his sources, and had he lived, would have supplied source credits for the others on his proofs. With help from Brother Patrick and Father Augustine of Gethsemani, the staff of Bellarmine-Ursuline College Library, and the Trustees of the Merton Legacy Trust, Miss Harr and I have provided source notes wherever we have been able to identify sources, either through recollections about the poet's reading or from his references in the notebook. I hope that readers able to identify still-unlisted sources will send them to me so that they may be included in later editions. Meanwhile I beg indulgence of authors and copyright owners of works from which passages or ideas may have been taken that are not yet specifically acknowledged. —J. LAUGHLIN

In reply to the Publisher's question as to whether from notes or conversations with Thomas Merton, I might be able to identify the name "Lograire," I recall that when he read me portions of the poem, then in progress, I asked him about the origin of the title, as I suspected it might have a connection with some mythical country in Arthurian Romance. He then explained that the real name of the French lyric poet, François Villon, was François *Des Loges,* and it was from this surname (really the name of a place) that he had "created" his own country of "Lograire" and that "loges" referred to little huts or cabins used by woodcutters or foresters. There is an immediate relevance not only to Merton's having been at one time chief forester of his Trappist community, with his lookout post in a tower on the highest hill, but perhaps more importantly to his own hermitage on a wooded rise near the Monastery of Gethsemani. The term "Des Loges" has certain interesting historical significances as well that seem pertinent. According to the *Grand Encyclopédie Larousse* it refers to a "pelouse" in the middle of the forest of Saint Germain, before the *Maison des Loges,* a monastery and royal residence destroyed during the Hundred Years War, that had replaced the original cabins or "loges." In 1644, Anne of Austria built a new monastery there which became a place of pilgrimage and of the "Fêtes des Loges."

SISTER M. THÉRÈSE LENTFOEHR

SOURCES

Page

475   *Thonga Lament.* Based on *The Life of A South African Tribe* by Henri Junod, London, 1927, II, p. 423.

476   *Hare's Message.* Based on *The Khoisan People of South Africa: Bushmen and Hottentots,* London, 1930, pp. 357-8.

477   *A Clever Stratagem.* Based on a passage in *The Soul of the Bantu* by W. C. Willoughby, Doubleday, Doran & Com-

pany, Inc., Garden City, 1928, page 135. (Copyright 1928 by Doubleday, Doran & Company, Inc.)

478 Notes for a New Liturgy. Probable source: B. G. M. Sundkler: *Bantu Prophets in South Africa,* Oxford University Press, 1961, pp. 103-13.

480 *Ce Xochitl.* Fray Bernardino de Sahagun (1499-1590) wrote the *Historia general de las cosas de Nueva España.* The lines on the Mayan festival honoring the god Xochilhuitl appear to have been taken from this work, especially from Book 4, Chapter 7. Merton seems not to have followed closely either the translation by Charles E. Dibble and Arthur J. O. Anderson (*General History of the Things of New Spain,* published by The School of American Research and The University of Utah, Monographs of the School of American Research and Museum of New Mexico, Santa Fe, No. 14, 1957) or the version of Fanny R. Bandelier (*A History of Ancient Mexico,* Fisk University Press, Nashville, 1932); Merton may have made his own translation from the Spanish or he may have used yet another English text.

482 Bishop Diego de Landa (1524-1579) wrote the *Relación de las cosas de Yucatan.* Merton probably used the translation by A. M. Tozzer, Papers of the Peabody Museum, Harvard, Volume XVIII, Cambridge, 1941. He may also have consulted the Spanish edition, with introduction and notes by Hector Perez Martinez, published by Editorial Pedro Robredo, Mexico, D. F., 1938. (Bishop Landa is also noted for having burned as many books of "heathen idolatry and diabolical superstition" as he could find; these were the priceless authoritative texts of the ancient Mayan holy writings, probably including some writings related to the *Chilam Balam* books which Merton quotes in succeeding passages.)

483 *The Ladies of Tlatilco.* The references to early Mexican

art are from *Indian Art of Mexico and Central America*
by Miguel Covarrubias. (© Alfred A. Knopf, Inc., 1957)
The Covarrubias book contains illustrations of animal-
shaped vessels and of a two-headed figurine. The text, espe-
cially on pages 13 through 27, discusses the pottery, food
and agricultural products, scant clothing and hair-bleaching
processes of the people of Tlatilco, as well as the possible
relation of their pottery to Picasso's work and to the idea
of twins. The quotation concerning the vessel with the
funnel-shaped tail and gurgling ears is from Covarrubias,
page 21. The lines satirizing contemporary American ad-
vertisements might have been inspired by those in *The
New Yorker.*

487   *Chilam Balam* and *Dzules.* Stanza 10 of *Dzules* is taken
490   from *The Book of the Jaguar Priest: a Translation of the
      Book of Chilam Balam of Tizimin,* with commentary by
      Maud Worcester Makemson, Henry Schuman, New York,
      1951. (Copyright 1951 by Henry Schuman, Inc.) Other
      portions (though not all) of these two sections may also
      have been derived from the Makemson book. Other pos-
      sible sources for the Yucatan sections include Ralph L.
      Roys, *The Book of Chilam Balam of Chumayel,* published
      by the Carnegie Institution of Washington, 1933, as Publi-
      cation No. 438; Ralph L. Roys, "The Maya Katun Proph-
      ecies of the Books of Chilam Balam, Series I," in *Con-
      tributions to American Anthropology and History,* Vol.
      XII, No. 57, 1954, published by the Carnegie Institution of
      Washington as Publication 606, 1960. Also, three articles
      in *Contributions to American Anthropology and History,*
      Vol. X, published by the Carnegie Institution of Washing-
      ton, 1949: "The Maya Chronicles," translated by Alfredo
      Barrera Vásquez and Sylvanus Griswold Morley, No. 48;
      "Guide to the Codex Perez," by Ralph L. Roys, No. 49;
      and "The Prophecies for the Maya Tuns or Years in the

Books of Chilam Balam of Tizimin and Mani," by Ralph L. Roys, No. 51. Also: *The Ancient Maya,* by Sylvanus Griswold Morley, 3rd ed., revised by George W. Brainerd, Stanford University Press, 1956. Merton's notebook contains many details noted from the Morley volume.

490 *Dzules.* Stanza 11 is taken from *El libro de los libros de Chilam Balam,* translated (into Spanish) by Alfredo Barrera Vásquez and Silvia Rendón, published by Fondo de Cultura Económica, Mexico and Buenos Aires, 1st edition, 1948, page 103. Other quotations in Spanish in this section may also be from this source.

517 "There is a grain of sand in Lambeth which Satan cannot find." William Blake: *Jerusalem,* II, 41, 15.

519 *The Ranters and Their Pleads.* The Ranters were a fanatical sect in England in the 17th century. They were antinomian, spiritualistic and pantheistic, believing that God is in every creature. They attacked the established church, the Bible, and the clergy, calling on people to listen only to the voice of Christ within them. The unrest which they generated, especially among the poor, led to accusations of sexual license and to the suppression of the sect. Merton's source is Norman Cohn, *The Pursuit of the Millennium,* Oxford University Press, New York, 1957. On pages 315-372, Cohn quotes at length from a number of seventeenth-century documents: writings of the Ranters, antiRanter tracts, reports of the arrest of Ranters and statements by Parliamentary acts and committees concerning them.
1. *The Routing of the Ranters.* An anti-Ranter tract, see Cohn, p. 328. The quoted paragraph, from court hearings, concerns a formerly-respectable matron allegedly corrupted by the Ranters.
2. Merton has condensed and rephrased material from

Cohn, p. 329, concerning eight Ranters arrested in London on November 1, 1650. Primary sources quoted by Cohn include: *The Arraignment & Tryall with a Declaration of the Ranters* . . . , 1650; *Strange News From the Old-bayly or The Proofs, Examinations, Declarations, Indictments and Convictions of the Ranters, at the Sessions of Gaole-Delivery, held in the Old Bayly, the 18, 19, and 20 of this instant January* . . . , *1651;* and *The Ranters Ranting: with The apprehending, examinations, and confession* . . . , 1650.

3. Selected and condensed from Cohn, pp. 319-320, 330. Primary sources include: Thomas Edwards, "Gangraena, or a Catalogue and Discovery of Many of the Errours, Heresies, Blasphemies and pernicious Practices of the Sectaries of this time, vented and acted in England in these four last years," 1646, pp. 21 sq.; Edward Hyde, D.D., "A Wonder and yet no Wonder: a great Red Dragon in Heaven," 1651, pp. 24, 35 sq.; and Richard Baxter, "Reliquiae Baxterianae," 1696, pp. 76-77.

4. Slightly edited quotations from a Ranter named Clarkson, see Cohn, p. 330.

5. From the title of a tract by Humphrey Ellis: *Pseudochristus; Or, A true and faithful Relation of the Grand Impostures, Horrid Blasphemies, Abominable Practices, Gross Deceits; Lately spread abroad and acted in the County of Southampton* . . . , 1650. See Cohn, p. 330.

6. The first three phrases are excerpted from an Act of Parliament of 9th August, 1650, for the "Punishment of Atheistical, Blasphemous and Execrable Opinions." Quoted by H. Scobell in *A Collection of Acts and Ordinances* . . . , 1658, Part II, pp. 124-126; quoted again in Cohn, p. 325.

The last paragraph is quoted from Cohn, p. 334. The primary source is an anti-Ranter tract entitled *The Ranters Religion or A faithfull and infallible Narrative of their*

damnable and diabolical opinions, with their detestable
lives and actions. With a true discovery of some of their
late prodigious pranks, and unparalleled deportments . . . ,
1650. Title of tract quoted by Cohn, p. 328.

7. First paragraph rephrased from Cohn, pp. 335 ff. Other
material quoted from a Ranter named Jacob Bauthemly
(or Bauthumley, or Bottomley), condensed from Cohn,
pp. 336-340.

8. First five phrases from titles of previously-noted tracts:
Strange News . . . , Arraignment and Tryall . . . , and
The Ranters Religion. . . . See Cohn, pp. 328-329. Other
material from Cohn, p. 323; the primary source is John
Holland, "Smoke of the Bottomlesse Pit or, A More true
and fuller Discovery of the Doctrine of those men which
call themselves Ranters: or, The Mad Crew," 1651. The
closing two lines of this stanza are from the titles of tracts
previously noted.

9. From the stated aim of a Parliamentary committee, ap-
pointed June 14, 1650, to consider this problem. See Cohn,
p. 325.

10. From the primary source by John Holland. See Cohn,
p. 324.

525 *Kane Relief Expedition.* This section is based on Dr. James
Laws' Journal of the Kane Relief Expedition, 1855, in the
Stefansson Collection at Dartmouth College Library.

538 *East with Ibn Battuta.* Ibn Battuta (1304-1369), a Muslim
from Morocco, left a colorful record of his *Travels in Asia
and Africa, 1325-1354.* In this section Merton worked from
the translation by H. A. R. Gibb, The Broadway Travellers
Series, Routledge & Kegan Paul Ltd., London, 1929. "Love
of the Sultan" (pp. 277 8); "Cairo 1326" (pp. 51-3);
"Syria" (page 61: "The Ten Companions": "the most
prominent members of Muhammad's entourage . . . greatly

revered by the orthodox [Sunnites]; the Shi'ites on the other hand, regard them much as Judas Iscariot is regarded in the Christian tradition. Their especial hatred is reserved for Omar, who was responsible for the election of the first Caliph and was himself the second, and whom they blame accordingly for the exclusion of Ali from the succession to which he was designated . . . by the Prophet." Gibb's note.); "The Nusayris" (pp. 62-3. "the Mahdi": the last iman, or leader of the faithful, whose appearance is awaited by the Sunnites.); "Mecca" (direct quotation from page 76); "Delhi" (page 226); "Calicut" (pp. 235 & 240-2). (An edition of *The Travels of Ibn Battuta,* edited by Gibb, is also published in this country by Cambridge University Press, two volumes, 1958 and 1962.)

545 *East with Malinowski.* This section is loosely based on Bronislaw Malinowski's South Sea Island journal, *A Diary in the Strict Sense of the Term,* published by Harcourt, Brace & World in 1967. (Copyright © 1967 by A. Valetta Malinowska) Merton, however, has done extensive rephrasing, condensation, and rearrangement.

547 *Cargo Songs.* Merton was deeply interested in the Cargo cults of Melanesia and read extensively on the subject. He taped a long lecture-essay on "Cargo Theology" which has not yet been published, basing his factual material principally on three books: *Mambu, A Melanesian Millennium* by K. O. L. Burridge, Methuen & Co., Ltd., London, 1960 (© Kenelm Burridge 1960); *Road Belong Cargo, A Study of the Cargo Movement in the Southern Madang District, New Guinea* by Peter Lawrence, Melbourne University Press & Manchester University Press, Manchester, 1964 (© 1964 Peter Lawrence); and *The Trumpet Shall Sound, A Study of "Cargo" Cults in Melanesia* by Peter Worsley, second, augmented edition, MacGibbon & Kee,

London & Schocken Books, New York, 1968 (Copyright © 1968 by Peter Worsley). In a letter to Naomi Burton Stone, dated February 27, 1968, Merton explained some of the special significance which the Cargo myths had for him:

"Cargo movements properly so called originated in New Guinea and Melanesia around the end of the 19th century and developed there especially after World War II. But analogous movements have been cropping up everywhere in formerly colonial countries, and starting from Cargo as such I tend to find analogies all over the place, not only in Black Power but even to some extent in Catholic renewal as practised by some types.

"A Cargo movement is a messianic or apocalyptic cult movement which confronts a crisis of cultural change by certain magic and religious ways of acting out what seems to be the situation and trying to get with it, controlling the course of change in one's own favor (group) or in the line of some interpretation of how things ought to be. In some sense Marxism is a kind of Cargo cult. But strictly speaking, Cargo cults are means by which primitive and underprivileged people believe they can obtain manufactured goods by an appeal to supernatural powers (ancestors, spirits, etc.) and by following a certain constant type of pattern which involves: a) a complete rejection and destruction of the old culture with its goods and values b) adoption of a new attitude and hope of immediate Cargo, as a result of and reward for the rejection of the old. This always centers around some prophetic personage who brings the word, tells what is to be done, and organizes the movement.

"Though all this may seem naive and absurd to western 'civilized' people, I, in common with some of the anthro-

pologists, try to spell out a deeper meaning. Cargo is
relevant to everyone in a way. It is a way in which primi-
tive people not only attempt by magic to obtain the goods
they feel to be unjustly denied them, but also and more
importantly a way of spelling out their conception of the
injustice, their sense that basic human relationships are
being ignored, and their hope of restoring the right order
of things. If they want Cargo it is not only because they
need material things but because Cargo will establish
them as equal to the white man and give them an identity
as respectable as his. But if they believe in Cargo it is
because they believe in their own fundamental human
worth and believe it can be shown in this way."

1. Sir William MacGregor. From Worsley, quoting Mur-
ray (page 51).
2. "The anthropologist lay low." Based on Malinowski's
Diary in the Strict Sense of the Term, pages 199-202.
Stanzas 5, 11, 17, 19, and 20 in this section are also based
on Malinowski; Malinowski's illnesses, his reading, his
reminiscences of friends and of his mother, the islander
Igua, and other relevant topics are mentioned recurrently
in the *Diary.* Merton, however, has done a great deal of
rephrasing and rearrangement.
3. "Meanwhile four natives must hang." Worsley (page
51).
Stanzas 6-10. Worsley (pp. 52-3).
12. *"Ein ganz eigentümlich Vorgang."* ("A very peculiar
event.") Worsley, quoting Wilhelm van Baar (page 108,
n.) "Blackfela Catholic Mambu." Worsley (pp. 106-7).
13. *"Ein undankbares, schweres Missionsfeld."* ("A thank-
less, hard field for missionaries.") Worsley, quoting
Höltker (page 107).
Stanzas 15, 16 and 18. Worsley (pp. 110-13).

552 *Place Names.* The chronology of European contacts in the Southern Madang District is based on Lawrence (pp. 34-7).

554 *Tibud Maclay.* Based on Lawrence (pp. 61-7). "Tibud": a god. "Djamans": Germans.

556 *Sewende (Seven Day).* 1. This section was suggested by an incident reported by Burridge (pp. 9-10). "Sewende": Pidgin for Seventh Day Adventist. "Big Belong": from *"bigpela bolong ol gat ap"* (God). 2. Based on Burridge (pp. 2-3). 3. Kaum. (Kaumaibu). A Kanaka Cargo prophet who led the Bagasin Rebellion of 1944 and was imprisoned by the Australian authorities. Kaum is treated in some depth by Lawrence (see the index to *Road Belong Cargo*) who tells of him: "He told [his followers] that while he had been in prison he had died as result of severe treatment by the native police. He had then gone to Heaven and seen God-Kilibob, who had given him a new skin—it would turn white in due course—a new name, Konsel (Councillor), and instructions to perform new ritual, which would bring ships and aircraft with cargo to Madang. . . . When the cargo arrived, God-Kilibob would cause an earthquake and tidal wave to destroy the Europeans." (page 163).

558 *Cargo Catechism.* Paragraphs 1-4 of this section are based on Lawrence's account of the "Third Cargo Belief" (pp. 15 *et seq.*). "Anut": God in the Madang area vernacular. In this myth, which the New Guineans invented from teachings of the missionaries, God punishes Ham (the ancestor of black people) for seeing his father Noah naked by taking away his "Cargo" (manufactured goods), which is then given only to his brothers, Shem and Japheth (the white man). "Heraus": New Guinea was first a German

606

colony; *"rausim"*: Pidgin for "root out." Paragraphs 5-10 are freely derived from the accounts in Lawrence and Burridge of the Cargo Cult leaders Manu and Yali.

561 *John the Volcano.* This entire section is either quoted or adapted, with imaginative additions, from an article by Jean Guiart, "The John Frum Movement in Tanna [New Hebrides]," in *Oceania,* published in Sydney by the Australian National Research Council, Volume XXII, Number 3, March, 1952. The letter in Stanza 9 is quoted verbatim from Guiart's appendix, where it has the heading: "Translation of Letter from Private Joe Nalpin to his Father Somo and to Sam Nako, Chief at Lenakel, Tanna." John Frum is also treated at length in Worsley (pp. 152-60).

569 *Dialog with Mister Clapcott.* See Worsley (pp. 148-9). A British planter, Clapcott, was murdered in 1923 at Tasmalum on the island of Espiritu Santo (New Hebrides) by the followers of a cult leader named Runovoro. He had promised that if the natives killed the Europeans, the dead would arise, and ancestors would return from a distant place where the whites had sent them, coming in a great white ship loaded with Cargo—for distribution to paid-up members of his movement.

571 *And a Few More Cargo Songs.* 1. From Worsley (page 152 n.), quoting Sir Harry Luke, *From a South Seas Diary.* 2 & 3. Mostly from Worsley (pp. 153-7) with perhaps some touches from Guiart.

575 *Day Six O'Hare Telephane.* The interpolated passages are from a relatively unknown Vedanta work, *Ashtavakra Gita,* translated by Hari Prasad Shastri and published by Shanti Sadan, London. Specifically quoted are: "The wise man who . . ." Chapter 17, verse 18; "Though appearing to . . ." chap. 17, v. 19; "It is not distant . . ." chap. 18, v. 5; "Having

finally recognized . . ." chap. 18, v. 8; "He who sees reality . . ." chap. 18, v. 15; His actions in this . . ." chap. 18, v. 13; "Not seeing, he . . ." chap. 18, v. 15.

587 *Ghost Dance: Prologue* and *Ghost Dance.* The Ghost Dance movement, a complicated series of interacting cults, apparently originated about 1869 among the Paviotso Indians near Walker Lake in Nevada. During the next thirty years, the religious movement spread in varying forms to the Washo, Klamath, Modoc, Shasta, Sioux and other tribes throughout nearly the entire western portion of the United States. Messianic in character, the Ghost Dance cults anticipated a time when the Indian dead would return, and when all white people would die or disappear. Such desperate and farfetched beliefs were probably stimulated and encouraged by the extreme deprivation and dislocation that many of the tribes were undergoing; the cults in turn were sometimes blamed for encouraging militancy among the Indians.

In terms of historical chronology, the section entitled *Ghost Dance: Prologue* should follow rather than precede *Ghost Dance* because it is based on events of the 1890 phase of the movement which spread chiefly east of the Rockies, while *Ghost Dance* refers to the 1870 phase of the movement, which flourished west of the Rockies. Although both phases originated among the Paviotso and sprang from a common cultural tradition, they were separate and distinct events, inspired by two different prophets.

589 *Ghost Dance: Prologue* is based on "Statement of American Horse, Delivered in council at Pine Ridge agency to Agent Royer, and forwarded to the Indian Office, November 27, 1890." Government Document 37002-1890. Quoted from James Mooney: *The Ghost-Dance Religion and the Sioux Outbreak of 1890,* edited by Anthony F. C. Wallace,

University of Chicago Press, 1965. (© 1965 by The University of Chicago) American Horse was a leader on the Sioux reservations in the Dakotas.

Merton's source for *Ghost Dance* is Cora DuBois, "The 1870 Ghost Dance," University of California Publications in Anthropological Records, Volume III (1939-1946), No. 1. Merton has used many phrases and direct quotations from the DuBois report, but he has also done a great deal of selection and condensation from her long and detailed account. "Doctor Sam," "Minnie Jo," "John Watchino," and "Annie Peterson" were DuBois' Indian informants. Wodziwob lived near Walker Lake in Nevada, about 1870. An adherent and assistant of his was apparently the father of Wovoka, also called Jack Wilson, who became known as "The Messiah," the most famous proponent of the later Ghost Dance cult of 1890. "Dr. Frank" was Frank Spencer, also widely known as Weneyuga. "Captain Jack," a leader of the Modocs, is also noted for leading his people in a fierce resistance to the whites. The quote from the *Cornwallis Gazette* (Stanza 23) is found in DuBois, page 26. "Coquille Charlie," actually named "Coquille Thompson," was one of DuBois' informants and had himself been a religious leader in his youth. His accounts of the Ghost Dance differ from those of Annie Peterson and other informants; he was apparently involved in one of the later and more corrupt manifestations of the cult. He should not be confused with earlier leaders such as "Depot Charlie" or "Klamath Charlie." The Warm House Dance, Dream Dance, and Feather Dance were later versions of the Ghost Dance ritual. DuBois points out that by the time of the Feather Dance, the religious significance was gone, and the "supernatural inspiration disregarded." (Dr. DuBois' material is used by permission of The Regents of the University of California.)

Appendix I
SENSATION TIME AT THE HOME
and other new poems
(1968)

THE ORIGINATORS

Because I chose to hear a special thunder in my head
Or to see an occipital light my choice
Suddenly became another's fate
He lost all his wheels
Or found himself flying.

And when the other's nerve ends crowed and protested
In the tame furies of a business gospel
His feeling was my explosion
So I skidded off his stone head
Blind as a bullet
But found I was wearing his hat.

Thus in art and innocence we fix each other fates
We drink each other to gravestones.

Brothers and Sisters I warn you my ideas
Get scarlet fever every morning
At about four and influence goes out of my windows
Over the suburbs
Get out of the way of my ideas.

I am wired to the genius you donated, the general demon.

So one man's madness is another man's police
With everybody's freedom we are all in jail
O Brothers and Sisters here we go again
Flip-flopping all over the circus
With airs of invention.

LUBNAN

Idris—Ilyas: two names
One star, one prophet
Throned in the sun (Idris)
And coming down
The ladder of alchemy and metals
To Baalbeck
Red hot earth
Whose temples are furnaces
He did not stop half way
To rutting Bedlam
Tried out all the dreams
Wasted his demon machine
In a university of lepers
And lost the faculty of speech.

One day the stonewall mountain
Cracked its blue dome
Let out a horse harnessed in flame
A car of fire
Which Ilyas happened to notice

Green green are the waters
Gone the rider in the green night
And Bedlam bells
Quiet

Far away the red saint rides the shouting fire of that horse
Idris—Ilyas one interpreter
May be back tomorrow morning
When the vision
Will be total.

WITH THE WORLD IN MY BLOOD STREAM

I lie on my hospital bed
Water runs inside the walls
And the musical machinery
All around overhead
Plays upon my metal system
My invented back bone
Lends to the universal tone
A flat impersonal song
All the planes in my mind
Sing to my worried blood
To my jet streams
I swim in the world's genius
The spring's plasm
I wonder who the hell I am.

The world's machinery
Expands in the walls
Of the hot musical building
Made in maybe twenty-four
And my lost childhood remains
One of the city's living cells
Thanks to this city
I am still living
But whose life lies here
And whose invented music sings?

All the freights in the night
Swing my dark technical bed
All around overhead
And wake the questions in my blood
My jet streams fly far above

But my low gash is no good
Here below earth and bone
Bleeding in a numbered bed
Though all my veins run
With Christ and with the stars' plasm.

Ancestors and Indians
Zen Masters and Saints
Parade in the incredible hotel
And dark-eyed Negro mercy bends
And uncertain fibres of the will
Toward recovery and home.
What recovery and what Home?
I have no more sweet home
I doubt the bed here and the road there
And WKLO I most abhor
My head is rotten with the town's song.

Here below stars and light
And the Chicago plane
Slides up the rainy straits of night
While in my maze I walk and sweat
Wandering in the low bone system
Or searching the impossible ceiling
For the question and the meaning
Till the machine rolls in again
I grow hungry for invented air
And for the technical community of men
For my lost Zen breathing
For the unmarried fancy
And the wild gift I made in those days
For all the compromising answers
All the gambles and blue rhythms
Of individual despair.

So the world's logic runs
Up and down the doubting walls
While the frights and the planes
Swing my sleep out the window
All around, overhead
In doubt and technical heat
In oxygen and jet streams
In the world's enormous space
And in man's enormous want
Until the want itself is gone
Nameless bloodless and alone
The Cross comes and Eckhart's scandal
The Holy Supper and the precise wrong
And the accurate little spark
In emptiness in the jet stream
Only the spark can understand
All that burns flies upward
Where the rainy jets have gone
A sign of needs and possible homes
An invented back bone
A dull song of oxygen
A lost spark in Eckhart's Castle.
World's plasm and world's cell
I bleed myself awake and well

Only the spark is now true
Dancing in the empty room
All around overhead
While the frail body of Christ
Sweats in a technical bed
I am Christ's lost cell
His childhood and desert age
His descent into hell.

Love without need and without name
Bleeds in the empty problem
And the spark without identity
Circles the empty ceiling.

A BAROQUE GRAVURE

(From a 17th-century Book of Piety)

She is devout and plump, but not happy:
Here is a *vie infortunée.*
But she will be patient:
She will bear life at Versailles.
No, she is not a Barbary slave:
But she, too, has her destiny, and the friendly engraver
Suggests a comparison: blackamoors
In chains. They are beaten.
A placid overseer
Raises his stick. One slave
Meek in coat and chain,
Waits.
      (Are you Madame,
      Sometime or other stung by wicked tongues?)

She, under the palm tree,
Great unfortunate peahen,
Sees none of this,
(Though three blacks in the next field
Are hooked up to a plow.)
No, she contemplates her own case,
And musters up her own resolutions.
      (*Plusieurs ont vu leurs peines terminées*
      Par leur patience et leur vertu.)

618

A resolution:
"Let each carry his own Cross!"

Two shiploads, there, arrive from Barbary.
(Is there patience under hatches?
Is there merit? Will virtue terminate
Their misfortunes?)
She does not inquire
She is carrying
Her own cross.
One independent Moor
Wearing an arbitrary uniform
Holds a bow and arrow
And (as if it had a meaning)
Views her sorrow.

SENECA

When the torch is taken
And the room is dark
The mute wife
Knowing Seneca's ways
Listens to night
To rumors
All around the house
While her wise
Lord promenades
Within his own temple
Master and censor
Overseeing
His own ways
With his philosophical sconce

Policing the streets
Of this secret Rome
While the wife
Silent as a sea
Policing nothing
Waits in darkness
For the Night Bird's
Inscrutable cry.

RILKE'S EPITAPH

"Rose, O pure
Contradiction
Longing to be nobody's
Sleep under so many
Lids."

Pierced by an innocent
Rose, (O pure
Contradiction)
Nobody's lids
And everybody's sleep

Death (Nothing but distance
And unreason)
You accept it,
You pluck it.

Music (O pure
Contradiction)
Everybody's
Vision.

620

READING TRANSLATED POETS, Feb. 1.

i

Now they are all moving
Out of unlocked rooms
Down stairways
Out of houses
We know their moods
As a matter of education.

Pumice and dry shell
Roses nails minerals
Lemon trees
(Poets of other countries
with burnt names.)

Water talks to them
It has sun in it
Girls love and are killed
Or simply known
Heard about

Brass trolleys
In the wealthy tourist sun
All are burned by this
It lasts
They turn to discern
The celebration of feathers
Girls youths peppers roses
Lemons.

Outside me is night
In which iron sleet
Talks everywhere.

Inside me ripen
The brass colors
Mineral landscape
And what the girls said
Is a second-hand celebration.

ii

In these other languages
They have kept words for tears
Salt blue tears
Mad as peacocks
Between the vain
Hot lashes.

iii

A battle in a stone garden
The sky and the scorched idol
A smoke fingerprint
On the sky
Marks the city cured by fire
And madness of weeping.

iv

Here I find
In the snow
A silver lemon-yellow
Wreck of feathers
The precise ruin of
Of an eaten kill.

v

There the low buildings are whitewashed.
It is a warmer season.
Black nuns and white walls
And hens in the sun
I learn of a conspiracy
And an incredible local Easter.
A warmer season.

THE GREAT MEN OF FORMER TIMES

Today I met Von Clausewitz
At the Stock Exchange
And said to him: "You're dead, man,
What are you doing here?"
And he replied
"I have nowhere else to go
Nowhere else to go."

I also saw Lord Nelson
The Duke of Wellington,
Napoleon and his Marshals
And many others with the names of Boulevards.
They all said the same.

And I said to Clausewitz
At the Stock Exchange:
"Don't you know, men,
That all the wars are over?
We fight no more:
It is sufficient to 'deter.'"

And they replied:
"You are wrong, and we will prove it
By killing you:
We will prove it by killing you."

Lord Nelson,
The Duke of Wellington
Napoleon and his Marshals
And many others with the names of Boulevards,
They all said the same.

Then I grew weary
Of my conversation
With these great men of former times,
And quickly leaving them
Went far from the Exchange
But I know that tomorrow
Or the next day
Or indeed next year, if I return,
I will find Von Clausewitz again
I will find him there again.

With Lord Nelson
The Duke of Wellington
Napoleon and his Marshals
And many others with the names of Boulevards
I will find them there again.

FIRST LESSON ABOUT MAN

Man begins in zoology
He is the saddest animal

He drives a big red car
Called anxiety
He dreams at night
Of riding all the elevators
Lost in the halls
He never finds the right door

Man is the saddest animal
A flake-eater in the morning
A milk drinker
He fills his skin with coffee
And loses patience
With the rest of the species

He draws his sin on the wall
On all the ads in all the subways
He draws mustaches on all the women
Because he cannot find his joy
Except in zoology

Whenever he goes to the phone
To call joy
He gets the wrong number

Therefore he likes weapons
He knows all guns
By their right names
He drives a big black Cadillac
Called death

Now he is putting anxiety
Into space
He flies his worries
All around Venus
But it does him no good

In space where for a long time
There was only emptiness
He drives a big white globe
Called death

Now dear children you have learned
The first lesson about man
Answer your test

"Man is the saddest animal
He begins in zoology
And gets lost
In his own bad news."

PICTURE OF A BLACK CHILD WITH
A WHITE DOLL

Carole Denise McNair, killed in Birmingham, Sept. 1963

Your dark eyes will never need to understand
Our sadness who see you
Hold that plastic glass-eyed
Merchandise as if our empty-headed race
Worthless full of fury
Twanging and drooling in the southern night
With guns and phantoms
Needed to know love

(Yet how deep the wound and the need
And how far down our hell

Are questions you need not
Answer now)

That senseless platinum head
Of a hot city cupid
Not yet grown to whore's estate
It glories and is dull
Next to your live and lovely shade
Your smile and your person
Yet that silly manufactured head
Would soon kill you if it could think
Others as empty do and will
For no reason
Except for that need
Which you know without malice
And by a better instinct
The need for love.

So without a thought
Of death or fear
Of night
You glow full of dark ripe August
Risen and Christian
Africa purchased
For the one lovable Father alone.

And what was ever darkest and most frail
Was then your treasure-child
So never mind
They found you and made you a winner
Even in most senseless cruelty
Your darkness and childhood
Became fortune yes became
Irreversible luck and halo.

TONIGHT THERE IS A SHOWING OF CHAMPION LIGHTS

Tonight there is a showing of champion lights
Gases and galaxies that are not where they went
And were not what the glass has seen.

These are a mathematical race of appearances
And algebraical retards
These wild vows on their infinite
Erratic run:
Admire the numbers!

Tonight there is a spectacle of excellent quantities
Getting out of sight:
But nothing must be said
About the quantum families.
No statement. Nothing.

O nothing is so clear
As the invisible ones
That cannot be denied
Because they cannot be detected:
These are reserved for politics!

Tonight there is a showing of the innocent void
Where relatives appear as spirals
And little chalk suns
Tiny and red are disappearing smokes
Of worlds in flight or in explosion
Before they came to be where they are seen
Light-years ahead of any popular equation.

They went before they were sent
To beep and collide

In the monotonous radio
Before two thousand billion years of *nada*.

And so, tonight, good men, there is a shining
Of skillful elements that disagree
And fly from an imaginary center
That was never well set.

"O look, look up at all the firefolk" sitting in the mind
Of the champion blackboard
Commanding all the follies
All the eventual statements
And the fate of us racers.

A SONG: SENSATION TIME AT THE HOME

When it is sensation time at the home
And the hundred-dollar bird from the pleasure company
Sings

Experts control
Spasms
Fight ennui
While giant smiles and minds
Relax limbs
Save $$$$$
(For a limited time)
In a smashing program
To resettle limbs and renew skin
Custom-made by the pleasure company and by nurse
In crash research to boost kicks
And save expert $$$$$

(It's all in the adjustment
And no good girl ever gets blue!)

Spasms are guaranteed
To relax giant smiles
And spastic minds
Free of ennui
On the sensation farm
For the whole family

When the hundred-dollar bird in fits of fun
Wins fortunes
It is easy to die of spasms
As experts do (for a limited time only)
When the expanded memory feels best
And boosts sales
On the platinum farm
Today, at sensation time, NOW!

When limbs and skins grow suddenly warm
Experts
Rosy with empathy
Win the war on ennui
With giant crash smiles and $$$$
And dual emphasis:
("Easy" and "Fun")

So optimism is remembered
By means of treatments and junkets:

Yes, but only at the home
And for sensation time
Only.

630

ELEGY FOR A TRAPPIST

Maybe the martyrology until today
Has found no fitting word to describe you
Confessor of exotic roses
Martyr of unbelievable gardens

Whom we will always remember
As a tender-hearted careworn
Generous unsteady cliff
Lurching in the cloister
Like a friendly freight train
To some uncertain station

Master of the sudden enthusiastic gift
In an avalanche
Of flower catalogues
And boundless love.

Sometimes a little dangerous at corners
Vainly trying to smuggle
Some enormous and perfect bouquet
To a side altar
In the sleeves of your cowl

In the dark before dawn
On the day of your burial
A big truck with lights
Moved like a battle cruiser
Toward the gate
Past your abandoned and silent garden

The brief glare
Lit up the grottos, pyramids and presences

One by one
Then the gate swung red
And clattered shut in the giant lights
And everything was gone

As if Leviathan
Hot on the scent of some other blood
Had passed you by
And never saw you hiding in the flowers.

A TUNE FOR FESTIVE DANCES IN THE NINETEEN SIXTIES

Now strike up a concert of action in the electric nest
In which the lighted eyes of deadly engines
Never doubt or admire
And the copper fire of defenders
Shows no sign of doubt or double desire.

This is no place for drugs or drink
Or human fright
(The one defectible link
Capable of pity or question
Is the no-lone intelligence: let it lie
Discarded like an undershirt.
Let it sleep in the glue of seconal
Although it moan and dream
That its inconsequential cities die.)

Let everybody sleep in the same glue. But the machine
Will stand out trim because it likes

All the numbers of the strong white spikes.
Its knowledge is alert all night
In this sweet chocolate spring
Calculating secrets for the moving
City of thunderbolts.
It feeds the million fueled implement.
Its dials smile. It loves the heavy beast
The enemy, who when our hemisphere is dark
Dares to lay open the abundant womb
Of war, and mark
Us for the storm and the fire-feast.

Let there indeed be a concert of action
In the electric lucky dream
When every man can violate the earth in sleep
And if he wakes may seem
Innocent as his lovable machine.

But no, one rotten wheel remains,
—Man—to be taken apart.
He is remembered and construed
By the magnetic engine; and its art
Can never forget. If it decide
That man is hesitant again, and tossing in his dream
(Reading the reasons of the wrong side)
Then the command will follow
And the hum be heard tonight
Of the immaculate beeline:
The drone of the butcher.
Thus one enduring light
Cancels the last mistake and gives itself thanks
That there can never be a failure
Within the plastic memory of such a future.

THE NIGHT OF DESTINY *

In my ending is my meaning
Says the season.

No clock:
Only the heart's blood
Only the word.

O lamp
Weak friend
In the knowing night!

O tongue of flame
Under the heart
Speak softly:
For love is black
Says the season.

The red and sable letters
On the solemn page
Fill the small circle of seeing.

Long dark—
And the weak life
Of oil.

Who holds the homeless light secure
In the deep heart's room?

Midnight!
Kissed with flame!

* "The Night of Destiny" celebrates the end of the Moslem fast, Ramadan, and commemorates the giving of the Koran to Mohammed. Hence it has something of the Spirit of Christmas, a feast when the heavens open and the "Word" is heard on earth.

See! See!
My love is darkness!

Only in the Void
Are all ways one:

Only in the night
Are all the lost
Found.

In my ending is my meaning.

LE SECRET *

Puisque je suis
Imaginaire
La belle vie
M'est familière,

Et je m'en vais
Sur un nuage
Faire un serein
Petit voyage.

Car le secret
Que je sais lire
Si je disais
Vous ferait rire.

Mon coeur est nu
Que rien ne cache

* For the English translation, by William Davis, see below, p. 827.

Et rien ne garde
Qu'il ne lâche,

Rien il ne sait
Rien il ne songe
Il ne vous dira
Nul mensonge.

Et mes deux yeux
Sont mappemondes
Tout je vois
Et rien ne gronde.

J'étais en Chine
Tout à l'heure
Et j'y ai vu
De grand bonheur.

J'étais au centre
De la terre
Où il n'y a pas
De misère.

Si je visite
Les planètes
Et les étoiles
Plus secrètes,

Dans la nuit
La plus profonde
Je suis personne
Et tout le monde.

Si je m'en vais
Sans souvenir

Comment pourrai-je
Revenir?

Ne cherchez pas
A me revoir
Je serai là
Sans le savoir:

Sans figure
Et sans nom
Sans réputation
Ni renom,

Je suis un oiseau
Enchanté:
Amour que Dieu
A inventé.

MAN THE MASTER

Here comes man the master
The all-time winner
With guns and vehicles
Ready to celebrate
Six billion busy selves
Here he comes
Bursting with individuals
All his bellies fat and clean
Umpire of the big skin game
With innumerable wits and plans
Nations and names problems and resolutions
With all his eyes on spaces

Here comes John the Master with his knuckles
And his skins all shaved
Shining and paid for
Assured he smells
Like a good example
Smart in the dream of dials
Where he is alone great
With all causes in his own hand
This is his lucky day

Here comes John with the chin
The all-time winner
To lead his squad against himself
Into the fiery question
(Each is his own question
Each pumps deadly lights
In honor of his own answer
Each is his answer)
John always plays to win
Because he is leader
In action and honor
Because he is Master he succeeds
Exploding all his selves
With ever greater distinction
Right in the center
Of his own building

Here he comes again
Ever more and more the Master
Father and cocky number one boy
Swinging and winning he will always enjoy
The fun-loving spread eagle that restores
And signals happiness
With punch and needle
On the weak vacation and he will spray

The enemy right on the table
Doctor Business is his smiling complaint
While the expensive whimper
Of each little hidden wish
Can tell mother
The model fantasy disease
Of old Father and young Number
(Even a billion more of the same)
Why it is so simple
Not to get well

So anyway he comes and comes with new planets
Master of classified intentions
With homeward roses and fibs
And plans redder than Mars for the female
He stands his drink alone or falls home
In graver trouble
Yes here comes big John the same
To his religious door with dagger and flu
Beefing and cross-eyed true to love and debt
Seeking to understand the Catholic home
The cornflake cathedral and brassy wedded nun
Who is insured but never nice and tame
To the Master to John's selves
Breeding when they like
Liking the OK canon and army

Such are the hopes such are the confusions
Such are the selves with shaved heads
With individual wants and certitudes
Each trying to define his own bravery
With "I-John   I-the Capital Person
I-Tarzan and Christian"
Ready to stick out all over
Keeping in full control of selves cancers

Weights taxes and debts
Braving the planets
And brand new disorders
The briskly blazing existential home
Till I continue in spite of all Master
Still drunk and all still anaesthetized
Co-pilot of my mangled star

ORIGEN

His sin was to speak first
Among mutes. Learning
Was heresy. A great Abbot
Flung his books in the Nile.
Philosophy destroyed him.
Yet when the smoke of fallen cities
Drifted over the Roman sea
From Gaul to Sicily, Rufinus,
Awake in his Italian room
Lit this mad lighthouse, *beatus*
Ignis amoris, for the whole West.

All who admired him gave him names
Of gems or metals:—"Adamant." Jerome
Said his guts were brass;
But having started with this pretty
Word he changed, another time,
To hatred.
And the Greeks destroyed their jewel
For "frightful blasphemy"
Since he had said hell-fire
Would at last go out,
And all the damned repent.

("Whores, heretics," said Bede,
Otherwise a gentle thinker.
"All the crowd of the wicked,
Even the devil with his regiments
Go free in his detestable opinion.")

To that same hell was Origen then sent
By various pontiffs
To try the truth of his own doctrine.
Yet saints had visions of him
Saying he "did not suffer so much":
He had "erred out of love."
Mechtilde of Magdeburg knew him altogether pardoned
(Though this was still secret
The Curia not having been informed).

As for his heroic mistake—the wild operation
Though brusque, was admitted practical
Fornicationem efficacissime fugiens.

In the end, the medieval West
Would not renounce him. All antagonists,
Bernards and Abelards together, met in this
One madness for the sweet poison
Of compassion in this man
Who thought he heard all beings
From stars to stones, angels to elements, alive
Crying for the Redeemer with a live grief.

FOR THE SPANISH POET MIGUEL HERNANDEZ

When the light spine of a society
Bends and crackles

There is needed space and sense
For some peculiar spark
In the free tenements.

They mock the bull in their jail.
And you resist so blunt and dumb
With married and deprived blood
To spend in death. And a bull's tongue
Wallowing around the heart
And the "loud west wind"
Around your neck.

The white spear. The Spanish dust.
The tongue swims up heavy
Out of the heart's appeal:
Time! Time!
To love again!

Another moment
And the head will spill all useless
Balls of flame and fruit:
Profusion of blasted gold
Apples and plums
In the storm of Hesperides.

They marked you for this
With steel, O Man!
Tossing your stupid head
Against command and the civilized
Spike!

Every man's last truth
Shines red like a rag
Snatched on the blade's end.

Life shudders at the point of the nation's tooth.

THE LION

High over the October wood the Lion
Climbs into the dark.
His soft burning silence
Threatened the still twins
But in the low regions
Of my planetary blood
There is nothing magnificent
Not stars, but glistening points
Of exasperation
I am a blind man dazzled
By nerves and fireflies.

All classic shapes have vanished
From alien heavens
Where there are no fabled beasts
No friendly histories
And passion has no heraldry.

I have nothing left to translate
Into the figures of night
Or the pale geometry
Of the fire-birds.
If I once had a wagon of lights to ride in
The axle is broken
The horses are shot.

And it does not really matter
I have arrived
Wounded with unimportance
At the end of my stale journey
Ashamed of being so tired

I find the frontier
To be after all neutral

Perhaps I will travel again
Watching the ambiguous signal

Is it after all a Lion?
If thou two stars are permanent:
Let us agree they are twins.

FALL '66

Arturumque etiam sub terris bella moventem.

Green bearded Arthur with his men still blinking from
    underground wars
Comes crawling out of the ivy. They fumble
With their weapons. Gather at the federal table
A party of ancient hoods
Nodding in the blue shadow
Pirates waiting for the new raids.
Infernal smoke
Fills Washington and Camelot
And ashes cut the sight of red-eyed intelligence.

Now Patria sets her stone vision
Toward the computer castles in the vortex;
Is critical of mist;
She alarms the police
And points a solid marble finger
In a general direction:
("There, in the Far East, are the malefactors!")

The granite nation is ugly now
But firm, consoled

By a coat of rhetoric
And soil of pigeons.

Local songs call guards to order.
The earth shakes. Will all the concrete
Stagger and fall?

Or will these armed phantoms
Swim death's ocean and win?

Win what? The earth shakes.
The war is busy in the underground
And hell is ready in the submarines.

SECULAR SIGNS

Three lost lights are blest by priests
With a salvo of savior rockets

An unknown temper
Is accused of loving peace

Lawgivers fill Valhalla
With a synod of meat-eating birds

A long fire is blest by priests

Penniless
Abandoned
Nine shades try to learn
One friendless hymn

Scribbled opinions of three smokes
Darkness blest by priests

Slender
Drest in dark flags
The wives of sable victims
Consider clean earth's
Six foot decisions

The child crowns his childhood with hate

My poor question leans out to understand the dead men

The intelligent furnaces burn blue
With omens

Long enough
The line of jets
The gentle obscurity of fumes

The proverbs of mistaken counsel
Blest by priests.

WELCOME

A ship, a forest of guilty masts
And climbing animals
Appears in the harbor.

The residence of shapes
Obscure
Is acclaimed.
It settles in the weeds.

A dusty shout
Hangs over the fortunate pier
"Stop" cries the Mariner.

"That flaming orpheum
That dwelling place of classic forms
Comes from the ranges of the south wind!"

"It comes in deadly style!"

It comes to this dear home
With enslaved tones
With tragic perfumes.

The seven towers of apprehension
Light their masts over the cool
Night channel.
All the houses of Love
Are afloat in odors
Charring the pupils
Of the night wind.

Then the cruiser in sunken mischief
Fills the bay with chances

Out of sight are the fortunes
The elegant memories
The Inca city of stone
The cyclone of plumes.

HOPELESS AND FELONS

The sun is down hopeless
And felons design war
Games against innocent owners

Stained so dark
They do not recognize
Their own faces

They will complain of ready
Missiles in everybody's air
Or fury of storms
They will all
Lose their minds
In the subway
The underworld of deadly confusions.

For they said they were friends of all men
Regardless of color etc
So friendly that they were regardless

Unfriendly felons
Work in classrooms
Learn Unreason
Spell Cyclone poems

They will speak
Their incoherence with
Sovereign disdain
Without apology
With no intelligible lesson
Till the night is full
Of racing cars smashed
Windows and alarms

The lunatic night alive
With broken bottles
And hot slogans of all
Who had a good time
When the innocent

Were found with no clothes on
In the Sunday paper.

A CAROL

When Jesus got my broken back for Christmas, Juniors,
He learned what bloody parties seed from my sun

He'd try my tissues with the simple question
About the fire and water mixing in fun

(O bloody water
Never trust
The military sun)

The chance of ages is a rock you'll jump from, Juniors,
When Jesus has my waterwings and is alone out there
Out in the sea where I must swim my Spanish
Around the Puerto and the lucky phare

(O bloody noses
Never trust
The military air)

And so I come to learn a new religion, Princess Mabel,
O heavy Princess let me leap as I feel
Over the burning houses and the drowned dinner table
With my skinny Baptist and my Catherine Cart-Wheel
While Elders sell the pieces of my automobile

(O never waste
Good money on
An automobile)

So Juniors see my borrowed body in the stable
Cutting one more cold night out of the funeral's domain
O Master of Timetables who will be the lucky one?

When Jesus gets my broken back for Christmas
And so many wizard babies of God are chosen
To ride in a runaway train?

(O bloody water
Never trust
The military rain).

EARLY BLIZZARD

No more loud Fall
October is suddenly over
Sunk in snow

It feels good to be without hearing
In the lone house
Loaded and warm

Or out following the hidden ways
The ways of instinct
A stranger in the double
Loneliness of snow

Ploughing the deep drifts
Of finding free footing
On shallow stone

All these trees
So heavily changed

650

Stupid
Bend and adore

The hills sleep
In frozen eiderdowns

I go knee deep in silence
Where the storm smokes and stings
The chattering leaves

You can't rule it
You can't tell it when
To come and go

Sink in the hidden wood
And let the weather
Be what it is

Let seasons go
Far wrong
Let freedom sting
The glad wet eye
Of winter.

PLESSY VS FERGUSON:
THEME AND VARIATIONS

1. "We consider the underlying fallacy of the plaintiff's argu-
ment to consist in the assumption that enforced separation of
the two races stamps the colored race with a badge of inferior-
ity. If this be so it is not by reason of anything found in the

act but solely because the colored race chooses to put that construction upon it."

Plessy vs Ferguson, 163. U.S. 537 (1896)

2. The whole issue is a question of choice. We are only giving you what you want. Why don't you make up your mind?

3. The trouble with your argument is an underlying fallacy which has the following characteristics:
   a) It underlies
   b) It consists
   c) It assumes
   d) It enforces
   e) It separates
   f) It stamps
Why don't you admit that all these things are your fault?

4. Analysis of the above.
   a) *Underlies*
   The fallacy underlies the plaintiff because he argues.

   But the plaintiff is only half white. When a half-white plaintiff puts forward an argument he had better take a look underneath it. He will discover an underlying fallacy. This is due to the fact that his argument is neither black nor white but mixed. If he were all black the fallacy would not be "underlying" but evident on the surface.

   Thus it follows that the fallacy of the plaintiff consists in his having chosen a half-white argument and stuck to it, in spite of the act which declares him equal.

5. Meanwhile, *who* is this that is found underlying the plaintiff? That is what this tribunal would now like to discover. How would you feel if it turned out to be your sister?

6. b) *Consists*
   The plaintiff is a living contradiction. The notion of consistency does not apply to his case.

7. c) *Assumes*

To assume is the same as "to consist in the assumption." But we have seen above that consistency is ruled out of the present case. So is the assumption. How can anything "consist in an assumption" which is at the same time "an underlying fallacy"?

8. d) *Enforces*

The court enforces the separation of the plaintiff from his own argument and thereby from the underlying fallacy. He is now liberated from all his mistakes. He does not have to go to jail. The court however enforces the separation of the races, the separation of the acts, the separation of the stamps, the separation of the badges, and the separation of the constructions. They are all equal.

9. e) *Separates*

Separation stamps: stamps separate. Consider yourself stamped.

10. f) *Stamps*

Here is your badge. Get back in the other car and stay there. Only there can you be equal. Don't you want to be equal?

11. The colored race is now in a separate toilet constructing what is not found in the act. This shall be made known to all by these presents as "Plessy's fallacy" (or his "underlying assumption").

12. Why did you choose that badge in the first place? Now that you have it, *wear* it. It stamps you with a unique choice.

13. We consider the overbearing fantasy of the plaintiff's argument to consist in an assumed pigmentation which forces him

to segregate. But this enforced separation is entirely voluntary. To be forced to separate is the only way to be free and equal.

14. If this be so, Plessy is found in the act.

15. He thought he was wearing a badge of inferiority but we taught him different.

16. We consider the plaintiff to consist of two separate and equal races. Thus he cleverly enforces his own assumptions. He is free twice. He is equal twice. This gives him an unfair advantage.

17. They get together in segregated schools and churches where they conspire to stamp each other with badges of inferiority. They undermine the American way of life.

18. Was anything of the sort ever found in the act? Only the colored race is found in the act. The white race is in the other car where no badge is necessary and nobody is ever stamped. There is indeed an act but nobody is found in it.

19. To wear a badge is the same as being found in the act. This is solely the construction of the colored race which began at the beginning and went on building.

20. (Years later, after many other acts, many other assumptions, decisions and, above all, constructions.)
Dear Mr. Ferguson:
Do you remember your decision?
It certainly was a good one, seeing that it outlasted all the other decisions meant to reverse it. Well, at present you have the suburbs and we have the cities. You now claim that we do not wish to join you in the suburbs because *de facto* possession of the cities gives us an unfair advantage. Therefore you insist

that the police must keep us segregated in the cities. The underlying fallacy of your argument is that the enforced separation of the two races stamps the colored race with a badge of superiority. If this be so it is not by reason of anything found in the act but solely because the colored race chooses to put that construction upon it.

21. (*Envoi:* Ferguson with judges)

We opened the door for the colored race. We knew it was their only way out. They themselves closed it. Perhaps they had misunderstood our motives. Thus we found ourselves all locked up together in the same construction. Only one question now remains: who will be the first to set fire to the building?

RITES FOR THE EXTRUSION OF A LEPER

Note:

These "rites" adjusted to the religious needs of contemporary man, are based on medieval *ordines* from the Churches of Angers, Rheims, Bourges, Sens, Amiens, and Chalons as found in Dom E. Martene's *De Antiquis Ecclesiae Ritibus* iii, x, (Bassanis, 1788, vol. ii). The use of the vernacular term "meazel" is neither arbitrary nor flippant. In the French vernacular passages (such as the various admonitions) the Leper if referred to sometimes as "mesel" and in one place he is reminded that all life demands the patient acceptance of "moult tristesse, tribulation, maladie, *meselerie,* et autre adversite du monde." *Meselerie* is sometimes thought to come from the Latin *miseria,* but the derivation of *mesel* from the Latin *misellus* (poor little chap) is more likely. After which *meselerie* would be the condition of the *mesel.* In

English we find *mesel* and also the following: *meosel, mesale, meseile, mezill,* and *meazel. The Mirrour of Saluacioun* (15th cent.) speaks of "Ane horrible seke mesel man" and Hoccleve in the same century speaks of one who "became a foul mesel". In the 18th Century *Exmoor Scolding* we find the word used broadly for any vile person: "What's mean by that ya long-hanjed Meazle?" So the word acquires wide extension, and in this we all concur quite readily. But one fine morning we discover that it has somehow, during the past dark hours when we were unaware, extended to ourselves. This very day the long-hanjed meazel is the one who is eating our breakfast: a reflection which tends to turn our coffee a little sour. So the present rite is a modest and we hope timely vernacular *ordo* suitable for some who may wish to celebrate our current measelries and find therein consolation, without however going to the lengths of those, for instance in the Churches of Bourges and Sens, who laid out their "meazel" with candles, shroud and coffin and sang over him the full liturgy of the dead. In other words the reader is exhorted to pick up his rattle and his barrel and walk off entertaining sentiments of hope. At least he can say to himself, "My parish seems to understand, and doubtless behind it all there is a reason."

1. A Leper is a Lazar or a Meazel. He is a sign of God to the people, for as Gregory teaches, his skin is patched pale and copper, that is to say, his sickness is a sign of the doubts that infect his parish. He is therefore to be extruded in honor of certainty. No man can be trusted in the company of others if he doubts his own skin.

2. In the extrusion of a Leper, Lazar or Meazel, whether to the common Lazar House or to a reclusory in the field, the Lords Vicar have forbidden that the Mass of the Dead be chanted, for the Meazel is not dead, he has only the Measelry or the Malaise. His color is no longer certain but he still lives,

though with one foot outdoors in eternity. Let there be chanted in the Church a Mass for the Sick or perhaps a Mass in time of Great Fear. And let him not be laid out under a shroud as some do, and let no candles be lighted around him since he is not a corpse. Indeed he is alive and all the world's doubts are fighting within him.

3. If the Meazel wishes to confess his sins let him now do so at the beginning of the Mass in the Church, the priest standing meanwhile at a reasonable distance and the Meazel shouting a little. But he cannot change his spots, nor resolve the doubts that are printed on his skin.

4. When the priest shall have celebrated Mass he shall put on his neck a stole and sprinkle the Meazel with some holy water and then accompany him to his hut in the field unless perhaps it happens to be raining. A Lazar is one for whom the rain no longer matters. But a cleric is tender and has other obligations.

5. Arriving at the hut the priest shall address the Leper as follows: "Brother Meazel, you are not encouraged to persecute yourself for your Malaise. It is useless to examine your skin or ask yourself any further questions. It is true you are now alone in your adversity in the company of Christ only, but the people of God shall also remember that your misgivings have become Sacred. Therefore the parish shall give you alms in the fear of Doomsday. But you are to have no fears since because of your hazards and meazelries you shall arrive spotless at Heaven's gate in a little while. Your uncertainty has become certain, a source of sacred dread to others, but to you a kind of hell in which absurdity itself is an earnest of salvation.

6. At this the priest shall advise the Meazel of the Rules of his new estate reading from Canon Law:

1. You shall enter no Church nor Minster nor Cloister nor go to any Fair or Market nor enter any Mill nor be in the company of humans.

2. You shall not be seen outside your hut without your Meazelcoat and you shall not go about without shoes, leaving upon the pavement marks of your doubt.

3. You shall not wash your hands nor anything of yours at any river or brookbank or spring, nor shall you drink therefrom, and if you desire a drink of water, dip into your barrel with your ladle. You shall not leave any of your questions in the public cistern. The river is not your friend.

4. If you bargain for anything or buy it you shall not lay hands on it before it is yours. Handle your money with gloves only and do not breathe upon it. You must see to it that you do not inject any of your doubts into the common stream of currency which is the life of the parish. Bad enough that we doubt ourselves and our Blessed God, without going to the very end and doubting even our money.

5. You shall not go into any tavern, and if you desire wine, whether it be sold you or given to you, take it first in your barrel. Then depart and sip it by yourself.

6. You shall not lie with any woman but your wife. We do not invite you to marry our sisters. If you have no wife yet and want to marry, seek one with your own problem.

7. If you go about the roads and meet anyone who speaks to you, you shall get down wind from him before you reply. For the wind can carry too many unsuitable suggestions. The wind can change the color of skins.

8. You shall not walk in narrow lands lest someone be the worse for having met you. Your face has become an accusation. It questions the general rule.

9. You shall touch no well nor bucket nor well-rope until you have first put on your gloves. And touch no children. Do not give anything at all to a child. The skin of a child is conscious.

10. You shall not eat or drink except from your own vessels and not in the company of others who are not also Meazels like yourself. We make no mention of those concerts which shall be eccentric, not celebrating our own regular systems.

7. Here follow the things a Lazar must have before he is put into his hut. A bell or tartarelle or a cliquette or rattle to ring or shake or clatter in warning of his arrivals. He shall be known by his vibrations. Shoes, breeches, robe, coat, hood, cape, drapes, blanket, barrel, dipper, strap, knife, spoon. All uncommon. Let there be made for him a house and a well. Over the door of the house shall be written "Responsibility". He must have a bed with a mattress of shucks, and cushion and cover and two pair sheets. An axe. A table, a stool, a light, a shovel and a basin. A pot to cook flesh in. A chest with lock and key in which to keep his memories of our parish. He shall have no weapons. And as long as he has fingers he may play the lute.

8. When all these implements are collected let them be placed on a table, let them be blessed by the priest, and afterwards conferred ceremoniously upon the Meazel for his encouragement. The extrusion of a Meazel thus acquires an air of ordination:

"Receive this hood as a sign of your Meazels and wear it at all times outside your hut in the name of the Father and of the Son and of the Holy Spirit, Amen.

"Receive this barrel in which the people of God will by means of a long hose give you to drink and know that you are forbidden to drink at common fountains, pumps and streams, or to dance at common festivals. Be content with your own vibrations.

"Receive bell, rattle, cliquette, tartarelle, to shake, ring, rattle and sound down wind from other people to warn of your arrivals.

"Receive this basket to take what is bestowed upon you by people with possessions and remember to pray God for your benefactors. (At this the Father places an alms in the basket motioning to the others to come and do likewise so that they may know their obligation to the Lazar.)

"Receive this lute. You are not forbidden to sing. Mourn for your doubts and also for our own, though they may differ. We no longer have even our doubts in common."

9. The Meazel Cottage is then incensed and sprinkled with holy water. The table covered with blessed implements is moved into the house. The priest stands for a moment of silence pointing to the word "Responsibility" which is over the door.

The Leper then enters his hut and sits, if he wishes, upon his stool. The Leper looks out through the door at the Father and the People who are standing back at a safe distance.

The Father addresses a few last words of comfort to the Leper, reminding him that though he will no longer see much of his friends, they will not cease to love him.

The Father warns the people that all are forbidden to despise the Meazel, that the children must not throw stones at him, and that no one is henceforth to insult or injure him in word or deed. All must bear in mind the judgment of God and contribute to his needs.

And if the Leper should fall more gravely ill it is hoped that some other priest will come to give him the sacraments, fortified by the thought that this would be an act pleasing to God.

When the Meazel shall have perished he shall be buried under the floor of his cottage and not in the church yard.

10. At last the Father admonishes some relatives of the Meazel, or if he has no relative some Friend, or if he has no Friend some Churchwarden, Beadle or Sexton, to stand by in

view of the Lazar Hut for some thirty hours or so lest the newness of his life and unaccustomed solitude might afflict this Lazar with too great a sorrow and thus whelm him and drown him in some grave peril of body or of mind.

11. After these thirty hours of comfort the Meazel, with God's help, will therefore cope with his uncertainties alone.

BEN'S LAST FIGHT

I

I suppose you never heard of Ben's first meeting with Shady Rovers. Or of his second, which was a beating in the night. Does anybody know his glorious third, a win in the lucky light? Now I will tell you about the first before the second and third, the one in the dark with the shady rovers. After that, between the first and the third, I will show you the second wallow in the rainstreets where they felled the old black bus. Then one all leads to the third win which, with Ben, is final. He takes the silver cup away of his own accord. One, two, three. With a word, we begin.

One evening Ben met the Shady Rovers at the waiting gate. (Pilgrim's wood was blue and foul, this tale should suppose an allegory!) They closed without warning all as planned! They held no hammerhands. They hailed him with a most unlucky smash. Ben's surprise was at his worst until he hit a better chance and caught one slipping after a foul. With a kick and a groan the whole hill went black. All seven grabbed for the ragweeds. Ben was up in a daze and lit out like a stream. Was the grass colored crimson that evening under the fast fog! Dark was lucky this time, for his antagonist. Ben had found his feet and now beat in solid, though he could not see. O it was tough where he landed. Fast as fast can he took hold of the brute's ear and heaved him up with main force to down him again in thunder. He got him up twice till his fists were half broken. It was the new fast force he would soon offer a crash with. He crashed himself ugly and splendid into the pig's great face. I raced in fast to get the end of the fight, and saw him out four down with a Japanese crack and throw them back into the new barley. Did he ever maim those rangy weeds! They were sorry now that they had begun, but it was too late: the whole wood rang with Ben's promising fun. Seven rovers sprung up again like seven hundred but Ben got stronger every time he swung. The whole hill shook. The whole land went west. Floods of flame, forests of smoke! Trees would lose their grip in the valley and the rocks themselves were less steady for the bouncing blows that fell. Everything had to move and move far. At last the rovers gathered for a final challenge, and Wham! It all came down at once on top of them like a collapsing mountain. On they went dizzying the gymns for weights and weights! They could not get away fast enough from Ben now. A smart blow on the bucket cried the fouls on the run! Scatter this way and that! Hill, hole, college and institute! No shelter for the tattered seven! Nine times nine ways home, or anywhere else out of sight of Ben! All laughed at the trim tucket sounded in the villages as seven gangs went through flying in every direction. Fans hailed the beaten throngs without plasters or poultices and helped them home with a kick and a run. Sure enough it was Ben's first and lively best, the youth of a lifetime, as he laughed with a bandaged hand. Down he danced the tall tame boulevard. Down he drank the winner's cup, while everybody cheered. Down came the glasses from the shelf and pictures fell from the wall. Down, down, gaudy, down the winner of a new year's first last riot! Down Ben went on a bet and sat up again in his own home bed, surprised as anyone might be, and only wishing it were true.

But it *was* true, though it was now morning. It had been a left bet, a win of a dime or a penny. Morning was another story: he had not won what he expected, and thought in his light head:

"I did not beat them as hard as I wanted, these hardy twisters in the pilgrim wood I have not saved myself yet from another licking, and if I hit hard I also have to hit more often."

Thus Ben's first test was all a dram he had drunk. A light in his thought, a flicker in his head, with visions in the night. Real good sport but a winner's illusion. O he had won, he had won: a dram of Hollands he had won. A dram of whiskey at his best. They owed him. They owed him more! There would be a quick revenge and a reckoning. It was not final yet, it was only Ben's first, best test.

II

. . . . I thought it was enough to race fast into the rainstreets of the wallow, where they felled the old bus. But Ben was up in a daze, and lit out like a locomotive. Fast as fast can he caught the brute and heaved himself up twice with main force. Then, boom! It all came down and they were razzing the stores for weights and weights. And sure enough, this was Ben's collapse! Down he went on a bet, and up he sat in his own home-bed, surprised as any day you or I might be. For it was morning, and it was all a left bet. Morning was yet another story. He had not won what he expected. He had not licked the twisters or saved his uncle from a smart bank. It was all in the whiskey he had drunk. How he failed to thunder was Ben's last test. . . .

. . . . He stayed where he stayed, and studied the rollers. Old Ben rolled home like an anchor, with every draught. Old fighting Ben was no more the monkey he had fought with his wrench. Old Ben was busted and lay untroubled by the darkness of his own thought, and it was very deep. They called him a philosopher and even a mystic, as he realized with a glint. A knowing glint had Ben's antagonist, Father Time. And when the times came round again, Ben was once again sunk, he had drunk his second dram, and the score was two all.

III

. . . . Thus we swung into the finals with mad excitement. The day was blue and the sun shimmered on all the tents. The flags went up all at once with the sound of an outburst. Ben fought the last time like a cloud. They all came up at him like trains and he threw them every one. He went past them all sides up and down like sunbeams he was so clever and they could not lay a hand on him he was light as a feather. For Ben had found a new technique. He was no longer present to their apprehensions and that was the way he finally one two three four and that is the end.

Such is the fable with the conclusion. Such is the melos with the dream. Look Northsoutheastwest and you will agree Ben is best. But who is Ben? Who are the Raiders? Who are the Shades and the Rovers? Where is the code to this winning adventure? Is man a creature fit to be baited by such brutes with never an explanation? Is it the wars you speak of? Is it the raids and the resolutions? Where have we lost our secrets?

Must you ask the author when Ben himself is sitting up in his bed interrogating the whiskey? Or does this upset my happy end? Have it the way you want: he was lighter than sunbeams and they never laid a hand on him. He had ascended into heaven.

Appendix II
UNCOLLECTED POEMS

ALL THE WAY DOWN

(Jonas Ch. 2)

I went down
Into the cavern
All the way down
To the bottom of the sea.
I went down lower
Than Jonas and the whale
No one ever got so far down
As me.

I went down lower
Than any diamond mine
Deeper than the lowest hole
In Kimberly
All the way down
I thought I was the devil
He was no deeper down
Than me.

And when they thought
That I was gone forever
That I was all the way
In hell
I got right back into my body
And came back out
And rang my bell.

No matter how
They try to harm me now

No matter where
They lay me in the grave
No matter what injustices they do
I've seen the root
Of all that believe.

I've seen the room
Where life and death are made
And I have known
The secret forge of war
I even saw the womb
That all things come from
For I got down so far!

But when they thought
That I was gone forever
That I was all the way
In hell
I got right back into my body
And came back out
And rang my bell.

[1966]

A NOTE IN HONOR OF MACHIAVELLI

And the keen hound overcomes fortune
   That fast Italian bitch   won in human and bestial combat

The good iron art of throngs, fist of troops by which
A clever Pope will govern
Sharpening the thousand tools of one collective wrong

This is policy, this is your one law: meet and offend.
Man is quick to reply: so he is afraid, this Prince
Who flings his shock and his fear
Bodily against a slack state and *fa paura*
He manufactures fear.
A prince's terror makes our whole world hell,
Whose torment must begin again tomorrow.
Be cruel every night
Bring out the instruments again and make the face,
    (the black mass of torture)
The rolling eyes of hell go light and dark together,
Make countenances glitter and flame
A gnash of wills and vile sentences
Broken with hate ends in vacant marks
                              courage is never enough:

(The victim was a lion only
and knew no better!)

ANTIPOEM I

O the gentle fool
He fell in love
With the electric light
Do you not know, fool,
That love is dynamite?

Keep to what is yours
Do not interfere
With the established law

See the dizzy victims of romance
Unhappy moths!

Please observe
This ill-wondered troth.

All the authorities
In silence anywhere
Swear you only love your mind
If you marry a hot wire.

Obstinate fool
What a future we face
If one and all
Follow your theology

You owe the human race
An abject apology.

[1964]

A RESPONSORY.

For Paul Hindemith

I

Chorus?
        Words and silence, standing face to face
        Weigh life and death. The hunters in the sky
        Seem to control our seasons.
        The trees stand where they were before,
        The stars pass by.

        Lord, when the skies fall down to hell
        Who will break the giant wheel

Who will stop the strict machine,
Who will save us from the mill?

Soloist?
or all the people?

We found no man to lead us
No man to teach us
No man to heal us.

Life and death are one
They said. Good and evil
Both are to be feared.
Life and death are terrible.

Night and morning,
Health and sickness
Not to be distinguished.
Both, they said, are terrible.
Both are to be feared,

Everything is dusk, they said:
Not light, not dark:
Nothing is defined.
Truth and lies are food of fear.
Things have lost their names
And all are terrible,
All, they said, are terrible.

There are no actions, only explanations.
No hope, no pity:
Only a setting sun.

Chorus

Who will define movement and rest?
Who will distinguish noise and fear?

Bring us a word that tells the mind
More than an echo in the ear?

Soloist or
all the people

> They give us numbers when we lose our
> names.
> No man tells us who we are.
> Numbers never let us know
> What we are for.
> Words are poured over us
> Like water. Words run down our necks
> Like sand. Sand and water
> All are one. They only touch our skins.
> No one tells us what the words are for.
> They give us numbers.

Chorus

> Lord, when the seas pour down to hell
> Who will save us from the sand?
> Who will keep us from our end,
> Dryness and fire on every hand?

II

All

> Washed in winters rivers
> Ancient seasons come
> Cancer and Orion
> The Bear and Capricorn.

Chorus

> Words and silence, standing face to face
> Fight for the earth, whose circles keep their peace

And dream of the tame seas, whose iron boils
  down
Draining the sand to spoil those shores again.

All

Washed is silent streams
The Lion and the Twins
Come crowned in diadems
With weapons in their hands.

Chorus

Old light, new darkness weigh is in their scales,
Deliver us to war-gods, or to men
Of war, men without wonder
Spawned by the Scorpion.
Our lives heave homeward on the wheel
That bears the stubborn stars,
Light and darkness know our poverty.
They plan our death, and mark our scars,

All

Storms and tides of spring
Divide their chains and come.
The Ram rides in their brine
Stronger than the sun.

Chorus

High seas draw backward for their bloodless war
Then bite their brothers' shoulders as they run.
Hand over hand the open harbor
Lands their enormous burdens one by one.

All

Washed in splendid rain
The stars and planets come:

                    The Crab, the Waterman,
                    And put their packages down.

Chorus

                    Now all is sand, or grass, or scandalous water
                    Where the rank marsh pulls down one crooked
                        gull.
                    Still the alarming heavens roll
                    Us earthward, wrestle our wordless time
                    And judge us dumb.

Soloist?

                    Insensate man! Words would make us human.
                    Killing our minds, we have denied our names.
                    Silence, if we remembered, was our Mother.
                    Shall we regain her, some more temperate time?

Soloist?

                    Trees stand where they were before
                    And villages are gone.
                    The plowman follows his machine
                    Across the edge of the sky.
                    The stars pursue their prey.

Chorus

                    Fire can quench water
                    Flame can stand upon foam
                    Blood lies on the sand
                    When the sea goes home.
                    Steel can give back thunder
                    Fire can spring from wood
                    And mercy from the heart of man
                    Though that heart be dead.

All

                    Washed in summer's peace
                    Both Mars and Jupiter come

The Virgin and the Bull
The wind and the bone moon.

III

Soloist

Now let no man pretend to tame
These innocent lights
Nor judge these ordered strangers.
Fate, when they were older than our earth,
Seemed to usurp their names
Making their skies the mothers of our acts.
They, too young to kill us, are too old to think
    of us.
Lighted children, friends of silence
They sing to us in fields and rooms.
They are the signals of our Christ
Who holds them in His hand.

Chorus

We waited for their light in winter
Learning discipline.
We worked until they came, in summer time
Reaping the words we planted
Under another season.
For the words of God were planted,
Working in word and silence
Barn and city, house and square:
The Mystery was in our wicked midst
And starlight beat like doves against our door.

All

His mercy heals the regions
Of the mind, Blessed by Him

Our acts are free.
Heard by Him our silences
Bear fruit, our words are true.

Chorus

Therefore we must renew
Labor and worship, work and blessing.
Cure the land with prayer and plow,
Cure the sea with wonder.
We must receive new seeds from an old harvest
Old truths out of a time newborn
If we would crown our timeless peace with
    timeless blossoms
When the strong Child climbs quietly to His
    throne.

[1953]

A ROUND AND A HOPE FOR SMITHGIRLS

Children the time of angry fathers
Is torn off the calendar
They turn to shadows in the spring

The city they thought theirs
They surrender to the gentle
Children that were
Unhappy in the electric flood
And emptiness

Believe him alone
The gentle One
You yourselves are

Believe yourselves
Arguments of a speechless
God lost in the
City of squares
Out of a job and looking
For his arm

Lost looking for believable
Joy to surface in the tame
Eyes of all his own

All who may mirror
His lost way to the elevator
Mad at failed lights

So they leave you alone
It is all right

All the windows (Look!) now awake
Are yours, O Flowers!

[1968]

ATLAS AND THE FATMAN

On the last day of a rough but fortunate voyage, near the farthest end of the known world, I found my way to the shores of a sentient mountain.

There stood the high African rock in the shadow of lucky rain: a serious black crag, at the tip of the land mass, with a cloud balanced on its shoulder.

O high silent man of lava, with feet in the green surf, watching the stream of days and years!

We saw the clouds drift by the face of that tame god, and held our peace. We placed our feet on the hot sands as the ship ran aground on the edge of night and of summer.

This was Atlas at his lonely work! I never thought I would have seen his face!

His head was hidden in cloud and night. His eyes were staring darkness. His thoughts were full of inscrutable waters. His heart was safe at the bottom of the green ocean. His spirit stood silent and awake in the center of the world.

He held everything in massive silence. In one deep thought without words he kept the continents from drifting apart. The seas obeyed not his eyes, not his words, but the beating of his heart.

His only utterance was one weak light in a lighthouse. Small sharp words, no commentary on the pure mystery of night, they left the mystery alone: touched it and left it alone.

From time to time he spoke (but only to the distance) with the short bass clangor of a bell. The neutral note was uttered, and said nothing.

Yet it was this dim bell in the heavens that moved the weather and changed the seasons. A new summer grew upon the ocean, before our eyes, closely followed by autumn, then winter.

The waves moved by with white hair. Time rode the secret waves, commanded only by Atlas and by his bell. There were ages passing by as we watched. Birds skimmed the white-haired ages. Young birds kept the morning young. The silence of this unvisited shore embraced the beginning of history and its end.

We made believe that it was five o'clock. We made believe that it was six o'clock. We made believe that it was midnight. Atlas must have deigned to smile on our efforts, since it was now dark. His eyes gave hope to the tumbling ocean. Once again, rain began to fall.

When it is evening, when night begins to darken, when rain is warm in the summer darkness and rumors come up from the woods and from the banks of rivers, then shores and forests sound around you with a wordless solicitude of mothers. It is then that flowering palms enchant the night with their sweet smell. Flowers sleep. Thoughts become simple. Words cease. The hollows of the mind fill with dreams as with water.

In the sacred moment between sleep and staying awake, Atlas speaks to the night as to a woman. He speaks freely to the night he loves, thinking no one is at hand.

He speaks of his heart at the bottom of the ocean. He speaks of his spirit at the center of the world. He speaks of fires that night and woman do not understand. Green fires that are extinguished by intelligence, that night and woman possess. Golden fires of spirit that are in the damp warm rocky roots of the earth. White fires that are clear outside of earth and sky which night and woman cannot reach. And waters that are common to night and to woman and to Atlas, ruled by a bell in the moon and by a bell in the sun.

Atlas puts out all those fires with his one bell, and looks at nothing. This is the work that supports the activity of seasons: Atlas looking at nothing.

"How lonely is my life as a mountain on the shore of ocean with my heart at the bottom of the sea and my spirit at the center of the earth where no one can speak to me. I ring my bell and nobody listens. All I do is look at nothing and change the seasons and hold up the sky and save the world.

"No one will come near to one so tall, no one will befriend one so strong as I, and I am forgotten forever. It is right that I be forgotten, for if I were not forgotten where would be my vigilance, and if I were not vigilant where would be the world? And if night and woman could understand my thoughts, where would be my strength? My thoughts would draw up my spirit from the center of the earth and the whole world would fall into emptiness.

"My stability is without fault because I have no connections. I have not viewed mankind for ages. Yet I have not slept, thinking of man and his troubles, which are not alleviated by the change of seasons. I wish well to mankind. I give man more seasons and pray that he be not left to himself. I want him not to see my far lights upon the ocean (this is impossible) or hear my dim bell in the heavens (this is not expedient). But I want him to rest at peace under a safe sky knowing that I am here with my lights and my bell and that the ends of the world are watched by an overseer and the seas taken care of.

"I do not tire easily, for this is the work I am used to. Though it is child's play, sometimes I hate it. I bear with loneliness for the sake of man. Yet to be constantly forgotten is more than I can abide.

"Thus I intend not only to watch, but to move watching, and I shall begin by moving the theaters."

At this there was a stir in all the distant cities of the world and the continents heaved up and down like the trays of a scale, as all the great countries were suddenly weighed by Atlas in the middle of the night: the lands of Europe and the lands of Asia were weighed in the hands of a tall hidden power, and knew nothing of it. The shores of America waited in the mist to be weighed in the same balance. It was Atlas, the guardian of nights and seas moving and watching.

We expected movement only after it had already begun and we looked for power when the strong were already overthrown. We saw the dance begin secretly in genteel houses, under the kitchen oilcloth, and leap to the tops of the most public monuments. Some buildings woke and walked downhill and would not stop until they came to water. Churches and banks begged pardon as they slipped and fell. People in the unsafe doors set out for earth that escaped them, and trod too late on streets that hurried away. It was more than most men could afford but far more than they could avoid. It was a lame evening. No taxi would take any man to the right place.

This was what happened everywhere when the movement began. The title of the earthquake was "Atlas watches every evening."

Then up jumped a great Fatman in one of the stadiums. He thought that he was god and that he could stop everything from moving. He thought that since he could, he had to. He cried out loud. He swore at the top of his voice. He fired off a gun and made the people listen. He roared and he boasted and made himself known. He blew back into the wind and stamped on the rolling earth and swore up and down he could make it all stop with his invention. He got up in the teeth of the storm and made a loud speech which everybody heard. And the first thing he said was this:

"If anything moves, I am the one to move it: and if anything stops, I am the one to stop it. If anything shakes, I am the one to shake it, and not one being is going to budge unless pushed."

At that moment everything stopped. No one had heard the dim bell at the edge of the sea (which Atlas had struck, in his dream, at this very moment). No one saw the lights in the dark at the edge of the ocean (which had gone on and off with a passing memory in that far place). No one thought of anything, the Fatman had all their attention.

Now this Fatman had been brought up on oats and meat and his name was secret. His father was a grocer and his mother was a butcher. His father was a tailor and his mother ran a train. His father was a brewer and his mother was a general in the army. He had been born with leather hands and a clockwork mind in order to make a lot of money. He hated the country and loved stadiums: a perfect, civilized man! His number was six hundred and sixty-six and he worked hard building up the stadium Atlas had destroyed.

All the people brought him money and played music to him because he was rich. And the music was so loud no one heard the bell ring again. Once again the houses began to tremble.

No one looked at anything, but fixed their eyes only on the Fatman in his rage. No one heard Atlas far off thinking in the smoke. All they knew was that the city began to fall again and the Fatman roared in the tumbledown theaters: "If I had my way there would be RAIN." He held up his hands and had his way. Rain came down as sudden as a black mountain. The clock struck ten. The world stopped moving. Everyone attributed this to the Fatman whose name was secret.

Then in the holes of the broken city the sergeants smiled safe and guns became a thing of the present. Gas was mercy then to many a Jew mother and a quick end came to more than a few as a gift of the popular state. "Here comes a chemical death, with the smile of the public Father. You shall be cheaply made extinct as a present from economy, and we will save your hair and teeth. Cyanide hopes are the face of a popular tomorrow, with ever more fun in the underwears. Everybody has dollars in the home of well-run Demos, and more for cars than for Sunday. But Sunday is public also where Fatman has his office. Only a different name, that's all.

"Here comes chemical Sunday, with a smile of the Fatman's ghost father. They take the girth of the Fat Father's own·gas, on top of the ancient marsh, in the name of a new culture. Toy thugs jump out of every cradle with weapons in their hands. They swing by hard and mean in the name of popularity and boy, that popularity is going to make you

*jump. It is already famous what they can do with guns, and
more so with a piece of small invented pipe, all for the fame
and benefit of the new police. Fatman, Fatman, blow us a
gassy kiss from the four chimneys of your new heaven!"*

*From the four sides of the wind there came together in
trolleys a set of delegations in the name of Dad. "Not for-
getting Mom," they blowed, "we come to hail the Fatman in
the name of Dad." And old Dad sat up high in the memories
of the police, a nineteenth-century legend, a corncob angle
measuring the west. A piece of trueblue oldgold faked-up
fortune. True Dad is all fixed up in the mind like a piece of
Real Estate, but Mom (cries the Fatman) Mom is real heart
and all soft in the easies. Mom is fat from toe to toe, and
slimmer than an ankle. Good old American Maw is Father's
boast on wedding-cake afternoon, in the days of Coca-Cola.
Maw is safe in the new car and Paw cares for corners. The
eyes of the innocent sergeant salute Maw with pride as they
draw Negro blood. And we will have a clean America for our
boys, clean as the toy toughs punished in rugged Lux. Tom-
boy Maw is the magic of Fatman's perpetual boast.*

Then the Fatman, moved by intuition, placed his feet in the
water and established contact with the spirit of night, and the
waves thrashed about his knees. All at once he began to grow.
He gave up meat to become an ascetic. He drank only the
most inexpensive mouthwash. He dealt with woman only by
mail. He tried out his hands on the sky and began to hold up
the firmament. He would hold up the sky and preach at the
same time, for he was suddenly religious. He began to list
all the dates of history and to tell men another word for love
and another word for death. He said he himself was the eldest
child of love and death, but principally of death. At this he
returned to his meat and dropped his letters and dealt with
woman once again directly. He said he could also tell them
another name for woman. The people took down notes of

what he said next, and he told them his own real name was god.

We who stood far off amid the tears of the African night, we who stood with our feet on a hot land, we knew who had rung the bell and changed the weather. We knew who had sent rain. We knew which was power and which was image, which was light and which was legend. And we knew which of the two had his heart at the bottom of the ocean. We knew who watched and who moved under the theaters every time the bell rang. We listened intently to the cloud and the darkness. We lived upon distance, and leaned upon emptiness until we heard our mountain think plain in his own cloud.

"Smoke is not measured by clocks," said Atlas. "Time is not told by disasters. Years are not numbered by the wars that are in them, days are not marked on the calendar for the murders that take place on them. What is it that you are measuring, Fatman? What is it that you are interpreting with your machine, meatman? What is it that you are counting, you square, serious stepson of death?

"I take my own time," said Atlas, "which is the time of the sea. The sea tells its own long time, not by the moon or by the sun or by any clock. The time of the sea is infinitely various, and out of it comes all life: but only when the time of the sea is the time of ·he sun. Not the time of rising and setting, but the time of light itself, which has no hours.

"The sea's time is the time of long life. The jungle's time is the time of many rains. The spirit of the trees takes up time out of the slow earth and the leaves are made of this earthtime turning into light. Longer life still undersea, for invisible Tritons. The long life of the earth. The life of spinning suns.

"The gods of the sea tell no time. They are busy with their own music. I, Atlas, improve the world with mists, evenings and colors. I have my own music of clouds, skies and cen-

686

turies. I strike music from far continents. Others do not hear. They have heard nothing of this for a long time. They have heard clock and cannon, not my music. They have eaten smoke and gone down by train to the last mute home of welfare, which is the end.

"Sad is the city of the Fatman, for all his industry. Snow cannot make softer the city of the Fatman, which is always black in its own breath. Rain cannot wash clean the city of the mercenary, which is always gray with his own despair. Light cannot make fair their houses or wine their faces, though they swim in millions they have won. The Fatman with his inventions is propping up a fallen heaven."

Shall we forget the periods of his earthly mischief, not with regret? Shall we forget the Fatman and his false rain? The people in that city shuddered and the rain ran down their necks and the Fatman struggled with his stadium.

"Fatman," said Atlas, "you are a faithless mad son of clocks and buzzers. I do not know what apparatus was your sire, you bastard of two machines, born with another million. Your mother is not the ocean, your father has not the sun in his heart, you do not know the smell of the earth, your blood is not your own; it is taken from armies. A red flash goes on and off for every thought in your head and a buzzer announces your latest word. I abhor the traffic that comes from such a mad, convulsive mouth. It is the mouth of a horde, the mouth of a system, the mouth of a garage, the mouth of a commission."

Atlas stopped speaking and the rain ended. The Fatman raged in his place and all the people sweated under attack. Crowds expected the Fatman to stand up for his honor and for the first time to move the world with his invention. Instead he only argued with himself and though he bragged he instantly called himself a liar. But in the same breath he accused Atlas of the most shameful infamies. "Atlas is responsible," he said, "for doors and windows, stairs, chimneys, and every other form of evil." In attacking Atlas he ended by moving no one but himself, and this was the burden of his display:

"Thirteen is an unlucky number and there are *thirteen in this theater.*" (This was his first bravery and very nearly his last, the heart of his argument. For though he said much more, he barely moved beyond this point: oh lucky thirteen!)

"Do you see," he cried, "do you see around me the thirteen beards of Victor Hugo and Karl Marx? Do you see around me the spectacles of Edison, Rockefeller, and behind me the comforting pokerfaces of Stakhanov and Patton? Do you see above my head the thirteen mustaches of Hitler and of Stalin? You who see these thirteen see me and my fathers. . . .

"Now I have fought the elements for thirteen days and nights with my invention. The elements will never be the same again. There were thirteen floods when the world was destroyed for the first time and thirteen sat together at supper in one room when very big business was done by my cousin Judas. (My cousins all prosper in business. We are not lucky in love.)

"Now that the fates are measuring more fires for the cities of men, and I myself am inventing more of them, and walls begin to shake at the work of the atheist Atlas, I stand here to defy walls, fires, earthquake and enemy. I stand here to defy Atlas. Yes I stand here in the name of clean government to defy this upsquirt downpush four-five-six confusion of aliens. Yes I maintain this Atlas is no longer public, and never was mechanical. Is he insured? Has he a license? Ask him for his card, his thumbprint, and his serial number. Has he been registered? Has he been certified? I have been all these things not once but thirteen times, which is fourteen stars on my best stripe. I am the auspicious beginning and the prosperous end, the lucky winner and the marvelous defeat. I am alone in the public eye on thirteen counts. Mine is the middle of the stadium.

"I alone shall shake walls in the future. I alone shall light thirteen fires. I alone shall determine right and wrong; establish time and season; plan day and night as I please, and the sex and the future of children. I alone shall spite or command sea, wind and element. And now by God I hear thirteen allegedly just men walking under the oilcloth and if they don't stop I'LL FIRE!"

Well, as you might expect, the citizens came out with bands to hail the Fatman, since this had been arranged. But the Fatman by now was lost in his own smoke. The strength ebbed out of his invention, and his hands fell slack; his eyes popped out and his fat began to get away from him in all the heat he had caused with his speech. The men in the bands continued to perspire and blow. Their horns would shiver till the drums fell in. There was no rain and the Fatman was smaller than a baby. Winds were still as death; buildings swayed for the last fall. Everyone knew the Fatman would not get out of the way in time. Generals cried to the Fatman as they left by all windows, telling him to jump, but nobody heard his answer.

Then Atlas stood over the world holding up the sky like a great wall of clear ice and the Fatman saw Atlas was not his friend. The Fatman was blinded by the glare of the ice and closed his eyes upon a world that had been made hateful by his own folly.

So winter comes to the ocean and the quiet city wears plumes of smoke upon helmets of ice. It is a time of golden windows and of a steel sun, a time of more bitter cruelty than before, though the Fatman is gone. For even the just man now kills without compunction, because it is duty to be hard and to destroy is mercy. Justice is a myth made of numbers. Mercy is love of system. Christmas goes by without a sound because there are no sinners any more, everyone is just.

No need of feast days when everyone is just: no one needs to be saved. No one needs to think. No one needs to confess.

689

The cold saints of the new age count with their machine the bitter, methodical sacrifices they are making in the Fatman's memory, and stand in line before his tomb. Sacrifice is counted in drops of blood (where blood is still left, for many can do without it).

Minutes are counted like Aztecs walking a man to his death with his heart out on top of a bad pyramid: such is order and justice. Such is the beauty of system.

So the children of scandal sit all day in the icy windows and try in vain to shed one tear: but in a time of justice tears are of no avail.

For the just man there is no consolation.

For the good there is no pardon.

For the holy there is no absolution.

Let no man speak of anything but Law, and let no work support anyone but the police.

These are the saints the Fatman has left us in the kingdom of his order. . . .

Yet Tritons under the sea must once again move. When warmth comes again to the sea the Tritons of spring shall wake. Life shall wake underground and under sea. The fields will laugh, the woods will be drunk with flowers of rebellion, the night will make every fool sing in his sleep, and the morning will make him stand up in the sun and cover himself with water and with light.

There is another kind of justice than the justice of number, which can neither forgive nor be forgiven. There is another kind of mercy than the mercy of Law which knows no absolution. There is a justice of newborn worlds which cannot be counted. There is a mercy of individual things that spring into being without reason. They are just without reason, and their mercy is without explanation. They have received rewards beyond description because they themselves refuse to be described. They are virtuous in the sight of God because their names do not identify them. Every plant that stands in the light of the sun is a saint and an outlaw. Every tree that brings forth blossoms without the command of man is powerful in the sight of God. Every star that man has not counted is a world of sanity and perfection. Every blade of grass is an angel singing in a shower of glory.

These are worlds of themselves. No man can use or destroy them. Theirs is the life that moves without being seen and cannot be understood. It is useless to look for what is everywhere. It is hopeless to hope for what cannot be gained because you already have it. The fire of a wild white sun has eaten up the distance between hope and despair. Dance in this sun, you tepid idiot. Wake up and dance in the clarity of perfect contradiction.

You fool, it is life that makes you dance: have you forgotten? Come out of the smoke, the world is tossing in its sleep, the sun is up, the land is bursting in the silence of dawn. The clear bell of Atlas rings once again over the sea and the animals come to the shore at his feet. The gentle earth relaxes and spreads out to embrace the strong sun. The grasses and flowers speak their own secret names. With his great gentle hands, Atlas opens the clouds and birds spill back onto the land out of Paradise.

You fool, the prisons are open. The Fatman is forgotten. The Fatman was only his own nightmare. Atlas never knew him. Atlas never knew anything but the ways of the stars, of the earth and of the ocean. Atlas is a friendly mountain, with a cloud on his shoulder, watching the African sun.

AUBADE: BERMUDA

Now at our island's shining rim
The waves upon their purpose run

Each one busy to consult
The mild opinions of the sun.

Within the darkling cedar tree
Catch the painted cardinal's wing
The delicate birds expect a signal
From their king before they sing.

Open your window to the bay
Reform the errors of the night
Then all the flowers will open their eyes
Gardens will dress themselves in light.

These flowers your wise subjects are
For theirs is only borrowed grace
And the small, glad birds are a queen's choir
Who hymn your beauty, not the day's.

[1939]

BE MY DEFENDER

(Psalm 4)

Lord, when there is no escape, be my Defender
When they crowd around me, Lord
Be my Defender,
Steal me out of here,
Have mercy Lord, show your power
Steal me out of here,
Be my Defender.

> Man
> Crowding all around
> Why are you
> So cold, so proud

Why is your tongue so mean
      Why is your hand
      So quick to harm
      Why are you like
      A rattlesnake
      So quick to strike?

Man
Crowding all around
You have children in your home
You have looked for happiness
      You have asked the Lord
      For better days
Kneel and tremble in the night
Ask my Lord to change your heart
Fear my Lord and learn the ways
Of patience, love and sacrifice.

Lord, when they all go by, riding high
Looking down on me, be my Defender
Be my Defender, Lord
And my secret heart will know
A sweeter joy, Lord, a sweeter joy
For I'll walk alone
With only you
I'll lie down to sleep in peace, in hope
For though I cannot trust in Man
I trust in you.

      Lord, when they all go by
      Riding high
      Looking down on me
      Be my Defender,
      Lord, be my Defender.

[1966]

BUREAUCRATS: DIGGERS

Oh curse them not nor rail
Upon nor arm against the mole.
And do not lift your spear
Against the poor pismire.

The mole digs underground
And hears no sound
Of Easter morning bell:
Pismire in his zeal
Learns the economy of the soil.
And oh, the mole crops tenderest shoots
And tells the time by twisted roots.
Some pismire's busy brain
Conceived the subway train.

These drizzling years
Make laughing moles and prosperous pismires.
Each careful digger lays his money by.
The wise pismire emperor shall be
With blind mole for secretary.

Oh curse them not etc.

[1939]

CEREMONY FOR EDWARD DAHLBERG

On this flashing afternoon of Ascension Thursday let me sit
    in my forest shade to praise a man of excellent language

694

Profuse and bushy is the eloquence of this Classic person, his talk is juiced with myth and with the lore of fathers who knew better than we

He makes all ears ring with the clamor of Romans we prefer to forget

What has he not done for us? Like Montaigne, Cervantes, Rabelais, he has dared unstop the more robust insanities of language

To ring changes on the hard metal of words and improve them with alchemy

To the drums of Cicero and Renaissance strings he has led forth in solemn procession dancing heroes that seem at first familiar

They summon one another in helmets and kilts from shadows of memory where there are no rigors but those of the dream

In which they remain lawless mummers of the unspoken

Teachers of no other sequences than those of invention

Who at once insult and charm the curious mind, disarming it with legitimate surprise

He writes of Kansas City as of fifteenth-century Bruges

He has the eye and pencils of Breughel or Bosch, the tongue of Thomas Browne, and sings the barbershops as Browne sang urn burial

Because he owns round words and rugous periods, experi-
ences the secret rigors of medieval physicians

For whom blood and urine were not yet abstractions

And his busy fires are stoked at the imaginative Etna of the
groin

When weary of the bickering of clerics and new lay-pontiffs,
I am glad of his harmonies

St. Fançois Rabelais, pray for him!

CHRISTINA

Then the old man flamed and prayed
In his stone cell and angry cloud
The mad fiend hanging on his back
The girl freezing in her closet. And owls
Sat on the psalter, looked out of blank orbs
Gold worlds

Wiping owlshit off the holy letters

[1963]

CHRISTMAS AS TO PEOPLE

Christmas is as Christmas does
And the wide world shudders now with woes.

Dance your Christmas with the bears
You stamp and sear the earth with wars.
For Christmas dinner lick your scars
Philosophize and pick your sores.

Wolves' strange philosophy
Makes them hate the Christmas tree.
Join the wolf to celebrate rage
You shake the bars of a Christmas cage.

Our wise men
Have built their den
So no star may shine on them.
The roof is strong, the walls are stout
And barred doors keep the angels out.
Invite the blind owl and the mole
To feed on owl food from their bowl;
For carols they sing theorems
To warm the ashes of their shame.

See no more the light of the sun
For in caves there can be none;
And sing no more, sing no more
The thief is at the wintry door.

But if the bear
Could shed one tear
Those ragged claws would wound no more.
If the wolf could learn to weep
He'd keep house with cows and sheep,
The sobbing babe could smile and sleep.

Thoughtful pen may write this glose
Christmas is as Christmas does.

[1939]

COMEDY CARD FOR A SERIOUS CASE

No smoke says law light-
Ning arrest alarm for
Thunder torpedo smells oxygen sub-
Marine warn tender sinker
Thousands envy dead

Warn unwelcome torpedo
(Smell oxygen)
Warn alert alone
Well careful pilot treads to land's end horizon:
Falls one match and striking the lightning dead

Slow sunboat goes by under an inventive bed
Rocksplit trumpet for laughing carload in the pit of souls
How clear the matching joker dies of reward!
Poor old vaudeville smoker, without an oath
Over and over down comedy canyon.

Bed is no safe engine in electric doom
As Daddy rides the sunbuilt air
Flashes in jet jokes
How he can swear!
His wits are all gone down the corridor
Or in the sunboat under Pharaoh's electric bed
Gone gone with the despairing breast
Stroke of the dead

So Spring bolt clarion hails expensive blood
Careful pilot steers away on tall-aired flood
And all the oxygen is good for chain volts
Drives Death boat down coronary night

So Daddy rides
(And lends light-)
Ning better than Ben Hur's
Sightless fates,

A roaring winner
In a legendary race.

CONVERSATIONS

Madam my action
Thankyo.

A little to one side
(Be my traum)

I am your Enrico
Don' you remembram?
Thankyo!

M-m-m-a-m.
Should we wait?

Madam it is my turn

I am your Enro.

(M-m-u-m-rico.)

Do you forgat? Is Muttons?

I am your Traum

A little to one side

Thankyo.

"Not too diplomatic!"

Madam Mein Traum
Ready in a moment.

A little to one side
(M'action!)

Thankyo
You are my lifetime Pigeon
I am your dream of flight

Madam: my action
Thankyo
(Sent from Enrico)
Interception by T. Muttons)

(To stop is a better mistake.)

[1968]

DARJEELING

And to dissolve the heaps. Afternoon lumber water filling
can full
Taxi call kids. Sharp cries spread rev motor whisper pony feet
        Hoo! Hoo!
Motor going gone (hill)
Looking back her long hair shining pattern of crosses
        unionjacks
shadows on the walk (Hoo! Hoo! Ponyfeet)
Ponysaddle afternoon all rich god Ganesha fills his waterpot.
All to dissolve the lagers (layers) spreads of sounds—waters,
        boards, planks, plankfall fur, voice near, man holds
        basket of green leaves. Going. Gone.
Sensations neutral low degree burn (sun) warmskin. Hears
        a little
water,
Again fills watercan the poor one—not rich Ganesha, he is
        gone in scarf
and glasses.
All come worship fun in the sun.
And to dissolve the fun. Worker basket empty and gone.
        Ganesha
gone in an
Oxblood muffler though not cold after good hot dinner
All come have fun dissolve values. Tibetan boss explains
        garden.
Layers of sounds hammer upon the ear spread selves away rich
roaring bark (spurs values) menaces bishop (Distances)
Image yards. Bogus is this freight!
Gate measure stransound gone taxi Water whumps in can
and fills softer, softer, gone of hearing.
Dog is crazy angry barkleap fighting any wires.
Gone basket of foliage
Bangs on an old bucket. *Inutile!*

700

Motorbike argues with some slops. Taxicry downhill in small city. Outcry!
Disarms v. chords.
Image yards spread wide open
Eye tracks work their way everywhere.
Mountain winds can harm voice.
Sensation neutral low four o'clock tone is general. Must call a nun on the telephone.
Two bad cheers for the small sun: burning a little life sunstorm: is not yet overcloudy winter!
Send aid ideas to dissolve heaps—to spread their freight.

[1968]

EARTHQUAKE

(Isaias 52)

Go tell the earth to shake
And tell the thunder
To wake the sky
And tear the clouds apart
Tell my people to come out
And wonder

Where the old world is gone
For a new world is born
And all my people
Shall be one.

So tell the earth to shake
With marching feet

Of messengers of peace
Proclaim my law of love
To every nation
Every race.

For the old wrongs are over
The old days are gone
A new world is rising
Where my people shall be one.

So tell the earth to shake
With marching feet
Of messengers of peace
Proclaim my law of love
To every nation
Every race.

And say
The old wrongs are over
The old ways are done
There shall be no more hate
And no more war
My people shall be one.

So tell the earth to shake
With marching feet
Of messengers of peace
Proclaim my law of love
To every nation
Every race.

For the old world is ended
The old sky is torn
Apart. A new day is born
They hate no more

They do not go to war
My people shall be one.

So tell the earth to shake
With marching feet
Of messengers of peace
Proclaim my law of love
To every nation
Every race.

There shall be no more hate
And no more oppression
The old wrongs are done
My people shall be one.

[1966]

EPITAPH FOR A PUBLIC SERVANT

In Memoriam—Adolf Eichmann

"Not out of mercy
Did I launch this transaction"

Relations with father mother brother
Sister most normal
Most desirable
Not out of mercy
A man
With positive ideas
(This transaction)
A Christian
Education

(Not out of mercy)
With private reasons
For not hating Jews

"Not out of mercy did I
Launch this"
Christian education
Without rancor
Without any reason
For hating

"I ENTERED LIFE ON EARTH
IN THE ASPECT OF A HUMAN BEING
AND BELIEVED
IN THE HIGHER MEANING"

Without ill-feeling
Or any reason for
This prize-winning transaction

"I ENTERED LIFE ON EARTH"
To launch a positive idea
"But repentance is for little children"

I entered life on earth
Bearing a ressemblance
To man
With this transaction
In my pocket
Relations most normal
Most desirable
Father mother brother sister
In the aspect
Of human beings
One and all without any reason

For ill will or discourtesy
To any Hebrew
Or to Israel
But without
Ideas

"Repentance is
For desirable
Little children"

Without any transaction.

ii

"I NEVER HARBORED ANY ILL FEELING
AGAINST THE JEWS DURING THIS ENTIRE
    TRANSACTION
I EVEN WALKED THROUGH THE STREETS
WITH A JEWISH FRIEND

HE THOUGHT NOTHING OF IT."

iii

Yet I was saddened at the order
I lost all joy in my
Work

To regain my joy
Without any reason
I joined the Party
I was swallowed by the
Party

Without previous
Decision and entered
Upon my apprenticeship
In Jewish
Affairs.

Saddened at the Order
And the merciless
Affairs
Of my learning
Fast
To forget
I resigned from various
Associations dedicated
To merriment lectures
And Humor refined
Humor!

From then on
Official orders
Were my only language

Repentance is for little children

iv

I lost all joy
In my work
And entered life on earth
In the aspect of a human
Believer.

They were all hostile.

The Leader's success alone
Proved that I should subordinate myself
To such a man
(Relations most normal)
Who was to have his own thoughts in such a matter?
In such a transaction?
Who was I
To judge
The Master?

I lost all joy
I believed in destiny.

I learned to forget
The undesirable Jew.

v

I was born among knives and scissors.

One of the few gifts fate
Bestowed on me is a gift
For truth in so far as it
Depends on myself.

I make it depend
On myself.

Gifted.

They were all hostile.

Repentance is
For little children

Depending on knives and scissors

vi

To grant a mercy death
Institutional care

Not out of mercy
Did I dare

To launch an institution
Or the gifted Leader's
Solution
Not out of mercy
Did I dare

O the carefree relation
The well-run institution
The well-planned
Charitable care

To grant a mercy killing summer
Vacation
To the hero nation
Not out of mercy
Did I dare

I welcomed one and all
To the charity ball
In the charitable foundation
For the chosen nation

708

I spent my sleepless nights
In care

Who was to have his own thoughts
I granted
To very many
A mercy death
With institutional
Care.

I never asked
For any reward.

vii

At the end
A leaderless life.

No pertinent ordinances
To consult

Not out of mercy
Did I launch this transaction

No pertinent orders
Lolita? "An unwholesome book"

Repentance is for little children

viii

As I entered it
So I left it

LIFE
In the aspect
Of a human
Being

A man with positive
Ideas
With no ill will
Toward any Jew

A man without reason
To hate his fellow citizen
Swallowed up by death
Without previous decision
A Believer

Long live Argentina
Long live Germany
We will meet again
And again
We have been chosen partners
Not out of mercy
Amid knives and scissors
In a positive transaction
Without any reason
For serious concern

WHO THEN SHALL CHERISH HIS OWN
    THOUGHTS?

Gentlemen Adios
We shall meet again

We shall again be partners
Life is short

Art is long
And we shall meet
Without the slightest
Discourtesy

Repentance is
For little children.

[1967]

EVENING PRAYER

(Psalm 140, 141)

Lord, receive my prayer
Sweet as incense smoke
Rising from my heart
Full of care
I lift up my hands
In evening sacrifice
Lord, receive my prayer.

When I meet the man
On my way
When he starts to curse
And threatens me,
Lord, guard my lips
I will not reply
Guide my steps in the night
As I go my way.

Maybe he belongs
To some other Lord

Who is not so wise and good
Maybe that is why those bones
Lie scattered on his road.

When I look to right and left
No one cares to know
Who I am, where I go.

Hear my prayer
I will trust in you
If they set their traps
On my way
If they aim their guns at me
You will guide my steps
I will pass them by
In the dark
They will never see.

Lord, to you I raise
Wide and bright
Faith-filled eyes
In the night
You are my protection
Bring me home.

And receive my prayer
Sweet as incense smoke
Rising from my heart
Free of care.

[1966]

FABLE FOR A WAR

The old Roman sow
Bears a new litter now

To fatten for a while
On the same imperial swill.
The cannibal wolf will dig
And root out Spanish bones beside the pig.

Germany has reared
A rare ugly bird
To screech a sour song
In the German tongue:
Tell me if there be
A sparrowhawk for such birds as he?

The parrots lift their beaks
And fill the air with shrieks.
Ambassador is sent
From the parrots' parliament:
"Oh see how fine I fly
And nibble crackers got in Germany."

Europe is a feast
For every bloody beast:
Jackals will grow fat
On the bones after that.
But in the end of all
None but the crows can sing the funeral.

Germany has reared
A rare ugly bird,
But crows ate Roman pig
Before this bird was egg.
And in the end of all
Crows will come back and sing the funeral.

[1939]

I HAVE CALLED YOU

(Isaias 43; 1)

Do not be afraid
O my people
Do not be afraid
Says the Lord:

I have called you
By your name
I am your Redeemer
You belong to me.

When you cross the river
I am there
I am with you
When your street's on fire
Do not be afraid
O my people
You belong to me.

Bring my sons from afar
Says the Savior
Bring them from that dark country
Bring them glad and free
Says the Lord
They belong to me.

Bring my sons and daughters
From that far country
From their house of bondage
Set them free
Bring them back in glory
Home to me.

Do not be afraid
O my people
I have called you by your name
You belong to me.

[1966]

KANDY EXPRESS

Inward parcels
Outward parcels
(Chamber of Horrors?)
Lordly blue ponds.
Men standing in river pouring water over
themselves from beat-up pails.
Coconuts, bananas, everywhere.
A Baur & Co Manure Works (Kelaniya)
Grand Land Auction
Little boy in yellow suit too big hat walks
tracks with brother
Schoolgirls walk tracks
Everybody walks tracks.

"Trespassers on the Railway will be prosecuted!"

2nd class on Kandy Express much more comfortable than
plane—entire compartment to myself—plenty of room, air,
see everything etc.

Enderamulla

Tall girl in green—lovely walks on tracks.
Bhikkhu with umbrella walks tracks.

Please refrain from
Traveling on footboards
Keeping carriage doors open
They are dangerous practices

Ragama
Man selling papers chants like sutras
"Never drink cold water lest the souls in it be injured."
(*Digha Nikaya*)

Little boy in tall grass near tracks waves
back delightedly when I wave.

Straw i.e. palm-mat flags scarecrows (or scaredemons?) in
    paddy.

Train speeds gladly amid paddy and
coconut—saying "Mahinda, Mahindi, Mahinda!"

Buffaloes swimming, great muzzles
yawning up out of the green-brown water.

Great train monster—Buddhabuddha!
Sawing everything down to tea's smallest leaf.

High blue mountains begin to show
their heads in distance.

Magelegoda. Buddha shrine on station platform.

"The people, pleased with one another and happy dancing
their children in their hands, dwelt with open doors!"

A white crane standing in sunny water
briefly shakes herself.
Another flies low over green paddy and alights.

Now the creeks are faster—begin to have rapids.
Hills. Irrigation tanks.

Ambepussa—slopes, tunnels, jungle.
Steep black rocks.

A lovely swift-flowing river with large sandbanks.
Jungle covered hills.

More coconut and paddy—bamboo and banana
Yellow robed bhikkhu walking away in coolgreen shadow

Far ahead—a big stone block of mountain
standing as monolithic as a fat lingam.
Polgahawela. (new station being built—obviously
                with endless delays)
Rambukkana.
A new side to the same mountain—it is two.
An interesting and massive shape.

White stupa in the midst of rice fields.
An enchanted dirt road winds (empty) into the hills.
Train slowly climbs.
Spear pointed peaks to the north.
Peaks everywhere—
Sweet cool smell of vegetation.
Tunnels.
Rock cluttered mountainsides.
Now we look down a hundred or two hundred feet
to paddy in the valley below.
Rock pools shaded by immense green leaves.
Longer and longer tunnels.
Deeper and deeper valleys.
Lovely pattern of terraced paddy

Waterfalls. White thatched houses far below.
Looking back—lingam from other side.
We have climbed the flank of it.
Ranges of peaks behind us. Deep valleys.
Two small boys with bundles on their heads
stand on path and watch train.
Black cliffs shine with water.
Small houses buried in masses of red flowers.
Kadugannawa.
Three pigeons sit motionless on the tile roof.
Men setting out rice seedlings.
First tea factory I've seen yet (about 1000 feet)
Others follow.
Man and dog walk quickly through paddy,
Fresh paddy set out in shallow water,
full of cloud reflections.
Women washing clothes in all the creeks.
We go faster—going down—the streams are with us,
rushing down the watershed to Kandy
(It is 10.30)
Tea set out everywhere in the shade of coconuts.
Women in a stream cover their breasts as train passes.

Graceful girl looks up at train, turns away, throws a bar of
red soap in the grass, takes bucket and stands in stream,
pours water suddenly over her head once—then moves out
and does it again and again rapidly, vigorously. Her wet
shift clings to her body. She is very beautiful—in her gestures.
Little boy comes to stream with a tiny puppy and a string.
Ties one end of string to puppy's neck, tethers him safely on
the bank, goes to wash.

Girl is beautifully cool and wet.
Boy flings clods of earth at tethered cow.

Woman scrubs another woman's back.
Bathers and launderers everywhere.

Peradeniya Junction. Kandy soon.

New white houses
Shady gardens
Red earth
We come to Kandy.

University in valley
Stupa on mountainside
Temple on a ridge
Radio tower on the top.

On August 3, 1858, Sir Henry Ward cut the first sod for the
railway line from Colombo to Kandy and forever ended a
long drawn out discussion which had gone on for about 40
years about a proposed railway connection to the hills.

Picks up spade, ends controversy

I now ride in car number 6700 (2nd class)
Amid the wet shadows of massive plantations
and cocoa trees.

Do not block corridors.
Proceed from talk to action.
"I am afraid, I am afraid of silence,"
Said the Vicar General,
"I was afraid of those Trappists."
Dark night of the soul:
"I too am disgusted:
But how avoid illusion?"

What if the mind becomes one-pointed
And the "one point" is then removed?

Return journey—heavy rains—a line of red oil barrels—a
crow flies down onto the rainy station platform—dances awk-
wardly along the edge, investigates a very wet sheet of news-
paper. He tries to pick it up. It falls apart. He flies up again
into the rain.

At the place where the girls were bathing the river is now
red and swollen with up-country storms. Rain falls—no hu-
man being is to be seen.

The mountains are all buried in rain-mist. The valleys are
full of it. The shadows of palms rise up in it near at hand,
then vanish in the clatter of a black cut full of ferns and
cobras.

Sanghamitta Poya. Full moon Poya day of Unduwap (Dec 4)
marks anniversary of establishment of bhikkhuism in Ceylon
at Anuradhapura, by Arhat Theri Sanghamitta. 245 B.C.

Rattling down the mountain the Kandy Express sings
Tsongkapa, Tsongkapa, Tsongkapa . . .
Praise of Yellow Hats.
Mirigama East.
Pink orchids among coconuts.
Veyangoda.

That which grew slowly toward me Friday
Flies rapidly away from me Tuesday.
I have seen that buffalo before
I have seen that boy before.

No man twice crosses the same river.

I have seen that felled coconut trunk before.

We rush blindly
In a runaway train
Through the great estates
Headlong to the sea.
That same sea which Queen Victoria
By a miracle of steam
Changed into sodawater.

[1968]

LAMENT FOR JAVIER HERAUD

Let a man alone in a cabin
In a house of rain
Of silence
Whose blind windows
Look south
and see nothing but night

Consider the void
You did not fear.

I have not seen the Andes
Or the jungle
Or those uniforms, those troubled eyes
those who took up weapons
And hunted you.

I do not know for what reason
You were killed

Except that all men are
Put to death without reason
As all Christs are slain
Without any reason
Only for the truth
Can there never be pity.

So we are one in this: we stand
Facing the one void
The one argument of death
The one extraordinary light and blinding flame
The one ferocity of hope
Unassailed by policies
By the lies of factions
Or by the doubt of hunters.

LETTERS TO CHE: CANTO BILINGUE

Te escribo cartas, Che,
En la sazón de lluvias
Envenenadas

They came without faces
Found you with eyeless rays
The tin grasshoppers
With five cornered magic
Wanting to feed you
To the man eating computer

Te escribo cartas, Guerrero,
Vestido de hojas y lunas

But you won and became
The rarest jungle tree
A lost leopard
Out of metal's way

Te escribo cartas
Hermano invisible
Gato de la noche lejana

Cat of far nights
Whisper of a Bolivian kettle
Cry
Of an Inca hill

Te escribo cartas, Niño,
De la musica callada.

[1967]

LIKE ILIUM

Is this the night the world must burn like Troy?
Is there no wise Aeneas
To look the Greek gift in its wooden teeth
Or fly the lovers of the hollow horse,
Loading his cross and sorrows
(With old Anchises) on his contrite shoulder?

Is there no priestly king
To crack the wooden wonder with his prophecy:
Does no one see the crowded sabres
Behind the lancets of those eyes?

The peace that sings like a muezzin
Upon that crenellated brow
Calls Troy to love a loaded citadel!

You who receive this idol full of pitch and matches
Yet curse Cross-branch and Calvary
Because you hate the nails and Blood
Refuse the peace price of that saving Wood,

Go, then, be deafened by the bonzes of your animal
Jumping and barking in the marble ruin
Too loud for you to hear the unborn armor
The steel heart bumping in that great
White horse's wooden drum.

Is this the night the world must burn like Ilium?

[1949]

LITANY

All holy souls
        pray for us fellows,
all Carmelites pray
all Third Orders,
all sodalities,
        all altar societies,
all action groups,
all inaction groups,
all beat up shut in groups,
all without money groups,

pray for the rich Trappist cheese groups
vice versa
mutual help,
    amen, amen.

LITANY

It yawns at me the cavernous gulf.
Find, find the nuns and make them pray.
De ore Leonis, libera nos Domine: and
    again, De manu canis unicam meam.
Hand of the dog reaching out
    from under fur, lousy false dog.
What is to be done?
Miserere.

All the goats, all the dogs, all the
    blank cattle, all the brute cattle, all
    the horned cattle, all the snarl,
all the fake,
all the bellow,
all the monster,
one horn, one man's foot,
one beast's claw, one hen's eye,
one yak's tooth,
one of everything mister,
one of everything.

These are my opinions of today's cosmos.
St. Giles, defend
        us.

LITANY

Sing miserere
For the men who must die
Taught that bone and blood
Made themselves of mud,
Or only know slime
To teach us whence we came.
Sing a litany
For their idolatry:
"Flesh can only die."

Thrushes, linnets sing
To Christ, Creator, King,
But men catch their breath
Attentive to death
While guns change every town
To a house of carrion.
To the grave we come,
(Earth, which was the womb)
And drums for death knell
March millions into Hell.

Then wounds cry your name
At this feast of the lame:
Speak now of mercy
Or all men must die.

[1939]

LONG ENOUGH

Flames of a blasted escape
Convert three warplanes into savior pyres.

726

Cries of a plummeting sign implore
The prayers of a marauder.

An unknown temper is accused of disarmament
The crew goes down in time with lighted heavens.
Dire powers meet and confirm
A synod of guards.

Fire
Studies the opinions of an inflexible Lawgiver
Penniless, abandoned
Nine shades try to understand
The friendless hymns of darkness

The child crowns his childhood with hate.

Slender, dressed in dark flags
The wives of sable victims consider
The clean earth and its decisions.

My poor question leans out to understand the dead men
Nameless are the fears.

The intelligent furnaces burn blue
With omens.

Long enough: the line of steamers
The gentle obscurity of fumes
The proverbs of mistaken counsel.

[1967]

MARTIN'S PREDICAMENT
OR ATLAS WATCHES EVERY EVENING

This is another, earlier treatment of the Atlas myth, less developed and less poetic. The themes of creativity, power, destruction and facticity are again evident—but the tone is intentionally trifling. These lines may be read as notes for a puppet show. It is nothing more.

I

Martin said "every sane man" would hesitate to believe what we were now about to see. For seeing is imagining. Imagining is make-believe. Who can make anyone believe that Atlas watches? Yet it is true; he watches every evening.

Watches what? This was to become Martin's big question.

II

The scene is a large gray yard with a view of the Atlantic. The waters clash, as in a dream. The ocean is before you with a boat and a bell and a cloud and a lighthouse. Look! It all moves!

Watch the tumbling shapes everywhere. The seas change their minds. Time goes past with white hair—Time's winged chariot which always goes too far. Time comes by from very far and keeps on coming. Be a witness!

Now make believe it is five o'clock; now make believe it is six o'clock; now make believe it is seven.

(We hear the great hollow pianos of the Atlantic. In the evening the waters address us with mindless solicitude, like that of programs.)

III

Wave after wave. Cloud upon cloud. Silence after silence. Shapes come in by every exit and go out by the door in the

728

roof. Our roof opens into the sky. The clouds know the way. East and West. Time flies, and Atlas watches.

IV

Martin, John, and Eva come by different doors into the room. There are chairs, a sofa, and a huge fireplace. There is a picture of Victor Hugo. Soon the four of them are alone with a piano. I shall never forget this afternoon: the snow that falls, the cards that are not played, the subtle movements of aggression that lead to every new phase in the conversation.

—Can't you stay still a minute? I want to take a photograph.

—Are you right to say such things about Father?

—Father would smile if he could hear you speaking now!

—But would we speak, unless Father were smiling?

Martin sits in the central chair and produces many tentative names for the personage who is the subject of their conversation: Father Mussorgsky; Father Van Tellen; Father Ed Coogan; Father Joy; Father Blue; Father Post; Father Grogan.

"Why," laughs Eva merrily, "I don't believe we even *have* a Father."

Here is a burst of sudden humor that dispels every cloud, so Martin sits down at the piano. Music goes on for a long time. A merry evening.

Long live the Queen!

Long live civilization!

V

Eva opens and reads aloud two letters she has received from Atlas:

"Far from my loved ones I eke out a laborious and distracted existence. Does anyone give me a thought? Does anyone recognize himself indebted to my care for the common comfort and security of the human race?"

And:

"Since I have been so completely forgotten I feel that it is time for me to move watching. Hitherto I have watched. Now I shall also move. I shall be called, "Moves Watching." I intend to begin with the theaters. I shall move all the theaters. I shall not betray your expectation. I shall begin tomorrow evening."

Eva looks significantly at the others who exclaim in unison: "At this very moment we are sitting in a theater."

It was already tomorrow evening.

VI

—I am concerned only with rewards and exiles.

—That explains your remorse.

—You touch me deeply. What did the girls say?

—Remember it has only happened once, but once is enough. If it has to happen more often, nobody will know what to think. But it did happen at least once, and for once all were ready with an explanation. In spite of a moment of doubt, reason surrendered and the whole thing was explained in terminology.

—There were lots of photographs; one would have been sufficient.

—Such luxuries are no longer expensive.

—But they will reassure Father and Mother.

—That is what the bells said.

—Good-by. See you in the mirror! (Ah! Civilization!)

VII

"If we were going to play a spelling game," says Eva, "we could spell things like 'civilization is hanging in the balance if not on the gallows.' But this is not the time for jesting since the movement we were expecting has already begun!"

In fact the earth has secretly moved. The carpets have stirred unnoticed under the feet of the visitors and the portrait of Victor Hugo has turned its face to the wall. Soon everybody will surprise everybody else in a meeting on all the roads out of town. Something is closing in upon human nature that is more than most men can afford, but it is too general to be avoided. They suffer the very insecurities they least expected. Their feet will not carry them to the right taxi and all the machinery is going backwards.

Then Eva knows by experience that Atlas moves watching, and that watching is moving without seeing—except to see that it is all moving.

"An odd philosophy," she thinks, as the wall parts in front of her, "But we must make the best of it now!"

VIII

Then Martin bravely dictates a telegram to Atlas in which he makes known all his qualifications for the new office of world-moderator. "For," he declares, "these movements must not be left to mere instinct." He is encouraged by Eva to "explain everything." He writes:

"I never had to exert myself in gymnasiums. Both strength and skill came naturally. I was majestic in the cradle, and knew it well. At the age of two I was able to cut my own hair but didn't as my parents were rich and we had many servants. When I was six I taught Greek in a small but decent college.

(Oh the perverse dignities of scholarship, thinks Eva aloud, over his shoulder.)

"In the most elegant houses I grew up out of the rain and had no holes in my stockings. I kept all the rain out of my room and out of my clothing. I was perfect in deportment.

731

I kept my friends and entertainers dry at all times in my limousines. I protected all because I was myself protected by all. Who could worry for a moment about the future? I grew up in the most distinguished vehicles. I grew up dry in the most expensive torrents of rain. I was hard to meet, of course, and seldom seen: rarely even in pictures. But imagine my strength! Imagine my hunger! Imagine my insatiable need for love! Imagine my demand for more than my own fair share of parents!

"Meanwhile I migrated from the scenic wonders and honeymoon cathedrals of antique overseas and settled in a fast-moving new continent where I developed a unique voice, the voice of the friend. I became a warmly trusted consultant of adult women and was kept so busy I developed bad eating habits. Yet I still loved pets. I became a seasoned traveler with an unpredictable schedule. I was connoisseur of versatile mixtures and occult taste-bud formularies, not to mention medicines! I was air-conditioned from stem to stern, a smooth sport, loving the surge of power under the pedal. I sent the no-risk reply-card to the jolly meat packers and re-read my own complete plays as an introductory gift. I married two eligible prospects simultaneously and we three walked hand in hand into the glorious but uncertain future.

"How can I avoid making friends when I need them so badly and am, in fact, almost never my own friend? I am so rich that I can buy up all their loneliness at once. All their solitudes are mine. I support them without being supported. I am alone. I am alone in the midst of those who love me. Now they are about to fall headlong into the hole. Can I prevent them? I must seek out the acquaintance of a man of power. Yet I myself am the only man of power.

"It is clear that with my immense wealth I can support Atlas, and thereby the whole grateful world. This is the rich song I have composed for the occasion:

By myself
in large numbers,
all together
by myself.
Growing daily richer
I'm a population
by myself.
I'm a one-man city
by myself.

This new song takes in the whole question of being so rich that you can supersede everybody else. I don't think that isn't pretty good."

No one can put into words the unspoken question: "Will Atlas answer? Can he even read this kind of language?"

IX

While they are waiting Eva smiles and says: "Victor Hugo has reserved for you a pleasant surprise: When the buildings moved he swam the ocean, and now he is *here!*"

—Well! He ought to go to confession!

As a matter of fact, the Great French Poet is now smiling in his beard.

X

"Do not be deceived," says Martin, who has worried silently for a long time: "if it moves it is mine. I am the one to tell it when to tick and when to sit still. We have seen that there was nobody watching in the ocean and there is no consciousness in the sky. Atlas has refused to answer letters. He cannot account for the present mood of exasperation. We have explored his presumed locality and found nothing. He has not moved on this or any other evening. If the movement seems to continue, as it unfortunately does, we must have a plan: *my* plan. We must have imperatives. And in fact we have them. I may humbly say that I am a man of imperatives. I am jokingly referred to as "Mr. Imperative." He stands up and begins to dictate telegrams: *Plan complete protection and worldwide total control remaining flexible while matching research with cosmic needs NOW! With treble and quadruple resources and split-second selection of non-motivated objectives we will upgrade dramatic DECISIONS and ACT GLOBALLY.*

We will not shrink from self-contradiction this or any other season, but we will implement a wide-open policy of antic dislocation focusing on round-the-clock professional carefree extermination programs. I proclaim this gala club opportunity and invite you to join me NOW!

XI

Eva picks up the telephone and dials Atlas but there is no answer.

Another wall collapses.

XII

Now it is John's turn.

"Smoke is not measured by minutes," he says quietly. "The sea tells its own long time, and not by the moon nor by any clock is the sea's time told. The sea's time is the time of a long life. The long life undersea of great invisible Tritons. The gods of the sea tell no time, busy themselves with their

734

own music. It is a music of mist and waves and clouds. It is a music of centuries. I have not heard any of this for a long time. I have heard the bells and the clocks but I have not heard this music. Martin, you are a faithless mad son of clocks and bells. I do not know who is your father, but your mother is not the ocean, and your father has not had the ocean in his heart; his heart has been possessed by clock and computer. A bell rings for every thought in his head and a light goes on for his approaching words. I avoid the traffic that comes out of such a mad mouth: it is the mouth of a horde, the mouth of a factory, the mouth of a station, the mouth of a slum.

"Snow is measured not by minutes but by winters. Seasons have no mechanical measure, their number is more like music. Drifting fog sings on over the cities and mercifully closes their eyes with no more new year and no more dateline.

"A new time has come. Atlas watches in his sleep."

But John is speaking in a foreign accent. How unfortunate!

XIII

After this calculated attack upon his philosophy everyone eagerly looks to see how Martin will stand up and for the first time move the world with his anger. But instead he only argues with himself. He cannot get clear of his own scruples, and though he brags, he instantly calls himself a liar almost in the same breath as he accuses John of the most shameful infamies. Martin, then, in attacking John, Eva, and even you, dear reader, ends by moving no one but himself. But here is what he says:

"This is a new game with new rules and I'm the one who plays the whole game and makes all the rules. That's why I regard myself as global imperative number one and I stand ready with new corporate enterprise without additional proof

that the product is either needed or desired. Skilled propagandists try to make you less willing to spend and I hear them all around us now walking up and down inside the last wall that is left standing. I warn you these agents are undermining the long-term dependability of my Hi-line global operation for service to friendly outlanders and even to natives. Who would refuse an instant connection with my staff of entertainment Kings and world famous playmates? Yet I am betrayed by indeterminate boyish-looking agents gnawing toward me under the oilcloth and if they don't stop I'LL FIRE!"

"Jump, you fool," cries John, scarcely hiding his merriment; but Martin replies that he cannot jump, "because," he says, "my foot's caught."

In this strange manner the whole human race comes to an end, and all because of our infatuation with numbers!

MERLIN AND THE DEER

After thrashing in the water of the reservoir
The deer swims beautifully
And so escapes
Limping across the country road into the little cedars.

Followed by Merlin's eye
Bewitched, a simple spirit
Merlin awakes
He becomes a gentle savage
Dressed in leaves
He hums alone in the glade
Says only a few phrases to himself

Or a psalm to his companion
Light in the wood.

Yes they can kill
The lovely doe and deer
In and out of season.

And messengers also
Come to bring him back
To hours and offices of men.

But he sees again
The curved and graceful deer
Fighting in the water
And then leaving

So he pulls out
Of all that icy water himself
And leaves the people

"Il revient a ses forets
Et cette fois pour toujours."

Now caught in many spells
Willing prisoner of trees and rain
And magic blossoms
The invisible people

Visit his jail
With forest stories
Tales without sound
And without conclusion
Clear fires without smoke
Fumbled prophecies
And Celtic fortunes.

MESSIAS

Stranger, the world expected You for long days,
We were all looking at the wrong horizon.
We came out and stood with our flags
In the gates of the wrong year.

We wanted to believe You with banners:
Our cannons prove us wrong.

God dwelt in our town without parades
Stood with the poor men on the river bank
Went down into the water before the blistered Baptist.

He came out of the river without armies and without money
But walked the red roads like a Conqueror.
No man starved when thousands
Sat down around Him on the land.
But His miracles were without sin
Without demonstration, without shame.

He did not despise the wild jasmine
Or turn His eyes away
From the young almond tree
Yet He has refused the crumpled roses
You offered Him for your own pleasure.
And by that act I'll swear that He is true.

If He had been born of our sorrow
He would have bombed the Samaritans with thunder
Made of Jerusalem a solfatara.

Without revenge He blessed our country.
But we have praised the chastity of God
With our own rotting lilies:

Those dirty trumpets turning brown
Those wide, white mouths, painted with golden meal!

The musicians have sighed at His picture with the noise
Of circus angels.
Painters have praised Him with heresy.
We have not known You, Virgin's Son!

He is the one clean King
With weapons in His hands
Rising in the night of our defeat
Armed with a Heart more burning than the sun.

Having ignored our ways, our gates
He entered by the center of the ruined capital
Stood like a giant in the smashed buildings
And burned the long converging streets with the gentleness of
    His expression.

The children praised Him with the voice of orchards
And clung to Him like vines and surrounded Him like birds
While death was being destroyed.

O Emperor! When will you come again?
When will we all sit down in thousands underneath the trees?
Some who have washed their hands with their own tears
Have said: "How shall we know Him when He comes?"

He is the light by which all truth is understood
The light inside us
Knowing His own truth in the true world, the mountains
    and the stars.
He has locked the sun and moon in His treasury.
Can my eyes see my own eyes?
How can I seize the light that knows me from within?

But we shall trace Him by the track of His own immortal
    music
Not count His wisdom by our own candlepower
Yet find Him in our own mansions
Catch Him in His own joy, and find Him in the echoes of
    his Father's feast.

[1948]

PAPER CRANES:

(The Hibakusha come to Gethsemani)

How can we tell a paper bird
Is stronger than a hawk
When it has no metal for talons?
It needs no power to kill
Because it is not hungry.

Wilder and wiser than eagles
It ranges round the world
Without enemies
And free of cravings.

The child's hand
Folding these wings
Wins no wars and ends them all.

Thoughts of a child's heart
Without care, without weapons!
So the child's eye
Gives life to what it loves
Kind as the innocent sun
And lovelier than all dragons!

POEM IN THE RAIN AND THE SUN

Watching the world from my peeled doorlight
Without my rain or my shame
My noonday dusk made steps upon the rock:
Tall drops pelted the steps with black jewels
Belonging to the old world's bones.

Owning the view in the air of a hermit's weather
I counted the fragmentary rain
In drops as blue as coal
Until I plumbed the shadows full of thunder.
My prayers supervised the full-armed atmosphere
And storms called all hounds home.

Then out of the towering water
Four or five mountains came walking
To see the chimneys of the little graves.
Flying the neutral stones I dwelt beneath the pines
And saw the countries sleeping in their beds,
Lands of the watermen, where the poplars bend.
Wild seas amuse the world with water:
No end to the surfs that charm our altars
And fatten the wide sands with their old foam and their old
    roar.

Thus in the boom of the wave's advantage
Dogs and lions come to my tame home
Won by the bells of this Cistercian jungle,
Where waves slow down their silence at my feet:
O love the livid fringes
In which their robes are drenched:

Songs of the lions and whales!
With my pen between my fingers,

Making the waterworld sing.
Sweet Christ, discover diamonds
And sapphires in my verse
While I burn the sap of my pine house
For the praise of the ocean sun!

I have walked upon the surf
Rinsing the bays with Thy hymns
My prayers have swept the horizons clean
Of ships and rain.
All the waters are slick as lacquer.
Upon these polished swells my feet no longer run:
Sliding all over the waves I come
To the hope of a slippery harbor.

The dogs have gone back to their ghosts
And the many lions, home.
But words fling wide the windows of their glassy houses—

Then Adam and Eve come out and walk along the coast
Praising the tears of the sun
While I am decorating with Thy rubies the bones of the
    autumn trees,
The bones of the homecoming world.

[1947]

PROLOGO

For Ludovico Silva

Curious to see oneself irresistibly alive in the middle of death.
It used to be more interesting. One knew oneself dead in the

midst of life, and one could sing it as a curse: *media vitae in morte sumus.*

Now it is reversed. In the Kingdom of Death the poet is condemned to sing that in the midst of death he, the unsuccessful, remains in the midst of life. All the others are embalmed in the vast whispering perfumed cybernetic silence of the millenium of death (Death the millionaire, Death the dictator, Death the engineer). It carries them away so smoothly into sweet poisoned smoke: O the great religious act of worship which is this rich society. In the midst of it we alone remain in life, the unfortunate ones, the ones whom the poison has not chosen but rejected and cursed.

Poet, here is your sentence: you are condemned to eat atomic ashes without antidote and remain alive, with the taste of all the poisons and all the components of the poisons alive in your mouth. I tell you it is a very funny existence, I am condemned to it also. It is very curious to find oneself laughing with a mouthful of ashes. Laughing because all the emissaries of Death the millionaire, Death the dictator, Death the engineer, are demanding that we sing something optimistic.

Here is your sentence: you can curse nothing that is not already ten thousand times cursed. You can't win.

You must face the banal existence of a poisoned life in which Death has failed. You and others, you and five poets, ten poets, twenty poets, skinny, disheveled roosters, singing together all at once with brass voices on the heap of atomic manure and then, suddenly, silent. Protest and complaint of life in the midst of death. It is interesting and acceptable to be corrupt: for death is a success. The poet must face the dreadful integrity of a poisoned life in which death has failed.

743

He is set apart from the happy ones who know why they hate, who know why they kill, who know what the missiles are for, who are precise about the justice of death. We, the unhappy, have been chosen inexorably by the injustice which is called life and which refuses to obey the laws which must align all equal and alike in the rich experience of finality which is death. Life on the other hand has this about it, that it is not final.

This is the beauty of the explosion: it meets the sweet exhilarating arrogant demand for *the end*. They all want *the end*. The end of the movie, the end of the ride, the end of the drink, the end of the boredom, the end of love. They even want to throw away the cigarette as soon as it is lit. Throw away everything, even the end.

For the huge chrome idol: worship: power: the atomic orgasm.

But we must continue to taste the lamentable experience of those in whom death has failed, O twenty poets, O ten poets, O five poets, O Ludovico Silva and Ernesto Cardenal: the idol refuses to shine in us. Shall we then run like the madman called Solomon Eagle who, in a year of plague in London, predicted a fire that would destroy London?
We shall run like him, with braziers on our heads, saying what he said.
I forget what he said.

Meanwhile Doctor Boom is everybody, and in his white coats he studies the dials and the clocks and the meters and the handles and the buttons and the lights and the screens.
Doctor Boom in his white white coats proposes an immediate therapy and Doctor Boom is always a perfect success.

744

READINGS FROM IBN ABBAD

1: *Ibn Abbad Described by a Friend* (Ibn Qunfud)

Among those I met at Fez, let me mention the celebrated
    preacher
The Holy Man Abu Abdallah Mahammad ben Ibrahim
    ben Abbad ar Rundi
Whose father was an eloquent and distinguished
    preacher.
Abu Abdallah is a sage,
A recollected man in whom renunciation and great kindness
    are one . . .
He speaks admirably of *Tasawwuf*.[1]
His writings are worthy to be read to the brothers as
    they practice *Dikr*.[2]
He never returns the visits of the Sultan
But he assists at spiritual concerts (*sama*) on the night
    of *Mawlid*.[3]
I have never found him sitting with anyone in a social
    gathering.
Whoever would see Abu Abdallah Mahammad must
    seek him out in his own cell.
At times I begged his prayers. This only made him
    blush with confusion.
Of all the pleasures of this world he permits himself none
Save only perfumes and incense
Which he uses lavishly:
Indeed, the Sultan tried to equal him in this
But failed.
And Abu Abdallah Mahammad has taught
That the Holy Prophet himself

[1] *Tasawwuf*—Sufism: the way of poverty and mystic enlightenment.
[2] *Dikr*—systematic method of prayer and concentration in which breathing techniques are united with rhythmic invocation of Allah.
[3] Feast of the nativity of the Prophet Mohammed.

Used incense copiously to prepare for his encounters
     with angels.
He takes care of his own household affairs
And has never taken a wife or a mistress
For above all things he prizes peace
And tranquillity of soul.
At home he wears patched garments
And, when he goes outdoors,
A white or a green mantle.

2: *The Burial Place of Ibn Abbad*

He was buried in a vacant property, for he was a
     stranger
And had not built himself a tomb in that city, or in any other.
After a few years the wall of the lot fell down
But later, the City Governor
Built the saint a small dome,
Confiding to his secretary the care
To take up the offerings left there
And send them to the saint's family.

Meanwhile the Guild of Shoemakers
Took him as patron. Each year
On the evening of his death in Ragab [4]

They come in procession for a vigil there
With lights, readings and songs,
For in his lifetime
The saint was their friend.
He sat in their shops, conversed with them.
He prayed for the apprentices
To save them from piercing awls

[4] *Ragab*—June.

And giant needles.
Often in the Mosque
He led the shoemakers in prayer.
Today, however, he is forgotten.

3: *Prayer and Sermon of Ibn Abbad*

O Mighty One:
Let me not constrain
Thy servants!

O men:
Your days are not without change and number.
Life passes more quickly than a train of camels.
Old age is the signal
To take the road.
It is death that is truth,
Not life, the impossible!
Why then do we turn away from truth?
The way is plain!

O men:
This life
Is only a blinking eye.

O men:
The last end of all our desire:
May He draw close to us
The Living, the Unchanging.
May He move toward us
His huge Majesty
(If it be possible to bear it!)
His Glory!

O men:
Burn away impure desire
In His Glory!

4: *Desolation*

For the servant of God
Consolation is the place of danger
Where he may be deluded
(Accepting only what he sees,
Experiences, or knows)
But desolation is his home:
For in desolation he is seized by God
And entirely taken over into God,
In darkness, in emptiness,
In loss, in death of self.
Then the self is only ashes. Not even ashes!

5: *To Belong to Allah*

To belong to Allah
Is to see in your own existence
And in all that pertains to it
Something that is neither yours
Nor from yourself,
Something you have on loan;
To see your being in His Being,
Your subsistence in His Subsistence,
Your strength in His Strength:
Thus you will recognize in yourself
His title to possession of you
As Lord,

748

And your own title as servant:
Which is Nothingness.

6: *Letter to a Sufi Who Has Abandoned Sufism to Study Law*

Well, my friend, you prefer jurisprudence to contemplation!
If you intend to spend your time collecting authorities
    and precedents
What advice do you want from me?
I can tell you this: each man, today,
Gets what he wants,
Except that no one has discovered a really perfect
Way to kill time.
Those who do not have to work for a living
Are engrossed in every kind of nonsense,
And those who must gain their livelihood
Are so absorbed in this that they
Have time for nothing else.
As to finding someone capable of spiritual life
Ready to do work that is clean of passion
And inordinate desire
Done only for love of Allah—
This is a way of life in which no one is interested
Except a few who have received the special
Mercy of Allah.
Are you aware of this? Are you sure of your condition?
Well then, go ahead with your books of Law,
It will make little difference whether you do this
Or something else equally trivial.
You will gain nothing by it, and perhaps lose nothing:
You will have found a way to kill time.

As you say: you prefer to spend your time doing things
    you are used to.
Drunkards and lechers would agree:
They follow the same principle.

7: *To a Novice*

Avoid three kinds of Master:
Those who esteem only themselves,
For their self-esteem is blindness;
Those who esteem only innovations,
For their opinions are aimless,
Without meaning;
Those who esteem only what is established;
Their minds
Are little cells of ice.

All these three
Darken your inner light
With complicated arguments
And hatred of Sufism.

He who finds Allah
Can lack nothing.
He who loses Allah
Can possess nothing.

He who seeks Allah will be made clean in tribulation,
His heart will be more pure,
His conscience more sensitive in tribulation
Than in prayer and fasting.
Prayer and fasting may perhaps
Be nothing but self-love, self-gratification,
The expression of hidden sin

Ruining the value of these works.
But tribulation
Strikes at the root!

8: *To a Novice*

Be a son of this instant:
It is a messenger of Allah
And the best of messengers
Is one who announces your indigence,
Your nothingness.
Be a son of this instant,
Thanking Allah
For a mouthful of ashes.

9: *To a Novice*

The fool is one
Who strives to procure at each instant
Some result
That Allah has not willed.

10: *Letter to One Who Has Abandoned The Way*

Our friend X brought me your letter—*one* letter—inform-
ing me of your present state. One letter, not two or three as
you contend. And thank God for it, since if there had been
two or three I would have had to answer them all and I have
no taste for that.

Since you have left me, your conduct is an uninterrupted
betrayal of Allah, the Prophet, the Law and the Way of Sufism.
And yet Allah had ennobled you in the state of poverty, and

had bound you more tightly than others to religion and *Tasawwuf,* so that your admiration of the friends of God had become your life's breath. Thus you were obligated to remain faithful and preserve this vocation from all that might corrupt it!

Yet you did nothing of the kind. You have taken the exact opposite path. You have made all reconciliation impossible. And worse: you have cast off religion entirely to run after trifles that even fools would despise, let alone men of reason.

And on top of all that you have betrayed me for an onion, for a turd, rather, since an onion can have some use!

Yet in spite of all this, there is the will of Allah which I do not measure; there is the power of Allah to which no limit can be imposed; and if Allah wishes to give the lie to my doubts of your possible conversion, that is not hard for Him to do.

As for me, I can help only by prayer.

But what help is that, if you do not help me by a sincere return?

ST. MAEDOC

(Fragment of an Ikon)

Maedoc of the floating stone
Of the fresh hazel
Son of a star

Bells will ring where
The wolves were
Ath Ferna
Of the green shore

Like sunlight in spring rain
Maedoc and his monks
Come through the wood
To the King's rock

Water and Spirit
Bright wave and flame
At the wood's edge
At Druim Lethan:
The chosen cell
The House of blessing

When Maedoc's sign
Halted an army
The King turned back:
"No fighting the saints
The Blessed Trinity
Or Meadoc's wonders."

Aed Duv son of Fergus
With a face like a board
Prayed and slept
In Maedoc's cowl
For a hideous man
A new fair form
A new name
Without despair

SONGS OF EXPERIENCE; INDIA, ONE

(Poem and Prayer to Golden Expensive Mother Oberoi)

O thou Mother Oberoi
Crosseyed goddess of death

Showing your blue tongue
Dancing upon Shiva or someone
With sharks in front gas—
Tanks empty the ambassadors
Coming tonight they
Shine you up
You Intercon—
Tinental Mam—
Moth Mother Kali Con—
Crete Oberoi not yet
Stained with the greygreen
Aftermoss of the monsoons
And a big clean pool
(Shacks out front and kids
In the red-flowers and
Goats) a big clean pool I say
With one American
General Motors type
Doing a slow breast—
Stroke in the chlorinated
Indigo water where no
Slate-blue buffalo has ever
Got wet
O thou merciful naked
Jumping millionaire
Rich in skeletons and buffets
You have taken
All our money away
Wearing a precious collar
Of men's heads
(Those blacks love you at night
In a trance of drums
Sitting with red headlights
Between their eyebrows)
With shacks out front

When kids are playing
With dusty asses
In scarlet flowers
While on your immaculate
Carpets all the am-
Bassadors from General Electric
Slowly chase their bluehaired wives
In high-heeled sneakers.

[1968]

SUBMERGED DRAGON

Clear green stars
Rise and set:
Peaceful dragon

He works and swims.
It is cool
His fragrant cauldron
The bright hieratic sea

Emerald fires appear
Wet lights
New stars without names
Is this the fortunate year?

His work is cosmic play
(O careless one!)
His water spout, his worship
His knowledge
Need no concern

He lives deep down
His thoughts no longer crease
The quiet water

Until the sea wakes up
In sunshowers of blazing spray.
His daily birth:
How free!

SUNDOWN

(Michaeas Ch. 3)

O sundown, sundown
Like blood on Sion!

The sun goes down
Upon the prophets;
Night is falling
And there is no answer.

O sundown, sundown
Like blood on Sion!

For men build Sion
Out of blood;
They build Jerusalem
With wrong

O sundown, sundown
Like blood on Sion!

They build the temple
With dead men's bones;

They build Jerusalem
With wrong

O sundown, sundown
Like blood on Sion!

Night has fallen
Is there still no answer?
O sundown, sundown
Like blood on Sion!

[1966]

THE EARLY LEGEND

Six Fragments of Work in Progress

"God alone is worthy of supreme seriousness. But man is made God's plaything and that is the best part of him. Therefore every man and woman should live life accordingly, and play the noblest games and be of another mind from what they are at present. . . For they deem war a serious thing, though in war there is neither play nor culture worthy the name, which are the things *we* deem most serious. Hence all must live at peace as well as they possibly can. What, then, is the right way of living? Life must be lived as play, . . . then a man will be able to propitiate the gods and defend himself against his enemies." Plato, *Laws,* VII, 803

I

Take thought, man, tonight. Take thought, man, tonight when it is dark, when it is raining. Take thought of the game you have forgotten. You are the child of a great and peaceful race. You are the son of an unutterable fable. You were discovered

on a mild mountain. You have come up out of the godlike
ocean. You are holy, disarmed, signed with a chaste emblem.
You are also marked with forgetfulness. Deep inside your
breast you wear the number of loss. Take thought, man, to-
night. Do this. Do this. Recover your original name. This is
the early legend that returns. This is the legend that begins
again. Remember the ancient dances. (He has remembered
the whole world at peace. He has remembered the world of
villages, of maize, of emeralds, of quiet mothers.
He has lifted up the world.)

*(They bring out drums and arrange them on the sand. They
begin to beat the drums. Three on one side, three on the
other side. They beat their drums by the ocean.)*

Take time to compose yourself.
(The deep air of the lifting night!)
Do this, do this, friend, while drums call to mind the deep
night. Lift up your heart! (My heart swims in the new tent
which is immense night!)
Now the mind's eye burns like sun in the chaos of forgetful-
ness. Whose great strength comes up out of the dark, sweeter
than this small sun? Breathe in, friend. Breathe in, friend. In-
hale the sweetness of Africa. You are the son of an unspeak-
able father.

Contemplation of water under the thunder, of fire under the
water, of air under the ocean, where time is born, the roots of
the sea. He watches the sunken ship. The night is older.
He has lifted up the night.
He has lifted up the ocean. (He will lift up the shaggy hull,
the dripping sun!) It is his heart, at the bottom of the sea, that
moves the waves of the thunder.

758

II

My birthday was in March, when the weather was furious. I was born in a scholar's town, a small town of famous men. The sign of the Ram. A choleric sign, it promised energy. I do not pretend to excuse all my actions: but from the first, I was a very merry, strong child.

My place of birth was a rich establishment called the "Hotel Everywhere."

Oh I remember well the golden hours of time all around me in the water, when I was still young! And I said to my mother: "Time is very warm!" "You must learn," said a certain mythical preceptor who had been assigned to me, "to run very far without tiring and to tell the truth." He had been the teacher of many heroes, whom I aspired to equal.
We sang music together by the river, I and my sisters, who were known later as nine mountains.

I became an unbloody priest. My hands and my hair turned into corn. I was given power to reconcile the earth with the seasons. I died repeatedly.

I died in the strong light of the sun, of thirst; the rocks all around me were crying out for summer. It was lovely to be twenty-one that morning! The whole world echoed to the dancing of my drum.

III

But did you ever know the whole world was once held prisoner in a bank?

Yes, it was on Cotton Street, and was called the Lotus Bank.
All the gold-barred windows used to jig with small-town tunes.
(These were the inmates' beau ideal.)
As to the police world, it wore a cowboy hat (to hide the bald head of finance and thoughts of impotence, together with the velleities of clever mechanical war).
The inmates were all white-haired juveniles with smooth repugnant chins weak-eyed economic wizards whom I refused to acknowledge as friends.

I made myself a black man so as not to be one of them.

They shined solemnly, they crowed at me, they spouted water, they roused up their dogs. They were glorious in their cells until the land rang with statements. But I had made myself black so as not to be one of them.

Now you will find the Lotus Bank on Cotton Street where happiness is on sale for the best of them only and the joy belongs to some. And you will find the Harmony Bank on Grunt Street where the drinks are liberal for a few and fortune rains full force on the shanks of the many. And you will find another bank on Riley Street, where the police dogs bury their bones and live the life appropriate to their address.

Each prison is built like a Corinthian temple. Each is solemn like the ghats. Each is pretty as the morning sun. And you will see the Magnolia Bank on Water Street to which the whole world turns for simple sustenance: it is built like the Temple of Victory, but the halls are without worship and without faith, only the sign says "Happiness for some." And the happiness sings a small-town tune of the old times not too long ago to be forgotten.

760

But I made myself into a black man so as not to join in their
song.

It is morning. Smoke goes up from the ghats. Sprinkle the
oily river, friend, with the ashes of the satisfied.

Brahmins in cowboy hats,
strumming on the old banjo,
light their cigars at the ghats
where happy Brahmins go.
These are the ashes of a civilization.
Or don't you know?

I turned myself into a man of Africa, so as not to mingle with
their ashes.

(Come on kid you may be right this could be a crematory
like you suggest but there just isn't anything that can't be
glamorized bring them all down to the ghats in bathing suits
there's always a new thrill why be a damn pessimist you may
be all right in your way but those people are basically different
sure you can tell by the smoke what is going on but it can be
glamorized there's nothing around here that can't be fixed
up by a sweet chick in a bikini.)

Well, I said nothing. I went to work on my drum.

IV

With great speed I set the young man free. He sat up and
spoke. The flowers were glad. Then there were people on the
sand, and ships coming over the ocean: for by now, my coun-
try lay over the ocean.

How they smiled! We have found, we have found, the places
where the rain is deep and silent. We have found the fountains
of the spring, where the Lord emerges refreshed every morn-
ing! He has laid His hand upon our shoulders, and our heart,
like a bird, has spoken!

His words were wild wrens, and had worlds rolling in their
throats: for He who sang in their bodies was the center of
planets!

His thoughts were quails on the palace wall at Knossos,
quails in the mountains behind Phaestos,
and which know him today, for the birds have not changed.

We have found the places where the Lord of Songs,
where the Nameless lies down in groves
making his light too shy. The valley flowers
with him. He sleeps in the sacred meadow,
he wakes in rain on the secular hill.
We have found him to be neither one nor the other,
neither sacred nor secular.

The quails whistling in the meadow
are the same as those on the palace wall.
The painted quail is sacred.
The live quail is neither sacred nor secular.

We have found places where the Lord of Songs
visits his beloved. Crossroads. Hilltops. Market towns.
Ball courts. Harbors. Crossroads. Meeting places.
Bridges. Places where the Lord of Songs
is refreshed. Crossroads.
It is when the Stranger is met and known

at the unplanned crossing
that the Nameless becomes a Name.

The silent plain. The bell in the morning.
The place where bread is broken,
where the host sees the pilgrim
and Man acquires a Name.
The Lord of Songs is always the familiar person,
neither sacred nor secular.

They came from the hill, Cretans, Minoans, Mayas, Incas,
to the crossing of the dusty stone god.
A little sweet smoke. Crickets in the field. They came from the
     hill city.
The smell of bread. The smell of maize. The Lord of the
     Songs
sought his beloved in the cornfield.
(The dusty stone is sacred.
The live maize is neither sacred nor secular.)
All the silent races came down from the hills
to the crossroads.

I went to them, I embraced my brothers whom I had now seen
for the first time. They laid upon my shoulders hands without
weapons and we saw one another in the eyes.

The plain where we met was high, among mountains: and
there was a ceremonial ball game, with music, such as we
played ten thousand years ago on our own mountain (yes,
this was our mountain!).

It was a game with four goals on the four sides of the field:
and the ball was supposed to be the universe, and the name of
the game was: Here is God Who plays among His own
children!

V

When night falls
beat one drum
in honor of night.

Maxims of the High Priest:
out of fire
the Bronze Word
"weapon."

The stranger
is holy.
With a consecrated blade
question his fountain
of sacred life.

Maxims of the High Priest:
strangers as sacrifice,
sacrum facere,
twice sacred.

Out of the fire
the iron question.
"Learn his source."

When night falls
beat one drum
in honor of night.

The High Priest
learns his maxims
in a secret dialogue
with fire.

764

Words of the forge:
discover
the stranger's origin;
you may find
his fountain.

Maxim:
try it again
with a double axe.

When night falls
beat one drum
in honor of night

VI

Out of the rain and the darkness and the depths, the bottom-
less holes in the green sea, the shadows of a religious chaos,
come fires holy and primitive, fires without voice, fires of
glory, of fury; sudden and lingering fires, coming and going,
hasty fires, fires printed on the horizon, starting and staying,
removing, lost, forgotten, remembered, parting and ascending,
vanishing over the water, emerging, and departing fires.

There is no voice with which to name these lightnings, there
is no eye to apprehend them, there is no thought traveling over
the water to the horizon, there is nothing in the air but rain.
There is no fear in the rain, there is no hesitation on the sea.
There is only one fire all over the sea running about in rain
upon the surface of the new world . . . and departing.

There is no way to compute the age of these unbounded fires,
there is no surmising the extent of their wandering courses, or

to find the origin of the waters either, the young waters, fresh and salt seas, thrashing together, shivering at times with blue and green ardors. None of this is heard. Nothing has been recorded. All has vanished. All has reappeared.

The flames sometimes have color without force. At other times heat without light, burning fiercely. Sometimes they are only seen and not heard, sometimes felt and feared at a great distance, sometimes they come across the waters like brass horses. Sometimes their heat is felt only in the iron caverns of the heart.

Out of the tornadoes and the shadow of the south, out of the heat of the equator into which the lightning has departed, out of the sea exploding on the western shore, naked fishermen leap from their boats into the surf, to come out covered with water and with pride. Trees are bent double at the constant murmur of fear and of contentment passing always like a flying bird's shadow across the countenances of the grass houses. These men have gone into the darkness and the familiarity of their houses and the world is now empty.

Out of the tornadoes of the equator come secret fires raging upon the calm waters of the Pacific.

The spirits have held out toward us in their hands in silence, and in their hands their orchids and oranges. They have mocked us and made a fable of our passing by, they have sung to us, they have followed us, friendly. They have left us, and returned to ensnare us again, they have surrounded us, they have kissed our feet, they have vanished. They have mutinied, they have repented, stolen up to us with prayers, they have licked our hands, they have laughed and rolled at our feet, they have fawned upon us like beasts, they have enticed us, they have flown seductively about our heads, they have vanished into the sky. We have not understood their playful modes. We have fought Eros.

They have ruined us with their fists and suddenly turned pale and friendly and have sung to us ancient songs of our own land mingled with foreign music. They have come boiling out of the earth to leave emeralds and gold mixed in the cooling lava. No one has seen the streams of clear water containing these emeralds. They roll in the bottom of the rivers and no one finds them. The fires are those of the land promised to my father and mother. And to their fathers and their mothers. The fires are those of the land shown to me in sleep. The fires are those of a new world that has not been discovered and of an old world that has never been known. I do not recognize the names of the men who come up out of those fires with diamonds in their hands, but I look up out of the sea and count the incredible mountains: Volcán Cayambe, Volcán Cotopaxi, Volcán Coliachi, Volcán Sangay . . . and after that the jungle.

THE LEGACY OF HERAKLEITOS

I

I have sought for myself.

The things that can be seen, heard and learned are what I value.

It is wise to hearken not to me but to my Logos (Word), and to confess that all things are one.

Though this Logos is at all times true, yet men are as unable to understand it when they hear it for the first time, as before they have heard it at all. For although all things come to pass in accordance with this Word, men seem as if they had no experience of them, when they make trial of words and deeds.

Fools, when they do hear, are like the deaf: of them does the saying bear witness that they are absent when present.

Eyes and ears are false witnesses to men if they have souls that do not understand their language.

The many do not pay attention to what is right in front of their nose: and when these things are pointed out to them, they do not take note of them though they think they do.

They are estranged from that with which they are always in contact.
The waking have one common world, but the sleeping turn aside each into a world of his own.
It is not right to act and speak like men asleep.

If you do not expect the unexpected, you will not find it, for it is hard to be sought out, and difficult.

The fool is fluttered at every word.

II

The mysteries practiced among men are unholy mysteries . . .
. . . Night walkers, Magians, Bakchoi, Lenai and the initiated . . .

And they pray to images as though one were to talk to a man's house, knowing not what Gods or Heroes are!

They vainly purify themselves by defiling themselves with blood, just as if one who had stepped in the mud were to wash his feet in mud. Any man who marked him doing thus would think him out of his mind.

III

Nature loves to hide.
It rests by changing.

IV

The Lord whose is the oracle at Delphi neither utters nor hides his meaning, but shows it by a sign,

And the Sybil, with raving lips, uttering things mirthless without adornment and without scent reaches over a thousand years with her voice, thanks to the god in her.

V

Wisdom is one thing: it is to know the thought by which all things are steered through all things.

The wise is one only. He is willing and unwilling to be called by the Name of *Zen* (i.e. the living one—sometimes translated as Zeus).

VI

Time is a child playing draughts.
The kingly power is a child's.

VII

The learning of many things does not teach understanding, or else it would have taught Hesiod and Pythagoras.

Pythagoras, son of Mnesarches, practiced scientific inquiry beyond all other men, and picking here and there in their writings, claimed for his own a wisdom that was nothing but a knowledge of many truths, and an imposture.

Hesiod is most men's teacher. Men are sure he knew very many things, a man who did not know day and night! They are one.

VIII

Homer was wrong in saying: "Would that conflict might perish from among gods and men." He did not see that he was praying for the destruction of the universe; for if his prayer were heard, all things would pass away.

(Men do not know how what is at variance agrees with itself. It is a harmony of opposite tensions, like that of the bow and lyre.)

Every beast is driven to pasture with blows!

IX

Of all those discourses I have heard, there is none who manages to discover that wisdom is apart from all.

X

The way of man has no wisdom, but the way of God has.

XI

All things are fire.

The cosmos, which is the same for all,
No one of the gods or men has made;
But it was ever, is now, and ever shall be an ever-living Fire
With measures of it flaming up
And other measures going out.

The transformations of Fire are, first of all sea;
And half of the sea is earth,
Half whirlwind.

All things are an exchange for Fire
And Fire for all things,
Even as goods for money,
And money for goods.

Fire is emptiness and fullness.

Fire in its advance will judge and convict all things:
How can one hide from that which never sets?

XII

God is day and night, winter and summer, conflict and peace,
   fullness and emptiness; but He takes various shapes, just as
   fire, when it is mingled with aromatic spices, is named ac-
   cording to the scent of each.

XIII

All things change.

The sun is new every day.

You cannot step twice into the same stream; for fresh waters
are ever flowing upon you.

We must know that conflict is common to all, and strife is
justice, and that all things come into being and pass away
through strife.

The straight and crooked path of the fuller's comb is one and
the same.

Asses would rather have straw than gold.
Oxen are happy when they find bitter weeds to eat.
To God all things are good and fair and right,
But men hold some things wrong, and some right.
Good and ill are one.

The way up and the way down are one and the same.
In the circumference of a circle the beginning and the end are
one.

It is not good for men to get all they wish to get.

It is the opposite which is good for us.

XIV

Souls smell in hades.

XV

The hidden harmony is better than the open.

You will not find the boundaries of the soul
By traveling in any direction,
So deep is the measure of it.

Man kindles light for himself in the night time when he
has died but is alive.
The sleeper whose vision has been put out lights up from the
dead.
He that is awake
lights up from sleeping.

XVI

It is hard to fight
against one's heart's desire.
Whatever the desire wishes to get
it buys at the soul's cost.

Unruly desire needs to be extinguished even more than a
house on fire.

XVII

The wisest man is an ape compared to God just as the most
beautiful ape is ugly compared to man.

XVIII

Dogs bark at everyone they do not know.

The Ephesians would do well to hang themselves, every
grown man of them, and leave the city to beardless lads; for
they have cast out Hermodorus, the best man among them,
saying: "We will have none who is best among us; if there
be any such, let him be so elsewhere and among others!"

XIX

Those who speak with understanding must hold fast to what
   is common as a city holds fast to its law, and even more
   strongly. For all human laws are fed by the one divine law.

Thought is common to all.
So we must follow the common,
yet though my Logos is common the many
live as if they had a wisdom of their own.
They are estranged from that with which
   they are in constant contact.
The waking have one common world, but the sleeping turn
   aside each into a world of his own.

The most esteemed of them knows only
   illusions and clings to them
Yet certainly justice shall overtake the makers
   of lies and the false witnesses.

The people must fight for its law as for its walls.
Gods and men honor those who are slain in battle.

One is as ten thousand to me, if he be the best.
And it is law, too, to obey the counsel of one.

In Priene lived Bias, the son of Teutamas,
Who is of more account than the rest.

XX

There await men when they die
such things as they look not for,
   nor dream of!

774

Greater deaths
win greater portions. . . .

. . . They (who die great deaths)
rise up and become the wakeful guardians
of the living and the dead.

THE LORD IS GOOD

(Psalm 71)

O the Lord is good
To the steady man
He is good
To the man of peace.

But I stumbled, I stumbled in my mind
Over those men
I did not understand
Rich and fat
With big cigars and cars
They seem to have no trouble,
Know no pain
I do not understand those men of war
Strong and proud
Rich and fat
The more they have
The more they hate
And hate rolls down their skin
Like drops of sweat.

I stumbled, I stumbled in my mind
Over those men of war

Full of power
Rich and fat
The more they have, the more they hate
And they jeered
At my people
Showed their power
Rolled their pile of fat
And my people
Listened to their threat
My people was afraid
Of those men of war
When hate rolled down their skin
Like drops of sweat.

My heart was sore
Seeing their success
"Does God care?
Has He forgotten us?"
Lord, I nearly fell
Stumbling in my mind
About those men of war
It was hard to see
Till you showed me
How like a dream
Those phantoms pass away.

[1966]

THE MOMENT OF TRUTH

For Alberto Girri

Man is an animal who thinks himself important
And his reason is right. His wit tells him the truth.

Ours is a new kind. Each one of us with good sense
Is greater than the race.

                        Some refuse to see
How whole mankind becomes great when it is smaller
Than each thinking part.

Some cannot bear the weight of being men.
They give their manhood to the corporation
Or political idol. They and the race alike
Suffer from this intemperance.

Others are strong enough to be sober,
Walk alone, see how man looks with God in him.

Man's home-made image is his enemy. This must be
    destroyed
With straight words and paradox.
Such is your religious work, merit and sacrifice.
Strike hard, Girri, with metaphysical grace!

THE OINTMENT

This day throw open all your houses, and forever.
And love, not fear, the many poor.
You who have sometimes fed the beggar in his tenement
And kept the mad in Bedlam, you would kill then
If they came too near to your day.

The smilers in the ticket windows, and the sellers at the
    counters,
The tellers in the friendly banks

All save behind their locks and iron shutters
Some holy pennies for a holy beggar:
But how they stare, with eyes like stones, for fear
When Jesus enters at the wealthy leper's door!

When God was in the leper's house at Bethany
There was a woman full of sin
Wasted a pound of ointment in a precious jar
In honor of His burying:
When with the lesson of that wasted ointment the whole house
    was sweetened
Look how the traps of the pious and the just were all laid
    bare.

For who came forward to proclaim the waste, but the
    betrayer,
Iscariot, who took the part of the poor.

We like St. Magdalen are poor and have no money
We have no merits, only our lives and our sins:
We have no food but daily take our bread
(When we grow hungry) from the hand of God.
We work in somebody else's vineyard
We sleep behind the just man's barn.

And look! The same betrayers come, and would accuse us
Because they say we spent the rain like money
And squandered the strong sun and threw away the trees
We worked all the olives of another man's garden
In oil of sacrifice for Jesus, teaching at the leper's table.
We took our dawn and broke it like a jar
And sweetened with that quiet light, a savior's sepulchre.
We took the flower of the alabaster spring
And the fruits of all our summers,
And threw them away, but not to the poor!

This way we all come happy with our empty hands,
And wait with nothing at the gate of heaven.

O we must quickly give away our lives before one night is
      over—
And waste our souls on Him, at this one supper:
This is the time of His betrayal by the lovers of the poor!

Now will we waste our works, knowing they cannot keep
      us hidden,
Put to no use our fruits, nor into barns our harvest
They'll never end our endless hungers! Let them go!

So we will give away our nights and days,
Waste them in tears and pour away our praises
Pour them upon our God, before the face of His betrayers
And throw them away for Jesus, to hallow His grave!

[1942]

THERE IS A WAY

(Isaias 35:8–10)

There is a way to glory
Clear and straight
But not for men of blood
They shall not stray
Upon my road
Nor the unclean
Whose hands have taken life:
They shall not find this holy way

To Jerusalem
Where the Lord of peace
Rules in glory.

Love is this way to glory
Truth and Mercy
No beast of prey
Shall be there
No angry wolf or bear
By my highway
Murder shall not stain
That way with blood
But forgiveness everywhere
Shall teach my people how
To go to glory.

Songs of love and joy
Echo everywhere
And the holy people
Travels there
Glad and free
Forgiving and forgiven
Riding on to Sion
Where the Lord of Peace
Their Defender, their Redeemer
Rules in glory.

[1966]

THESE YEARS A WINTER

What armies ride November clouds
And white apocalypse on the sky,

Ruin the walls of glorious Rome
And in the birch woods burn down Troy?

"Ubi sunt" in antiphon
The wood sings to the curlew's cry
When perilous knifelight upwood strikes
At pale shreds of a winter day.

The wild guest wings his glorias far
From lean hedgerow and pillaged choir
Yet silent fields intone a hymn.

Beyond the hills a sudden star
Walks upon the winter clear
Calling Kings to Bethlehem.

[1939]

WHAT TROUBLES I HAVE SEEN IN BIRDLEGGED SPRING

I

Coming by noon to all the branches
and every girl
holding a stone
where there are book-
shelves bewildered men
in soft blue beards
with such fright
behind big lenses and
the nymphs

Speak above the dry furniture
of a library
(to every girl a source
a kind of home)
speaking I say
with the gentle
voices of paper
way down home

In Egypt land I seek a spring of cards
from a young woman who is a library
of beautiful notes and legs

Devotion to sofas
to longprinted afternoon
and poems of hair
while old Doc Williams said in a letter
I'd gone to be a half assed monk
O God the troubles I have seen in birdlegged spring

II

Way down in Egypt land
where the longprinted girls
dream in the sources of their lighted hair
and devotion is to the bare branches
of Utopian spring.

Dryland here for singles.

Arrival of teachers
in Utopia
in Egypt land
to every history a land.

782

Every girl
holding a stone
guards a source
defying the committees.

Way down home
by the branches
jungle cards
will teach the way
to sunburn saying
      Tac-
      tile
      sun-
      burn
      tac-
      tile
      sun
      says ravishing time.

III

Every girl
defends a store
of time she has saved
from a committee

Listening to gentle
verbs of hair
and hair alone

For all day volumes of the people
bloom in Egypt land

writing the histories
of everybody's God

what troubles I have seen in birdlegged spring.

[1968]

[UNTITLED]

Berceuse: to end the sorrow of mortals: talelo, riding the bull.
Talelo. Riding the great blue buffalo. Talelo! They kill swine.
They break the bone, eat the marrow of sorrow. The Tamil
page cures in the dry wind, the inner aviation. You striding
baby, you three-step world surveyor.

Weep not. Talelo.
Love has lotus feet
Like the new blossoms
Bells are on her ankles.
Talelo.

You who came to drink on earth
Poisoned milk
Weep no more. Talelo?
The carp is leaping
In the red-rice. Talelo.
And in the open lotus
Stays the blackgold bee
The slow cows come
Heavy with milk
(Come, doll. Talelo.)
Kiss kiss one sandy sparrow

And coins tinkle on the wrist
Bells on the ankles of girls at the churns.
Talelo.

You little thundercloud
With red eyes
Lotus buds
Lion cub of yasoda
The girls go
To wash in the river
But for you
They do not pencil
Their eyes.

[1968]

[UNTITLED]

Five breaths pray in me: sun moon
Rain wind and fire
Five seated Buddhas reign in the breaths
Five illusions
One universe:
The white breath, yellow breath,
Green breath, blue breath,
Red fire breath, Amitabha
Knowledge and Desire
And the quiescence
Of Knowledge and Desire.

[1968]

[UNTITLED]

Hrishikesa, destoyer of Titans, ogres and canailles,
Slaves flee the old group, embracing the feet of Hrishikesa,
    flying from Wallace,
Free champagne is distributed to certain air passengers
"Ad multos annos," sings the airline destroyer of ogres
    and canailles
In the sanctuary of the lucky wheel
Blazing red circle in the fire
We are signed between the eyes with this noble crim-
Son element this Asia,
The lucky wheel spins over the macadam forts
Showering them with blood and spirits
The thousand bleeding arms of Bana
Whirl in the alcohol sky
Magic war! Many armies of fiery stars!
Smash the great rock fort in the Mathura forest
Baby Krishna plays on his pan-flute
And dances on the five heads
Of the registered brass cobra
Provided free by a loving line of governments.

[1968]

[UNTITLED]

King Solomon: my master and the imbeciles
with drapes and crowns, with comets in their eyes,
Present him one by one their sentences
and the dead king is my authority

All is approved and all is empty
    and all his monkeys are impartial
    Heroes of history
While this parliament of grackles
Cry out together Jefferson
and Marx and Popes and Zen
(all is approved and certified together—
    It's all in the applause!)
Meanwhile the roof caves in upon
King Solomon who is my master
Sitting in the nightclub with a vacant face
approving Popes and bombs and gin
While anthropoids in linen suits
    bring him the latest noises of his streets
"J'appreuve tout; en tout, tout est sonore!"

[UNTITLED]

Mothers you have met before still need you
Well-wishers meet you full on defying comprehension

Our scene is foggy we are asking you to clarify
Explain the geometry of life at Catholic Worker
The night court, the mumbling judge: confused!
With our mouths full of cornflakes we are expecting an
  emergency.

Cynics declare you are in Greece.

We read poetry at the lunch club not for fun

Come on we know you have seen Popes.

It rains too hard untouchables exclaim

Soldiers: harbingers of change

Come back before the place is used up.

Sir what do I hold in my hand?

[UNTITLED]

1. Now you are all here you might as well know this is
America we do what we like.
2. Be spontaneous it is the right way.
3. Mothers you have met before still defy comprehension.
4. Our scene is foggy we are asking you to clarify.
5. Explains geomoetry of life. Where? At Catholic Worker.
6. Very glad you came. With our mouths full of cornflakes
we were expecting an emergency.
7. Cynics declare you are in Greece.
8. Better get back quick before the place is all used up.
9. The night court: the mumbling judge: confused.
10. Well-wishers are there to meet you head on.
11. For the journal: soldiers, harbingers of change.
12. You came just in time, the score is even.
13. None of the machines has yet been broken.
14. Come on we know you have seen Popes.
15. People have been a little self-conscious around here in
the emergency.
16. Who cares what the cynics declare. But you have been in
Greece.

[UNTITLED]

O Cross, more splendid than all the stars,
Glorious to the world,
Greatly to be loved by men,
More holy than all things that are,
Thou who alone wast worthy to weigh the gold
    of the world's ransom,
Sweet tree, beloved nails,
Bearing the Love-Burden,
Save us who have come together here, this day,
In choirs for Thy Praise!
Alleluiah, alleluiah, alleluiah!

[UNTITLED]

O small Saint Agnes dressed in gold
With fire in rainbows round about your face,
Sing with the seven martyrs in my Canon.

Come home, come home O centuries
Whose soundless islands ring me from within,
Whose saints come down this winter morning's iris
To wait upon our prayers with hyacinths.

I speak your name with wine upon my lips
Drowned in the singing of your lovely catacomb
My feet upon forget-me-nots.
I sink this little frigate in the Blood of Peace

And put my pall upon the cup
Working our peace, our mystery, who must
Run down and find you, saint, by Saint John's stairs.

No lines, no globes,
No compasses, no staring fires
No candle's cup to swing upon my night's dark ocean
No signs, no signals claim us.

There the pretended horns of time grow dim.
The cities cry like peacocks in their sleep

I speak your name with blood upon my wrist
With blood upon my breast
O small Saint Agnes dressed in martyrdom
With fire and water waving in your hair.

[UNTITLED]

The moon smiles like a queen,
(says the voice in my vision)
The star sings in the gate,
(shines the speech in my ear)
The waves all clap hands
(says the voice in my vision)
And the sleeping capes
(shines the speech in my ear)
Awake as shrill as children,
The sleeping capes awake as innocent
as children, lifting up their
Hands to high heaven,
(says the voice in my vision).
The queen of light comes shining like a ship.
The green hills sing hymns.
The rocks cry out like glass.
Leviathan plays in the gates of the ocean.

The man on the mast cries land!
(shines the speech in my ear)
The man on the mast cries land!

[UNTITLED]

There is a little ceremony to be performed, the fingers are washed in silence over an earthenware bowl before entering, before vesting. There is a moment of prayer before vesting.

The chapel is as clean and well-lit as a child's room. From very high it overlooks a wet field lined with blossoming trees. Beehives stand in low grass waiting for the sun. The trees and hives are silent. The chapel is silent. I speak in Latin. The acolytes respond in Latin.

The Gospel is for Abbots and Apostles, for men who have renounced lands, wives, houses for Christ. They have left houses to follow Him who has no den to sleep in. They have followed the Great Bird who has no nest.

[UNTITLED]

The silver bird is E backward in cool pond water.

The paper bird is a pale leaf in browneyed water
She lies limp over the dish or upturned face
An underwater sun,
Out of this braided disk

Three eyes or hosts look out noplace or upward
Through filtered light
There will be no shadow on this rufous paten.
The limp bird lies in air or water elsewhere.
Cast like a letter
Of some language impossible and perfect. Where E in a mirror
Says more than everything.
In a water world that is not alien
But infinitely human: it has wood in it
And the wood has been sawed
And the bird is cut like a letter
Both bird and tree are Saviors
Three white hosts of wood are branded on the sweet humus

And the stones of a paradise city see themselves backward
Spelling certainties in frugal water.

[1963]

[UNTITLED]

Things and people goodbye
It is not that I prefer
The singleness of death
Where no companions are,
Yet things and "you" and "I"
The "he" the "she" the "they"
Must all go off alone
In common, not to be—
And not in company.

[1964]

[UNTITLED]

What is beyond reproof
Is done in this building
Care is taken for each to feel noble.
Whoever is without blame
Shall be commended in these halls.

Whatever is beyond reproof
Comes from behind that door.
All decisions are in the papers:
No more day and night, the managers decree.

O if the world had a center
And if Paradise were true
If there some sacred spring
To wash away blame.

Appendix III
HUMOROUS VERSE

A PRACTICAL PROGRAM FOR MONKS

1

Each one shall sit at table with his own cup and spoon, and
    with his own repentance. Each one's own business shall be
    his most important affair, and provide his own remedies.
They have neglected bowl and plate.
Have you a wooden fork?
Yes, each monk has a wooden fork as well as a potato.

2

Each one shall wipe away tears with his own saint, when three
    bells hold in store a hot afternoon. Each one is supposed
    to mind his own heart, with its conscience, night and
    morning.
Another turn on the wheel: ho hum! And observe the Abbot!
Time to go to bed in a straw blanket.

3

Plenty of bread for everyone between prayers and the psalter:
    will you recite another?
Merci, and *Miserere.*
Always mind both the clock and the Abbot until eternity.
Miserere.

4

Details of the Rule are all liquid and solid. What canon was
the first to announce regimentation before us? Mind the
step on the way down!
Yes, I dare say you are right, Father. I believe you; I believe
you.
I believe it is easier when they have ice water and even a
lemon.
Each one can sit at table with his own lemon, and mind his
conscience.

5

Can we agree that the part about the lemon is regular?
In any case, it is better to have sheep than peacocks, and cows
rather than a chained leopard says Modest, in one of his
proverbs.
The monastery, being owner of a communal rowboat, is the
antechamber of heaven.
Surely that ought to be enough.

6

Each one can have some rain after Vespers on a hot afternoon,
but *ne quid nimis,* or the purpose of the Order will be
forgotten.
We shall send you hyacinths and a sweet millennium.
Everything the monastery provides is very pleasant to see and
to sell for nothing.
What is baked smells fine. There is a sign of God on every
leaf that nobody sees in the garden. The fruit trees are

there on purpose, even when no one is looking. Just put
the apples in the basket.
In Kentucky there is also room for a little cheese.
Each one shall fold his own napkin, and neglect the others.

7

Rain is always very silent in the night, under such gentle
cathedrals.
Yes, I have taken care of the lamp. *Miserere.*
Have you a patron saint, and an angel?
Thank you. Even though the nights are never dangerous, I
have one of everything.

CHEE$E

Joyce Killer-Diller

I think that we should never freeze
Such lively assets as our cheese:

The sucker's hungry mouth is pressed
Against the cheese's caraway breast

A cheese, whose scent like sweet perfume
Pervades the house through every room.

A cheese that may at Christmas wear
A suit of cellophane underwear,

Upon whose bosom is a label,
Whose habitat:—The Tower of Babel.

Poems are nought but warmed-up breeze,
Dollars are made by Trappist Cheese.

MESSAGE TO BE INSCRIBED ON
MARK VAN DOREN'S HAMILTON MEDAL

You think we don't have messages in Kentucky? Here is one I got by hounds, on the day of a blizzard.

Hounds, hounds, with lolling heads of snow! See them signal:

"Mark's one doorway has opened to the Hamilton medal, a huge fabulous piece of gold given away each year for letters."

"Great gold," I cry, "an up-country treat!"

"Country nothing" frown the two efficients, "Mark is a metropolitan winner. He is feasted by mayors in city halls, for personal eminence."

"Yes" I concur "his eminence may be great, but greater is his friendship. For eminence let him be paved all over with gold medals. For friendship let him receive alphabets and inscriptions from friends on the sea, in the air, and in monasteries."

"Let lenten monks meditate upon Mark and the meats of the banquet."

"Bring me a piece of coal and a strip of birch bark and I will praise Mark's doorway to joy in the Alphabet Medal.

"I will praise Mark all day long for the twenty six medals of his alphabet.

"...riters I know Mark is the only one with
...et."

[1959]

BABYSITTER IN A
...M

...ter in a thunderstorm you do not know
...ng as God started all the thunder
...tion
...s to call on the phone

Never call a babysitter in the summer rain
When the baby has torn a hole in the ceiling
And the house is full of water all the lights are fused
You won't hear much on that phone

Tell her in vain to put the baby in the icebox
To keep him cool and dry
He will tear the icebox to pieces
And destroy the telephone

It is therefore useless to express your love
When the implacable baby strong as a tank
Plows through the walls of the house and blocks the highway
Yelling for shelter you can forget that phone

Never call a babysitter when the revolution
Is in full swing
Baby has hoisted the black flag and taken over
The telephone company and everything

When baby is holding off the police
With molotov cocktails bazookas and hand grenades
You can forget about calling the babysitter
He has stuck a bottle of milk in her mouth
You'll never hear what she is saying

In short my boy be careful of love
It fills the world with this destruction
Millions of small pocket cyclones
Have fouled up communication with loves
Inexhaustible demanding rage

Rather than call her on the telephone
Which would only be an act of war
Go sell your car your golf clubs your tennis racket and
    your TV
Try to raise a little money
And pay the baby to set her free.

OLD

old fun is too true for the truth
and spokes is out of kilter with the cloth
but if you will sell me an easy chay
I will find you a better and cheaper way
Meanwhile in the end of the older grove
you must look for a houseboat lying in a cove
and there you will understand some other day
how easter and wester is a holiday
they put on their best and their newest vest
in order to observe the day of rest.

PROVERBS

For Robert Lax

1. I will tell you what you can do ask me if you do not understand what I just said

2. One thing you can do be a manufacturer make appliances

3. Be a Man-u-fac-tu-rer

4. Make appliances sell them for a high price

5. I will tell you about industry make appliances

6. Make appliances that *move*

7. Ask me if you do not understand what is move

8. First get the facts

9. Where to apply? Ask industry

10. Do not expect to get by without Mr. and Mrs. Consumer

11. Man-u-fic-tion

12. I am wondering if you got the idea be a manu

13. MAKE FALSE GODS

14. Apply mind energy they will move

15. Mention one of the others see what happens

16. Now apply that to our problem

17. Try not to understand

18. Be a mounte-fictioner

19. Surpass all others in price and profit

20. Assail the public with lies

21. Home-spun-facts-are-more-fun repeat this

22. Prevent spreading on garments

23. Breathe more than others

24. Supply movement and traction

25. Our epidemix will exceed

26. A homemade appliance: no honorable mention

27. Now you can refer to garments and spread out

28. But there are still more facts

29. For excitement: say whose epidemic may be next

30. Apply this to the facts and see what happens

31. Wear dermal gloves in bed

32. Here is an appliance that will terrorize mothers

33. And fight the impossible

34. Man-u-fac-ture: wear it on your head

35. Beat it here come the mothers

[1968]

PSALM 132: A MODERN MONASTIC REVISION

David ben Jungfreud

Ecce quam leve et quam jocosum
Cruciari fratres in Capitulo!

Ave cadaveres laniatos filmorum Cain!
O jucunda ninis clamor praelii
O delicata confusio tremendi commercii!

Surgit Sadius iste, percutit baculo
Manu, pede, hic illic, nimis ardenter!

Immolat fratres Sadius gaudens, necnon Masoch
Vult vapulare, vult, et participat!

Die felix Purgatorium noctu exultans
Animas devorat!

Ah! What a thrill it is for us all,

descendants of Adam—
by way of Cain and the Marquis de Sade—

to dwell together
and kick each other into heaven,

while Leopold von Sacher-Masoch
observes us understandingly.

PUBLIC AFFAIRS

The Magistrate spoke
Said the future was going to be for the public
The Magistrate he said he was for the future
              and had it in his cage
He was converting expert
Affairs in this same cage.

He himself threw an egg at the public saying "It is future."

The Magistrate spoke
Said the future was filled with meaty affairs
And he was for it since the public
Is always right
He would help the public by throwing an egg
("The future of affairs")

He himself would provide for the chicken anytime
The Magistrate spoke entirely for the future
"In future we will all lay eggs."
The public agreed that it would be good business.

Plucking his (future) chicken the Magistrate
Looked hard at the fresh laid egg rolling over the floor.
He said "It will never be safe
On the outside of a jail"

The public agreed it would be a bad egg
Without the benefit of Public Premises

So the Magistrate took the chicken out of its cage
And threw it at the public
Is not our Magistrate a public servant of the future?

"REDUCED TO THIS"

Alone
With nothing to say
Which is better?
Which is right?
Alone
Able to listen.
This is right.
I hear you
Others singing
Reduced to singing
With nothing to say
Reduced to this
In everything
So we say nothing
We can forget about it
      And sing.

Reduced
Re-
Duced - Re-juiced
(Cut it out!)
"Well
Music always
Makes me cry."

We are reduced to this
(Forget it!)
      Spring

SOLITARY LIFE

White-collar man blue-collar
Man I am a no-collar man
(least of all a *Roman* collar!)
Shave twice a week
Maybe.

Hear the trains out there
Two miles away
Trucks too
The road not near.

Hear the owls in the wood and pray
When I can
I don't talk
About all that
What is there to say?

Yes, I had beer in this place
A while back and once
Whiskey.

And I worry about the abbot
Coming up here to
Inspect
And finding
A copy of *Newsweek*
Under the bed.

Now it's another
Morning and the doves
Boom softly and the world
Goes on it seems
Forever.

[1963]

SONGS

Man in a window?
    When dead men sing
    Everybody listens.

Man on a bridge?
    If dead men play
    Everybody dance.

Man with a gun?
    When dead men sing
    Everybody listens.

Man with another gun?
    If dead men play
    Everybody dance.

TWENTY THREE POINT PROSPECTUS FOR SMALL COLLEGE IN THE BADLANDS

For Robert Lax as Writer in Residence

1. GET SMART WITH GENERAL BIGGLE IN THE QUADRANGLE OF MATH AND FUN

2. GET NEXT TO BEADLE AND WATCH LIFE AND LETTERS GO BY

3. LEARN YOUR WAY THROUGH MAZE OF CULTURE STRAIGHT TO BOVT MINOTAUR

4. LIGHT LAMP OF CIV WITH GENERAL ALMA AND WATCH MATER RUN

5. COME TO BIGGLE'S OASIS AND HEAT UP DAKOTA

6. CULTIVATE EXCESS WITH BIGGLETY HIP

7. RIDE ALL AROUND BEAGLE ON YOUR POTAMUS

8. SEARCH BIGGLE AND WREST FROM HIM THE AXIOM

9. COME TO GENL B. AND SUBMIT TO TRAINERS

10. MAKE BIGGLE MORE IMPORTANT LIKE PENTAGON

11. NEVER WANTING IS A CONFLICT WITH V-CONGS.

12. GENERAL BIGGLE VAMPS CONGS DAILY

13. IF YOUR ARM HURTS ASK GENL BOODLE TO PRAY OVER IT

14. I WISH TO MEET GENL BEAGLE SORRY HE IS BUSY CHASING A RABBIT

15. GENERAL BEADLE COLLEGE IS ATTENDED EXCLUSIVELY BY WILD LIFE

16. AMID HIM (BIGGLE) IS RELIGION GONE OVER THE FALLS

17. TOO MUCH NIBBLING OF MARSBARS ALL OVER THE CAMPUS

18. GENL BEADLE TO THE VAMPS: GET YOUR ASS OFF'N THIS CAMPUS AND STAY THERE

19. BUILD WITH GENL B. THE PALACES OF IN- VENTION

20. IGNITE WITH BOOGLE THE ROCKETS OF IMAGINATION

21. EVERYBODY KNOWS THAT GENL BEAGLE COLLITCH IS REALLY BOYSTOWN

22. ETC THIS AND MANY OTHER PERT MAXIMS WILL PUT GENL BUGGLE ON THE MAPS

23. TRY IT AND FIND OUT WITHOUT EXPENSE.

WESTERN FELLOW STUDENTS SALUTE
WITH CALYPSO ANTHEMS
THE MOVIE CAREER OF ROBERT LAX

". . . a personal poem sent to a friend who lives in Greece, a poet, who is not a movie star but who wrote me some obscure information about 'being in a movie.' This epic news occasioned the poem. I am still in the dark about the movie however."

We western fellow students salute with Calypso anthems
Your movie career in Greece oh famous Robert with
    your hat

Your sense of humor and your wry antics
Have made you notorious on the screens and TV's do
  not forget
It was your ancient association with Columbia U
That has placed you upon the top pinnacle where you are
  now at
Give sensitive response and grateful testimonies at
  ALMA MAT.

Now that you are a movie king and move with the elite
With that imposing *barba* contrasting with the white hat
Your sense of humor and your college capers for the screen
  public
Will appear like a vision in the eyes of the multitude
While you are portrayed in love with a stellar pulchritude
All for the visions of the less fortunate
Who lurk in the shadows of the cinema and view
(As once you did The Marx Brothers) who else but You?
This is principally (you must admit it) due
To the radical and wholesome influence of creative
  Columbia U
So astounding are you on the pinnacle of fame where you
  are now at
Do not forget your former fellow students nor your
  Alma Mat.

We on the other hand abiding on the distant progressive
  shore
Of our impressive continent hail more and more
The waving flag and the principle of might is right
Having little time for art and music, but only to create
New marvels of engineering and technology we are up
  to date

812

Though we may not appear in films or on the TV we
    tirelessly remain
In business offices and old folks homes and automats
We too are a modest credit to Alma Mat.

I most of all with consummate fellow feeling and warm
    religious glow congratulate
Your religious witness and achievement for the Cat-
lick Church among the Greek Orthodox with the black hat
You are besides being a poet and a well known wit
Doing in your own inimitable way your ecumenical bit
Thus as for the Greek film you fail to dodge the custard pie
You retain a glint of hesychasm in your eye
To show the Orthos that you know where you are at
You are on the very summit of Mount Ararat
Thinking at once of Noah and of Alma Mat.

Thus in a kindred spirit of faith and pat-
riotism I climb my religious dolmen and raise the stu-
    pendous flag
I salute you where I wrestle on the ascetic mat
I fling ashes in the air over my greying eremitical head
I holler at the other dervishes and beat my pet cat
All in the name of fellowship and the right hand
Proffered in communion to every living man woman and
    child

Regardless of color creed or ugly face
I am in a condition of ecstasy over the human race
In whose history this important and significant date
Will surely substitute universal love for universal hate
The weapon will drop from the hand and the hand will
    stretch out
In friendship while a smile untwists the distorted mout'

Your film will surely make for camaraderie between mouse
    and cat
Provided only you are respectful and not oblivious of
    Alma Mat.

[1967]

[UNTITLED] *

Special continuations: the Gethsemani racetrack:
HELLO ARNOLD HELLO ROGER HELLO ISIDORE
    HELLO ODILO AND HELLO MEIN LIEBER
AUGUSTIN STOP HELLO WILFRID HELLO LEO
    AND HELLO FERDINAND AND ZACHARY AND
DONALD THE BRAVE GANG IN THE OLD BACK
    ROOM

Continuation for more races to the Gethsemani Track and
    acknowledgments
time out for customer identification:

HELLO CASSIAN HELLO CHARLES HELLO
    MARTIN HELLO RODERICK STOP THERE ARE
PLENTY OF OTHERS BUT IT IS A RARE SHOP

Hello all the boys in the barbershop

[1968]

* This poem, originally a section of *The Geography of Lograire* but not
included in the final manuscript, is a listing of Father Merton's fellow monks
at Gethsemani.

The old monk is turned loose
And can travel!
He's out to see the world.
What progress in the last thirty years!
But his mode of travel
Is still the same.

Photograph by Robert Lax

The old monk is turned loose
And can travel!
He's out to see the world.
What progress in the last thirty years!
But his mode of travel
Is still the same.

Appendix IV
A FRENCH POEM

LES CINQ VIERGES *

Pour Jacques

Il y avait cinq vierges
Hurluberlues
Qui sont venues aux Noces de l'Agneau
Avec leur motos en panne

Et leurs bidons de petrole
Vides

Mais puisq'elles savaient
Danser
On leur dit quand même
De rester:

Et voila: il y avait
Cinq vierges hurluberlues
Sans petrole
Mais bien engagées
Dans le mouvement.

Il y avait donc dix vierges
Aux Noces de l'Agneau.

* For the English translation, by William Davis, see below, p. 826 ("The Five Virgins").

Appendix V
TRANSLATIONS OF FRENCH POEMS
BY THOMAS MERTON

CABLES TO THE ACE 35 *

I read you the sonnets of a blind captain. He has eyes full of brilliance. He celebrates the division of electric communions. Gold and money tinkle like chimes on the top of a Building about to terminate itself.

It is the hour of melted wagons in the night of the city. In the caves, the secret voices of bulls having nightmares; the ocean climbs into the hallways of the eye until the dawn of the mornings: and they are there, both of them: the Sun and the Outspoken Rifleman.

Imprisoned in wholesale mud, Poseidon eats the flags on the stage of the wars. He ponders the ruins which he loves. He considers the regulations of shipwrecked outlaws. He meditates on the seaweed business. He hears the sound of pearls.

The uncertain dawn catches fire from too many people breathing. The burn is terrible. The slow fire of slang eats up conversations. The decorated escalator of futile questions leads to the Judge who has a bench on the most informal layers of opinion. A message from the women! You can wait for us in the shadowy mirror. You make us adore the products of the stars, the dynamic Babylonian construction firms.

The proper words come down the escalator from the floor where the angels have their sports games. Now they find themselves among the swallows.

* For Merton's original French in *Cables to the Ace,* see above, p. 393. This translation is by William Davis.

Plato is there with the girls. He listens to them. He encourages them. He travels incognito. Art becomes benevolent in the circuses of winter. In the valley of tears, the championship game of the Smile.

To the abyss: the eyes of fire, the lamps with bony wings, the escapes around the Equator. The brown sun of the antipodes is equipped with arrows; it pursues the naïve bird into a cablegram decorated with storms. It is time for the nerve which electrocutes. The mass flash of feeling. Everything is recorded on a memorandum pad. Hell summons the neuter verb. The bird rests finally atop a thunderbolt.

The ascetic beauty of the awakened arsenal. The little bearded Consul of Copper chews up the silent smoke. He thinks about flying buttresses, the broken-hearted bridges, the goats going crazy. These are some of the children of his age: these fickle sailors. He has seen the fire of their nostrils, the flame at the bottom of the pier. The amateur! He dreams of his coat edged with blood. He walks through the targets. Stuffed full of pins, he inhales the rising salt. He enters into the traffic of weddings. He is swallowed up there, stuffed with pagan songs.

The Red Sea of the Pharaohs, where the spectacle vanishes in an unemployment of fireworks: the sudden disappearance of the wisemen. Hieroglyphics riot in the temples of the octopi. The masked high priest walks again to the end of the rivers to search for the lost Moses.

The mothers. They live on the roofs. They mold little birds. They have understood the wisdom of the egg. They offer you patience of ecstasy. They smile at you intimately at the moment of your choice. Do not choose the neuter. The sold forehead cannot look at you O flowers! you clues of pleasure!

The turtle is proud of her jewels. She stretches out her palms to show them to the rain.

Fantoche is beat up in the hoarfrost. You have embalmed us like a few verses on a piece of silk. Go look for your Apocalypse in the unexplored subways!

I sit in my green field like a quiet diamond. I engulf the blue domain of naked air. Light! and all the letters add up to this: music is a joy invented by silence. Daisies. A geography of little unknown girls present in the grass. Charm the baby monsters! I hear the great red bell of summers, the messenger of deep times.

Cloud and testament. I am quiet about the ghosts of tears. I complain about the useless muscle which cries: "Me."

The frontier. A little further. It is green-clear. The summit. Nothing. The little silent girls enter into the shadow by the door of the chosen.

I BELIEVE IN LOVE *

I believe in the love
which sleeps and wakes up,
caught in the sperm of the seasons.

When I breathe my spring
on the fresh liturgical peaks of the hills

* For Merton's original French in *The Tears of the Blind Lions,* see above, p. 217 ("Je crois en l'Amour"). This translation is by William Davis.

seeing all the trees and the green corn,
the anxious essence of my being
awakens with gaping yawns
and the adoration sounds like the legendary clocks
who ring their heavy chants in the womb of the ocean.

And when the looming sun of my summer
has stripped the gold flesh from my wheat
I find I have become rich: my song is pure,
this skeletal praise of Our Lady is my money.

O brothers, come with me.
Drink the wine of Melchisedech
while all the giant mountains
dressed in the vines of Isaias
sing peace.

Poems are born because love is like this
in the hollow heart of a man
and in the breast of my own broken rock.

THE FIVE VIRGINS *

For Jacques

There were five howling virgins
Who came
To the Wedding of the Lamb
With their disabled motorcycles

* For Merton's original French, see above, p. 819. This translation is by
William Davis.

And their oil tanks
Empty

But since they knew how
To dance,
A person says to them
To stay anyhow.

And there you have it:
There were five noisy virgins
Without gas
But looking good
In the traffic of the dance.

Consequently
There were ten virgins
At the Wedding of the Lamb.

THE SECRET *

Since I am
Somebody's dream,
I have a good life.

Sometimes I go away in my sailboat on a cloud
and take a quiet little trip.

I have a secret
which I have learned how to read inside myself;

* For Merton's original French in *Sensation Time at the Home*, see above
p. 635 ("Le Secret"). This translation is by William Davis.

if I told it to you,
it would make you laugh.

My heart is naked
and no one can put clothes on it,
and nothing can be put on
that will not immediately fall off.

My secret is ignorant,
it doesn't sing songs,
no lie,
it has nothing to tell you.

My two eyes
are maps of the planet—
I see everything
and nothing upsets me.

Just now
I was in China
and saw there a great piece of happiness
that belonged to one man.

And I have been to the center of the earth,
where there is no suffering.

If on your loneliest nights,
I visit other planets
and the most secret stars of all,

besides being no one,
know that I am you
and everybody.

But if I go away
without giving you a name to remember me with,

how will I find
the right dream to return to?

You won't have to mark down
on your calendar that I am coming back;
don't bother to write me into your notebooks.
I will be around
when you aren't thinking about me,

without hair or a neck,
without a nose and cheeks
no reputation—
there won't be anything.

I am a bird
which God made.

Appendix VI
TRANSLATIONS

FROM THE SPANISH OF RAFAEL ALBERTI

ROMAN NOCTURNES

1

Nights belong to
What hurts
Rome
Loveless city

After twelve
Everybody gone
Dead
Not even a dead cat
For not even cats
Make love
Wider the cracks
In the unsafe
Dark houses
Like quiet graves
Dead of sorrow
Only the garbage
Sighs and stinks.

Rome, loveless city

2

From empty windows
Voice of dead eyes

Low, hushed, in the night
Next door someone
Lives, some few
Are sleeping
Quiet in bed
Rooms they have
Rescued from death
But there is ever
The menace the splintered
Man of bone
Who never sleeps

3

You did not come to Rome to dream
After all this time you wonder
What you are doing
Busting your feet against stones
Running head first
Into the walls
Giving yourself to every devil
Amid the shadows
Wearing out your old flesh until clean bones
Show in the air
Unwinding all around
Knowing what you hope for
Though it never comes?
You did not come to Rome to dream
Dreams have kept so distant
You no longer descry them
And they no longer come after you
For they no longer know you.

4

The other night I saw . . .
Who did I see?

I saw the one who bit me
I saw the one who ate me
It was life I saw

In a murky puddle
There he was, murky
Watching, swollen
Small and swollen
Right there

What are you doing
Here in Rome
Is Rome dead?
Tell me

Don't pollute the air
Leave the air alone
If I push you in the river
The river will be poisoned
Get the hell out!

You slug, you louse
You fat slug
Nobody killed you
Who would bother
To kill you?
The other night I saw . . .
I won't say who.

5

Take, O take the key of Rome
For in Rome there is a street
In the street there is a house
In the house there is the bedroom
In the bedroom is a bed
And in the bed a lady
A lady in love
Who takes the key
And leaves the bed
Who leaves the bedroom
Who leaves the house
Who goes out in the street
Who picks up a sword
Who runs in the night
Killing the passers-by
Who returns to her street
Who returns to her house
Who goes up to her bedroom
Who gets into her bed
Who hides the key
Who hides the sword
And Rome is left
With no passers-by
With no death
No night
No key and
No lady.

FROM THE LATIN OF ST. AMBROSE

SPLENDOR PATERNAE GLORIAE

Fourth Century

Thou splendor of the Father's glory,
Pouring upon us light drawn from Thy Light:
Thou art the Light of lights, the fount of brightness
And to our days the daylight-giving Day.

O Thou true Sun,
Shine down in everlasting glory,
And with the radiance of Thy Spirit
Flood our souls!

Cry we, then, in our prayers, to the Father,
Father of glory everlasting, and of mighty grace
To save us from the treachery of sin:

Confirm our souls in works of strength
And blunt the teeth that hate our life,
And contradict our evils into blessings
Giving us grace to do His will.

Govern our spirits, rule them Father!
Build in our chaste and unrebellious bodies
Fires of faith!
Nor let the poison of betrayal chill our blood.

And may Thy Christ our life-bread be,
His faith our drink:
Then slake we our glad spirits
Wisdom's mighty wine.

So may this day go by in joy,
And may our cleanness be like its clean dawn
Our faith like the high noon:
But let no evening shroud our minds in dusk.

But now the dawn begins to show:
O may our true Day soon shine full upon us:
The Day which is the Father in the Son,
The Son in Him, His Word, entire.

And so, to God the Father, glory,
And to His only Son,
Together with the Spirit, the Paraclete,
Now and forever and ever.

Amen.

FROM THE PORTUGUESE
OF CARLOS DRUMMOND DE ANDRADE

MEMORIES OF THE ANCIENT WORLD

Clara walked in the garden with the children.
The sky was green, over the grass,
Water ran golden under the bridges
And other elements were blue, or pink or orange,
The policeman smiled, and bicycles went by
The little girl ran on the grass to catch a bird,
The whole world, Germany and China, all was quiet around
    Clara.

The little ones looked up at the sky: it was not forbidden.
Mouths, nostrils and eyes were wide open: There was no
    danger.

The only dangers Clara feared were influenza, hot weather,
    insects.
Clara feared to miss the 11 o'clock bus
And hoped for letters that were slow in coming.
She was not always able to wear a new dress.
But she walked in the garden, in the morning!

For, in those times, there were gardens, and there were
    mornings.

SONG OF PURIFICATION

After many battles
The good angel killed the bad one
And threw his body in the river.

The waters were stained
With blood that did not give them any special color.
The fishes all died.

Then a light—no one could tell
Where it came from—
Appeared and lit up the world.
Another angel came to bandage
The wounded angel of battles.

FROM THE SPANISH
OF JORGE CARRERA ANDRADE

A MAN FROM ECUADOR BENEATH
THE EIFFEL TOWER

You turn into a plant on the coasts of time
With your goblet of round sky,
Your opening for the tunnels of traffic.
You are the biggest ceiba tree on earth.

Up go the painter's eyes
By your scissor-stair, into the blue.

Over a flock of roofs
You stretch your neck, a llama of Peru.

Robed in folds of winds,
A comb of constellations in your hair,
You show yourself
To the circus of horizons.

Mast of an adventure above time!
Pride of five hundred and thirty cubits.

Pole of the tent set up by men
In a corner of history,
Your gaslit drawing in the night
Copies the milky way.

First letter of a cosmic alphabet,
Pointing in the direction of heaven,
Hope standing on stilts,
Glorification of the skeleton.

Iron to brand the flock of clouds
Or dumb sentinel of the industrial age.
The tides of heaven
Silently undermine your pillar.

COCOA TREE

Cocoa tree,
Archangel tutor of the green parrot,
Cool doctrine in a tropic land,
Adding colors, subtracting sounds
In a total of shade,
With a heavenly vocation you dictate
Fragrant lessons.

On your knees, hands joined,
Hearing the hum of secret hives of bees
You let your happiness grow.

Rich in almond-shaped thoughts,
You write, upon the pages of the air,
The virgin jungle's novel
Even to the sweet smell of grandmothers' cups
In dining rooms, with silent doors,
Where the wall clock drips
Like a half-orange.

NOTES OF A PARACHUTE JUMPER

All I met were two birds and the wind,
The clouds with rolled-up maps
And a few flowers of steam that opened to seek me
In heavenly travel, straight down.

For I come out of heaven
As in prophecies and hymns,
Messenger from on high with my uniform of leaves,
My supply of deaths and lives.

Down from heaven, descending like daylight,
I moisten the eyelids
Of all who await me. I come
Via the roads of light and rain.

Friendly shrub, break my fall.
Earth, tell your wet furrows to receive me.
Tell that fallen tree to teach me
Color of a motionless form.

Here I am, farmers of Europe.
I come in the name of bread, of the mothers of the world,
In the name of all that is white and bare,
The heron, the lily, the lamb, the snow.

Ruined cities, torn families
Scattered over the earth, strengthen my arm:
Children and red countries living, now for years.
Ages of night and blood.

Farmers of the world, I have brought down the sky
Like a white umbel, a jellyfish swimming on air.
Hidden lightnings I bring, a store of deaths,
But I also bring another year's harvests.

I bring the quiet crop empty of soldiers,
The windows lighted again, driving out night,
Routed forever. I am
The new angel of our time.

Citizen of air and clouds,
I yet have earthly blood
Which knows the way and enters every house,
The road that flows beneath cars,

The waters that pretend to be the same
And that passed by before
The earth of animals, of plants, with tears,
Whither I go to light the day with my hands.

RADICALS

Comrade locust sings
With a splinter in his throat.

Hatching plots in the weeds
Against the dictator: Man.

A broken cart, bumping along,
Locust goes no place, singing his song.

Ranting as he goes.
Ministry of Propaganda!

Proclaims on a cabbage leaf:
"It's a hard life and a hot sun!"

Worker locust, you are right
To undermine the state
With your sagacious song.
We have one same song to sing,
Comrade! We are the world's
Extreme left wing.

THE MIRROR'S MISSION

When all things forget color and shape,
When walls, pressed by night, fold in
And all else yields, or kneels, or blurs,
You, O lucid presence, you alone stand!

You make the shadows yield to your bright will.
Your mineral silence glows in the dark.
Sweet messages to other objects
Fly out of you (your sudden pigeons).

Each chair opens out, waits in the night
To seat some unreal guest before a dish of shadows.
You alone, transparent witness,
Recite your lesson learned by heart—your lesson of light.

THE WEATHERCOCK ON THE
CATHEDRAL OF QUITO

The cock on the weather vane
Cannot flap his wings
Even though today is a feast day.

The sun spreads his great yellow
Carpet in the courtyard
As Anna del Campo passes by.

Gold quilts on the balconies,
Diamonds on the roofs,
Domes and towers.

Anna del Campo has come
With her nose in the air,
A dew damsel.

The cock would like to crow,
Poor tin Don Juan,
Stuck on his belfry.

Clouds wheel round him.
In his blue henyard,
The burning bird flashes.

Silver cock in the wind,
Sun cock, paralyzed
In a desert of roofs.

Cathedral ascetic,
He knows no other corn
Than the sky's kind: hail.

Anna del Campo goes by.
He flashes sun signals
To his friend, the lightning rod.

Anna, take me to the door
Of your house of flowers
Where bliss never ends.

Give me your cool dew
For my throat of sand.
Give me your lily field!

FROM THE SPANISH OF ERNESTO CARDENAL

DRAKE IN THE SOUTHERN SEA *

For Rafael Heliodoro Valle

I set out from the Port of Acapulco on the twenty-third of
    March
And kept a steady course until Saturday, the fourth of April,
    when
A half hour before dawn, we saw by the light of the moon
That a ship had come alongside
With sails and a bow that seemed to be of silver.
Our helmsman cried out to them to stand off
But no one answered, as though they were all asleep.
Again we called out: "WHERE DID THEIR SHIP COME FROM?"
And they said: Peru!
After which we heard trumpets, and muskets firing,
And they ordered me to come down into their longboat
To cross over to where their Captain was.
I found him walking the deck,
Went up to him, kissed his hands and he asked me:
"What silver or gold I had aboard that ship?"
I said, "None at all,
None at all, My Lord, only my dishes and cups."
So then he asked me if I knew the Viceroy.
I said I did. And I asked the Captain,
"If he were Captain Drake himself and no other?"

---

* This poem is based on a strictly historical account of the encounter with
Drake written by a Spanish captain, in a letter to the Viceroy of New Spain,
dated Realejo (Nicaragua), 1579.

The Captain replied that
"He was the very Drake I spoke of."
We spoke together a long time, until the hour of dinner,
And he commanded that I sit by his side.
His dishes and cups are of silver, bordered with gold
With his crest upon them.
He has with him many perfumes and scented waters in
    crystal vials
Which, he said, the Queen had given him.
He dines and sups always with music of violins
And also takes with him everywhere painters who keep
    painting
All the coast for him.
He is a man of some twenty-four years, small, with a reddish
    beard.
He is a nephew of *Juan Aquinas,** the pirate.
And is one of the greatest mariners there are upon the sea.
The day after, which was Sunday, he clothed himself in
    splendid garments
And had them hoist all their flags
With pennants of divers colors at the mastheads,
The bronze rings, and chains, and the railings and
The lights on the Alcazar shining like gold.
His ship was like a gold dragon among the dolphins.
And we went, with his page, to my ship to look at the coffers.
All day long until night he spent looking at what I had.
What he took from me was not much,
A few trifles of my own,
And he gave me a cutlass and a silver brassart for them,
Asking me to forgive him
Since it was for his lady that he was taking them:
He would let me go, he said, the next morning, as soon as
    there was a breeze;

* John Hawkins

For this I thanked him, and kissed his hands.
He is carrying, in his galleon, three thousand bars of silver
Three coffers full of gold
Twelve great coffers of pieces of eight:
And he says he is heading for China
Following the charts and steered by a Chinese pilot whom
      he captured . . .

SELECTIONS FROM "GETHSEMANI, KY"

I

Spring has come with its smell of Nicaragua:
Smell of earth recently rained on, and smell of heat,
Of flowers, of disinterred roots, wet leaves,
(And I have heard the lowing of distant cattle. . . .)
Or is it the smell of love? But this love
Is not yours. Love of country, is the Dictator's love
The fat Dictator with his sports clothes and panama hat:
He was the one who loved the country, stole it,
And possessed it. In that earth he lies embalmed:
While love has taken you away to a strange land.

2

Like the flights of ducks
That go over calling
That in the autumn nights go over calling
To lagoons in the south they never saw,
And do not know who takes them, nor where they go,
So we are carried to Thee not knowing where.

Just like the flights of ducks that come from the south
And pass over Kentucky calling in the night.

3

Every evening the L&N
Goes singing through these Kentucky fields
And I seem to hear the little train at home
In Nicaragua, when it borders the Managua Lake
Across from the volcano, just before
Mateare, going around the bend
Across from Bird Island, piping and singing
Its iron song of wheels and rails,
With the first lights of Managua there
Far off, shining in the waters. . . .
The L&N goes off
Into the distance with its song.

4

The sound of passing cars, (if a car comes)
On the highway outside the noviciate
Is like sea surf. You hear one begin
To come far off and the sound grows
More and more, the motor roars,
Tires sing on the damp tar
And then it goes away, dies down,
Is no longer heard. Later some other engine
In the distance, begins to come again.
Like waves in the sea. And I, like waves
In the sea, once ran along tar roads that go
To no definite place. And still at times
It seems I go by the same roads

And do not stop going and arrive at no place,
That I am not the one in the noviciate
Seeing the cars pass,
But that I have seen the noviciate
Through the window of that car that just went by.

5

When the first signs go on
When they light up the marquees
Of the movie theaters
Here we hear nothing but swallows.
At 7 p.m. the Trappists go to bed
In broad daylight, like noon,
And with a full moon like midnight.
The horses are quiet in the stable.
The trucks sleep in the garage.
The tractors are still
Before the barn.
Above the water tank: the aluminum moon.

6

The long freight train
Wakes me in my cell
I hear it coming from far off
In the night. It passes and passes, whistling,
Seeming that it will never all get past:
Cars and cars and cars bumping along!
I fall asleep again, and it is still passing
Panting in the distance and still whistling,
And between dreams I ask myself
Why they still have trains

And where they take their freight, and what freight,
Where the cars come from
And where they can possibly go.

7

The zinc roofs in the moonlight
And the tin shop, the gas tank
And the water tank, all look like silver.
Like a star, like a cigarette,
Far out, over Nally's hill,
A passenger plane
Passes and flashes in the night.

8

A dog barks far out
Behind the black wood.
Further still
Behind another wood,
Another dog answers.

9

Like empty beer cans, like cigarette butts;
My days have been like that.
Like figures passing on a TV screen
And disappearing, so my life has gone.
Like cars going by fast on the roads
With girls laughing and radios playing.
Beauty got obsolete as fast as car models
And forgotten radio hits.

Nothing is left of those days, nothing,
But empty beer cans, cigarette butts,
Smiles on faded photos, torn tickets
And the sawdust with which, in the mornings,
They swept out the bars.

10

I turned out the light to see the snow,
And I saw snow through the window and a new moon.
But I saw that both snow and moon
Were also a window pane
And that behind that pane you were watching me.

11

I do not know who is out in the snow
All that is seen in the snow is his white habit
And at first I saw no one at all:
Only the plain white sunlit snow.
A novice in the snow is barely visible.
And I feel that there is something more in this snow
Which is neither snow nor novice, and is not seen.

12

That auto horn sounds familiar.
So does this wind in the pines.
This zinc noviciate roof
Reminds me of my house at home.
They are calling me with the auto horn.
But my house, near the road

Where the cars went by all day
Was sold years ago. Strangers live there.
This was no known car. It is gone.
The wind is the same. Only the sighing
Of this rainy autumn evening is well known.

THREE EPIGRAMS

i

Suddenly in the night the sirens
Sound their alarm, long, long alarm:
The siren's miserable howl
Of fire, or death's white ambulance
Coming and coming down the avenues
Along the buildings, it rises, rises, falls
Grows, grows, falls and is near
Growing and dying. Neither a fire nor death:
                The Dictator flashes by.

ii

Shots were heard last night
Out by the burial ground;
No one knows who killed, or was killed.
No one knows a thing,
Shots were heard last night.
That is all.

iii

We wake up with guns going off
And the dawn alive with planes—
It sounds like a revolution:
It is only the Tyrant's birthday.

FROM THE FRENCH OF RENÉ CHAR

ALLEGIANCE

In the streets of the city: there is my love
No matter where he goes in the divided time. He is no
    longer my love;
anyone can speak to him. He no longer remembers:
    who loved him anyway?

He seeks his like in the vow of eyes. The space he travels
    is my
fidelity. He sketches a hope, leads it lightly away.
    He is preponderant
yet takes no part!

I live in his depths like glad drift wood. My loneliness
    is his fortune:
he does not know! In the great meridian where his flight
    is charted, my
freedom tunnels him.

In the streets of the city: there is my love.
No matter where he goes in the divided time. He is no
    longer my love;
anyone can speak to him. He no longer remembers
    who loved him anyway,
and who lights him from far so that he does not fall.

AT THE GATES OF AEREA

Happy time. Each walled town was a big family which fear kept together; the singing of hands at work and the living night of the sky gave light to it. The pollen of the mind kept its share of exile.

But the everlasting present, the instantaneous past, under Mistress Weariness, took it apart.

Forced march scattering at the end. Beaten children, golden thatch, festering men, all get the work done! Shot by the iron bee the weeping rose lies open.

CELEBRATING GIACOMETTI

This late afternoon of April 1964 the despotic old eagle, the kneeling iron worker under the fire-cloud of his invectives (his work, his own self, never stopped lashing him with insults) uncovered for me down by the very paving-stones of his workshop the face of Caroline his model, the face painted on canvas of Caroline—after how many clawings, woundings, blood blisters?—fruit of passion among all the love objects, winner over the false giantism of the junk-piles of death, winner over the barely separate parcels of light, ourselves, his witnesses in time. Out of his honeycomb of cruelty and desire. This fine face with no yesterday which was going to kill sleep reflected itself in the mirror of our look, provisional world-wide receiver for all future eyes.

COME DANCE IN BARONIES

In an olive-tree dress
                    The Amoureuse
had said:
            'Trust my very childlike
                                loyalty"
            And after that
an open valley
                a shining slope
a path of union
                broke into town
where pain runs free under the quick of water.

CONVERGENCE OF THE MANY

This man was generous not because he wanted to see him-
self as generous in his own looking-glass. He was generous
because he came from the Pleiades and abhorred himself. One
same prodigal shadow with phalanxes of upraised fingers
joined us together. Him and me. A sun which was not for us
broke away from it like a guilty or unsatisfied father.

FACTION DU MUET

The stones huddled together on the ramparts and men lived
off the moss of the stones. Deep night carried a gun and the
women did not give birth. Disgrace had the look of a glass of
water.

858

I joined up with the courage of a few beings, lived violently, growing no older, my mystery in their midst, I shuddered for the existence of all the others like an unchaste vessel riding over cloistered deeps.

FIGHTERS

In the sky of men the bread of stars seemed to me shadowy and hardened but in their narrow hands I read the jousting of these stars, inviting others: still dreaming emigrants from the deck; I gathered up their golden sweat and because of me the earth stopped dying.

SEPTENTRION

I went walking (said the girl)
on the edge of madness.

She, my companion, gave way
to the questions of my heart
when my heart did not ask
any questions:
Such is the inventiveness of absence.
Then her eyes, at ebbtide like the violet Nile
Seemed to count their wages endlessly
Reaching under the cool stones.

Madness dressed her hair
With long and cutting rushes.
Somewhere this stream lives its double life.
The cruel gold of its invading name
Came to give battle to unfriendly fortune.

FROM THE CHINESE OF CHUANG TZU

ACTION AND NON-ACTION

The non-action of the wise man is not inaction.
It is not studied. It is not shaken by anything.
The sage is quiet because he is not moved,
Not because he *wills* to be quiet.
Still water is like glass.
You can look in it and see the bristles on your chin.
It is a perfect level;
A carpenter could use it.
If water is so clear, so level,
How much more the spirit of man?
The heart of the wise man is tranquil.
It is the mirror of heaven and earth
The glass of everything.
Emptiness, stillness, tranquillity, tastelessness,
Silence, non-action: this is the level of heaven and earth.
This is perfect Tao. Wise men find here
Their resting place.
Resting, they are empty.

From emptiness comes the unconditioned.
From this, the conditioned, the individual things.
So from the sage's emptiness, stillness arises:
From stillness, action. From action, attainment.
From their stillness comes their non-action, which is also
    action
And is, therefore, their attainment.

For stillness is joy. Joy is free from care
Fruitful in long years.
Joy does all things without concern:
For emptiness, stillness, tranquillity, tastelessness,
Silence, and non-action
Are the root of all things.

ACTIVE LIFE

If an expert does not have some problem to vex him,
    he is unhappy!
If a philosopher's teaching is never attacked, he pines away!
If critics have no one on whom to exercise their spite,
    they are unhappy.
All such men are prisoners in the world of objects.

He who wants followers, seeks political power.
He who wants reputation holds an office.
The strong man looks for weights to lift.
The brave man looks for an emergency in which he can
    show bravery.
The swordsman wants a battle in which he can swing
    his sword.
Men past their prime prefer a dignified retirement, in which
    they may seem profound.
Men experienced in law seek difficult cases to extend
    the application of laws.
Liturgists and musicians like festivals in which they parade
    their ceremonious talents.
The benevolent, the dutiful, are always looking for chances
    to display virtue.

Where would the gardener be if there were no more weeds?
What would become of business without a market of fools?
Where would the masses be if there were no pretext
    for getting jammed together and making noise?
What would become of labor if there were no superfluous
    objects to be made?

Produce! Get results! Make money! Make friends!
    Make changes!
Or you will die of despair!

Those who are caught in the machinery of power take no joy
except in activity and change—the whirring of the machine!
Whenever an occasion for action presents itself, they are com-
pelled to act; they cannot help themselves. They are inexorably
moved, like the machine of which they are a part. Prisoners
in the world of objects, they have no choice but to submit to
the demands of matter! They are pressed down and crushed
by external forces, fashion, the market, events, public opinion.
Never in a whole lifetime do they recover their right mind!
The active life! What a pity!

ADVISING THE PRINCE

The recluse Hsu Su Kwei had come to see Prince Wu.
The Prince was glad. "I have desired," he said,
"To see you for a long time. Tell me
If I am doing right.
I want to love my people, and by the exercise of justice
To put an end to war.
Is this enough?"

"By no means," said the recluse.
"Your 'love' for your people
Puts them in mortal danger.
Your exercise of justice is the root
Of war after war!
Your grand intentions
Will end in disaster!

"If you set out to 'accomplish something great'
You only deceive yourself.
Your love and justice
Are fraudulent.
They are mere pretexts
For self-assertion, for aggression.
One action will bring on another
And in the chain of events
Your hidden intentions
Will be made plain.

"You claim to practice justice. Should you seem to succeed
Success itself will bring more conflict.
Why all these guards
Standing at attention
At the palace gate, around the temple altar,
Everywhere?

"You are at war with yourself!
You do not believe in justice,
Only in power and success.
If you overcome
An enemy and annex his country
You will be even less at peace
With yourself than you are now.
Nor will your passions let you
Sit still. You will fight again

And again for the sake of
A more perfect exercise of 'justice'!

"Abandon your plan
To be a 'loving and equitable ruler.'
Try to respond
To the demands of inner truth.
Stop vexing yourself and your people
With these obsessions!
Your people will breathe easily at last.
They will live
And war will end by itself!"

A HAT SALESMAN AND A CAPABLE RULER

A man of Sung did business
In silk ceremonial hats.
He traveled with a load of hats
To the wild men of the South.
The wild men had shaved heads,
Tattooed bodies.
What did they want
With silk
Ceremonial hats?

Yao had wisely governed
All China.
He had brought the entire world
To a state of rest.
After that, he went to visit
The four Perfect Ones
In the distant mountains
Of Ku Shih.

864

When he came back
Across the border
Into his own city
His lost gaze
Saw no throne.

APOLOGIES

If a man steps on a stranger's foot
In the marketplace,
He makes a polite apology
And offers an explanation
("This place is so terribly
Crowded!").

If an elder brother
Steps on his younger brother's foot,
He says, "Sorry!"
And that is that.

If a parent
Treads on his child's foot,
Nothing is said at all.

The greatest politeness
Is free of all formality.
Perfect conduct
Is free of concern.
Perfect wisdom
Is unplanned.
Perfect love
Is without demonstrations.

Perfect sincerity offers
No guarantee.

AUTUMN FLOODS

The autumn floods had come. Thousands of wild torrents
poured furiously into the Yellow River. It surged and flooded
its banks until, looking across, you could not tell an ox from
a horse on the other side. Then the River God laughed, de-
lighted to think that all the beauty in the world had fallen
into his keeping. So downstream he swung, until he came to
the Ocean. There he looked out over the waves, toward the
empty horizon in the east and his face fell. Gazing out at
the far horizon he came to his senses and murmured to the
Ocean God: "Well, the proverb is right. He who has got
himself a hundred ideas thinks he knows more than anybody
else. Such a one am I. Only now do I see what they mean by
EXPANSE!"

• • •

The Ocean God replied:
"Can you talk about the sea
To a frog in a well?
Can you talk about ice
To dragonflies?
Can you talk about the way of Life
To a doctor of philosophy?

"Of all the waters in the world
The Ocean is greatest.
All the rivers pour into it
Day and night;

It is never filled.
It gives back its waters
Day and night;

It is never emptied.
In dry seasons
It is not lowered.
In floodtime
It does not rise.
Greater than all other waters!
There is no measure to tell
How much greater!
But am I proud of it?
What am I under heaven?
What am I without Yang and Yin?
Compared with the sky
I am a little rock,
A scrub oak
On the mountain side:
Shall I act
As if I were something?"

Of all the beings that exist (and there are millions), man
is only one. Among all the millions of men that live on earth,
the civilized people that live by farming are only a small pro-
portion. Smaller still the number of those who having office
or fortune, travel by carriage or by boat. And of all these,
one man in his carriage is nothing more than the tip of a
hair on a horse's flank. Why, then, all the fuss about great
men and great offices? Why all the disputations of scholars?
Why all the wrangling of politicians?

There are no fixed limits
Time does not stand still.

Nothing endures,
Nothing is final.
You cannot lay hold
Of the end or the beginning.
He who is wise sees near and far
As the same,
Does not despise the small
Or value the great:
Where all standards differ
How can you compare?
With one glance
He takes in past and present,
Without sorrow for the past
Or impatience with the present.
All is in movement.
He has experience
Of fullness and emptiness.
He does not rejoice in success
Or lament in failure
The game is never over
Birth and death are even
The terms are not final.

CONFUCIUS AND THE MADMAN

When Confucius was visiting the state of Chu,
Along came Kieh Yu
The madman of Chu
And sang outside the Master's door:
       "O Phoenix, Phoenix,
         Where's your virtue gone?

It cannot reach the future
Or bring the past again!
When the world makes sense
The wise have work to do.
They can only hide
When the world's askew.
Today if you can stay alive
Lucky are you:
Try to survive!

"Joy is feather light
But who can carry it?
Sorrow falls like a landslide
Who can parry it?

"Never, never
Teach virtue more.
You walk in danger,
Beware! Beware!
Even ferns can cut your feet—
When I walk crazy
I walk right:
But am I a man
To imitate?"

The tree on the mountain height is its own enemy.
The grease that feeds the light devours itself.
The cinnamon tree is edible: so it is cut down!
The lacquer tree is profitable: they maim it.
Every man knows how useful it is to be useful.

No one seems to know
How useful it is to be useless.

CRACKING THE SAFE

For security against robbers who snatch purses, rifle luggage,
    and crack safes,
One must fasten all property with ropes, lock it up with locks,
    bolt it with bolts.
This (for property owners) is elementary good sense.
But when a strong thief comes along he picks up the whole lot,
Puts it on his back, and goes on his way with only one fear:
That ropes, locks, and bolts may give way.
Thus what the world calls good business is only a way
To gather up the loot, pack it, make it secure
In one convenient load for the more enterprising thieves.
Who is there, among those called smart,
Who does not spend his time amassing loot
For a bigger robber than himself?

            • • •

In the land of Khi, from village to village,
You could hear cocks crowing, dogs barking.
Fishermen cast their nets,
Ploughmen ploughed the wide fields,
Everything was neatly marked out
By boundary lines. For five hundred square miles
There were temples for ancestors, altars
For field-gods and corn-spirits.
Every canton, country, and district
Was run according to the laws and statutes—
Until one morning the Attorney General, Tien Khang Tzu,
Did away with the King and took over the whole state.
Was he content to steal the land? No,
He also took over the laws and statutes at the same time,
And all the lawyers with them, not to mention the police.
They all formed part of the same package.

Of course, people called Khang Tzu a robber,
But they left him alone

To live as happy as the Patriarchs.
No small state would say a word against him,
No large state would make a move in his direction,
So for twelve generations the state of Khi
Belonged to his family. No one interferred
With his inalienable rights.

. . .

The invention
Of weights and measures
Makes robbery easier.
Signing contracts, settings seals,
Makes robbery more sure.
Teaching love and duty
Provides a fitting language
With which to prove that robbery
Is really for the general good.
A poor man must swing
For stealing a belt buckle
But if a rich man steals a whole state
He is acclaimed
As statesman of the year.

Hence if you want to hear the very best speeches
On love, duty, justice, etc.,
Listen to statesmen.

But when the creek dries up
Nothing grows in the valley.
When the mound is levelled
The hollow next to it is filled.
And when the statesmen and lawyers
And preachers of duty disappear
There are no more robberies either
And the world is at peace.

Moral: the more you pile up ethical principles
And duties and obligations
To bring everyone in line
The more you gather loot
For a thief like Khang.
By ethical argument
And moral principle
The greatest crimes are eventually shown
To have been necessary, and, in fact,
A signal benefit
To mankind.

CUTTING UP AN OX

Prince Wen Hui's cook
Was cutting up an ox.
Out went a hand,
Down went a shoulder,
He planted a foot,
He pressed with a knee,
The ox fell apart
With a whisper,
The bright cleaver murmured
Like a gentle wind.
Rhythm! Timing!
Like a sacred dance,
Like "The Mulberry Grove,"
Like ancient harmonies!

"Good work!" the Prince exclaimed,
"Your method is faultless!"
"Method?" said the cook

Laying aside his cleaver,
"What I follow is Tao
Beyond all methods!

"When I first began
To cut up oxen
I would see before me
The whole ox
All in one mass.

"After three years
I no longer saw this mass.
I saw the distinctions.

"But now, I see nothing
With the eye. My whole being
Apprehends.
My senses are idle. The spirit
Free to work without plan
Follows its own instinct
Guided by natural line,
By the secret opening, the hidden space,
My cleaver finds its own way.
I cut through no joint, chop no bone.

"A good cook needs a new chopper
Once a year—he cuts.
A poor cook needs a new one
Every month—he hacks!

"I have used this same cleaver
Nineteen years.
It has cut up
A thousand oxen.
Its edge is as keen
As if newly sharpened.

"There are spaces in the joints;
The blade is thin and keen:
When this thinness
Finds that space
There is all the room you need!
It goes like a breeze!
Hence I have this cleaver nineteen years
As if newly sharpened!

"True, there are sometimes
Tough joints. I feel them coming,
I slow down, I watch closely,
Hold back, barely move the blade,
And whump! the part falls away
Landing like a clod of earth.

"Then I withdraw the blade,
I stand still
And let the joy of the work
Sink in.
I clean the blade
And put it away."

Prince Wan Hui said,
"This is it! My cook has shown me
How I ought to live
My own life!"

DUKE HWAN AND THE WHEELWRIGHT

The world values books, and thinks that in so doing it is
valuing Tao. But books contain words only. And yet there is
something else which gives value to the books. Not the words

only, nor the thought in the words, but something else within the thought, swinging it in a certain direction that words cannot apprehend. But it is the words themselves that the world values when it commits them to books: and though the world values them, these words are worthless as long as that which gives them value is not held in honor.

That which man apprehends by observation is only outward form and color, name and noise: and he thinks that this will put him in possession of Tao. Form and color, name and sound, do not reach to reality. That is why: "He who knows does not say, he who says, does not know."

How then is the world going to know Tao through words?

• • •

Duke Hwan of Khi,
First in his dynasty,
Sat under his canopy
Reading his philosophy;
And Phien the wheelwright
Was out in the yard
Making a wheel.
Phien laid aside
Hammer and chisel,
Climbed the steps,
And said to Duke Hwan:
"May I ask you, Lord,
What is this you are
Reading?"
The Duke said:
"The experts. The authorities."
And Phien asked:
"Alive or dead?"
"Dead a long time."
"Then," said the wheelwright,
"You are reading only
The dirt they left behind."

Then the Duke replied:
"What do you know about it?
You are only a wheelwright.
You had better give me a good explanation
Or else you must die."
The wheelwright said:
"Let us look at the affair
From my point of view.
When I make wheels
If I go easy, they fall apart,
If I am too rough, they do not fit.
If I am neither too easy nor too violent
They come out right. The work is what
I want it to be.
You cannot put this into words:
You just have to know how it is.
I cannot even tell my own son exactly how it is done,
And my own son cannot learn it from me.
So here I am, seventy years old,
Still making wheels!
The men of old
Took all they really knew
With them to the grave.
And so, Lord, what you are reading there
Is only the dirt they left behind them."

GOOD FORTUNE

Master Ki had eight sons.
One day he called in a physiognomist, lined the boys up,
    and said:
"Study their faces. Tell me which is the fortunate one."

After his examination the expert said:
"Kwan is the fortunate one."

Ki was pleased and surprised.
"In what way?" he inquired.
The physiognomist replied:
"Kwan shall eat meat and drink wine
For the rest of his days
At government expense."

Ki broke down and sobbed:
"My poor son! My poor son!
What has he done to deserve this misfortune?"

"What!" cried the physiognomist,
"When one shares
The meals of a prince
Blessings reach out
To all the family,
Especially to father and mother!
Will you refuse
Good fortune?"

Ki said: "What makes this fortune 'good'?
Meat and wine are for mouth and belly.
Is good fortune only in the mouth,
And in the belly?
These 'meals of the prince'—
How shall he share them?

"I am no shepherd
And a lamb is suddenly born in my house.
I am no game-keeper
And quails are born in my yard.
These are awful portents!

"I have had no wish
For my sons and myself,
But to wander at liberty
Through earth and heaven.

"I seek no joy
For them and for myself
But joy of heaven,
Simple fruits of earth.

"I seek no advantage, make no plans,
Engage in no business.
With my boys I seek Tao alone.

"I have not fought life!
Yet now this uncanny promise
Of what I never sought:
'Good fortune!'

"Every strange effect has some strange cause.
My sons and I have done nothing to deserve this.
It is an inscrutable punishment.
Therefore I weep!"

And so it happened some time afterward that Ki sent his
son Kwan on a journey. The young man was captured by
brigands who decided to sell him as a slave. Believing they
could not sell him as he was, they cut off his feet. Thus,
unable to run away, he became a better bargain. They sold
him to the government of Chi, and he was put in charge of
a tollgate on the highway. He had meat and wine, for the
rest of his life, at government expense.

In this way it turned out that Kwan was the fortunate
one!

GREAT AND SMALL

When we look at things in the light of Tao,
Nothing is best, nothing is worst.
Each thing, seen in its own light,
Stands out in its own way.
It can seem to be "better"
Than what is compared with it
On its own terms.
But seen in terms of the whole,
No one thing stands out as "better."
If you measure differences,
What is greater than something else is "great,"
Therefore there is nothing that is not "great";
What is smaller than something else is "small,"
Therefore there is nothing that is not "small."
So the whole cosmos is a grain of rice,
And the tip of a hair
Is as big as a mountain—
Such is the relative view.

You can break down walls with battering rams,
But you cannot stop holes with them.
All things have different uses.
Fine horses can travel a hundred miles a day,
But they cannot catch mice
Like terriers or weasels:
All creatures have gifts of their own.
The white horned owl can catch fleas at midnight
And distinguish the tip of a hair,
But in bright day it stares, helpless,
And cannot even see a mountain.
All things have varying capacities.

Consequently: he who wants to have right without wrong,
Order without disorder,
Does not understand the principles
Of heaven and earth.
He does not know how
Things hang together.
Can a man cling only to heaven
And know nothing of earth?
They are correlative: to know one
Is to know the other.
To refuse one
Is to refuse both.
Can a man cling to the positive
Without any negative
In contrast to which it is seen
To be positive?
If he claims to do so
He is a rogue or a madman.

Thrones pass
From dynasty to dynasty,
Now in this way, now in that.
He who forces his way to power
Against the grain
I called tyrant and usurper.
He who moves with the stream of events
Is called a wise statesman.

Kui, the one-legged dragon,
Is jealous of the centipede.
The centipede is jealous of the snake.
The snake is jealous of the wind.
The wind is jealous of the eye.
The eye is jealous of the mind.
Kui said to the centipede:

"I manage my one leg with difficulty:
How can you manage a hundred?"
The centipede replied:
"I do not manage them.
They land all over the place
Like drops of spit."
The centipede said to the snake:
"With all my feet, I cannot move as fast
As you do with no feet at all.
How is this done?"
The snake replied:
"I have a natural glide
That can't be changed. What do I need
With feet?"
The snake spoke to the wind:
"I ripple my backbone and move along
In a bodily way. You, without bones,
Without muscles, without method,
Blow from the North Sea to the Southern Ocean.
How do you get there
With nothing?"
The wind replied:
"True, I rise up in the North Sea
And take myself without obstacle to the Southern Ocean.
But every eye that remarks me,
Every wing that uses me,
Is superior to me, even though
I can uproot the biggest trees, or overturn
Big buildings.
The true conqueror is he
Who is not conquered
By the multitude of the small.
The mind is this conqueror—
But only the mind
Of the wise man."

GREAT KNOWLEDGE

Great knowledge sees all in one.
Small knowledge breaks down into the many.

When the body sleeps, the soul is enfolded in One.
When the body wakes, the openings begin to function.
They resound with every encounter
With all the varied business of life, the strivings of the heart;
Men are blocked, perplexed, lost in doubt.
Little fears eat away their peace of heart.
Great fears swallow them whole.
Arrows shot at a target: hit and miss, right and wrong.
That is what men call judgment, decision.
Their pronouncements are as final
As treaties between emperors.
O, they make their point!
Yet their arguments fall faster and feebler
Than dead leaves in autumn and winter.
Their talk flows out like piss,
Never to be recovered.
They stand at last, blocked, bound, and gagged,
Choked up like old drain pipes.
The mind fails. It shall not see light again.

Pleasure and rage
Sadness and joy
Hopes and regrets
Change and stability
Weakness and decision
Impatience and sloth:
All are sounds from the same flute,
All mushrooms from the same wet mould.
Day and night follow one another and come upon us
Without our seeing how they sprout!

Enough! Enough!
Early and late we meet the "that"
From which "these" all grow!

If there were no "that"
There would be no "this."
If there were no "this"
There would be nothing for all these winds to play on.
So far can we go.
But how shall we understand
What brings it about?

One may well suppose the True Governor
To be behind it all. That such a Power works
I can believe. I cannot see his form.

He acts, but has no form.

IN MY END IS MY BEGINNING

In the Beginning of Beginnings was Void of Void, the
    Nameless.
And in the Nameless was the One, without body, without
    form.
This One—this Being in whom all find power to exist—
Is the Living.
From the Living, comes the Formless, the Undivided.
From the act of this Formless, come the Existents, each
    according
To its inner principle. This is Form. Here body embraces and
    cherishes spirit.
The two work together as one, blending and manifesting their
Characters. And this is Nature.

But he who obeys Nature returns through Form and Formless
    to the Living,
And in the Living
Joins the unbegun Beginning.
The joining is Sameness. The sameness is Void. The Void is
    infinite.
The bird opens its beak and sings its note
And then the beak comes together again in Silence.
So Nature and the Living meet together in Void.
Like the closing of the bird's beak
After its song.
Heaven and earth come together in the Unbegun,
And all is foolishness, all is unknown, all is like
The lights of an idiot, all is without mind!
To obey is to close the beak and fall into Unbeginning.

KENG'S DISCIPLE

A disciple complained to Keng:
"The eyes of all men seem to be alike,
I detect no difference in them;
Yet some men are blind;
Their eyes do not see.
The ears of all men seem to be alike,
I detect no difference in them;
Yet some men are deaf,
Their ears do not hear.
The minds of all men have the same nature,
I detect no difference between them;
But the mad cannot make
Another man's mind their own.
Here am I, apparently like the other disciples,

But there is a difference:
They get your meaning and put it in practice;
I cannot.
You tell me: 'Hold your being secure and quiet,
Keep your life collected in its own center.
Do not allow your thoughts
To be disturbed.'
But however hard I try,
Tao is only a word in my ear.
It does not ring any bells inside."

Keng San replied: "I have nothing more
To say.
Bantams do not hatch goose eggs,
Though the fowl of Lu can.
It is not so much a difference of nature
As a difference of capacity.
My capacity is too slight
To transform you.
Why not go south
And see Lao Tzu?"

The disciple got some supplies,
Traveled seven days and seven nights
Alone,
And came to Lao Tzu.
Lao asked: "Do you come from Keng?"
"Yes," replied the student.
"Who are all those people you have brought with you?"
The disciple whirled around to look.
Nobody there. Panic!
Lao said: "Don't you understand?"
The disciple hung his head. Confusion!
Then a sigh. "Alas, I have forgotten my answer."
(More confusion!) "I have also forgotten my question."

Lao said: "What are you trying to say?"
The disciple: "When I don't know, people treat me like a fool.
When I do know, the knowledge gets me into trouble.
When I fail to do good, I hurt others.
When I do good, I hurt myself.
If I avoid my duty, I am remiss,
But if I do it, I am ruined.
How can I get out of these contradictions?
That is what I came to ask you."

Lao Tzu replied:
"A moment ago
I looked into your eyes.
I saw you were hemmed in
By contradictions. Your words
Confirm this.
You are scared to death,
Like a child who has lost
Father and mother.
You are trying to sound
The middle of the ocean
With a six-foot pole.
You have got lost, and are trying
To find your way back
To your own true self.
You find nothing
But illegible signposts
Pointing in all directions.
I pity you."

The disciple asked for admittance,
Took a cell, and there
Meditated,
Trying to cultivate qualities
He thought desirable

886

And get rid of others
Which he disliked.
Ten days of that!
Despair!

"Miserable!" said Lao.
"All blocked up!
Tied in knots! Try
To get untied!
If your obstructions
Are on the outside,
Do not attempt
To grasp them one by one
And thrust them away.
Impossible! Learn
To ignore them.
If they are within yourself,
You cannot destroy them piecemeal,
But you can refuse
To let them take effect.
If they are both inside and outside,
Do not try
To hold on to Tao—
Just hope that Tao
Will keep hold of you!"

The disciple groaned:
"When a farmer gets sick
And the other farmers come to see him,
If he can at least tell them
What is the matter
His sickness is not bad.
But as for me, in my search for Tao,
I am like a sick man who takes medicine
That makes him ten times worse.

Just tell me
The first elements.
I will be satisfied!"

Lao Tzu replied:
"Can you embrace the One
And not lose it?
Can you foretell good things and bad
Without the tortoise shell
Or the straws?
Can you rest where there is rest?
Do you know when to stop?
Can you mind your own business
Without cares, without desiring reports
Of how others are progressing?
Can you stand on your own feet?
Can you duck?
Can you be like an infant
That cries all day
Without getting a sore throat
Or clenches his fist all day
Without getting a sore hand
Or gazes all day
Without eyestrain?
You want the first elements?
The infant has them.
Free from care, unaware of self,
He acts without reflection,
Stays where he is put, does not know why,
Does not figure things out,
Just goes along with them,
Is part of the current.
These are the first elements!"

The disciple asked:
"Is this perfection?"

888

Lao replied: "Not at all.
It is only the beginning.
This melts the ice.

"This enables you
To unlearn,
So that you can be led by Tao,
Be a child of Tao.

"If you persist in trying
To attain what is never attained
(It is Tao's gift!)
If you persist in making effort
To obtain what effort cannot get;
If you persist in reasoning
About what canot be understood,
You will be destroyed
By the very thing you seek.

"To know when to stop
To know when you can get no further
By your own action,
This is the right beginning!"

KENG SANG CHU

Master Keng Sang Chu, a disciple of Lao Tzu, became fa-
mous for his wisdom, and the people of Wei-Lei began to
venerate him as a sage. He avoided their homage and refused
their gifts. He kept himself hidden and would not let them
come to see him. His disciples remonstrated with him, and
declared that since the time of Yao and Shun it had been the

tradition for wise men to accept veneration, and thus exercise a good influence. Master Keng replied:

"Come here, my children, listen to this.
If a beast big enough to swallow a wagon
Should leave its mountain forest,
It will not escape the hunter's trap.
If a fish big enough to swallow a boat
Lets itself be stranded by the outgoing tide,
Then even ants will destroy it.
So birds fly high, beasts remain
In trackless solitudes,
Keep out of sight; and fishes
Or turtles go deep down,
Down to the very bottom.
The man who has some respect for his person
Keeps his carcass out of sight,
Hides himself as perfectly as he can.
As for Yao and Shun: why praise such kings?
What good did their morality do?
They knocked a hole in the wall
And let it fill up with brambles.
They numbered the hairs of your head
Before combing them.
They counted out each grain of rice
Before cooking their dinner.
What good did they do to the world
With their scrupulous distinctions?
If the virtuous are honored,
The world will be filled with envy.
If the smart man is rewarded,
The world will be filled with thieves.
You cannot make men good or honest
By praising virtue and knowledge.
Since the days of pious Yao and virtuous Shun

Everybody has been trying to get rich:
A son will kill his father for money,
A minister will murder his sovereign
To satisfy his ambition.
In broad daylight they rob each other,
At midnight they break down walls:
The root of all this was planted
In the time of Yao and Shun.
The branches will grow for a thousand ages,
And a thousand ages from now
Men will be eating one another raw!"

LAO TZU'S WAKE

Lao Tan lay dead
Chin Shih attended the wake.
He let out three yells
And went home.

One of the disciples said:
Were you not the Master's friend?
"Certainly," he replied.

"Is it then sufficient for you
To mourn no better than you have just done?"

"In the beginning," said Chin Shih, "I thought
He was the greatest of men.
No longer! When I came to mourn
I found old men lamenting him as their son,
Young men sobbing as though for their mother.
How did he bind them to himself so tight, if not

By words he should never have said
And tears he should never have wept?

"He weakened his true being,
He laid on load upon
Load of emotion, increased
The enormous reckoning:
He forgot the gift God had entrusted to him:
This the ancients called 'punishment
For neglecting the True Self.'

"The Master came at his right time
Into the world. When his time was up,
He left it again.
He who awaits his time, who submits
When his work is done,
In his life there is no room
For sorrow or for rejoicing.
Here is how the ancients said all this
In four words:
            'God cuts the thread.'

"We have seen a fire of sticks
Burn out. The fire now
Burns in some other place. Where?
Who knows? These brands
Are burnt out."

MAN IS BORN IN TAO

Fishes are born in water
Man is born in Tao.

If fishes, born in water,
Seek the deep shadow
Of pond and pool,
All their needs
Are satisfied.
If man, born in Tao,
Sinks into the deep shadow
Of non-action
To forget aggression and concern,
He lacks nothing
His life is secure.

Moral: "All the fish needs
Is to get lost in water.
All man needs is to get lost
In Tao."

METAMORPHOSIS

Four men got in a discussion. Each one said:
"Who knows how
To have the Void for his head
To have Life as his backbone
And Death for his tail?
He shall be my friend!"

At this they all looked at one another
Saw they agreed,
Burst out laughing
And became friends.

Then one of them fell ill
And another went to see him.

"Great is the Maker," said the sick one,
"Who has made me as I am!

"I am so doubled up
My guts are over my head;
Upon my navel
I rest my cheek;
My shoulders stand out
Beyond my neck;
My crown is an ulcer
Surveying the sky;
My body is chaos
But my mind is in order."

He dragged himself to the well,
Saw his reflection, and declared,
"What a mess
He has made of me!"

His friend asked:
"Are you discouraged?"

"Not at all! Why should I be?
If He takes me apart
And makes a rooster
Of my left shoulder
I shall announce the dawn.
If He makes a crossbow
Of my right shoulder
I shall procure roast duck.
If my buttocks turn into wheels
And if my spirit is a horse
I will hitch myself up and ride around
In my own wagon!

"There is a time for putting together
And another time for taking apart.
He who understands
This course of events
Takes each new state
In its proper time
With neither sorrow nor joy.
The ancients said: 'The hanged man
Cannot cut himself down.'
But in due time Nature is stronger
Than all his ropes and bonds.
It was always so.
Where is there a reason
To be discouraged?"

OWL AND PHOENIX

Hui Tzu was Prime Minister of Liang. He had what he be-
lieved to be inside information that Chuang Tzu coveted his
post and was intriguing to supplant him. In fact, when
Chuang Tzu came to visit Liang, the Prime Minister sent out
the police to apprehend him. The police searched for him
three days and three nights, but meanwhile Chuang presented
himself before Hui Tzu of his own accord, and said:

"Have you heard about the bird
That lives in the south
The Phoenix that never grows old?

"This undying Phoenix
Rises out of the South Sea
And flies to the Sea of the North,

Never alighting
Except on certain sacred trees.
He will touch no food
But the most exquisite
Rare fruit,
Drinks only
From clearest springs.

"Once an owl
Chewing a dead rat
Already half-decayed,
Saw the Phoenix fly over,
Looked up,
And screeched with alarm,
Clutching the rat to himself
In fear and dismay.

"Why are you so frantic
Clinging to your ministry
And screeching at me
In dismay?"

PERFECT JOY

Here is how I sum it up:
    Heaven does nothing: its non-doing is its serenity.
    Earth does nothing: its non-doing is its rest.
    From the union of these two non-doings
    All actions proceed,
    All things are made.
    How vast, how invisible
    This coming-to-be!

All things come from nowhere!
How vast, how invisible
No way to explain it!
All beings in their perfection
Are born of non-doing.
Hence it is said:
"Heaven and earth do nothing
Yet there is nothing they do not do."

Where is the man who can attain
To this non-doing?

STARLIGHT AND NON-BEING

Starlight asked Non-Being: "Master, are you? Or are you
not?"

Since he received no answer whatever, Starlight set himself
to watch for Non-Being. He waited to see if Non-Being
would put in an appearance.

He kept his gaze fixed on the deep Void, hoping to catch
a glimpse of Non-Being.

All day long he looked, and he saw nothing. He listened,
but heard nothing. He reached out to grasp, and grasped
nothing.

Then Starlight exclaimed at last: "This is IT!"

"This is the furthest yet! Who can reach it?
I can comprehend the absence of Being
But who can comprehend the absence of Nothing?
If now, on top of all this, Non-Being IS,
Who can comprehend it?"

SYMPHONY FOR A SEA BIRD

You cannot put a big load in a small bag,
Nor can you, with a short rope,
Draw water from a deep well.
You cannot talk to a power politician
As if he were a wise man.
If he seeks to understand you,
If he looks inside himself
To find the truth you have told him,
He cannot find it there.
Not finding, he doubts.
When a man doubts,
He will kill.

Have you not heard how a bird from the sea
Was blown inshore and landed
Outside the capital of Lu?

The Prince ordered a solemn reception,
Offered the sea bird wine in the sacred precinct,
Called for musicians
To play the compositions of Shun,
Slaughtered cattle to nourish it:
Dazed with symphonies, the unhappy sea bird
Died of despair.

How should you treat a bird?
As yourself
Or as a bird?

Ought not a bird to nest in deep woodland
Or fly over meadow and marsh?
Ought it not to swim on river and pond,
Feed on eels and fish,

Fly in formation with other waterfowl,
And rest in the reeds?

Bad enough for a sea bird
To be surrounded by men
And frightened by their voices!
That was not enough!
They killed it with music!

Play all the symphonies you like
On the marshlands of Thung-Ting.
The birds will fly away
In all directions;
The animals will hide;
The fish will dive to the bottom;
But men
Will gather around to listen.

Water is for fish
And air for men.
Natures differ, and needs with them.

Hence the wise men of old
Did not lay down
One measure for all.

TAO

Cocks crow
Dogs bark
This all men know.
Even the wisest

Cannot tell
Whence these voices come
Or explain
Why dogs bark and cocks crow
When they do.

Beyond the smallest of the small
There is no measure.
Beyond the greatest of the great
There is also no measure.

Where there is no measure
There is no "thing."
In this void
You speak of "cause"
Or of "chance"?
You speak of "things"
Where there is "no-things."
To name a name
Is to delimit a "thing."

When I look beyond the beginning
I find no measure.
When I look beyond the end
I find also no measure.
Where there is no measure
There is no beginning of any "thing."
You speak of "cause" or "chance"?
You speak of the beginning of some "thing."

Does Tao exist?
Is it then a "thing that exists."
Can it "non-exist"?
Is there then "thing that exists"
That "cannot not exist"?

To name Tao
Is to name no-thing.
Tao is not the name
Of "an existent."
"Cause" and "chance"
Have no bearing on Tao.
Tao is a name
That indicates
Without defining.

Tao is beyond words
And beyond things.
It is not expressed
Either in word or in silence.
Where there is no longer word or silence
Tao is apprehended.

THE BREATH OF NATURE

When great Nature sighs, we hear the winds
Which, noiseless in themselves,
Awaken voices from other beings,
Blowing on them.
From every opening
Loud voices sound. Have you not heard
This rush of tones?

There stands the overhanging wood
On the steep mountain:
Old trees with holes and cracks
Like snouts, maws, and ears,
Like beam-sockets, like goblets,

Grooves in the wood, hollows full of water:
You hear mooing and roaring, whistling,
Shouts of command, grumblings,
Deep drones, sad flutes.
One call awakens another in dialogue.
Gentle winds sing timidly,
Strong ones blast on without restraint.
Then the wind dies down. The openings
Empty out their last sound.
Have you not observed how all then trembles and subsides?

Yu replied: I understand:
The music of earth sings through a thousand holes.
The music of man is made on flutes and instruments.
What makes the music of heaven?

Master Ki said:
Something is blowing on a thousand different holes.
Some power stands behind all this and makes the sounds die
    down.
What is this power?

THE EMPTY BOAT

He who rules men lives in confusion;
He who is ruled by men lives in sorrow.
Yao therefore desired
Neither to influence others
Nor to be influenced by them.
The way to get clear of confusion
And free of sorrow
Is to live with Tao
In the land of the great Void.

If a man is crossing a river
And an empty boat collides with his own skiff,
Even though he be a bad-tempered man
He will not become very angry.
But if he sees a man in the boat,
He will shout at him to steer clear.
If the shout is not heard, he will shout again,
And yet again, and begin cursing.
And all because there is somebody in the boat.
Yet if the boat were empty,
He would not be shouting, and not angry.

If you can empty your own boat
Crossing the river of the world,
No one will oppose you,
No one will seek to harm you.

The straight tree is the first to be cut down,
The spring of clear water is the first to be drained dry.
If you wish to improve your wisdom
And shame the ignorant,
To cultivate your character
And outshine others;
A light will shine around you
As if you had swallowed the sun and the moon:
You will not avoid calamity.

A wise man has said:
       "He who is content with himself
       Has done a worthless work.
       Achievement is the beginning of failure.
       Fame is the beginning of disgrace."

Who can free himself from achievement
And from fame, descend and be lost

Amid the masses of men?
He will flow like Tao, unseen,
He will go about like Life itself
With no name and no home.
Simple is he, without distinction.
To all appearances he is a fool.
His steps leave no trace. He has no power.
He achieves nothing, has no reputation.
Since he judges no one
No one judges him.
Such is the perfect man:
His boat is empty.

THE FIGHTING COCK

Chi Hsing Tzu was a trainer of fighting cocks
For King Hsuan.
He was training a fine bird.
The King kept asking if the bird were
Ready for combat.
"Not yet," said the trainer.
"He is full of fire.
He is ready to pick a fight
With every other bird. He is vain and confident
Of his own strength."
After ten days, he answered again:
"Not yet. He flares up
When he hears another bird crow."
After ten more days:
"Not yet. He still gets
That angry look
And ruffles his feathers."

Again ten days:
The trainer said, "Now he is nearly ready.
When another bird crows, his eye
Does not even flicker.
He stands immobile
Like a cock of wood.
He is a mature fighter.
Other birds
Will take one look at him
And run."

THE FIVE ENEMIES

With wood from a hundred-year-old tree
They make sacrificial vessels,
Covered with green and yellow designs.
The wood that was cut away
Lies unused in the ditch.
If we compare the sacrificial vessels with the wood in the ditch
We find them to differ in appearance:
One is more beautiful than the other
Yet they are equal in this: both have lost their original nature.
So if you compare the robber and the respectable citizen
You find that one is, indeed, more respectable than the other:
Yet they agree in this: they have both lost
The original simplicity of man.

How did they lose it? Here are the five ways:
Love of colors bewilders the eye
And it fails to see right.
Love of harmonies bewitches the ear
And it loses its true hearing.

Love of perfumes
Fills the head with dizziness.
Love of flavors
Ruins the taste.
Desires unsettle the heart
Until the original nature runs amok.

These five are enemies of true life.
Yet these are what "men of discernment" claim to live for.
They are not what I live for:
If this is life, then pigeons in a cage
Have found happiness!

THE FLIGHT OF LIN HUI

Lin Hui of Kia took to flight.
Pursued by enemies,
He threw away the precious jade
Symbol of his rank
And took his infant child on his back.
Why did he take the child
And leave the jade,
Which was worth a small fortune,
Whereas the child, if sold,
Would only bring him a paltry sum?

Lin Hui said:
"My bond with the jade symbol
And with my office
Was the bond of self-interest.
My bond with the child
Was the bond of Tao.

"Where self-interest is the bond,
The friendship is dissolved
When calamity comes.
Where Tao is the bond,
Friendship is made perfect
By calamity.

"The friendship of wise men
Is tasteless as water.
The friendship of fools
Is sweet as wine.
But the tastelessness of the wise
Brings true affection
And the savor of fools' company
Ends in hatred."

THE IMPORTANCE OF BEING TOOTHLESS

Nieh Ch'ueh, who had no teeth,
Came to P'i and asked for a lesson on Tao.
(Maybe he could bite on *that!*)

So P'i began:
"First, gain control of the body
And all its organs. Then
Control the mind. Attain
One-pointedness. Then
The harmony of heaven
Will come down and dwell in you.
You will be radiant with Life.
You will rest in Tao.
You will have the simple look

Of a new-born calf,
O, lucky you,
You will not even know the cause
Of your state . . ."

But long before P'i had reached this point in his sermon, the
toothless one had fallen asleep. His mind just could not bite
on the meat of doctrine. But P'i was satisfied. He wandered
away singing:

"His body is dry
Like an old leg bone,
His mind is dead
As dead ashes:
His knowledge is solid,
His wisdom true!
In deep dark night
He wanders free,
Without aim
And without design:
Who can compare
With this toothless man?"

THE INNER LAW

He whose law is within himself
Walks in hiddenness.
His acts are not influenced
By approval or disapproval.
He whose law is outside himself
Directs his will to what is
Beyond his control

And seeks
To extend his power
Over objects.

He who walks in hiddenness
Has light to guide him
In all his acts.
He who seeks to extend his control
Is nothing but an operator.
While he thinks he is
Surpassing others,
Others see him merely
Straining, stretching,
To stand on tiptoe.

When he tries to extend his power
Over objects,
Those objects gain control
Of him.

He who is controlled by objects
Loses possession of his inner self:
If he no longer values himself,
How can he value others?
If he no longer values others,
He is abandoned.
He has nothing left!

There is no deadlier weapon than the will!
The sharpest sword
Is not equal to it!
There is no robber so dangerous
As Nature (Yang and Yin).
Yet it is not nature
That does the damage:
It is man's own will!

THE JOY OF FISHES

Chuang Tzu and Hui Tzu
Were crossing Hao river
By the dam.

Chuang said:
"See how free
The fishes leap and dart:
That is their happiness."

Hui replied:
"Since you are not a fish
How do you know
What makes fishes happy?"

Chuang said:
"Since you are not I
How can you possibly know
That I do not know
What makes fishes happy?"

Hui argued:
"If I, not being you,
Cannot know what you know
It follows that you
Not being a fish
Cannot know what they know."

Chuang said:
"Wait a minute!
Let us get back
To the original question.
What you asked me was
How do you know

What makes fishes happy?'
From the terms of your question
You evidently know I know
What makes fishes happy.

"I know the joy of fishes
In the river
Through my own joy, as I go walking
Along the same river."

THE KINGLY MAN

My Master said:
That which acts on all and meddles in none—is heaven . . .

The Kingly Man realizes this, hides it in his heart,
Grows boundless, wide-minded, draws all to himself.
And so he lets the gold lie hidden in the mountain,
Leaves the pearl lying in the deep.
Goods and possessions are no gain in his eyes,
He stays far from wealth and honor.
Long life is no ground for joy, nor early death for sorrow.
Success is not for him to be proud of, failure is no shame.
Had he all the world's power he would not hold it as his own,
If he conquered everything he would not take it to himself.
His glory is in knowing that all things come together in One
And life and death are equal.

THE LOST PEARL

The Yellow Emperor went wandering
To the north of the Red Water

To the Kwan Lun mountain. He looked around
Over the edge of the world. On the way home
He lost his night-colored pearl.
He sent out Science to seek his pearl, and got nothing.
He sent Analysis to look for his pearl, and got nothing.
He sent out Logic to seek his pearl, and got nothing.
Then he asked Nothingness, and Nothingness had it!

The Yellow Emperor said:
"Strange, indeed: Nothingness
Who was not sent
Who did no work to find it
Had the night-colored pearl!"

THE MAN OF TAO

The man in whom Tao
Acts without impediment
Harms no other being
By his actions
Yet he does not know himself
To be "kind," to be "gentle."

The man in whom Tao
Acts without impediment
Does not bother with his own interests
And does not despise
Others who do.
He does not struggle to make money
And does not make a virtue of poverty.
He goes his way
Without relying on others

And does not pride himself
On walking alone.
While he does not follow the crowd
He won't complain of those who do.
Rank and reward
Make no appeal to him;
Disgrace and shame
Do not deter him.
He is not always looking
For right and wrong
Always deciding "Yes" or "No."
The ancients said, therefore:
"The man of Tao
Remains unknown
Perfect virtue
Produces nothing
'No-Self'
Is 'True-Self.'
And the greatest man
Is Nobody."

THE MAN WITH ONE FOOT
AND THE MARSH PHEASANT

Kung Wen Hsien saw a maimed official
Whose left foot had been cut off—
A penalty in the political game!

"What kind of man," he cried, "is this one-footed oddity?
How did he get that way? Shall we say
Man did this, or heaven?"

"Heaven," he said, "this comes from
Heaven, not from man.
When heaven gave this man life, it willed
He should stand out from others
And sent him into politics
To get himself distinguished.
See! One foot! This man is *different*."

The little marsh pheasant
Must hop ten times
To get a bite of grain.

She must run a hundred steps
Before she takes a sip of water.
Yet she does not ask
To be kept in a hen run
Though she might have all she desired
Set before her.

She would rather run
And seek her own little living
Uncaged.

THE NEED TO WIN

When an archer is shooting for nothing
He has all his skill.
If he shoots for a brass buckle
He is already nervous.
If he shoots for a prize of gold
He goes blind
Or sees two targets—
He is out of his mind!

914

His skill has not changed. But the prize
Divides him. He cares.
He thinks more of winning
Than of shooting—
And the need to win
Drains him of power.

THE TOWER OF THE SPIRIT

The spirit has an impregnable tower
Which no danger can disturb
As long as the tower is guarded
By the invisible Protector
Who acts unconsciously, and whose actions
Go astray when they become deliberate,
Reflexive, and intentional.

The unconsciousness
And entire sincerity of Tao
Are disturbed by any effort
At self-conscious demonstration.
All such demonstrations
Are lies.

When one displays himself
In this ambiguous way
The world outside storms in
And imprisons him.

He is no longer protected
By the sincerity of Tao.

Each new act
Is a new failure.

If his acts are done in public,
In broad daylight,
He will be punished by men.
If they are done in private
And in secret,
They will be punished
By spirits.

Let each one understand
The meaning of sincerity
And guard against display!

He will be at peace
With men and spirits
And will act rightly, unseen,
In his own solitude,
In the tower of his spirit.

THE TRUE MAN

What is meant by a "true man"?
The true men of old were not afraid
When they stood alone in their views.
No great exploits. No plans.
If they failed, no sorrow.
No self-congratulation in success.
They scaled cliffs, never dizzy,
Plunged in water, never wet,
Walked through fire and were not burnt.

Thus their knowledge reached all the way
To Tao.

The true men of old
Slept without dreams,
Woke without worries.
Their food was plain.
They breathed deep.
True men breathe from their heels.
Others breathe with their gullets,
Half-strangled. In dispute
They heave up arguments
Like vomit.

Where the fountains of passion
Lie deep
The heavenly springs
Are soon dry.

The true men of old
Knew no lust for life,
No dread of death.
Their entrance was without gladness,
Their exit, yonder,
Without resistance.
Easy come, easy go.
They did not forget where from,
Nor ask where to,
Nor drive grimly forward
Fighting their way through life.
They took life as it came, gladly;
Took death as it came, without care;
And went away, yonder,
Yonder!

They had no mind to fight Tao.
They did not try, by their own contriving,
To help Tao along.
These are the ones we call true men.

Minds free, thoughts gone
Brows clear, faces serene.
Were they cool? Only cool as autumn.
Were they hot? No hotter than spring.
All that came out of them
Came quiet, like the four seasons.

THE TURTLE

Chuang Tzu with his bamboo pole
Was fishing in Pu river.

The Prince of Chu
Sent two vice-chancellors
With a formal document:
"We hereby appoint you
Prime Minister."

Chuang Tzu held his bamboo pole.
Still watching Pu river,
He said:
"I am told there is a sacred tortoise,
Offered and canonized
Three thousand years ago,
Venerated by the prince,
Wrapped in silk,
In a precious shrine

On an altar
In the Temple.

"What do you think:
Is it better to give up one's life
And leave a sacred shell
As an object of cult
In a cloud of incense
Three thousand years,
Or better to live
As a plain turtle
Dragging its tail in the mud?"

"For the turtle," said the Vice-Chancellor,
"Better to live
And drag its tail in the mud!"

"Go home!" said Chuang Tzu.
"Leave me here
To drag my tail in the mud!"

THE USELESS

Hui Tzu said to Chuang Tzu:
"All your teaching is centered on what has no use."

Chuang replied:
"If you have no appreciation for what has no use
You cannot begin to talk about what can be used.
The earth, for example, is broad and vast
But of all this expanse a man uses only a few inches
Upon which he happens to be standing.

Now suppose you suddenly take away
All that he is not actually using
So that, all around his feet a gulf
Yawns, and he stands in the Void,
With nowhere solid except right under each foot:
How long will he be able to use what he is using?"

Hui Tzu said: "It would cease to serve any purpose."

Chuang Tzu concluded:
     "This shows
     The absolute necessity
     Of what has 'no use.' "

THE USELESS TREE

Hui Tzu said to Chuang:
I have a big tree,
The kind they call a "stinktree."
The trunk is so distorted,
So full of knots,
No one can get a straight plank
Out of it. The branches are so crooked
You cannot cut them up
In any way that makes sense.

There it stands beside the road.
No carpenter will even look at it.

Such is your teaching—
Big and useless.

Chuang Tzu replied:
Have you ever watched the wildcat
Crouching, watching his prey—
This way it leaps, and that way,
High and low, and at last
Lands in the trap.

But have you seen the yak?
Great as a thundercloud
He stands in his might.
Big? Sure,
He can't catch mice!

So for your big tree. No use?
Then plant it in the wasteland
In emptiness.
Walk idly around,
Rest under its shadow;
No ax or bill prepares its end.
No one will ever cut it down.

Useless? You should worry!

THE WOODCARVER

Khing, the master carver, made a bell stand
Of precious wood. When it was finished,
All who saw it were astounded. They said it must be
The work of spirits.
The Prince of Lu said to the master carver:
"What is your secret?"

Khing replied: "I am only a workman:
I have no secret. There is only this:
When I began to think about the work you commanded
I guarded my spirit, did not expend it
On trifles, that were not to the point.
I fasted in order to set
My heart at rest.
After three days fasting,
I had forgotten gain and success.
After five days
I had forgotten praise or criticism.
After seven days
I had forgotten my body
With all its limbs.

"By this time all thought of your Highness
And of the court had faded away.
All that might distract me from the work
Had vanished.
I was collected in the single thought
Of the bell stand.

"Then I went to the forest
To see the trees in their own natural state.
When the right tree appeared before my eyes,
The bell stand also appeared in it, clearly, beyond doubt.
All I had to do was to put forth my hand
And begin.

"If I had not met this particular tree
There would have been
No bell stand at all.

"What happened?
My own collected thought

Encountered the hidden potential in the wood;
From this live encounter came the work
Which you ascribe to the spirits."

THREE FRIENDS

There were three friends
Discussing life.
One said:
"Can men live together
And know nothing of it?
Work together
And produce nothing?
Can they fly around in space
And forget to exist
World without end?"
The three friends looked at each other
And burst out laughing.
They had no explanation.
Thus they were better friends than before.

Then one friend died.
Confucius
Sent a disciple to help the other two
Chant his obsequies.

The disciple found that one friend
Had composed a song.
While the other played a lute,
They sang:

> "Hey, Sung Hu!
> Where'd you go?

Hey, Sung Hu!
Where'd you go?
You have gone
Where you really were.
And we are here—
Damn it! We are here!"

Then the disciple of Confucius burst in on them and
Exclaimed: "May I inquire where you found this in the
Rubrics for obsequies,
This frivolous caroling in the presence of the departed?"

The two friends looked at each other and laughed:
"Poor fellow," they said, "he doesn't know the new liturgy!"

TWO KINGS AND NO-FORM

The South Sea King was Act-on-Your-Hunch.
The North Sea King was Act-in-a-Flash.
The King of the place between them was
No-Form.

Now South Sea King
And North Sea King
Used to go together often
To the land of No-Form:
He treated them well.

So they consulted together
They thought up a good turn,
A pleasant surprise, for No-Form
In token of appreciation.

"Men," they said, "have seven openings
For seeing, hearing, eating, breathing,
And so on. But No-Form
Has no openings. Let's make him
A few holes."
So after that
They put holes in No-Form,
One a day, for seven days.
And when they finished the seventh opening,
Their friend lay dead.

Lao Tan said: "To organize is to destroy."

WHEN A HIDEOUS MAN...

When a hideous man becomes a father
And a son is born to him
In the middle of the night
He trembles and lights a lamp
And runs to look in anguish
On that child's face
To see whom he resembles.

WHEN KNOWLEDGE WENT NORTH

Knowledge wandered north
Looking for Tao, over the Dark Sea,
And up the Invisible Mountain.
There on the mountain he met
Non-Doing, the Speechless One.

He inquired:
"Please inform me, Sir,
By what system of thought
And what technique of meditation
I can apprehend Tao?
By what renunciation
Or what solitary retirement
May I rest in Tao?
Where must I start,
What road must I follow
To reach Tao?"

Such were his three questions,
Non-Doing, the Speechless One,
Made no reply.
Not only that,
He did not even know
How to reply!

Knowledge swung south
To the Bright Sea
And climbed the Luminous Mountain
Called "Doubt's End."
Here he met
Act-on-Impulse, the Inspired Prophet,
And asked the same questions.

"Ah," cried the Inspired One,
"I have the answers, and I will reveal them!"
But just as he was about to tell everything,
He forgot all he had in mind.
Knowledge got no reply.

So Knowledge went at last
To the palace of Emperor Ti,

And asked his questions of Ti.
Ti replied:
"To exercise no-thought
And follow no-way of meditation
Is the first step toward understanding Tao.
To dwell nowhere
And rest in nothing
Is the first step toward resting in Tao.
To start from nowhere
And follow no road
Is the first step toward attaining Tao."

Knowledge replied: "You know this
And now I know it. But the other two,
They did not know it.
What about that?
Who is right?"

Ti replied:
Only Non-Doing, the Speechless One,
Was perfectly right. He did not know.
Act-on-Impulse, the Inspired Prophet,
Only seemed right
Because he had forgotten.
As for us,
We come nowhere near being right,
Since we have the answers.
"For he who knows does not speak,
He who speaks does not know"
And "The Wise Man gives instruction
Without the use of speech."

This story got back
To Act-on-Impulse

Who agreed with Ti's
Way of putting it.

It is not reported
That Non-Doing ever heard of the matter
Or made any comment.

WHEN THE SHOE FITS

Ch'ui the draftsman
Could draw more perfect circles freehand
Than with a compass.

His fingers brought forth
Spontaneous forms from nowhere. His mind
Was meanwhile free and without concern
With what he was doing.

No application was needed
His mind was perfectly simple
And knew no obstacle.

So, when the shoe fits
The foot is forgotten,
When the belt fits
The belly is forgotten,
When the heart is right
"For" and "against" are forgotten.

No drives, no compulsions,
No needs, no attractions:

Then your affairs
Are under control.
You are a free man.

Easy is right. Begin right
And you are easy.
Continue easy and you are right.
The right way to go easy
Is to forget the right way
And forget that the going is easy.

WHERE IS TAO?

Master Tung Kwo asked Chuang:
"Show me where the Tao is found."
Chuang Tzu replied:
"There is nowhere it is not to be found."
The former insisted:
"Show me at least some definite place
Where Tao is found."
"It is in the ant," said Chuang.
"Is it in some lesser being?"
"It is in the weeds."
"Can you go further down the scale of things?"
"It is in this piece of tile."
"Further?"
"It is in this turd."
At this Tung Kwo had nothing more to say.
But Chuang continued: "None of your questions
Are to the point. They are like the questions
Of inspectors in the market,

Testing the weight of pigs
By prodding them in their thinnest parts.
Why look for Tao by going 'down the scale of being'
As if that which we call 'least'
Had less of Tao?
Tao is Great in all things,
Complete in all, Universal in all,
Whole in all. These three aspects
Are distinct, but the Reality is One.

"Therefore come with me
To the palace of Nowhere
Where all the many things are One:
There at last we might speak
Of what has no limitation and no end.
Come with me to the land of Non-Doing:
What shall we there say—that Tao
Is simplicity, stillness,
Indifference, purity,
Harmony and ease? All these names leave me indifferent
For their distinctions have disappeared.
My will is aimless there.
If it is nowhere, how should I be aware of it?
If it goes and returns, I know not
Where it has been resting. If it wanders
Here then there, I know not where it will end.
The mind remains undetermined in the great Void.
Here the highest knowledge
Is unbounded. That which gives things
Their thusness cannot be delimited by things.
So when we speak of 'limits,' we remain confined
To limited things.
The limit of the unlimited is called 'fullness.'
The limitlessness of the limited is called 'emptiness.'
Tao is the source of both. But it is itself

Neither fullness nor emptiness.
Tao produces both renewal and decay,
But is neither renewal or decay.
It causes being and non-being
But is neither being nor non-being.
Tao assembles and it destroys,
But it is neither the Totality nor the Void."

WHOLENESS

"How does the true man of Tao
Walk through walls without obstruction,
Stand in fire without being burnt?"

Not because of cunning
Or daring;
Not because he has learned,
But because he has unlearned.

All that is limited by form, semblance, sound, color,
Is called *object*.
Among them all, man alone
Is more than an object.
Though, like objects, he has form and semblance,
He is not limited to form. He is more.
He can attain to formlessness.

When he is beyond form and semblance,
Beyond "this" and "that,"
Where is the comparison
With another object?
Where is the conflict?
What can stand in his way?

He will rest in his eternal place
Which is no-place.
He will be hidden
In his own unfathomable secret.
His nature sinks to its root
In the One.
His vitality, his power
Hide in secret Tao.

When he is all one,
There is no flaw in him
By which a wedge can enter.
So a drunken man, falling
Out of a wagon,
Is bruised but not destroyed.
His bones are like the bones of other men,
But his fall is different.
His spirit is entire. He is not aware
Of getting into a wagon
Or falling out of one.

Life and death are nothing to him.
He knows no alarm, he meets obstacles
Without thought, without care,
Takes them without knowing they are there.

If there is such security in wine,
How much more in Tao.
The wise man is hidden in Tao.
Nothing can touch him.

FROM THE GREEK OF CLEMENT OF ALEXANDRIA

SOLDIERS OF PEACE

Now the trumpet sounds with a mighty voice calling the sol-
 diers of the world to arms, announcing war:
And shall not Christ who has uttered His summons to peace
 even to the ends of the earth
Summon together His own soldiers of peace?
Indeed, O Man, He has called to arms with His Blood and
 His Word an army that sheds no blood:
To these soldiers He has handed over the Kingdom of Heaven.
The trumpet of Christ is His Gospel. He has sounded it in
 our ears
And we have heard Him.
Let us be armed for peace, putting on the armor of justice,
 seizing the shield of faith,
The helmet of salvation,
And sharpening the "sword of the spirit which is the Word of
 God."
This is how the Apostle prepares us peaceably for battle.
Such are the arms that make us invulnerable.
So armed, let us prepare to fight the Evil One.
Let us cut through his flaming attack with the blade which the
 Logos Himself has tempered in the waters (of Baptism).
Let us reply to His goodness by praise and thanksgiving.
Let us honor God with His divine Word:
"While thou art yet speak," He says, "Here I am."

THE DIATRIBE AGAINST THE OLD GODS

1. Zeus Is Dead

Zeus is snake no longer, nor swan, nor eagle
Nor erotic man.
He does not fly as god, nor chase boys
Nor make love, nor fight:
Yet there are now far more lovely women
Sweeter than Leda, more seductive than Semele . . . .
Where then is that eagle: Where that swan?
Where Zeus?
He and his wings have moldered;
He has, no doubt, not repented of loving and not learned
    temperance.
The myth is unveiled: Leda is dead.
And you are looking for your Zeus? Look not in heaven
But on earth. The Cretans, in whose island he lies buried,
They will tell you of him. Listen to Callimachus
In one of his hymns:
"The Cretans, Lord, have built thy tomb."
For (pardon me) Zeus, like Leda, is dead
Dead as a swan, dead as eagle, as erotic man,
And dead as serpent!

2. The Idol of Sarapis

Who was the great devil who, we are told, was judged worthy
    beyond others in the veneration of all?
That Egyptian Sarapis, of whom it is claimed that he had an
    image made without hands?
And yet Athenodoros, son of Sandon, trying to prove the an-
    cient origin of Sarapis,

Goes and contradicts himself by showing that it was a statue
with a definite origin.
For he tells us that Sesostris the Egyptian King, having con-
quered most of the peoples of Greece, came back to Egypt
bringing with him skilled artists.
He commissioned them to make a costly statue of Osiris his
forefather.
Bryaxis the demiurge, not the Athenian but another by the
same name, fashioned this statue.
He employed, in his creative work, a mixture of various
materials.
For he was able to get some filings of gold, silver, iron, lead
and even tin.
Not one precious stone of Egypt was lacking to him:
Dust of sapphires, hematite, emeralds and topaz.
He crushed this all together and tinted it with blue, which
made the surface of the figure turn out black.
Then having tempered all this with drugs that remained from
the embalming of Osiris and Apis, he formed his Sarapis.
This name signified that the work of his hands resulted from
a pooling of the honors and the funeral materials,
The combination of Osiris and Apis ending up as Osirapis.

3. The Priests of the Old Gods

Just take a look at the servants of the idols:
Filthy hair, soiled and torn clothes,
They are total strangers to the bathtub,
Their nails are like the claws of wild animals.
Many of them are even emasculated.
These facts show that the sacred precincts of the idols are
nothing more than tombs or prisons.
Such people mourn their gods instead of honoring them.

Their lives are more worthy of pity than of pious respect.
Seeing this can you still remain blind?
You do not turn your eyes toward the Master of all,
The Lord of the universe?
Will you not take refuge in the
Pity that comes from heaven, in order that you may escape
    these prisons?
For God in His great love for man, stays very close to man
Like the mother bird when the fledgling falls from the nest.
God the Father seeks His creature, heals it when it falls,
Chases away the wild beast, picks up the little one
And encourages him to fly back into the nest.

THE LOGOS OUR TEACHER

Now it seems to me that since the Word Himself has come
    down from heaven to us, we no longer have any need for
    the schooling of men,
Nor need we get excited any more over Athens or the rest of
    Greece, or Ionia either.
For if we have as Master the One who fills all things with His
    sacred strength by the Creation, salvation and the doing of
    all good,
By His laws, prophecies and teachings,
He is our teacher in all things,
And the whole world is now become Athens and Greece be-
    cause of the Word.
Do not then give your belief to the poetic myth of Minos the
    Cretan living in fellowship with Zeus, and refuse us your
    belief when we have become the disciples of God.
For we hold in trust the only true wisdom
Which the greatest philosophers have barely glimpsed

936

But which the disciples of Christ have received and announced to the world.

And indeed the whole Christ, if I may say so, is not divided.

He is not Barbarian or Jew or Greek, not man or woman.

He is the new man, made over entirely by the Holy Spirit of God.

Philosophy, the ancients tell us, is a prolonged consideration, aimed at attaining the eternal love of wisdom.

But the commandment of the Lord shines from afar, enlightening our eyes.

Receive Christ, receive sight, receive your light "in order to know well God and man" (*Iliad* 5:28).

"Delightful" is the Word that has enlightened us, "beyond gold and precious stones. More to be desired than honey and the honeycomb."

How indeed should He not be desirable who has enlightened the mind that was buried in darkness,

Who has given sharp perception "to the light-bearing eyes of the soul?" (Plato) Just as "without the sun the other stars would leave the world plunged in night" (Herakleitos).

So too if we had not known the Word and had not been illumined by His rays,

We would be no different from poultry stuffed with food in the dark,

For we would be in darkness, overfed and fattened for death.

Let us receive the Light, so that we may receive God.

Let us receive the Light and become disciples of the Lord.

For He has made this promise to the Father:

"I will make thy name known to my brothers: in the midst of the Church I will praise thee."

Sing to God thy Father and make Him known to me.

Thy words will save me, Thy song will teach me.

Up until now I have wandered far from the path in seeking God.

But since Thou dost enlighten me, O Lord, I find God through
Thee,
I receive the Father from Thee,
I have become co-heir with Thee since Thou art not ashamed
of Thy brother.
Let us put an end to our forgetfulness of truth.
Let us be rid of the ignorance, the darkness which veil our
eyes like fog, and look upon the true God,
Acclaiming Him with the cry of "Hail, O Light."
Light from Heaven has shone upon us who were buried in
the dark and prisoners in the shadow of death:
A Light purer than the sun, and sweeter than the life of this
earth.
This light is life everlasting, and everything that shares in it,
lives.
But night avoids the light, hides in fear, and gives way to the
Day of the Lord.
All has become unfailing Light, and the place of the setting
sun has become the place of its rising.
Such is the meaning of the "new creature."
For the "sun of justice" passing over the whole world in its
course, impartially visits all the family of man
In imitation of His Father "who makes His sun to rise upon
all alike."
And He distills for them the dew of truth.
He it is who has changed the place of the sun's setting into a
new east, death into life by His crucifixion.
Snatching man away from perdition He gives him a sure place
in heaven.
He takes up corruption and plants it in incorruption.
He transforms the earth into heaven.
He is God's farmer who sets up favorable signs and "calls the
peoples forth to work" (Aratos) at good.
He reminds them of the way of life according to truth.

He endows us with a truly great, divine inheritance, coming
    from our Father,
An inheritance that cannot be lost.
He divinizes men by a heavenly teaching,
Giving laws to their intellect and writing these laws in their
    heart.
What laws does He write in their hearts? These:
"All of them shall know God, from the little ones to the great
    ones."
"I shall be propitious to them," says God,
"And I shall no longer keep any memory of their sins."

THE NEW SONG

Amphion the Theban and Arion the Methymnian were both
    mythical and both singers
(So runs the song of the Greeks, still chanted in choirs);
By the power of music the latter charmed a dolphin and the
    former raised the walls of Thebes.
A Thracian, a skilled singer, (this also is a Greek myth)
    tamed the wild animals with nothing but song,
And trees, oak trees, he transplanted with his music!
I could also relate to you still another myth, brother of the
    above, about Eunomos the Locrian and the cricket of
    Delphi.
A Greek celebration of the dragon's death had brought them
    all together at Delphi
And they were applauding as Eunomos performed, the song
    being some hymn or lamentation
For the dragon (how should I know what?), but in any case
    it was a contest.

Eunomos was accompanying his song on the lyre and the day
was blazing hot.

Crickets were singing among the leaves all up the mountain-
side, burning in the sun.

They were singing, not indeed for the death of the dragon,
the dead Pythian, but

They hymned the all-wise God, in their own mode, far su-
perior to that of Eunomos.

A harp string breaks on the Locrian.

A cricket flies down on top of the lyre. She sings on the
instrument as though on a branch. The singer, harmoniz-
ing with the cricket's tune, goes on without the lost string.

Not by the song of Eunomos is the cricket moved, as the myth
supposes, or as is shown by the bronze statue the Delphians
erected, showing

Eunomos with his harp and his companion in the contest!

The cricket flies on her own and sings on her own.

The Greeks suppose her none the less to have sung *their*
music . . .

Very different from the mythical singer is the one I now pro-
pose to you:

He comes and instantly dissolves the bonds of bitter slavery to
the demon tyrants,

And with the kind and humane rule of piety

He leads back to heaven those who have been thrown down
upon the erath.

He alone has truly tamed the hardest of animals to subdue—
man.

For the lightminded among men are birds,

The deceitful are snakes,

The violent are lions,

Pleasure-lovers are swine

And the rapacious are wolves.

The senseless ones are wood and stone.

Even more senseless than stone
Is man sunk in error!

As witness to our words let the voice of the Prophets come
forth
Singing in harmony with Truth
Lamenting over those who spend their whole life in igno-
rance and folly.
"God is able from these stones to raise up children to Abra-
ham."
He it is who, pitying the manifold ignorance
And the hard hearts of those who have become stones as re-
gards the truth,
Has brought to life a God-fearing seed sensitive to virtue
In those very stones, the stone-worshipping nations.

See what power the new song has!
From stones, men,
From beasts it has made men.
Those otherwise dead, those without a share in life that is
really life
At the mere sound of this song
Have come back to life . . . .
Moreover He has structured the whole universe musically
And the discord of elements He has brought together in an
ordered symphony
So that the whole Cosmos is for Him in harmony.
Though He has left the sea unchained
He forbids her to trespass on the land.
The land too, instead of floating about
Is stabilized and placed by Him as the sea's boundary.
He it is also who has, with air,
Quieted the surge of fire
As though combining the Dorian and the Lydian modes,
And He has tamed the freezing rigors of the air

By the dancings and crossings of fire,
Thus blending together in one harmony
Those, among all the world's voices, which are most extreme.
And this pure song, sustaining all,
Uniting everything in harmony
Disposed from the center to the periphery
And from the ends to the center
Has brought into harmony this vast universe
Not according to Thracian music (which resembles Tubal
    Cain's)
But according to the fatherly will of God
Which David so eagerly sought.
And this One Who is from David and before David
This Word of God, looking beyond lyre and harp, mindless
    instruments,
By His Holy Spirit tunes the Cosmos
Especially this little cosmos, man, mind and body;
And He sings to God with this many-voiced instrument—
He accompanies His song with the instrument of man:
"For thou art to me a harp, a flute and a temple"
A harp by the unity of parts in one whole
A flute by the living breath
A temple by thy reason:
A harp that rings in harmony
A flute that breathes melody,
A temple that is the Lord's house.

FROM THE SPANISH OF ALFONSO CORTES

AEGEUS IN PRISON

Room of the guilty one
Evil place of bad luck
No presentiment of this
Was possible,
Now double your deathly terror,
Lend thy attraction to my works,
That my soul, thrust out of land and home,
May not dread a king's torment.

AIR

A child's song sounds behind the mud walls
The Plaza leads patrols of ancient ecstasy
As far as my house.

When the child's air, with little tired steps,
Wheels with the oboe dying along roofs,

And peoples with an ecstasy of dusk
The garden, full of distresses,
Wanting to speak
Words said among leaves. . . .

While in the mists
White folds of souls spume
Twist in mad delightful movements
When rubbed by winds. . . .

DIRTY SOULS

To silence I open the inertia of fluid
Distance we don't see, between one life and the next
Behind which the things we see observe us. . . .

I will raise up vast essences which keep
Secrets of dreams in the enormous heart,
I will unite details of Form, Light and Accent
Which wind's pale distances make one.

Between, above and under skies,
The distance of which I tell you,
Is the idea giving fragrance
To subtle relationships, slab
Stones,

Silence,
Stillness belonging to the soul of things!

Year 13.

GREAT PRAYER

Time is hunger, space is cold
Pray, pray, for prayer alone can quiet
The anxieties of void.

Dream is a solitary rock
Where the soul's hawk nests:
Dream, dream, during
Ordinary life.

ORGAN

I had a barrel organ and I cranked its distant tones
Watching, dog-eyed, how a blue day
Died among the old oak trees

And if a group of lovers came laughing through the roses
My voice shrilled like a bloody knife,
And over my soul's dust
The song wept;

Over my soul's dust in which my troubles
Played in yellow light;
Over my soul's dust where come
Like howls the voices of the little town.

SPACE SONG

The distance that lies from here
To some star that never existed
Because God has not yet managed
To pull the skin of night that far!

And to think we still believe greater
More useful world peace
Than the peace of one lone savage . . .

This relativity craze
In our contemporary life: There's
What gives space an importance
Found only in ourselves!

Who knows how long we'll take to learn
To live as stars—
Free in the midst of what is without end
And needing no one to feed us.

Earth knows nothing of the paths it daily travels—
Yet those paths are the conscience of earth. . . . But if
This is not so, allow me just
One question:—Time, you and I
Where are we,
I who live in you
And you who do not exist?

SUNDOWN

Sundown, white with ecstasy, hold
One minute more your step
In the blue, do not plunge altogether down
Your tranquil fortune,
O sundown,
The hour, sad in time, calls back to life the strong
Sight of Bethlehem:
The hound of night bays in this sky of a long
Time ago,
And down to the horizon goes
A troop of unknown bodies and shadows. . . .

946

THE FLOWER OF THE FRUIT

In the silence of flowers is found a sacred love
That changes the future.
Being is, for its own road, the end
If some grace grants it
Fragrance and quiet.

Sweet blood explodes upon the tongue
When you break
The body of fruit:
This is the word, vivid and absolute
With which each tree tries out its virtue.

Man is mystic tree and barely grasps
Space and Time if he can turn himself
Into soul's flower and veins' fruit;

For, from his double essence, unconfused
The bees of death draw honey
And the roses of life their fragrance.

THE THREE SISTERS

Hada is light, Estela is harmony
Theresa is grace. And in Theresa,
In Estela and Hada shines out that
Feast of love that crowns the day.

One sings. The other dreams. The other
Confides to wandering time unscathed illusions,

And in the smile of three
The ultimate truth of poetry appears.

Those three sisters in felicitous hours
Spin their lives on distaffs of invention
Like the incarnation of three twin
Dawns, and in their dances, in their games
They advance toward hope
Preceded by a glad
Chorus of blind infants.

THE TRUTH

Fate is dead. God is in man
What man is in God. Art caves in
Upon itself. Truth is a name
Reason a dilemma: all is a tomb.

The only law that centers you in virtue
Prophet, wise man, artist, proletarian,
Is mystery: if a womb is with child
If a tree with fruit: if the sun is every day.

No good more actual than the present now
No good future better than
Your good guess today,
Work is more useful than the dawn;
Stronger than destiny is pain.

Ideals? For what, if they are dreams?
Memories? What do they matter to what lies ahead?
Future is half the past: an end
Is what is every minute made real.

WHEN YOU POINT YOUR FINGER

For Margarita Debayle

When you point your finger
Oblivion stops short, surprised, and if you call
The Future turns around and lies at your feet.

Spring is nothing but
One of your words. The moon is nothing
But a memory of yours you left
Hooked in the bramble sky.

Beneath your heart there beats a
Sweet and constant living clock:
Time would fall apart
If this should stop.

Your step is fine and brief as if
Caught on the ground each time by sighs
Of sorry angels. When you go
By there stay perfumes swim-
ming in the air and talking about you!

There's a divine delight,
A flower of your soul, clearly declares
The day you love, love will be made over
Into something new!

In your body of harmonies is
Found all the geometry of heaven. In your soul
Is met the music of God!

If someone asks your origin, say
It is from Him you come. To those who do not know your
    way
Answer you go toward Thyself.

FROM THE SPANISH OF PABLO ANTONIO CUADRA

CUP WITH A JAGUAR FOR THE DRINKING OF HEALTH

He has stamped the clay with his hostile
But harmonious mark

And I with clay and blood
Upon this amphora
Copy his claw!

A ball of rage
Clenched over the earth
For the wine of the drunken accident
Hailed by your death.

FACES OF GIRLS LOOKING AT THEMSELVES IN THE RIVER

I view, in the flying time
Of this stream, my face unmoving.
The River of the East carries away the dead, but holds
Life in its transient mirror.
Tomorrow you shall hear my song
Upon the lips of girls
As they go down
To the river.

950

And in the waters of the East
Those faces shall pass away
That vanish, today, in my song . . .

LAMENT OF A MAIDEN FOR
THE WARRIOR'S DEATH

Ever since the old days
The rain weeps.
       And yet
Young is the tear,
Young is the dew.

Ever since the old days
Death has stalked.
       And yet
Your silence is new,
And new is my pain!

MEDITATION BEFORE AN ANCIENT POEM

The flower asked: "Will my scent,
Perhaps, survive me?"

The moon asked: "Shall I keep
Some light after perishing?"

But man said: "How is it that I end
And that my song remains among you?"

NAHOA URN, FOR A WOMAN

Two ways only
For the weary lover:

That of your face,
Which troubles my rest;

That of your heart,
Which gives rest.

Where is a word
To reach your heart's blood?

PAIN IS AN EAGLE CLINGING TO YOUR NAME

Whose is my pain, if I reject it
And it belongs to me? I bear
Upon my back an eagle, and his eye
Nails being onto my name.
Yet I am the "other" fleeing from his talon.
I carry the eagle on my shoulder. Liberty
Is torment.
        Nailed into my flesh,
His claw goads me to move
And reassures me: I am alive!

But his cry brings death.

THE BIRTH OF THE SUN

I have invented new worlds. I have dreamed
Nights built out of ineffable substances.

I have made burning stars, subtle lights
Next to half-closed eyes.

               Yet never
Can I recover that first day when our fathers
Emerged, with their tribes, from the humid jungle
And looked to the East. They listened to the roar
Of the jaguar, the song of birds; and they saw
Rise up a man with a burning face,
A youth with a resplendent face,
Whose looks, full of light, dried up the marshes,
A tall, burning youth whose face was aflame:
Whose face lit up the whole world!

THE DESPAIRING MAN DRAWS A SERPENT

I went up the hill
At moonrise.

She swore that she would come
By the south way.

A dusky hawk
Caught up the path
In his talons.

THE EYE IS A DOG HOWLING
IN THE DISTANCE

The jaguar king sent to my eyes
Two raging dogs.

He knew the poet
Was a hunter of magic birds,
Tracker of secret spoors,
Wandering archer.

But I said, when youth was over, to the perverse magician:
—"Chain these dogs of mine. I am
Weary. Let me rest under the trees."

—"Leave them," he said, "they would bite
The ankles of the goddess who forsakes you.
My sister, the stained moon, is glad
When a tired heart hastens onward."

THE JAGUAR MYTH

Rain, the earliest creature,
(Made even before the stars) said:
"Let there be moss that feels, and is alive."

And the jaguar's hide was made. But
Lightning struck its flint, saying:
"Let there be also his claw." Then came
The talon with cruelty sheathed in a caress.

"Let him move," said the wind
Upon its flutes, "with the rhythms of the breeze."
            And he started off
Like harmony, like the measures
With which the gods foreshadowed our dances.

But fire saw this and stayed his advance:
And went to the place where "yes" and "no" were parted

(The place where the serpent's tongue received its division).
Fire said: "Let his coat be made of light and shadow."

So his kingdom was death, indistinct
And blind.
            But men mocked
The inexorable, calling it "mad,"
When it united accident and crime.

Now not necessity with its devouring law
(Not the moon eaten by the earth to fill her hungry nights
Nor the weak one feeding with his blood
The glory of the strong)
But mystery, presiding over destruction. Fortune,
Fate blindfolding Justice—gods—
The rebels cried: "We will read in the stars
The hidden laws of destiny."

Lightning in his sleepless pallor,
Heard their clamor. He said:
"Alas for man!"
And kindled in the jaguar's empty sockets
The deadly nearness of a star.

THE SECRET OF THE BURNING STARS

For Mario Cajina-Vega

To him who fought for liberty
Was given a star next door
To the shining mother
Dead in giving dawn to life.

—"Was it great, your suffering?" asked
The Warrior.
                    —"Not so great as the joy
Of giving a new man to the world."
—"And your wound," she asked,
"Was it deep? Did it burn?"
                    —"Not so much
As the joy of giving a new world to man."
—"And did you know your son?"
                    —"Never."
—"And did you know the fruit of your battle?"
                    "I died too soon."
—"Do you sleep?" asked the Warrior.
The mother replied: "I dream."

THE WORLD IS A ROUND
EARTHENWARE PLATE

A mean fate surrounds our life with fear.
Whichever way we turn, we meet
Beasts lying in wait.

The bat, in the East, seeks
Possession of your shadow.
In the West, the crocodile
Fishes for your secrets.
Eagles, in the South, destroy
All traces of your history.
In the North, the jaguar
Chases your future star.

Ah, tell me,
Who can protect my inmost heart?

956

URN WITH A POLITICAL PROFILE

The chief is silent:
—(I draw his silent face.)

The chief is powerful:
—(I draw his mighty hand.)

The chief is leader of armed men:
—(I draw the skulls of dead soldiers.)

WRITTEN NEXT TO A BLUE FLOWER

"I fear to draw the wing of the sparrow
Lest my brush harm
His tiny liberty."

  Let the man of power
Remember this law of the master
When he legislated for the weak.

  Let the maiden pay attention
To this potter's proverb
When my lips approach her.

FROM THE SPANISH OF MIGUEL HERNANDEZ

THE TWO PALM TREES

Love rose up between us
Like the moon between the two palm trees
That never embraced

Private rustling of the two bodies
Flowing in waves, to a gentle song—
The hoarse voice was torn,
Tormented. The lips were stone.

The need to clasp: it stirred flesh
Lit up bones with flame
But arms wanting to reach
Died amid arms

Love, the moon, passed
Between us. Devoured
Our lonely bodies.
We are two specters seeking
Each other: Finding
Each other far.

THE GLORIA IN EXCELSIS

Roman Missal

Glory to God in the highest
And peace on earth
To men of good will.

We praise Thee; we bless Thee; we adore Thee;
We give Thee glory;
We give Thee thanks for Thy great glory.

Lord, God, heavenly King,
God, Father almighty.

Lord, God, Lamb of God,
The Father's Son:

Who takest away the world's sins,
Have mercy on us.

Who takest away the world's sins,
Receive our prayer.

Who sittest at the Father's right hand,
Have mercy on us:

For Thou only
Art holy;

Thou alone
Lord;
Thou alone Most High,
Christ Jesus,
With the Holy Ghost
In God the Father's glory.

Amen.

PROSE IN ADVENT TIME

11th century, French-Roman Missal

Let us sing together to our God, Who made all things
And Who created time,
Who made the sky, and filled it with much light
And with the different stars—
Who made the sun, for the world's finery:
The moon, the grace of night, and all things shining:
The sea, the land, the highlands, and the level places,
And the deep rivers:
The air, whose open distances birds, in their flights,
And winds traverse, and showers of rain.

O all these things together, God, Our Father,
Are marshaled under Thy command:
Now, and forever, and never an end to their service,
World without end!
Their praise is Thy glory.
Who, for our salvation,
Didst send to earth, to suffer, guiltless, but for our sins,
Thine only Son.

960

Thee, Holy Trinity, we pray
To rule and guard our souls and bodies
And grant us pardon for our sins.

Amen.

Jubilemus omnes una Deo nostro qui creavit omnia,
Per quem condita sunt saecula;
Coelum quod plurima luce coruscat, et diversa sidera;
Sol mundi schema, noctium decus luna, cunctaque
     splendentia,
Mare, solum, alta, plana et profunda flumina;
Aeris ampla spatia: quae discurrunt aves, venti atque pluvia.
Haec simul cuncta tibi soli Deo Patri militant,
Nunc et in aevum, sine fine, per saecula:
Laus eorum tua gloria:
Qui pro salute nostra Prolem unicam,
Pati in terra misisti sine culpa, sed ob nostra delicta.
Te, sancta Trinitas, precamur ut corpora nostra et corda regas
     et protegas et donas peccatorum veniam.

Amen.

FROM THE FRENCH OF RAISSA MARITAIN

AUTUMN

Branch on bird
Singing and losing leaves
Autumn held the bow
Of the whimpering violin
In wind out of the west
Murmuring sad things
The bird wept by itself
Flowering the dark elm
With tears in blossoms
Of glass and new gold
Both branch and sparrow
In mist grey and pure
Marry their homesickness
With the night's mystery

CHAGALL

Chagall came with long strides
Out of melancholy Russia
With a pack on his back
Full of violins and roses
With lovers lighter than angels
And frock-coated beggars

Musicians and archangels
And synagogues

He has meadows and villages
Rocking in the storm
Inns dances and beauties
Windows in the rainbows
Lily thrones for the brides
Under the silk scarlet canopy
The whole Bible in pictures
All the great personages
Longbearded and longrobed
With their lambs and pigeons
Spangled cocks and cows
Animals from the Ark and La Fontaine

Crowds and weddings kisses and tears
Chimerical horses
Ladies and cavaliers
Circuses
He has painted all the world
And nothing is left out
All the colors of the sun
Are dancing there

Then he has a Christ
Spread across a lost world
In a vast ivory space
At His feet a candlestick is lit
With six candles by mistake
While in the sky desolate men
Watch what goes on

At the four quarters of the horizon
Fire and flame

Poor Jews from everywhere go their way
No one asks them to stay
They have no place left on earth
Not a stone to rest on
Hence they must lodge at last in heaven
The wandering Jews
Whether alive or dead
With those friends of Chagall
Who here below have it so bad
They are always in the air on clouds
These pensive rabbis
And players of violins
Who make music
On their own hearts
In the snow

EURYDICE

Eurydice is impossible
If Orpheus looks away
Eurydice doubts and weeps
If Orpheus looks at her
Eurydice dies

GLASS ORCHARD

Glass orchard
Snow blossoms
In the firmament

Of tears
The clean star
Guards us
From veils of sleep

MOSAIC: ST. PRAXED'S

So like a quiet pigeon in a hollowed rock
You stand there in the wall's curve
Made of stone needled tapestry
In this dim sheltered paradise
Mary made of love art and poetry

In the obscure and flaming chapel
Where gold and ruby hold the azure
Conch of sweetly burning peace
You welcome me refuge pure
To see you O soul's delight

Deeply forgetful of the evil by our side
We sail above our strange agony
Chained utterly Mary to your joy

PILLARS

Pillars of vanquished lands
O lonely thought-filled ones
Crowned with massive leaves
With you the unsubmitting heart

Proud outraged queens
Uprooted pillars
Views a forbidden world
Sky earth and isles
All made of my exile

RECIPE

Not heart not soul—some spirit
Very little azure—a lot of palms

THE GLOVE

A silk glove at my window
Forgotten by destiny
Will this glove fit my hand
Which one right or left
The liar glove has no more fingers
Destiny got the wrong window
And left me too little silk

THE CLOUD

A cloud in the sky
The vehicle of Ezechiel

In the meadow
Under the peach tree

Roses shine
You appear

Tears flow
In the gentle air
On your face
O messenger

THE LAKE

The lake full of glass houses
Rocking their frail mass
Home of sincere persons
Who dwell there as on islands
Silent so very long

Moon and sky there swing
Oars go in the windows
Sails shiver in this mirror

And those persons recall
Very old adventures
In houses on the land

THE PRISONER

Thy servant is in irons
In the shadow of death
Lord deliver him
I see his face behind bars
Like a saint's face in holy pictures

His wide face protruding eyes
Fringe of black hair on his brow
Streaked with white wool
He looks like the Christ
Of Quentin Matsys
He gazes straight in front
Stunned at his misfortune
He sees God's sky
And that all will go well
No he is not yet painted
In the holy pictures
He sits on his bed
His head in his arms
He weeps
Alone among enemies
Who hate all he loves
For whom his kindness his intelligence
Are objects of contempt
Prisoner of his innocence
He keeps patience
Like his Master Jesus Christ
Like Him sorrowful unto death
He has so loved Justice
He is like the Christ
Of Quentin Matsys
He is learning
The language of heaven

THE RESTORATION OF THE PICTURES

We were in Rome not far from the Piazza di Spagna in the midst of a thick and restless crowd, and we too were anxious.

Was war coming? Then, to the left in the sky, appeared a mass of light. Amid the clearness of daylight it came forth quite distinct. As it came, it looked at first like a mass of stars. The stars gradually increased in size and we saw they were a cohort of angels. And all at once the angels were among us. They marched in closed ranks like an army of young men clothed in black and white. Grace and joy spread everywhere as they passed. Everything became beautiful with a resplendent beauty, extremely well defined.

So then we found ourselves once more in the Palazzo Taverna, still in the same aura of great, mysterious meaning. The walls of the reception rooms painted with mythological scenes, shone with a singular beauty, now no longer the light and gracious and somewhat dimmed beauty which they have, but magnificently. Each design was set out with a gold line and stood forth in relief like Cordova leather. Thus, in every room we traversed, each object, great or small, books, furniture, the crowded desk in the study, the Biblical scenes painted in a cold flat style on the walls of my own room, everything was transfigured, picked out with a gold line, dazzling, delicately modeled and as it were ennobled with an inexhaustible significance. All things, and the least things, were radiant with grave light, rich with fullness, warm as bronze and gold. Our hearts overflowed with joy reaching out toward a beneficent mystery whose immensity flooded us with peace.

After a fairly long time the angelic cohorts began to leave us and the joy began to pass from our souls. When we had traversed with the angels the rooms in which we lived we felt their presence without seeing them. We saw them once again as they took their leave. They comforted us by saying: we will be back again soon. I awoke happy, sorrowful with my regret at the departed light, fortified by the grace of the dream.

FROM THE CHINESE OF MENG TZU

THE OX MOUNTAIN PARABLE

i

Master Meng said: There was once a fine forest on
    the Ox Mountain,
Near the capital of a populous country.
The men came out with axes and cut down the trees.
    Was it still a fine forest?
Yet, resting in the alternation of days and nights,
    moistened by dew,
The stumps sprouted, the trees began to grow again.
Then out came goats and cattle to browse on the young shoots.
The Ox Mountain was stripped utterly bare.
And the people, seeing it stripped utterly bare,
Think the Ox Mountain never had any woods on it at all.

ii

Our mind too, stripped bare, like the mountain,
Still cannot be without some basic tendency to love.
But just as men with axes, cutting down the trees
    every morning
Destroy the beauty of the forest,
So we, by our daily actions, destroy our right mind.

Day follows night, giving rest to the murdered forest,
The moisture of the dawn spirit
Awakens in us the right loves, the right aversions.

With the actions of one morning we cut down this love,
And destroy it again. At last the night spirit
Is no longer able to revive our right mind.

Where, then, do our likes and dislikes differ from those
    of animals?
In nothing much.
Men see us, and say we never had in us anything but evil.
Is this man's nature?

iii

Whatever is cultivated rightly, will surely grow.
Whatever is not cultivated rightly must surely perish.
Master Kung (Confucius) said:
    Grasp it firmly and you will keep it.
    Grasp it loosely, and it will vanish out of your hand.
    Its comings and goings have no fixed times:
    No one knows its country!

Of man's right mind, of this only does he speak!

FROM THE SPANISH OF NICANOR PARRA

BUTTERFLY

In the garden that seems an abyss
A butterfly catches the eye:
Interesting, the zigzag flight
The brilliant colors
And the black circles
At the points of the wings.
Interesting
The form of the abdomen.

When it turns in the air
Lit by a green ray
As when it gets over the effect
Produced by dew and pollen
Clinging to the obverse of a flower
I do not let it out of sight
And if it disappears
Beyond the railings of the garden fence
At an excessive speed
Or because the garden is small
I follow mentally
For a moment or two
Until I recover
My reason.

I MOVE THAT WE ADJOURN THE MEETING

Ladies and Gentlemen:
I am going to ask just one question:
Are we children of the Sun
Or children of the earth?
Because if we are children only of the earth
I see no reason
Why we should go on shooting the film:
I move that we adjourn the meeting.

MUMMIES

One mummy walks on snow
Another mummy walks on ice
Another mummy walks on sand.

A mummy walks through the meadow
A second mummy goes with her.

One mummy talks on the phone
Another mummy views herself in the mirror.

One mummy fires her revolver.

All the mummies change places
Almost all the mummies withdraw.

A few mummies sit down at the table
Some mummies offer cigarettes
One mummy seems to be dancing.

One mummy older than the others
Puts her baby to her breast.

PARADISE OF SQUARES

Whoever wants to make it
To the paradise of squares
Must take the road of art
For art's sake and swallow
A lot of spit.
The novitiate has practically
No end.

List of things he needs to know:
Artfully tying the necktie
Passing out his card
Shaking off his shoes for comfort
Looking in full-length mirrors
Self-study front and profile
Downing a dose of cognac
Telling a viola from a violin
Receiving visitors in pajamas
Prevention of falling hair
And swallowing a lot of spit.

Everything has to be in his files
if his wife gets interested in somebody else
I recommend the following tricks:
Shaving with razor blades
Admiration of the beauties of nature
Crackling a piece of paper
Carrying on a telephone conversation

Shooting off a parlor rifle
Fixing his nails with his teeth
And swallowing a lot of spit.

If the square desires to make an impression
In society
He must know how to
Go on all fours
To sneeze and smile at the same time
To waltz on the edge of the cliff
Worship the organs of sex
Take his clothes off in front of a mirror
Remove the petals of a rose with a pencil
And swallow a lot f spit.

After all this we might inquire
Was Jesus Christ in middle-class society?

As you see, in order to make it
To the paradise of squares you need to be
A: accomplished acrobat
In order to make it to paradise you need to be
An accomplished acrobat.

With what good reason does the true artist
Spend his time killing dragonflies!

To get out of the vicious circle they recommend
the *acte gratuit:*

To appear and disappear
Walk in a cataleptic trance
Waltz on a pile of junk
Cradle an old man in one's arms
Without removing one's eyes from his

Ask the time from a man about to die
Spit in the hollow of your hand
Show up in tuxedo at a fire
Cut through a funeral procession
Go beyond the feminine sex
Lift the burial slab to see
If they are growing trees in there
Cross from one sidewalk to the other
Without explaining why or when
By the sole power of your word
With your movie-star mustache
At the speed of thought.

POETRY ENDS WITH ME

I do not claim to put an end to anything
I have no illusions in this matter
I would like to go on with my verses
But inspiration has come to an end.
Poetry has enjoyed good health
My health has been
Terribly bad.

What do I gain by saying
I have been in good health
Poetry has been sick
When all know that I am the guilty one.

So that's fine: I pass for a fool!

Poetry has been in the best of health
My health has been
Terribly bad.
Poetry ends with me.

SODA FOUNTAINS

I take advantage of breakfast time
To examine my conscience
How many arms do I still have to open?
How many black petals still to close?
Like as not I am a survivor!

The radio reminds me
Of my duties: classes, poems
With a voice that seems to come
From the bottom of the grave.
The heart knows not what to think.

I make out I am looking in the mirrors.
A customer sneezes at his wife
Another lights a cigarette
Another reads the news.

What are we to do, trees without leaves,
On such a cruel day.
So cowardly and ceremonious a night!

Answer, dark sun
Turn on for a moment
Even if then
You go out forever.

THE IMPERFECT LOVER

A pair of newlyweds
Halt before a tomb
She is in severe white.

To observe without being seen
I hide behind a pillar.

While the sad bride
Weeds her father's grave
The imperfect lover devotes himself
To reading a magazine.

WHAT THE DECEASED HAD TO SAY ABOUT HIMSELF

With great satisfaction I take
This marvelous opportunity
Offered me by the science of death
To make a few clarifications
Concerning my adventures on earth.
Later on, when I have time,
I shall speak of life beyond the grave.

I want to laugh a little
The way I did while living:
Knowledge and laughter are one.

When I was born my mother asked:
What am I to do with this tadpole?
I applied myself to filling sacks of flour
I applied myself to breaking windows
I hid behind the rosebushes.

I started out in business
But commercial documents
Gave me goose flesh.

My worst enemy was the telephone.

I had two or three natural children.

A shyster fresh out of hell
Was furious at me for "the crime
Of abandoning your first wife"
He asked, "Why did you abandon her?"
I replied, smashing the desk with my fist,
"That woman abandoned herself."

I almost went out of my mind.

My relations with religion?
I crossed the Andes on foot
Disguised as a Capuchin friar
Changing rats into doves.

I no longer remember how or why
"I embraced the literary career."

I wished to startle my readers
Through humor
But I made a most unfortunate impression.

I became known as a nervous wreck
And of course I was sent to the penitentiary
For sticking my nose into the abyss.

I lay on my back and fought like a cat.

I wrote in Araucanian and in Latin
While the others wrote in French
Verses that made you shake all over.

In these unusual verses
I mocked sun and moon
I mocked sea and cliff

But the silliest thing of all
I mocked death.[1]
Childishness, perhaps? No,
Tactlessness
But I made fun of death.[2]

My inclination for the occult sciences
Earned me a note of infamy
As an eighteenth-century charlatan
But I am sure
The future may be read
In smoke, clouds, flowers.
In also profaned altars
Until taken in the act.
Moral: watch out for the clergy!

I wandered in parks and gardens
As a new Quixote
But I never fought a windmill
Never got mad at sheep.

Do I make myself clear?

I was known in the whole district
For my childish extravagances
I who was a venerable old man.

I lingered talking with beggars
Not for religious reasons
But only to abuse patience.

In order not to have difficulties with the public
I pretended to have clear ideas

[1] Mortals imagine themselves immortal.
[2] I thought everything was funny.

980

I expressed myself with great authority
But the situation was delicate
I had Plato mixed up with Aristotle.

In desperation, totally insane,
I invented the artificial woman.

But I was not a clown after all
Because I got serious all of a sudden [3]
I plunged into a dark abyss
I put on the light at midnight
A prey to blackest thoughts
Which seemed sockets without eyes
I hardly dared to move a finger
Fearing to vex the spirits
I remained gazing at the vial.

You could make a movie
Of my adventures on earth
But I do not want to make my confession
I only want to say these few words:

Absurd erotic situations
Repeated attempts at suicide
Yet I died a natural death.

The funeral was very nice
The casket was, I thought, perfect.
Though I am not a race horse
Thanks for the pretty wreaths.

Don't go laughing in front of my grave
I might break through the coffin
And take off for heaven like a rocket.

[3] Being a cherub or defeated demon.

FROM THE LATIN OF PAULUS DIACONUS

"UT QUEANT . . ."

Hymn for the Feast of St. John the Baptist's Nativity. 8th century.

(Vespers)
Now that thy servants all may sing
The wonder of thy works, O great Saint John,
With liquid voices, fine and free,
Deliver all our lips from sin!

Lo, then, the messenger, from high heaven coming,
Tells to thy father, in due order,
First thy birth, now near at hand, thy name,
And then thy life's appointed mission.

But he does not believe
The promises of heaven:
Therefore the fluent syllables of speech die in his throat
Thou at thy birth didst soon restring
The instrument of his robbed voice.

Curled in the secret cradle of the womb
Thou wast aware of the great King His bride-bed keeping
And the two mothers, each enlightened by her infant
Sudden saw clear what mystery was there.

(Matins)
Even in thy frailest years, thou soughtest haven,

Far from the squadrons of the city
In a desert cavern
There to keep thy clean life unstained
Even by lightest sin, by slip of tongue.

O Prophet, there the camel offered thee
His coarse coat, for thy shoulders' covering:
And goatskin girt thee.
Thou drankest at rare pools:
Honey and locusts were, together, all thy dinner.

The other prophets only sang
With future-seeing hearts, that Light was coming:
But O! Thy long forefinger
Finds out the very Lamb,
Who comes to take away the whole world's sins.

Nowhere, across the earth, in its vast compass
Was ever born a holier than John,
Who was held worthy to baptize in water
The One who was to wash away the crimes of Time.

(Lauds)
O man of boundless joy, of mighty merits
Knowing no fault to stain thy snowy cleanness,
Martyr most powerful, and dweller in the woods,
Thou art the greatest prophet!

Ten times three, or twice as much again
Are some men crowned with interest, on their talents,
The threefold sown in thee, at birth, harvests a hundred,
Piling thy brows with bands of glory.*

   * Cf. Mark 4:8–20.

983

O now, thou strong in merits, come
Break up our hearts' resisting stone:
Smooth out our rugged roads, make plain
Our twisting and uncertain courses,

So that, when the compassionate Creator
And Redeemer of the world comes down
He may find all our souls' ways clean of sin,
And deign to place His blessed feet, and walk therein.

Let all the citizens of heaven hymn Thee with their praises
O God, One, in simplicity, and Three
And we Thy suppliants, beg Thee pardon for our sins:
Praying Thee, spare us whom Thou hast redeemed.

Amen.

FROM THE PERSIAN

TOMB COVER OF IMAM RIZA

At Meshed, Iran

Here is the threshold of holiness in the dust of the road
    where mighty kings have laid their heads and crowns
Men and spirits, birds and beasts, fairies and demons
    all have laid their heads down in the court of His presence.
No wonder that they lay the head of service and obedience
    on the threshold of Him descended from the prophet
For having laid the hand of seeking on the skirt of Haidar
    their desire is fulfilled
Seeking for grace the holy cherubim have spread
    their pinions under the footsteps of His visitors.

For the being of Abbas the nine round canopies of heaven
    were raised
    for the life of Abbas and the enduring of his line.

In the hand of heaven the radiant sun was fixed
    to light the steps of those who came before His court
The dust of their passing is a lure baited with mush
    and the earth of their footsteps a snare with ambergris
They are drunk as with wine in union with the Friend's
    beauty
    or even as if they had set foot in paradise

Without weariness of the road they reach the fountain of life
  and leave to Alexander for his portion the realms of
    darkness.
Greater joy than the water of life is their pleasure
  who give their hearts to the winebearer of Kanthar.

FROM THE PORTUGUESE
OF FERNANDO PESSOA

TWELVE POEMS FROM
THE KEEPER OF THE FLOCKS

1

My gaze is clear as a sunflower.
My way is to walk the roads
Looking right and left
And sometimes looking behind me . . .
What I see at each moment
Is that which I never
Caught sight of before.

I have the knack of full awareness
The knack of essential astonishment
That an infant might experience
If at birth he were aware
That he was actually born!
I feel myself born at each moment
Into the everlasting newness
Of the world.

I believe in the world
As I believe in a daisy
Because I see it.
But I do not think about it
Because to think is to not-understand.

The world was not made
For us to think about it
(To think is to have sick vision)
But for us to look at it and assent.

I have no philosophy: I have senses . . .
If I talk of nature, that is not because
I know what nature is
But because I love it, and love is for this only:
For he who loves never knows what he loves
Or why he loves, or what love is.

Loving is eternal innocence
And the only innocence is not-thinking.

2

Lightly, lightly, so lightly
A light wind goes by
And goes on going by
Always so lightly;
And I know not
What I am thinking
Nor do I attempt
To find out.

3

I do not bother with rhymes.
Seldom do you see two trees, identical,
Side by side.

I think and write
The way flowers wear their
Color
Yet less perfectly in my mode of expression.
I lack the divine simplicity
Of being entirely my own exterior
And nothing more.

I look, I am moved.
I am moved as running water moves
When the ground slopes,
And my verse is as natural
As the breeze rising.

4

The Tagus is finer than the creek
That runs through my village
But the Tagus is not finer than the creek
That runs through my village
Because the Tagus is not the creek
That runs through my village.

The Tagus has big boats on it
And on it sails still
(For those who see everything
That is not there)
The memory of frigates.

The Tagus comes down out of Spain
And the Tagus enters the sea in Portugal:
This everybody knows.

Few know about my village creek,
Where it comes from, where it goes.
Because of this, belonging to few
My village creek is
Greater, more free.

Down the Tagus you go out into the world:
Beyond the Tagus lies America,
With fortune for such as find it.
No one ever thought what might exist
Beyond my village creek.

My village creek makes no one think of anything:
He who is by it, is by it.

5

What we see of things is the things themselves.
Why should we see one thing if another were there?
Why should seeing and hearing delude us
If seeing and hearing are seeing and hearing?

The main thing is knowing how to see
Knowing how to see without being in thought:
To see when you see—
And not to think when you see
Or see when you think.

But (woe to us with dressed-up souls)
This demands deep study
Learning to unlearn,
Confinement in the freedom of that convent

Whose perpetual nuns (the poets say) are the stars
And flowers the Magdalens convinced for a day
But where, in the end, the stars are stars only
And flowers are flowers only
Which is why we call them
Stars and flowers.

6

If peope insist on my having
Mysticism, all right, I have it
I am a mystic, but of the body only.
My soul is simple
It does not think.

My mysticism is in not wanting to know—
Living without reflection.

I do not know what nature is: I sing nature.
I live on top of a hill
In a lonely whitewashed house
And that is my definition.

7

If I sometimes say that flowers smile
And if I happen to say
That rivers sing,
This does not mean I think there are smiles in flowers,

Songs in the running of rivers . . .
Such is my way to make false men aware
Of the truly real existence
Of rivers and flowers.

Since I write for them to read me, I sacrifice myself at times
To the stupidity of their feelings . . .
In this I do not agree
With myself: yet give myself
Absolution: I am that serious being
Nature's spokesman,
Since there are men who do not know
Nature's language—
Which is no language at all.

8

Last evening a city man
Was talking in the hotel door
To everyone, including me.

He talked of justice, of the struggle to obtain
Justice, of the workers
Suffering: of unending work
Of hungry men, of rich men turning
Their backs to it all.

Then, looking at me, he saw me with tears
In my eyes. He smiled, happy,
Thinking I felt the same hatred he felt
And the compassion
He claimed to feel.

(But I was hardly listening to him.
What do I care about people
And what they suffer, or suppose they suffer?
Let them be like me—they will not suffer.
All the ill in the world comes from people interfering
With one another:
Wanting to do good, wanting to do evil.
Our soul, heaven and earth, these are enough:
To want more is to lose these and be wretched.)

What I was thinking when this friend of man
Spoke (and this moved me to weep)
Was that the far murmur of cowbells
In the evening air
Was nothing like small chapel bells
Where flowers and brooks might have heard Mass
Along with simple souls
Simple as mine.

(Praise be to God I am not good and have
The natural selfishness of flowers
And rivers, going on their way
Concerned only, and not knowing it,
To flower and go.
This is the only mission in the world:
This—to exist clearly
And to know how
Without thinking about it.)

The man fell silent,
He viewed the setting sun.
But what have sunsets to do
With haters and lovers?

9

Rather the flying bird, leaving no trace
Than the going beast
Marking the earth with his track.

The bird flies by and forgets
(As is only right). The beast
Where he no longer is
(And is therefore no use)
Marks that he was there before
(Which is also no use).

For to remember is to betray
Nature, since the nature of yesterday
Is not nature.
What has been, is nothing.
Remembering
Is failure to see.

Move on, bird, move on, teach me
To move on.

10

Poor flowers in geometric beds
Of formal gardens:
They seem to dread the police . . .
And yet so fair, they flower in the same way,
With the same ancient smile
They had for the gaze of the first man
When he saw they were out
For the first time, and lightly touched them
Wondering if they spoke!

11

The "mystery of things"—where is it found?
Where is it, that it does not appear
At least long enough for us to see
It is a mystery?
What does the river, what does the tree
Know about it?
And, I who know no more about it than they,
What do I know about it?
Whenever I look at things and think
What men think about them,
I laugh like the stream
Falling with a cool sound
Over the stones.
For the only hidden meaning things have
Is that they have no hidden meaning.
Stranger than all that is strange,
Than poets' dreams and philosophical ideas
Is this: things are actually
Just what they appear to be
And there is nothing about them to understand.
Yes, here is what my senses learned
All by themselves:
Things do not have meanings: they have existence.
Things are the only hidden meanings of things.

12

The bus has gone by
Down the street and vanished:
By which the street is neither improved

Nor, for that matter, spoiled.
So with every act of man
All over the world:
We take nothing away
Leave nothing behind.
We pass and forget.
As for the sun—each morning
It rises on time.

FROM THE LATIN OF SEDULIUS

A SOLIS ORTUS CARDINE

4th century—Hymn for Lauds, Christmas Day

Nor from the compass-quarter of the rising sun
To the world's end, we sing
Our Christ and King
Born of the Virgin Mary.

The Blessed Maker of the universe
Puts on the garment of His servant's body,
And, lest He lose His handiwork,
He comes among us, saving flesh with Flesh.

Grace of heaven enters His chaste Mother's womb,
And mysteries beyond her fathoming
Deep in her girl-life bide and grow.

Her virgin body's house has suddenly become
God's Temple!
Her innocence, that knows not man,
Is quickened at a word, and bears His Son.

And now the birth that Gabriel foretold
Is come to pass:
This is the One Whom John, unborn,
Hailed with a leap in womb-house hiding.

He let them put His Body in the straw
He did not hate His crib
And He by Whom even the birds are fed,
Is happy with a little milk.

The heaven-dwelling citizens rejoice in choirs
And angels sing to God,
And shepherds come to view
The Shepherd, the Creator of the world.

We give Thee glory, Lord,
Born of the Blessed Virgin,
And to the Father and to the Holy Ghost,
World without end,

                        Amen.

FROM THE SPANISH OF CÉSAR VALLEJO

ANGER

Anger which breaks a man into children,
Which breaks the child into two equal birds,
And after that the bird into a pair of little eggs:
The poor man's anger
Has one oil against two vinegars.

Anger which breaks a tree into leaves
And the leaf into unequal buds
And the bud into telescopic grooves;
The poor man's anger
Has two rivers against many seas.

Anger which breaks good into doubts
And doubt into three similar arcs
And then the arc into unexpected tombs;
The poor man's anger
Has one steel against two daggers.

Anger which breaks the soul into bodies
And the body into dissimilar organs
And the organ into octave thoughts;
The poor man's anger
Has one central fire against two craters.

BLACK STONE ON TOP OF A WHITE STONE

I shall die in Paris, in a rainstorm,
On a day I already remember.
I shall die in Paris—it does not bother me—
Doubtless on a Thursday, like today, in autumn.

It shall be a Thursday, because today, Thursday
As I put down these lines, I have set my shoulders
To the evil. Never like today have I turned
And headed my whole journey to the ways where I am alone.

César Vallejo is dead. They struck him,
All of them, though he did nothing to them.
They hit him hard with a stick and hard also
With the end of a rope. Witnesses are: the Thursdays,
The shoulder bones, the loneliness, the rain and the roads. . . .

ESTAIS MUERTOS

You people are dead.
What a strange manner of being dead. Anyone might say that
you were not.
But, in truth, you are dead.

You float like nothing behind that membrane which, sus-
pended from zenith to nadir, comes and goes from dusk to
dusk, trembling in front of the sonorous box of a wound
which to you is painless. Well, I assure you that life is in
the mirror and that you are the original: death.

While the wave goes and while the wave comes, with what
impunity one can be dead! Only when the waters swell and

break on the shores in front of them, and when the waves pile one on top of the other, then you transfigure yourselves and, imagining you are about to die, you discover the sixth string which does not belong to you.

You are dead, never having at any time before this been alive. Anyone might think that since you do not exist now, you might have existed at some other time. But in truth you are the cadavers of a life that never was. Pathetic fate, never to have been anything at any time, but only dead! To be a dry leaf without ever at any time having been a green one. Orphaned beyond all other orphans!

Yet for all that the dead are not, and cannot be, cadavers of a life they have not lived. They have forever died of life. You are dead.

PEACE, THE WASP . . .

Peace, the wasp, the bung, the hillsides,
The dead man, the ten liter bottles, the owl,
Places, the spider, the tombs, the tumbler, the dark women,
Unknowing, the kettle, the acolyte,
Drops, forgetfulness,
Power, the cousins, the archangel, the needle,
The parish priests, ebony, lack of skill,
The part, the type, the stupor, the soul. . . .

Easy to handle, covered with saffron, everlasting, spotless,
Easy to carry, old, thirteen, covered with blood,
They have been photographed, made ready, they have
    swollen up,

Joined together, broad, they have put on ribbons, they are
    perfidious. . . .

Burning, comparing,
Living, flying in a rage,
Striking, analyzing, listening, meddling,
Dying, bearing up, getting themselves a place, weeping. . . .

After, these here,
After, up above,
Perhaps, while, behind, so much, so never,
Below, maybe, far,
Always, that one, tomorrow, how much,
How much . . . !

The horrible, the sumptuary, the very slow,
The portly, the fruitless,
The ill-fated, causing us to twitch, the wet, the fatal,
The all, the most-pure, the gloomy,
The bitter, the satanic, the tactile, the profound. . . .

Appendix VII
DRAFTS AND FRAGMENTS

A PRAYER OF THANKSGIVING WRITTEN
FOR VICTOR HAMMER

O Tu Pater splendoris Dator luminis
Ad Te gaudens precor restituto lumine
Da quaeso mihi servulo tecum perpetuam
Nox ubi non contristet corda vel umbra diem.

O Thou Father of splendor, Giver of light
To Thee I pray in joy, with light restored
Grant I beg to me Thy servant everlasting
Day in which no night makes sad the heart, and no shadow.

APRIL 4th 1968

For Martin Luther King

On a rainy night
On a rainy night in April
When everybody ran
Said the minister

On a balcony
Of a hotel in Tennessee
"We came at once
Upstairs"

On a night
On a rainy night in April
When the shot was fired
Said the minister

"We came at once upstairs
And found him lying
After the tornado
On the balcony
We came at once upstairs"

On a rainy night
He was our hope
And we found a tornado
Said the minister.

And a well dressed white man
Said the minister.
Dropped the telescopic storm

And he ran
(The well-dressed minister of death)
He ran
He ran away

And on the balcony
Said the minister
We found
Everybody dying

GOD SAID "THEY DID NOT HEAR . . ."

They did not hear my children
Singing in the jungle

They did not hear my sons
Singing in the tropical rain
They did not see my chosen ones
Dance to my dream.

LISTEN, SAINTS—

To Peter on holy problems
Or to Paul, about cares

Narcissa wants to know about the Pontiff
De Deo, de carminibus.
De risibus et hymnis
To Cyprian in perplexity
Misfortunes! let changes happen.

Immobility is worse.
Only God remains

Madre Teresa
A gift of pears:
Keep busy!

NEW RIBBON

It is quick it is far it is over it is
Forty-five miles long

Ten or twenty people there every Sunday

It is deep it is low it is out of hand
It is a Long Island

Ten or twenty thousand every Sunday

It is sandy it is full of dead grass
There has been no rain but there is
Salt water

The clock strikes ten. The island is
Full of people, drinking beer out of cans
And singing very badly.

Smoke goes up from the Island,
Wind blows the sand away from
Ten or twenty thousand good-byes.

It was a nice sandy Island.

New Ribbon ii

Broken glass
Foreheads
Putty motes up sawmill lame
Post of Father's gate
Drop four and I'll tell
You the code number
Brush
Full of topes,
Tropes, a kind of
New Art on the
Blackfingered spool.

New Ribbon iii

You put your leg in the water and it bends see you
Put your hand in the water and it bends.
Trees bend in the sky. You put your hand in the
Sky it does not bend, see you
Put your leg in the sky, yes, you can bend it.
Or not, whichever way you
Like it to be in the air.

Come on Blackfriars, count your ten fingers in the air
Count your ten eyes in the stars.
Is that enough?
(They stalled in the middle of counting).

New Ribbon iv

Come everybody we got to help Johnson
We got to help him with his boat and with his
Fishing pole, we got to help Johnson out of his
House and into the dam boat with his
Fishing pole.

Come on everybody to the communal sports,
Everybody in the water, everybody out of the water,
One two three, everybody out of the rain.

One man stays out in the rain, Johnson, the indi-
Vidualist does not write think or spell like other
People, stands in the rain unlike the other.

Come on everybody help Johnson back into the house
With his boat and his fishing pole, one two three
Help him (struggling) through the door

(He says he hates the dam house)

Come on everybody help Johnson not to be an
Individual, one two three help Johnson
Back into the bar.

Come on everybody it is raining and so we got to
Help Johnson.

[UNTITLED]

All of the branches
None of the roots.
    All of the words—
    Freedom branches
    All of the words
    Happiness branches
    All of the words
    Equality branches
    None of the roots.
All of the branches
None of the roots.

[UNTITLED]

Famous engines support type B network

Valve parts easily flake but
An economy way is more pressure says heavy.

Close down pin trail and it stays! and pass it through
Supposes troop. Runs free like class seven.

Acid treat is homogen for vita-twin spores
Cork it then, and sonotrap clings
Flush home: double expenses anticipated
But the result no finer barbs
No smoke, no clinker, & no foil & no more ice.

[UNTITLED]

It would be wrong to let one man
Contain all natures
Be a body of worlds and stars

Too primitive!
Moons, metals, animals, seas
All in the Form of Man

Fire speaking with a man's voice
The Sun
With a man's face

Let there be no more man
Nail him up
Let him tick like a clock.

Nature? Has man a nature?
Has he a human essence?
Nature is birds
Essence is French for gasoline

He is a machine of nerves
He runs on hot fuels
Better break his liquid sun
And spill the essence.

Man is only when he works
Nail him up
Let him tick for profit

Better close his stars
Better take him down from there

Do not leave his body
Where the wind may burn it
Do not leave his signature
Where he is known

He has signed all things
With his own name
So destroy them
Do not leave this woman where like my mother
She weeps for the world's body

[UNTITLED]

Marks and numbers
Cut in skin
Official wires
Can be destroyed
His austere look
Is carved in salt
He counts the steps

Of haywire bails
Black wasps
Dance on stones
And hot brass luck
Is tame with sun
They have grown old
In war and fun.

[UNTITLED]

Now the official nerve is analyzed
The loved machine
Dances on a blue spark
Go mark the man's skin with the following numbers 2, 4, 6, 8.

His wires are then counted, his eyes lit, turn the switch
His look is cut in salt, his word melts, his thought falls loose
His hot brass luck is suddenly tame
This captain has grown old in war and fun.

[UNTITLED]

The bees love grass
Wet with urine
On which they grow angry.
Sing like poison
Ready to attack
Gone
Back again

Ready uncertain gone
Change of scent
Gone
Grass is mortal.

[UNTITLED]*

Then from tomorrow
Topping scared woods
And empty houses

Wounded by sunstroke
(therefore sacred)
Silence is his way

O blessed
Invulnerable OM!
O Festival secret
Unplanned Saturday!

[UNTITLED]

What are the marks of the enemy?
He has no wit.

What are the marks of his message?
He demands immediate compliance.

* The text of this fragment is transcribed from a poem in Merton's hand on
the book jacket of *Zen Buddhism and Psychoanalysis*, edited by Erich Fromm,
et al., Harper and Brothers, Publishers, 1960.

What is his face?
Hairless clean as glass
No lip. So mathematical
Is that face.

What is his expression?
Expression four.

What are the marks of the enemy?
He has no face.

What is his message?
An immediate reply
"Haywire!"

What is his wit?
Counts everything.
Can't be scrapped.

What are the marks on his face?
Three eyes. No lips.
Expression four.

[UNTITLED]

When class was in the garden at Greylands
And we tried to translate Euripides
Not knowing Greek

We cared little for a dead hero
However mad
Or for his mad language

Prefects and cricketers
We were alive & sane and careless in our own strength.
We spoke English.
We smiled
At the Master's cat.

Holidays came,
We left the crazy Titan
Before the hot shirt
Drove him to kill his own children.

We were alive & sane
Sons of a cool & gentle England.

That was in 1931. Since then
There have been hotter seasons
We go on translating
More & more Euripides
With less & less Greek.

The fury of Herakles
Has swollen beyond bounds.
And now we are never out of danger
We have forgotten our smiles & our strength

A SELECTION OF CONCRETE POEMS

```
H U R L U B
    E R L   U H
U R L     U   B   E       R
L     U     H U R   L
U     B   E R   L         U
    H   U     R   L
              U
B E R   L     U H   U
R L U B E R         L U U
U   U   U   U   U U U U
H U R L U B E R       LU
B B B E B B E B E R B E
R L U L E R L U B   E R
LU LUH LU LHU LU LUH HU

    H U R L U B E
    E R L U H U H
        UH
    BERLULULUBEREL
        U
```

SEMIOTIC POEM FROM RACINE'S "IPHIGENIE"

```
c e s        m o r t s
c e t t e    l e s b o s
c e s        c e n d r e s
c e t t e    f l a m m e
```

```
        C E S
        C E T T E
        C E S
        C E T T E
    M O R T S
    L E S B O S
    C E N D R E S
    F L A M M E
        C E S
        C E T T E
        L E S

        b o s
        e e e e
        o e e l
        s t s t
        r s n a
          t t
          e e
        s o r m
        l e s b o
        m o r f a
        f l a m m a
    M O R S

        L E S B O S
        C C C C C C
        E E E E E E
        S T S T S T
C E S M O R T S C E T T E
        L E S B O S

        c e n d r e s
```

```
W H I S K E
W H I   S K
W H I S S S
  K E   E   Y
  S H K E E Y
W H I S K W
H I S K W Y
W H I S K Y


whisk   E Y
EYE   hisky
W H I S K W
aaaa s h ky
w h I S  key
w h i S K y
YK e h w ik


W H I S K I
h s e y k W
H I s k e y
W I S H K I
```

BROnze fasHIONs
    RONZEfa shIONS BR
        onzeFAS hionSB RONZE FA
SHI onsbr ONzeFabrASH FASHio
    BRonzefa shIONSB rasho FONZE R
AshION
        ONZE mash
                        FAbra SHION MA
ROnsha FashbrON
    BRA shon RONZE Fashbra RASha
BRonsh
        ASHMA frabshon BRASS on
HIONBronza FAShibro Ronzba BRASFO
Nshion
        RASHA MO BARiosh Ronza Br
ONZE Fa shio nbr
                    onZE FAZESH
ON BR ONZA Fonze FASHIO Nsbronze
RasHMA   Fashio BRASH a fonz
        RONza   BRONZA
                    Fash ION
NIObr ONfaSH NOBro ShF ia BRONZE
FASHIONSBRONZEFASHIONSBRON   ZEF
ASHio nbron nbrsh BROnsh Bronsh FAS
FASFASFAS   GASGASGAS FASFASFASFAS
BRONZEFAShionshionshoniashioniasha
BRON Zefa FaRonZE FAsb RONZ eashBR
            O N Z E

FOUND MACARONIC ANTIPOEM

Amicorum communia ſunt omnia
  Mein gůt iſt dein gůt.
Stateram ne tranſgrediaris.
  Hau nicht vber die ſchnůr.
  Vbermachs nit.
  Trit nicht ůßer das zyl.
Cor ne edito
  Bekümer dich nit zůfaſt.
Per publicam viam ne ambules
  volg nit dem gemainen pôfel.
Aduerſus ſolem ne loquitor
  widerſtreß nit dem offenßarn.
A prora & puppi perit
  der verdirbt in grundt.
  der iſt fertig von tach an vnd von keller.

Friends have all in common
  My gutt is thy gutt
Don't mess with the scales
Don't slice over the line
  Nix overmake
Don't drive through the back
  Of the garage
Keep your silly ideas to yourself
Don't get in such a sweat
Don't amble down the highway
Follow not common piffle
Don't contradict the sun
Don't deny the obvious
Wrecked from stem to stern
Rotten to the core
He's through with his
Beef and beer.

(From an Elementary Reader, Augsburg, 1514)

```
                              M m m m u
                              V i i e s

                              N A T U R
                              A A B H O
                              R R R E T
                              M U V I E
                              E E E E S

                              M O V I E
                              P I C T R
                              A A B H O
n a t u r                     R R R E T
                              N A T U R
a a b h o

r r r e t

v a c u u                     n a t u r

u u u u m                     a a b h o

                              r r r e t

                              v a c u u

                              u u u u m




N A A T U

R A A B H

O O R R R

RRRRR E T

V A A A C

UUU  UUUM


N A T U R

A A B H U

R R H U I

T V A C M



V a a a c
M m m m m
U u u u u
```

                    N O R M S

Graa aa aa lll   aa GRA aa aa ll aaal aaalGRaa
     aal Graalaal

              Graa aal aa aal aa
                      g r a a a a

                  N O R M S

                            a a a a l graalaallaa
                      gralalagralala   gralala
                              graal   graaalaaal

                                      graalaalaa

              N O R M S

                            grgraa grgraagr
                                grgr grgr grl
                                    gralalagr

G R A A a a a   g r a a
              gra aa aa
              N O R M S

                            AA AA AA
                                LL LL LL AA
                                        G R   G R
                      AAA AAA AAA   aa aa aa aa aa lllll
              n o r m s .
                      GRAA AA AA GRAA AA AA GR AA GR
                          A A A A A L L
                          G R A A A A
                            G R A A A A A A A
                                G R AA   AA   AA   AA

```
wundiwundiwundiwundiwundiwundi
wundiwundiwun   diwundiwundiwun
wundiwundiwun   diwundiwundiwu
wundiwundiwu    ndiwundiwundiwu
wundiwundi      wundiwundiwundi
wundiwund       wundiwundiwun
wundiwun        diwundiwundiwun
wundiwu         ndiwundiwundiw
wundiw          undiwundiwundiw
wundiwu         ndiwundiwundiwu
wundiwundi      wundiwundiwund
wundiwund       iwundiwundiwundi
wundiwun        diwundiwundiwun
wundiwu         ndiwundiwundiw
wundiwund       iwundiwuindwuind
wuindwui    ndwuidnwuindwuindw
wuindwuind  wuindwuindwuindwui
wuiwuinwui  wuiwuinwuiwuiwjinw
wuiwuinw dnud wuiwuinduwuindwu
wuindwuin  dwui wuindwuindwuin
wuin  wuin   wuind wuind wuind
wui  wuin wuid   wuin wuindwuk
wundiwuind      wuindwuindwuindw
wundiwundiwu    ndiwundiwundiwu
wuindwuin       dwuindwuindwuind
wundiwundiwundi  wuindwuindwui
wuiwuindwui   ndwuind uindwuin
wuinwuinw    wuinwuinw   wuinwu
wuindwuin    wuindwuind wuinwui
wundiwundiwu    ndiwundiwundiwu
wundiwundiwundiwundiwundiwundi
```

OVID	DIVO
VOID	DIOV
IDOV	IOVD
VIDO	OVID
VOID	DIOV
DVOI	OIVD
IDVO	OVID
OIDV	VOID
IVOD	DOVI
VIDO	OVID
OVID	VIDO
DOVI	IVOD
DVOI	VOID
IDVO	VIDO
OIDV	IDOV
VOID	DIVO
OVID	DIVO
VOID	DIOV
IDOV	IOVD
VIDO	OVID

G 16

```
A W F U L M U S I C A W
F U L MUSIC
A W F U L M U S I C A W F
U L MU    SIC
S I C M U W A F U L M U S I
C A W F U L M
        U S I C  AWFULMUSIC
AWFULMUSICAWFULMUSICAWFULMUS
IC IC IC IC A W F U L  I C I
M U S I S I S I I I C    A W
FUL MUS ICA WFU MUL SIC LUMA
SWA MUC ICU AWF LUM ASW UFLM
AWFULMUSICAWFULMUSICAWFULMUSIC




        A W F
        U L M
        U S I
        C A W
        F U L
        M U S
        I C A
```

```
vicovicovicovicovicovicovicovicovic
vicovicovicovicovico  vicovicovicov
vicovicovicovico           vicovicovi
vicovicovicov                  icovicov
vicovixovix                  ovixovixovi
vicovicovi                  vicovicovicovi
vicovicov                     icovicovic
vicovicovic                 ovicovicovicov
vixovixovi              xivoxivoxivoxivox
visovisovisoviso     visovidovifodio
visccidoei                    vixodisoriso
vicovicovicovico    vicovico  vicovi
vicovicovicovi          covico    vicovi
vicovico  vicovicovico              vico
vicovicovixovixovixovixovixovixo vixovi
vicovix ovix ovixovixovicovixo vixo
vicovixovixovicovixovicovixovicovix
```

T H W P R V N C L

The Provincial has

left with a woman

The Provincial has

run off with a

woman the pro vincial has run

out wi tha wo man   the V E R T

he has gone and   W E N T

T H W P R V cl hs lft wth a wmn

Psst he has   L F F T

WNT WTH a L A D Y who?

THE VERY REV FR PRVNCL SJ

he flew wth a lady

to tropical cancer

THE VERY REV has flown

away with a lady to the trpc

of cncr THE VERY has fled

wth a wmn to the trpc of CONCERN

Psst he has LUFT too well he has

LUFTLUFT LUFT LIFT the very rev

TROPICAL PROVINCE HAS LUFT

        wth a wmn

INDEX OF TITLES AND FIRST LINES